HOW AND WHY ARE SOME THERAPISTS BETTER THAN OTHERS?

HOW AND WHY ARE SOME THERAPISTS BETTER THAN OTHERS?

Understanding Therapist Effects

Edited by Louis G. Castonguay and Clara E. Hill

American Psychological Association • Washington, DC

Copyright © 2017 by the American Psychological Association. All rights reserved. Except as permitted under the United States Copyright Act of 1976, no part of this publication may be reproduced or distributed in any form or by any means, including, but not limited to, the process of scanning and digitization, or stored in a database or retrieval system, without the prior written permission of the publisher.

Published by
American Psychological Association
750 First Street, NE
Washington, DC 20002
www.apa.org

To order
APA Order Department
P.O. Box 92984
Washington, DC 20090-2984
Tel: (800) 374-2721; Direct: (202) 336-5510
Fax: (202) 336-5502; TDD/TTY: (202) 336-6123
Online: www.apa.org/pubs/books
E-mail: order@apa.org

In the U.K., Europe, Africa, and the Middle East, copies may be ordered from
American Psychological Association
3 Henrietta Street
Covent Garden, London
WC2E 8LU England

Typeset in Goudy by Circle Graphics, Inc., Columbia, MD

Printer: Sheridan Books, Chelsea, MI
Cover Designer: Nicci Falcone, Gaithersburg, MD

The opinions and statements published are the responsibility of the authors, and such opinions and statements do not necessarily represent the policies of the American Psychological Association.

Library of Congress Cataloging-in-Publication Data

Names: Castonguay, Louis Georges, editor. | Hill, Clara E., 1948- editor.
Title: How and why are some therapists better than others? : understanding therapist effects / edited by Louis G. Castonguay and Clara E. Hill.
Description: First Edition. | Washington, DC : American Psychological Association, [2017] | Includes bibliographical references and index.
Identifiers: LCCN 2016052063 | ISBN 9781433827716 | ISBN 1433827719
Subjects: LCSH: Psychotherapy—Research. | Psychotherapists—Training of—Research.
Classification: LCC RC337 .H69 2017 | DDC 616.89/14072—dc23 LC record available at https://lccn.loc.gov/2016052063

British Library Cataloguing-in-Publication Data
A CIP record is available from the British Library.

Printed in the United States of America
First Edition

http://dx.doi.org/10.1037/0000034-000

10 9 8 7 6 5 4 3 2

À la memoire de mon père, Roméo, qui aurait pu être un grand thérapeute,
mais qui fut bien plus.
(To the memory of my father, Roméo, who could have been a great therapist,
but who was much more.)
—*Louis G. Castonguay*

To all the therapists I've had and trained, because I know that who the
therapist is makes a big difference.
—*Clara E. Hill*

CONTENTS

Contributors xi

Preface xiii

Introduction 3
Louis G. Castonguay and Clara E. Hill

I. Empirical Foundations 11

Chapter 1. Therapist Effects, Effective Therapists, and the Law of Variability 13
Michael Barkham, Wolfgang Lutz, Michael J. Lambert, and David Saxon

Chapter 2. What Characterizes Effective Therapists? 37
Bruce E. Wampold, Scott A. Baldwin, Martin grosse Holtforth, and Zac E. Imel

Chapter 3.	Who Works for Whom and Why? Integrating Therapist Effects Analysis Into Psychotherapy Outcome and Process Research	55
	Michael J. Constantino, James F. Boswell, Alice E. Coyne, David R. Kraus, and Louis G. Castonguay	

II. Conceptual Contributions 69

Chapter 4.	Appropriate Responsiveness as a Contribution to Therapist Effects	71
	William B. Stiles and Adam O. Horvath	
Chapter 5.	Therapist Presence, Absence, and Extraordinary Presence	85
	Jeffrey A. Hayes and Maria Vinca	
Chapter 6.	Inner Experience and the Good Therapist	101
	Charles J. Gelso and Andres E. Perez-Rojas	
Chapter 7.	The Role of the Therapist's Attachment in the Process and Outcome of Psychotherapy	117
	Bernhard M. Strauss and Katja Petrowski	
Chapter 8.	The Role of Therapist Skills in Therapist Effectiveness	139
	Timothy Anderson and Clara E. Hill	
Chapter 9.	The Contributions of Client Culture to Differential Therapist Effectiveness	159
	Jeffrey A. Hayes, Jesse Owen, and Helene A. Nissen-Lie	
Chapter 10.	Therapist Negative Reactions: How to Transform Toxic Experiences	175
	Abraham W. Wolf, Marvin R. Goldfried, and J. Christopher Muran	
Chapter 11.	Professional Expertise in Psychotherapy	193
	Franz Caspar	

Chapter 12.	Gaining Therapeutic Wisdom and Skills From Creative Others (Writers, Actors, Musicians, and Dancers) 215
	Barry A. Farber

III. Empirical Contributions 233

Chapter 13.	Effective Therapists in Psychodynamic Therapy for Depression: What Interventions Are Used and How? 235
	Nadia Kuprian, Harold Chui, and Jacques P. Barber

Chapter 14.	Effective and Less Effective Therapists for Generalized Anxiety Disorder: Are They Conducting Therapy the Same Way? 259
	Soo Jeong Youn, Henry Xiao, Hanjoo Kim, Louis G. Castonguay, Andrew A. McAleavey, Michelle G. Newman, and Jeremy D. Safran

Chapter 15.	Something to Laugh About: Humor as a Characteristic of Effective Therapists 285
	Sarah Knox, Meghan C. Butler, Dakota J. Kaiser, Graham Knowlton, and Clara E. Hill

IV. Implications and Conclusions 307

Chapter 16.	The Implications of Therapist Effects for Routine Practice, Policy, and Training 309
	James F. Boswell, David R. Kraus, Michael J. Constantino, Matteo Bugatti, and Louis G. Castonguay

Chapter 17.	Therapist Effects: Integration and Conclusions 325
	Clara E. Hill and Louis G. Castonguay

Index 343

About the Editors 355

CONTRIBUTORS

Timothy Anderson, PhD, Ohio University, Athens
Scott A. Baldwin, PhD, Brigham Young University, Provo, UT
Jacques P. Barber, PhD, Adelphi University, Garden City, NY
Michael Barkham, PhD, University of Sheffield, Sheffield, United Kingdom
James F. Boswell, PhD, University at Albany, State University of New York
Matteo Bugatti, MA, University at Albany, State University of New York
Meghan C. Butler, MA, Marquette University, Milwaukee, WI
Franz Caspar, PhD, Bern University, Bern, Switzerland
Louis G. Castonguay, PhD, Pennsylvania State University, University Park
Harold Chui, PhD, Adelphi University, Garden City, NY, and The Chinese University of Hong Kong, Shatin, Hong Kong
Michael J. Constantino, PhD, University of Massachusetts Amherst
Alice E. Coyne, MS, University of Massachusetts Amherst
Barry A. Farber, PhD, Teachers College, Columbia University, New York, NY
Charles J. Gelso, PhD, University of Maryland, College Park
Marvin R. Goldfried, PhD, Stony Brook University, Stony Brook, NY
Martin grosse Holtforth, PhD, University of Bern, Bern, Switzerland
Jeffrey A. Hayes, PhD, Pennsylvania State University, University Park
Clara E. Hill, PhD, University of Maryland, College Park

Adam O. Horvath, EdD, Simon Frasier University, Vancouver, British Columbia, Canada, and University Catolica, Santiago, Chile
Zac E. Imel, PhD, University of Utah, Salt Lake City
Dakota J. Kaiser, MS, Marquette University, Milwaukee, WI
Hanjoo Kim, MS, Pennsylvania State University, University Park
Graham Knowlton, MS, Marquette University, Milwaukee, WI
Sarah Knox, PhD, Marquette University, Milwaukee, WI
David R. Kraus, PhD, Outcome Referrals, Framingham, MA
Nadia Kuprian, MA, Adelphi University, Garden City, NY
Michael J. Lambert, PhD, Brigham Young University, Provo, UT
Wolfgang Lutz, PhD, University of Trier, Trier, Germany
Andrew A. McAleavey, PhD, Weill-Cornell Medical School, New York, NY
J. Christopher Muran, PhD, Derner Institute, Adelphi University, Garden City, NY
Michelle G. Newman, PhD, Pennsylvania State University, University Park
Helene A. Nissen-Lie, PhD, University of Oslo, Oslo, Norway
Jesse Owen, PhD, University of Denver, Denver, CO
Andres E. Perez-Rojas, PhD, New Mexico State University, Las Cruces
Katja Petrowski, PhD, University Hospital Carl Gustav Carus, Dresden, Germany
Jeremy D. Safran, PhD, New School for Social Research, New York, NY
David Saxon, MSc, University of Sheffield, Sheffield, United Kingdom
William B. Stiles, PhD, Miami University, Oxford, OH, and Appalachian State University, Boone, NC
Bernhard M. Strauss, PhD, Institute of Psychosocial Medicine and Psychotherapy, Jena, Germany
Maria Vinca, PhD, Independent Practice, State College, PA
Bruce E. Wampold, PhD, University of Wisconsin, Madison, and Modum Bad Psychiatric Center, Vikersund, Norway
Abraham W. Wolf, PhD, Case Western Reserve University, Cleveland, OH
Henry Xiao, MS, Pennsylvania State University, University Park
Soo Jeong Youn, MS, Pennsylvania State University, University Park

PREFACE

The origins of this book can be traced to our long-standing hope that psychotherapy can be improved by the integration of clinical and research knowledge. Over the last few years, we have become convinced that an exciting opportunity for such an integration can be built on the convergence between what we, and many of our colleagues, have seen in supervising therapists of different levels of experience, and what research has now demonstrated: Not all therapists are equal. By relying on conceptual, clinical, and empirical knowledge and the perspective of a diversity of experts, this book is aimed at describing what we know about the fact that some therapists are better than others at helping clients, and that some therapists are substantially less effective, and even more harmful, than the majority of practitioners. We also aim to better understand why and how such differential levels of effectiveness, or therapist effects, take place in psychotherapy.

The impetus for this book was a series of biannual meetings, called the Penn State Conferences on the Process of Change, that we have been organizing for the past 15 years. Reminiscent of the famous Nebraska conferences that shaped social psychology many years ago, these meetings have been described as a "think tank" of psychotherapy.[1] The first two sets of conferences focused on insight and corrective experiences, each of them leading to a book.[2,3] This current book is the result of the third set of conferences, which involved a total of three meetings.

As with the past two sets of conferences, the meetings on therapist effects involved a large contingent of scholars from eastern North America (participants were originally selected based on their expertise and, for economic reasons, driving distance of their academic institution from Penn State!). Because of the current worldwide attention to the topic of therapist effects, however, contributors to this book include highly respected and influential researchers from North America and Europe.

We invited these scholars to focus on several questions aimed at better understanding and maximizing the effectiveness of therapists: How have therapist effects been studied? What are the personal features of good therapists? What are therapists doing, thinking, and feeling (or not doing, thinking, or feeling) when they are conducting a good session or a good treatment? What factors facilitate or interfere with effective performance during a session or treatment? And what are the best ways to identify good therapists and assess their performance?

This book is not a compilation of conference proceedings, or a transcription of exchanges that took place during meetings. Rather, the conferences served as opportunities to stimulate and exchange ideas, clarify and sharpen thoughts, generate new ways of thinking, and debate alternative views with the ultimate aim of setting up, building, and receiving feedback about conceptual and empirical projects conducted by members between meetings. In this book, we showcase these innovative projects, and then present the consensus reached by the group in terms of defining therapist effects and clarifying the factors that explain these effects.

We are grateful to all of our contributors who have provided knowledge and creative insights to our collaborative efforts to shed light on the intriguing, but largely unexplained phenomenon, of therapist effects. We also owe tremendous gratitude to Brian Rabian, who, on behalf of the Psychology Clinic at Penn State, provided us with most of the funding for the conferences. We also want to thank Susan Reynolds for her support and guidance as senior acquisitions editor at the American Psychological

---

[1]Hatcher, S. L. (2007). Epiphanies on insight: A review of Castonguay and Hill (2006). *PsycCritiques*, 52(13), 1–5. Retrieved from https://www.apa.org/pubs/books/4317122c.pdf
[2]Castonguay, L. G., & Hill, C. E. (Eds.). (2006). *Insight in psychotherapy*. Washington, DC: American Psychological Association.
[3]Castonguay, L. G., & Hill, C. E. (Eds.). (2012). *Transformation in psychotherapy: Corrective Experiences across cognitive behavioral, humanistic, and psychodynamic approaches*. Washington, DC: American Psychological Association.

Association. Our thanks also go to our current and former doctoral students (several of whom have authored chapters in this book), as well as our mentors, for their collaborative spirit. Having worked with them for many years has contributed significantly to our personal understanding of the role of therapists, mentors, clients, and students. And as for all aspects of our professional engagement, we are most grateful for our spouses (Michelle and Jim) for backing us up, challenging us, and nurturing us. Finally, we would like to express our love and gratitude for close family members, those who are still with us and those who have gone before us.

HOW AND WHY ARE SOME THERAPISTS BETTER THAN OTHERS?

INTRODUCTION

LOUIS G. CASTONGUAY AND CLARA E. HILL

We have clearly established through research that several treatment approaches are successful for a wide range of psychological disorders, that a number of client characteristics are related to the process and outcome of therapy, and that a host of relationship variables are predictive of beneficial or harmful effects of psychotherapy (Castonguay & Beutler, 2006; Chambless & Ollendick, 2001; Norcross, 2011). Interestingly, however, *therapist effects* are one of psychotherapy research's most intriguing paradoxes: Although we know intuitively and anecdotally that therapists differ in their effectiveness, we are only beginning to demonstrate the phenomenon statistically, and our empirical understanding of what explains such differences is limited.

What we mean by therapist effects is that a number of clinicians in a diversity of data sets (as part of randomized clinical trials and studies in naturalistic settings) have been found to be better at fostering symptomatic

http://dx.doi.org/10.1037/0000034-001
How and Why Are Some Therapists Better Than Others? Understanding Therapist Effects, L. G. Castonguay and C. E. Hill (Eds.)
Copyright © 2017 by the American Psychological Association. All rights reserved.

change, whereas, unfortunately, other clinicians have produced less beneficial change in their clients. At this point in time, however, it is mostly unclear how and/or why this happens.

We know that therapists vary in terms of their therapeutic intentions. For example, Fuller and Hill (1985) found that when working with the same clients, some experienced therapists strived to give more information to their clients, whereas other therapists were more intent on getting information from their clients. Particular therapists, within and across different theoretical orientations, might also be focusing more on some processes or techniques than others (e.g., exploring what is taking place in the therapeutic relationship, facilitating a more positive view of self, helping clients to think about meaning in life and death anxiety, fostering the resolution of painful feelings toward parents). However, we can only rely on a paucity of empirical findings to show whether or not these intentions and interventions, as well as several other ways of being, thinking, and acting, are responsible for the fact that not all therapists are equal in their outcomes.

The goal of this book is to address this gap in knowledge by relying on the expertise and collaboration among highly influential scholars and researchers from different theoretical orientations (e.g., cognitive–behavioral, humanistic, psychodynamic) and research traditions (e.g., quantitative, qualitative, randomized clinical trials, naturalistic investigations, cases studies). All of the chapters in this book are designed to address one or two fundamental questions: What might explain, at least in part, why some therapists are better or worse than others? What are the ways by which therapists might get more positive and less negative outcomes? All chapters have been written to be clinically relevant and meaningful because we want this book to be a source of innovative and creative strategies to help clinicians examine and improve their practice.

We believe that the clinical insights and guidelines that can be derived from these chapters are relevant to the practice of clinicians, irrespective of their professional background and level of experience. Similarly, this book was written to be helpful to early and well-seasoned researchers interested in clarifying how, with whom, and under what circumstances individual therapists make a difference in the outcome of psychotherapy.

The book is composed of four sections. Part I includes introductory chapters about the empirical foundations of our current knowledge. The next two sections focus on general characteristics, ways of being, and clinical competencies of effective therapists. The chapters included in Part II examine these issues from a conceptual perspective, whereas the chapters in Part III show how clinically relevant studies can delineate factors that may explain therapist effects and help clinicians to become more effective. Finally, implications and conclusions are presented in the chapters of Part IV.

PART I: EMPIRICAL FOUNDATIONS

The first three chapters of the book include reviews of the empirical literature about therapist effects.

In Chapter 1, Michael Barkham, Wolfgang Lutz, Michael J. Lambert, and David Saxon first define key concepts in this line of research. They then summarize the evidence that some therapists are more effective than others, and some are more harmful than others. On the basis of six major conclusions that they derived from current research, Barkham et al. provide recommendations for future investigations, as well as suggestions for the clinical applications of our scientific knowledge.

Chapter 2, by Bruce E. Wampold, Scott A. Baldwin, Martin grosse Holtforth, and Zac E. Imel, begins with the assumption that there are therapist effects, and then goes on to address the next obvious question of who the best therapists are and what they are doing in therapy. After describing conceptual and methodological difficulties related to understanding what sets these therapists apart, Wampold et al. review the characteristics and competencies that have currently been shown to contribute or not contribute to therapist effects (a number of these characteristics and competencies are examined in detail in later chapters of the book).

Building on Chapter 2, Michael J. Constantino, James F. Boswell, Alice E. Coyne, David R. Kraus, and Louis G. Castonguay discuss various complexities of between-therapist effects on client outcomes in Chapter 3. They outline two categories of promising determinants of these effects and provide a detailed map (and numerous examples) for investigating therapist effects and their determinants. Specifically, this chapter offers a conceptual (rather than a technical) description of design and statistical strategies for future research on therapist effects.

PART II: CONCEPTUAL CONTRIBUTIONS

The second section of the book explores in depth a number of individual characteristics, general ways of being, attitudes, and skills that likely differentiate effective and ineffective therapists. These factors go above and beyond demographics (e.g., gender, age, professional background), which have not been shown to be reliably linked with treatment outcome. All of the chapters in this section present clinical variables that are explicitly relevant to many, if not all, therapeutic contexts.

In Chapter 4, William B. Stiles and Adam O. Horvath argue that in all forms of therapy skillful and successful clinicians are responsive to their clients' immediate and long-term needs. Responsiveness for them involves appropriately doing the right thing at the right time by choosing and implementing interventions on the basis of a range of contextual variables. With the goal of expanding previous conceptual and research work, they propose that the therapeutic effect of such responsiveness is mediated by good therapeutic processes, such as the formation of a strong and positive working alliance.

Closely related to the notion of responsiveness is the concept of presence, or the capacity of therapists to be aware of and open to their experience and the client's experience in the here-and-now of the therapeutic interaction. The role of presence, especially as a precondition of empathy, as well as factors that occur before and during sessions that can influence therapist presence, is described in Chapter 5 by Jeffrey A. Hayes and Maria Vinca. Hayes and Vinca also boldly suggest that a state of "extraordinary presence" may distinguish the most effective therapists from others.

Chapter 6, by Charles J. Gelso and Andres E. Perez-Rojas, focuses on specific types of inner experience (especially affective experience) that therapists, irrespective of their conceptual allegiance, have when working with clients. Gelso and Perez-Rojas argue that therapist effects can be explained in part by therapists' ability to experience and communicate attitudes of empathy, positive regard, and authenticity. They also suggest that effective therapists are able to accept "taboo" feelings of hate and love toward their clients, and understand and regulate these emotions as they occur in the therapeutic relationship. Gelso and Perez-Rojas then describe specific strategies to therapeutically manage countertransference and provide suggestions for how to investigate these phenomena.

Therapists' regulation of emotions and their interaction with clients are also explored in Chapter 7 by Bernhard M. Strauss and Katja Petrowski. On the basis of their review of the emerging research on this topic, Strauss and Petrowski propose that differential attachment (secure or insecure) may explain one important aspect of therapist effects: Therapist effects are stronger for highly impaired and distressed clients than for highly functioning clients. With these distressed clients, secure therapists (who are less prone to react defensively and with negative countertransference) may foster more positive alliance and outcome.

Timothy Anderson and Clara E. Hill describe four sets of intertwined therapeutic skills in Chapter 8: technical, relational, conceptualization, and cultural. Although each of these skill sets is important for novice and experienced therapists to develop, Anderson and Hill argue that highly successful treatment requires a combination of these skills. They further suggest that therapeutic mastery is reflected by a personalized integration of highly advanced and nuanced skills. They illustrate how the different skill sets can be integrated using a conceptual model.

Focusing on the cultural component of psychotherapy, Jeffrey A. Hayes, Jesse Owen, and Helene A. Nissen-Lie review the empirical evidence supporting the differential effectiveness of therapists with minority clients in Chapter 9. Hayes et al. also identify a number of myths about therapist multicultural expertise. As an alternative to the predominant conceptualization of cultural competence as performance (what to do), they suggest a more general orientation (how to be). They present research on key characteristics of this way of being in therapy (an attitude of cultural humility, an engagement in opportunities to explore cultural issues, and a sense of cultural comfort), as well as examples of microaggressions that can result from difficulties in relating in a culturally oriented way with clients.

In Chapter 10, Abraham W. Wolf, Marvin R. Goldfried, and J. Christopher Muran focus on the inability to deal appropriately with negative reactions triggered by some clients as a type of mistake, or technical and relational skill deficit, which might distinguish less effective, or even harmful, therapists from other more helpful therapists. Wolf et al. first review the empirical literature about these negative reactions (especially anger and frustration) and their toxic impact on the therapeutic relationship and outcome. On the basis of converging recommendations from experienced therapists of different orientations, they then present strategies on how to handle negative reactions, including the awareness, regulation, and transformation of hostile affects into empathy and compassion for clients.

Chapter 11 is aimed at opening new horizons in our understanding and improving of therapist effectiveness. On the basis of the literature in fields such as chess, athletics, and music, as well as a number of psychotherapy studies, Franz Caspar argues that expert therapists display superior information processing abilities, as reflected, for example, in the development of rich and complex case formulation. He also argues that these abilities can be learned and refined by repetitive and deliberative practices, during and after formal training.

Also as a way of opening new windows of thinking, Chapter 12 by Barry A. Farber shows how therapists can gain wisdom and knowledge about human suffering and healing from creative and artistic thinkers outside the field of psychotherapy. Through interviews with writers, actors, dancers, and musicians who became therapists, Farber describes numerous ways by which the engagement in creative thinking and activities can increase therapist awareness, understanding, and ability to work with a wide range of human experiences and ways of being. He also makes specific suggestions for how therapists can foster and make use of their creative sensibilities to improve their effectiveness.

PART III: EMPIRICAL CONTRIBUTIONS

In the third section, studies examining interventions used in particular orientations and in the treatment of specific client populations are presented, as well as ways of being or relating that cut across all psychotherapies. These studies provide examples of how therapist effectiveness can be investigated.

Chapter 13 by Nadia Kuprian, Harold Chui, and Jacques P. Barber examines the use of techniques focused on clients' relationships and interpersonal functioning. Using data for a subset of three therapists from a randomized clinical trial for psychodynamic treatment of depression, Kuprian et al. show that the most effective of the three therapists focused significantly more on interpersonal issues than did the other two therapists. They also present clinical vignettes showing how such interpersonal interventions might be used optimally in psychodynamic treatment.

Similarly, in Chapter 14, Soo Jeong Youn, Henry Xiao, Hanjoo Kim, Louis G. Castonguay, Andrew A. McAleavey, Michelle G. Newman, and Jeremy D. Safran present quantitative and qualitative analyses about three therapists who demonstrated differential levels of effectiveness as part of a randomized clinical trial for an integrated treatment of generalized anxiety disorder. Examining technical and relational skills, Youn et al. describe how the less effective therapist committed errors of commission (using interventions that were inconsistent with the change mechanisms in the treatment approach and being overly controlling) and errors of omission (not responding to markers indicating that specific interventions were required).

Ending Part III on a positive note, Sarah Knox, Meghan C. Butler, Dakota J. Kaiser, Graham Knowlton, and Clara E. Hill offer a chapter on therapist humor in Chapter 15. Knox et al. report a qualitative analysis of 11 therapists' perceptions of why, when, and how they use humor in general, as well as their description of specific humor events (positive and negative). The chapter illustrates that therapists might foster the process of change (e.g., reduce client anxiety, increase alliance, provide new perspectives) when they use humor in a way that is consistent with their personality, responsive to the client's attitude toward humor, and used in appropriate relationship contexts.

PART IV: IMPLICATIONS AND CONCLUSIONS

The fourth and final section is devoted to the effort of having a broader impact on psychotherapy practice. In Chapter 16, James F. Boswell, David R. Kraus, Michael J. Constantino, Matteo Bugatti, and Louis G. Castonguay discuss a wide range of implications raised by the collection of process and outcome data on therapist effects in day-to-day clinical practice. Boswell et al. make recommendations about what should and should not be done with these data in terms of issues such as referrals, case assignments, supervision, and postgraduate training. They base these suggestions on the needs and concerns of multiple stakeholders (clients, trainers, administrators, third party payers, and policymakers) involved the delivery of mental health care. They also describe problems and solutions regarding how to collect and use data about therapist effects.

The aim of the final chapter, Chapter 17 by Clara E. Hill and Louis G. Castonguay, is to provide an integration of what we have learned throughout this process. What do we know about therapist effects? What do we know about therapist variables that might explain therapist effects? What are the implications of therapist effects? What are the next steps in this line of research? The culmination of deliberations by a group of scholars about the state of the art in the field, this final chapter provides a starting point for future research on therapist effects.

REFERENCES

Castonguay, L. G., & Beutler, L. E. (Eds.). (2006). *Principles of therapeutic change that work*. New York, NY: Oxford University Press.

Chambless, D. L., & Ollendick, T. H. (2001). Empirically supported psychological interventions: Controversies and evidence. *Annual Review of Psychology, 52*, 685–716. http://dx.doi.org/10.1146/annurev.psych.52.1.685

Fuller, F., & Hill, C. E. (1985). Counselor and helpee perceptions of counselor intentions in relationship to outcome in a single counseling session. *Journal of Counseling Psychology, 32*, 329–338. http://dx.doi.org/10.1037/0022-0167.32.3.329

Norcross, J. C. (2011). *Psychotherapeutic relationships that work: Evidence-based responsiveness* (2nd ed.). New York, NY: Oxford University Press. http://dx.doi.org/10.1093/acprof:oso/9780199737208.001.0001

I
EMPIRICAL FOUNDATIONS

1

THERAPIST EFFECTS, EFFECTIVE THERAPISTS, AND THE LAW OF VARIABILITY

MICHAEL BARKHAM, WOLFGANG LUTZ,
MICHAEL J. LAMBERT, AND DAVID SAXON

During the past 50 years, clinicians and researchers have made huge steps toward devising and testing more effective psychological therapies, with their implementation into practice settings supported by national policy bodies (e.g., the Substance Abuse and Mental Health Services Administration in the United States, the National Institute for Health and Care Excellence in the United Kingdom, the Agency for Healthcare Research and Quality in Australia). However, the focus on treatment models and interventions has masked a focus on the role and contribution of therapists, a result that is surprising given that they are the most valuable and costly component in the delivery of psychological therapies. Accordingly, the focus of this chapter is on *therapist effects*, the contribution made by therapists to client outcomes as opposed to the effects of specific treatments or client factors.

As the chapter title suggests, there are two key components that are related but subtly different to therapist effects. The first is *effective therapists*,

---

http://dx.doi.org/10.1037/0000034-002
How and Why Are Some Therapists Better Than Others? Understanding Therapist Effects, L. G. Castonguay and C. E. Hill (Eds.)
Copyright © 2017 by the American Psychological Association. All rights reserved.

which refers to the finding that some therapists are more effective than others, and the second is *variability*, which refers to the natural phenomenon that pervades almost all human endeavors, such that achieving similar levels of skills within a profession is nigh on impossible. In this chapter, we first set out more fully the central definitions and concepts relating to therapist effects, effective therapists, and variability. We then provide a brief history of research in this field, focus on how research studies are moving toward placing therapists at the center of research—what we term *therapist-focused research*—and identify one situation where therapist effects appear most apparent. We draw together six substantive conclusions concerning our current view of therapist effects and flag key directions for improving research before concluding with a section on applying research in this field to key areas of practice.

Our aim is to introduce readers to the conceptual issues that underpin implications for practitioners, policymakers, and researchers. However, this chapter focuses primarily on therapist effects and is, therefore, only a starting point. For specific perspectives, we direct interested readers to more detailed accounts within this volume (e.g., Chapters 2 and 3 address characteristics and behaviors of effective therapists, as well as statistical and methodological strategies to identify these therapist factors; Chapter 16 discusses what to do with data related to therapist effects in terms of practice, training, and policymaking).

DEFINITIONS AND CONCEPTS

The term *therapist effects* encompasses conceptual, clinical, and statistical phenomena that refer to "the contribution that can be attributed to therapists when evaluating the efficacy of a psychological intervention" (Lutz & Barkham, 2015, p. 1). In this sense, therapist effects can be distinguished from reporting on the effectiveness of therapists. Therapist effects refer to the contribution made to the outcome variance that can be apportioned to therapists rather than to other variables, primarily the client. For example, an article might report that 8% of outcome variance was attributable to therapists. This would be sufficient for a clinic to take note and appreciate that it is not just the treatment or therapy that is important for client outcomes. It is predominantly a term used in research but which has widespread implications for clinical practice and policy. The term *therapist effects* captures the variability that is attributable to therapists. If there was no therapist effect, all therapists would yield identical client outcomes (i.e., there would be no variability). In this scenario, it would not matter which therapist clients see, as outcomes would not vary between therapists.

In simple terms, therapist effects are akin to the range of effectiveness in a sample of therapists. The implication of therapist effects is that it matters which therapist clients see. However, stating that there are therapist effects does not identify the degree to which therapists in a sample are effective. By contrast, research on effective therapists focuses on the extent to which therapists are effective. For example, data might show that 75% of a therapist's clients recover or improve. Research focusing on effective therapists often seeks to identify what makes therapists more effective and may support efforts to modify the selection and training of therapists.

Hence, we see the three phenomena of therapist effects, effective therapists, and variability as capturing concepts at differing levels: Variability is the overarching natural phenomenon within which resides therapist effects, and within therapist effects there are effective therapists, whose work with clients is either more or less effective on the basis of some agreed criterion.

Therapist Effects and Variability

Therapist effects is one manifestation of the more general phenomenon of *variability*. As stated by William Osler (1904), one of the four founding professors of Johns Hopkins Hospital and sometimes referred to as the father of modern medicine, "variability is the law of life, and as no two faces are the same, so no two bodies are alike, and no two individuals react alike and behave alike" (p. 348). From this statement, and consistent with our perspective, it follows that variability between clients and between therapists is a natural phenomenon. As such, our task as practitioners and scientists is to identify and understand the extent of this phenomenon. It may be the case that there are situations where the extent of variability is less (e.g., where practitioners are assessed as being highly competent or where they are following a specific treatment protocol). However, regardless of the extent of variability, it would seem unlikely that this phenomenon is not present to some degree in all therapeutic situations. Our view is that to help build a more accurate science of the psychological therapies, we need to have a greater understanding of the phenomenon of variability and how it affects therapists and the outcomes of their clients in therapy.

From this perspective, two central points follow. First, any estimate of therapist effects indicates variability between therapists, and the size of the effect indicates the extent of that variability within a particular client population, clinic, or research sample. Second, to the extent that therapists have a varying effect on outcomes in addition to the effects of clients and treatments, therapist effects need to be designed into studies, evaluations, or trials of psychological therapies that seek to understand causality rather than be viewed as errors. If therapist effects are ignored or excluded from analyses, this simply attributes any therapist effect to the treatment.

The view that therapist effects are errors has largely derived from the litany of trial methodology where clients are randomly assigned to therapists, thereby reducing any systematic bias. Such procedures create a comparison in which no systematic difference occurs between Condition A and Condition B other than the treatments themselves. Hence therapists are trained to a specified standard and are monitored in terms of their adherence and competence to ensure uniform delivery across clients. Although such training may reduce variability between therapists, it is highly improbable that it will remove it.

Therapist Effects and Effective Therapists

A simple and logical consequence of variability is that some therapists are more effective than others. This observation will be true in any situation if the outcomes of therapists in any clinical setting are ranked on the basis of their clients' outcomes. Ranking, by definition, places people—in this case therapists—in an order, which will have upper and lower portions. Depending on the specific outcome criterion used, therapists will be ranked relative to other therapists, and their ranking may well fluctuate in response to different criteria. But it is also possible that therapists may be ranked consistently at one end or the other regardless of the criterion used. Of course, the range between upper and lower portions might be very small or very large, and therapists ranked lowest in one clinical setting might, in absolute terms, have better outcomes than therapists ranked highest in another clinical setting. However, although all therapists can, by definition, be ranked according to their client outcomes, we would want to be able to identify those therapists who are consistently effective. Indeed, there may be therapists whose client outcomes appear to be so consistently and markedly better than others that these therapists might be described as *exceptional*. The same also will be true for therapists who might have exceptionally poor client outcomes.

The recognition that some therapists have exceptional outcomes appears to have been first commented on by Frank D. Ricks in a text published in 1974. Ricks described an exceptional therapist who saw 15 emotionally disturbed delinquent boys of whom only four (27%) went on to develop schizophrenia in adulthood, as opposed to another therapist who saw 13 boys of whom 11 (85%) went on to develop schizophrenia in adulthood. The boys at the center called the first therapist *supershrink*. Although effectiveness was determined by the outcomes obtained years later, the boys recognized aspects of the therapist's actions or presence that led them to naming him so. These actions and aspects have been summarized in terms of the therapist providing greater "effort, greater support of clients' autonomy, use of resources outside of therapy, and better relationships with clients' parents" (Najavits & Strupp, 1994, p. 115). By contrast, Ricks indicated that the other therapist became depressed and had very little energy for the most disturbed cases. Of particular note was the observation that the difference between the two therapists occurred in response to the more severely disturbed boys.

The distinction between effective and exceptional therapists can be highlighted by the comparison of the two therapists in Ricks' (1974) account. Although one therapist's clients clearly had better adult functioning than the other's (i.e., the therapist would be placed higher in any ranking system), the location of any therapists within the population or distribution of therapists and their outcomes relative to other therapists is crucial. Therapists with an 85% recovery rate might be exceptional if average therapists have a recovery rate of 50%, but less so if average therapists return a 75% recovery rate.

Whether a therapist is deemed effective or exceptional, both terms apply to the outcomes of multiple clients from a specific therapist, rather than a single case study with a very good outcome. The implication is that because the level of effectiveness is replicated across many clients, there is a contribution to these outcomes that can clearly be attributed to the therapist. If we also find variability (i.e., differences between therapists), then the key questions become: What is it that the effective therapists are doing in their sessions that the less effective therapists are not? Or, what qualities do more effective therapists bring to their sessions, in contrast to less effective therapists, that yield consistently good outcomes for their clients? When there is a discovered therapist effect (discovered by examining multiple client outcomes within the case load of each of several therapists), this allows us to set a cutoff for defining exceptional therapists (e.g., the top 10%) and then making comparisons with other therapists (e.g., the bottom 10%). As we will show, however, there are less arbitrary methods for identifying therapists whose work could inform the profession or whose work appears to need improvement.

THERAPIST-FOCUSED RESEARCH: A BRIEF HISTORY

As noted earlier, the Ricks (1974) text appears to be one of the first reports focusing on the phenomenon of a very effective and also a seemingly ineffective therapist. Although the study included just two therapists and a small number of clients who were not randomly assigned to a therapist, the Ricks study was important because it illustrated the possible consequences different therapists could have on long-term adjustment. Amidst a prevalent culture that presumed therapists to be uniform (Kiesler, 1966), the Ricks study brought researchers' attention to the fact that this assumption was erroneous. Despite warnings and dramatic illustrations, like those provided by Ricks, little change could be noted in the research literature. Martindale (1978) again brought attention to the fact that psychotherapy research was failing to consider therapist variability. His review showed that of 33 studies, the majority (63%) ignored the practitioner factor and just one study (3%) treated practitioners as if drawn randomly from the population of practitioners, thereby meaning that results could be generalized. In light of this observation, Martindale noted that researchers were inappropriately generalizing findings beyond the practitioners involved in studies.

A meta-analysis by Crits-Christoph et al. (1991) marked the first summary quantitative statement of the research evidence regarding therapist effects, although a major argument and statement as to the role of therapist effects appeared in Wampold's *The Great Psychotherapy Debate: Models, Methods, and Findings* (2001), which indicated that therapist effects accounted for approximately 8% of the outcome variance and effects of specific treatments hovered around 0%. Okiishi, Lambert, Nielsen, and Ogles (2003) highlighted the extent of variability between therapists in the outcomes of therapists from a single clinic. Figure 1.1, taken from the Okiishi et al. study, shows the extent of the difference between the three therapists ranked top versus those ranked bottom in terms of their client outcomes. These results are consistent with findings from additional studies sampling beyond a single clinic. Brown, Lambert, Jones, and Minami (2005) found that the clients seen by the most effective therapists from a variety of treatment settings showed 3 times as much change as other clients. Wampold and Brown (2005) also found that the most effective therapists were similarly effective over time.

A debate focusing on the presence or not of therapist effects arose from the reanalyses of the National Institute for Mental Health Treatment of Depression Collaborative Research Project (TDCRP) carried out by Elkin,

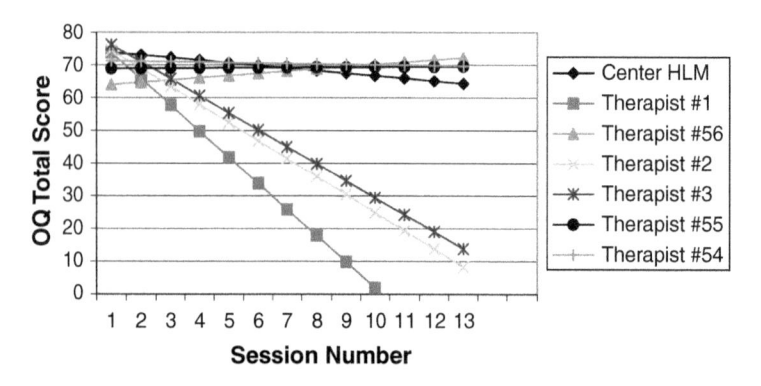

Figure 1.1. Hierarchical linear modeling growth curves for three best and worst therapist outcomes compared with the center mean. From "Waiting for Supershrink: An Empirical Analysis of Therapist Effects," by J. Okiishi, M. J. Lambert, S. L. Nielsen, and B. M. Ogles, 2003, *Clinical Psychology & Psychotherapy, 10*, p. 366. Copyright 2003 by Wiley. Reprinted with permission.

Falconnier, Martinovich, and Mahoney (2006; Elkin and other colleagues conducted the original study) and also by Kim, Wampold, and Bolt (2006). Although the two research groups analyzed the identical dataset, they arrived at very different results. Kim et al. yielded therapist effects of 8%, whereas Elkin et al. found no evidence of therapist effects. One explanation for the disparity includes the different statistical analyses carried out by the two groups: Kim and colleagues used two levels (clients and therapists; clients nested within therapists), whereas Elkin and colleagues used three levels (sessions, clients, and therapists; sessions nested within clients who nested within therapists). However, our view is that the TDCRP was designed specifically as a treatment study with the resulting sample size of therapists and clients being too small from which to generate a robust debate concerning the existence or not of therapist effects.

In 2013, Baldwin and Imel provided a summary of the therapist effects literature. The authors identified 25 studies using fixed effects (where comparisons are restricted to the sample of therapists used in each individual study) and 46 studies using random effects (where results can be generalized to the population of therapists). The median number of therapists for the 25 studies using fixed effects was 9 (4–696). Although a total of 696 therapists in one study is exceptional, there was a trade-off as each therapist had a minimum of 10 clients (Kraus, Castonguay, Boswell, Nordberg, & Hayes, 2011). In only two studies did the mean number of clients per therapist exceed 30 (Okiishi et al., 2006; Project MATCH Research Group, 1998). Although the results from studies were reported individually rather than as an overall effect, findings suggested that there was variability in clients' outcomes across therapists and that where these occurred, certain therapists were about twice as effective as other therapists.

The 46 studies using random effects yielded a total of 1,281 therapists and 14,519 clients. However, the median number of therapists per study was 9 (range: 2–581) and in only two studies did the mean number of clients per therapist exceed 30 (Cella, Stahl, Reme, & Chalder, 2011; Dinger, Strack, Leichsenring, Wilmers, & Schauenburg, 2008). Of the 46 studies, 29 were efficacy studies (i.e., trials) yielding therapist effects of approximately 3%, and 17 were classed as naturalistic or effectiveness studies yielding therapist effects of 7%. As would be expected, therapist effects are suppressed in trials because of factors such as the provision of treatment manuals and adherence monitoring. Overall, therapist effects were 5%.

Baldwin and Imel (2013) concluded that there is a need for future studies to be designed as therapist effect studies. This statement is our rallying call from which we consider, in the remaining sections of this chapter, initial steps toward achieving the aim of moving from a focus on treatments to a focus on therapists—therapist-focused research.

DESIGNING THERAPIST-FOCUSED RESEARCH

In response to Baldwin and Imel's (2013) call for future studies to be designed as therapist effect studies, we draw on three studies that exemplify how research in this field has been moving toward placing therapists rather than treatments as the central focus of attention. The first study focuses on effective therapists and variability (Okiishi et al., 2006). The second focuses on therapist effects and variability (Saxon & Barkham, 2012). The third study focuses on the relationship between therapist effects and aspects of the therapy session and of the therapeutic delivery system (Lutz et al., 2015).

These three studies use multilevel modeling, which is sometimes termed hierarchical linear modeling (Raudenbush & Bryk, 2002; Snijders & Bosker, 2004). These statistical methods recognize the hierarchical structure in the data, where clients are nested within therapists. These methods allow for the partitioning of the variance in client outcomes between the different levels in the data (e.g., client level, therapist level), with the therapist effects being the proportion of the total variance that is at the therapist level. Readers interested in a conceptual and statistical description of these methods are directed to Chapter 3 of this volume and Adelson and Owen (2012), respectively. As an additional aid, we display a visual representation of therapist effects in Appendix 1.1.

Effective Therapists and Variability

In the first study, Okiishi et al. (2006) extended their earlier work (Okiishi et al., 2003) by using a larger sample of 71 therapists, each of whom saw a minimum of 30 clients. A key focus was the variability between therapists. The authors ranked the therapists according to (a) the extent of change from pre- to posttherapy (i.e., effectiveness) and (b) the extent of change per session over the number of sessions delivered (i.e., efficiency). When a combination of these two indices was used to rank therapists, those in the top 10% ($n = 7$) were twice as effective and had half the client deterioration rates compared with therapists in the bottom 10% ($n = 7$). Practically speaking, the top-ranked therapists had the best rate of improvement and total change, whereas the bottom-ranked therapists produced the worst rates of improvement and total amount of change. However, only three therapists were in the top 10% for each of the two change indices (amount of change and rate of change). Remembering that these outcomes are based on a minimum of 30 clients, these three therapists might be viewed as not only effective but also, perhaps, exceptional in that they delivered effective and efficient therapy consistently across many clients.

However, there were also marked differences according to the two indices of change (amount of change and rate of change). For example, two therapists were ranked 5th and 14th, respectively, according to rate of change (i.e., efficiency) but ranked 63rd and 66th with regards to the total amount of change achieved (i.e., effectiveness). This pattern of practice indicates therapists whose clients respond to treatment quickly but who, on average, leave treatment with little improvement gained. One possible general implication of these findings is that if therapists see many clients who are not very disturbed at the onset (relative to other therapists in a sample), they will be ranked worse on change per session (slope) and amount of change produced over a relatively large number of sessions. In our opinion, both indicators of outcome should be used to estimate therapist effects because they provide different markers.

Therapist Effects and Variability

One advantage of using the rate of change is that the statistical procedures use all the session-by-session data from every client to calculate change, whereas pre- and posttherapy methods use only the intake level of disturbance and the final level of disturbance at termination. Hence, more information is being used to derive this index. However, many clinical settings only have pre- and posttreatment methods available. Saxon and Barkham (2012) analyzed such a dataset comprising 119 therapists and 10,786 clients with all therapists seeing at least 30 clients each (M = 90). A specific reason for selecting this study is that it uses one of the highest numbers of therapists and clients in a study of therapist effects. For the specific purposes of this chapter, in contrast to the published article, we present the results here using a simpler analysis that only controlled for client intake severity.

Overall, the Saxon and Barkham (2012) study yielded therapist effects of 8.3%. Figure 1.2 presents the degree to which therapists' outcomes varied from the average (denoted by the horizontal dotted line) and is represented by the various symbols denoting individual therapists together with their 95% confidence intervals (CIs). This form of display is often referred to as a *caterpillar plot*. The distance therapists lie from the average is termed a *residual*, which can be viewed as the additional impact of therapists on client outcome after controlling for other factors (e.g., level of severity).

Figure 1.2 shows the pre- to posttreatment change on a standard outcome measure, the Clinical Outcomes in Routine Evaluation–Outcome Measure (CORE-OM; Barkham et al., 2001). Because the outcome index is the extent of change achieved, negative residuals appear on the left of the figure and indicate therapists who yield client change that is less (i.e., poorer) than the average (n = 23; 19.3%), whereas therapists who increase client

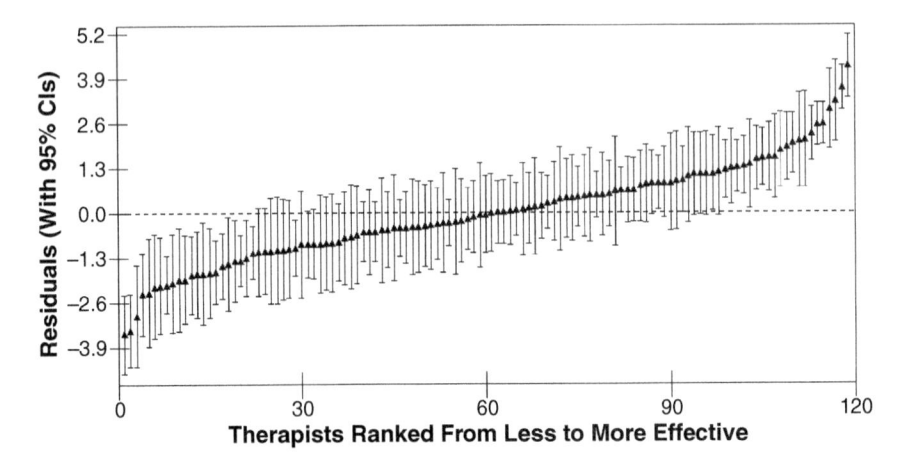

Figure 1.2. Caterpillar plot of intercept residuals for therapists (*n* = 119) ranked with 95% confidence intervals (CIs). Data from Saxon and Barkham (2012).

change more (i.e., better) than the average (*n* = 23; 19.3%) are on the right of the figure. Each group is identified by the 95% CIs not crossing zero. The fact that these percentages are identical is pure chance. The remaining therapists (*n* = 73; 61.3%) are deemed not to be reliably different from average because the 95% CIs cross zero. This latter group of therapists—by far the largest group—might be deemed to be effective with the other two smaller groups being termed *less effective* and *more effective*, respectively.

Importantly, however, the terms *less* and *more effective* are relative to the specific sample of 119 therapists. That is, therapists are less or more effective in relation to the average. We therefore sought to relate this representation to standard rates of effectiveness by calculating the recovery rates of each practitioner, defined as the percentage of a therapist's clients whose posttreatment score met the criteria of reliable improvement (change of more than 5 on the CORE-OM) and clinically significant improvement (postscore falls to less than 10 on the CORE-OM; Jacobson & Truax, 1991). Figure 1.3 presents the therapist residual scores from Figure 1.2 plotted against therapist recovery rates. The mean recovery rate was 58.8% (*SD* = 13.7), yielding lower and upper limits for the average (effective) group of therapists to be 43.8% and 75.9%, respectively. The Pearson correlation (1-tailed) between therapists' residuals and recovery rates was 0.93. The mean recovery rate for the less effective therapists was 40.4% (*SD* = 7.6) with a range of 23.5% to 52.6%, whereas the recovery rate for the more effective therapists was 76.3% (*SD* = 8.7) with a range 64.7% to 95.6%. A comparison between the less and more effective categories shows that the ranges do not overlap (i.e., they are two distinct groups) and that the average

Recovery Rate (Percent)

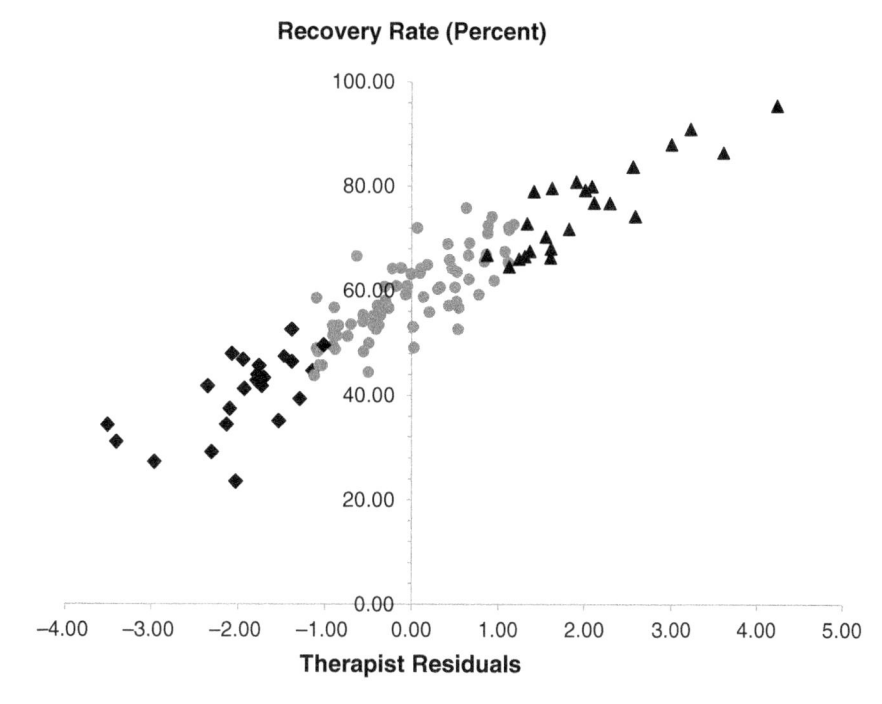

Figure 1.3. Scatterplot of residuals for therapists (*n* = 119) against therapist recovery rates. Data from Saxon and Barkham (2012).

recovery rate for the more effective therapists is almost twice that of the less effective group.

In short, both representations of the outcomes for therapists convey the same effect. There is considerable variability in outcomes summarized as therapist effects of approximately 8%. Indeed, it is interesting how close the correlation is given that the recovery rates using the Jacobson and Truax (1991) method do not, by definition, include clients below the clinical cutoff at intake. That is, the plot of recovery rates is based on the clinical subgroup of clients who scored at or above the clinical cutoff at intake (i.e., equal to or more than 10), whereas the residuals are based on all of the therapists' caseload. In addition, the latter takes into account case-mix factors that have a significant impact on outcomes. Accordingly, the residuals together with their CIs that are produced by the multilevel model provide a greater degree of certainty as to whether their outcomes are located in one category or another (e.g., below average, average, or above average). The fact that the CIs provide a 95% certainty that therapists' outcome actually lie within the category therapists are assigned to provides therapists and clinical settings with more information than merely ranking therapists.

Therapist Effects and Delivery of Psychological Therapies

What both these studies show very clearly is that variability (i.e., therapist effects) exists in relation to client outcomes. But the move toward designing studies that focus on therapist effects also means considering the impact of therapist effects on other aspects in the delivery of psychological therapies, as well as locating studies within standard clinical settings where the number of therapists may be lower and where the number of clients per therapist may be less than 30. Lutz et al. (2015) examined therapist effects not only in relation to treatment outcome but also for treatment length in a German feedback study that analyzed a sample of 349 clients and 44 therapists in outpatient psychotherapy under routine conditions. The therapists saw between five and 18 clients each, which may be more representative of samples drawn from clinical settings. In addition, the average length of treatment was approximately 40 sessions. The authors considered several predictors of treatment outcome and length including therapist effects, psychometric feedback, and therapists' attitudes toward feedback. Approximately 6% of the variability in treatment outcome and 9% of the variability in length could be attributed to therapists.

In an additional analysis, significant variability in dropout rates by therapists was also found. Furthermore, therapists' attitudes (a composite index of feedback usage and satisfaction with the feedback system) was a differential predictor in terms of treatment outcome, which indicates therapist variability in using psychometric feedback, being satisfied with it, and being able to handle such feedback successfully. In this study, significant therapist variability could be found in terms of treatment outcome, duration, and dropout. But there was no correlation between the average effectiveness of therapists, the average length of their treatments, or their dropout rate. This meant that being an effective therapist with respect to outcome does not mean being effective in terms of dropout (i.e., having a low rate) or treatment duration (i.e., providing fewer sessions). Future research should investigate this relationship further. For example, therapists with a high individual effect size but also a high dropout rate may treat only clients (on purpose or not) for whom they are effective, whereas clients for whom therapists are ineffective will not remain with the therapists and drop out of therapy.

CLIENTS' PRESENTING SEVERITY

The research reported in this chapter attests to a small but statistically significant effect for therapists. However, one observation on the size of the effect—in the region of 5% to 8%—is that this is an average figure across therapists and conditions. Our view is that, although this figure is significant and meaningful, it may disguise the fact that therapist effects are more salient in some contexts than others. In other words, we want to know more about the practice or clinical conditions in which therapist effects are most likely to occur. Recalling the observation that the difference between the two therapists in the Ricks (1974) study was influenced by the severity of the adolescents' presentation, in this section we consider the contribution of client severity to therapist effects.

To investigate the role client severity may play, we constructed a dataset from the United States, United Kingdom, and Germany comprising three separate datasets using four different outcome measures. The specific measures and sample sizes for therapists (N_T) and clients (N_C) were as follows: the Brief Symptom Inventory (Derogatis, 1975; $N_T = 97$; $N_C = 667$), the Inventory of Interpersonal Problems (Horowitz, Rosenberg, Baer, Ureño, & Villaseñor, 1988; $N_T = 97$; $N_C = 667$), the CORE-OM (Barkham et al., 2001; $N_T = 119$; $N_C = 10,786$), and the Outcome Questionnaire–45 (OQ-45; Lambert, Kahler, Harmon, Burlingame, & Shimokawa, 2011; $N_T = 146$; $N_C = 2,811$). The therapist effects for each of these four measures were 7.9%, 8.5%, 7.6%, and 1.3%, respectively. The first three values closely approximate the average or expected value reported in the literature (see Wampold, 2001) and would suggest that therapist effects transcend countries and outcome measures. However, the result for the OQ-45 (1.3%) differs and, although statistically significant, is noticeably smaller than the results from the other measures.

However, when we considered the extent of therapist effects as a function of initial client severity, the outcomes from all four outcome measures were virtually identical in that they all showed that the higher the initial client severity level, the greater the therapist effects. In other words, the higher the initial client severity score, the more it matters which therapist clients see. In short, severity matters. This effect is shown in Figure 1.4, in which we have selected the OQ-45 as a representative example. Figure 1.4 shows that with increasing client severity (x-axis), the therapist effect percentage increases (y-axis) such that an OQ-45 score of 80 (x-axis) yields a therapist effect of approximately 4% (y-axis) while a score of 120 yields a potential therapist effect of approximately 16%.

The finding that the size of therapist effects is a function of client initial severity makes good clinical sense. In relation to symptom presentation, if clients present with a low level of severity, it might be that the required level of clinical skill is more generic to most practitioners. By contrast, as clinical cases become more severe and more complex, a range of unspecified skills will be required from therapists. It is likely that the manifestation of such skills will be more variable.

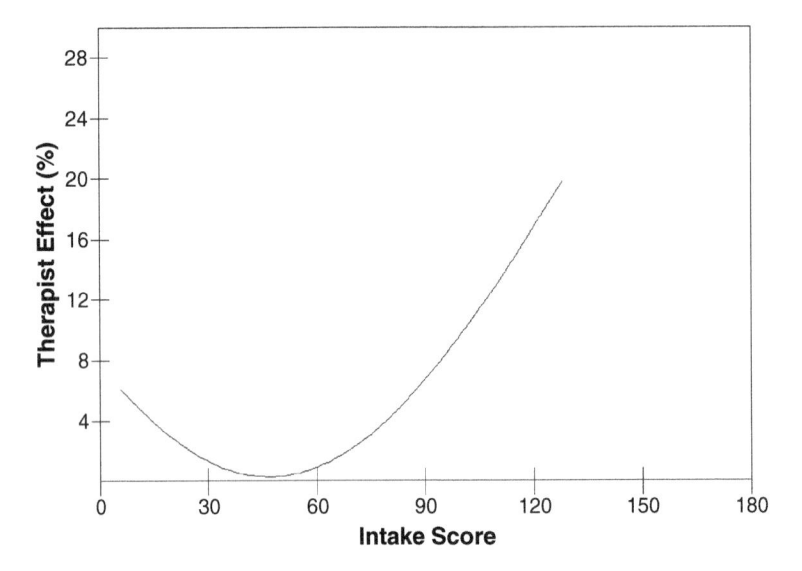

Figure 1.4. Therapist effects across increasing client severity levels for the Outcome Questionnaire–45.

TOWARD IMPROVING THERAPIST-FOCUSED RESEARCH

We draw six substantive conclusions from the state of the reported research. First, it is clear from the data presented there is variability in client outcome as a function of which therapist offers treatment. In fact, it appears to be at least, or maybe more, important who clients see rather than what specific therapy is offered. The implications are considerable in terms of the selection and training of therapists and also monitoring their outcomes.

Second, nevertheless, therapist effects are limited to accounting for about 8% of the variance in outcome, meaning that other factors combined (e.g., client characteristics) account for far more variability. This is a clear call for expanding the research effort to gain a fuller understanding of the factors that lead to client change.

Third, to a large degree, the middle two thirds of therapists cannot be confidently and reliably distinguished from each other with regards to the amount of change they facilitate in their clients. This message is reassuring to the large portion of therapists who are effective and doing a good job. It is also a warning against the use of oversimplified rankings of therapists according to their outcomes that do not use CIs. Without the CIs, some people may believe that therapists could be ranked directly against each other. The use of CIs protects therapists from crude comparisons and enables us to talk with confidence about broad classes of therapists.

Fourth, around 15% to 20% of therapists have distinguishably better outcomes, and 15% to 20% of therapists have distinguishably poorer outcomes. These two classes of therapists are the most interesting and should be the focus of future research efforts. The question we must ask is, what is it that the more effective and less effective therapists are consistently doing or not doing that differentiates them so markedly even when controlling for case-mix?

Fifth, the position of these individual therapists appears to remain relatively constant over time. The implication may be that effectiveness is a relatively stable state.

Sixth, much of the effort yielding better outcomes can be linked to how the exceptional therapists deal with the more severely disturbed individuals. This is the area in which therapist effects appear to be most apparent and may, therefore, be an area to target research that could have a real impact on client outcomes.

Focusing on Client Severity

Given the preceding six conclusions, it would seem that if we want to examine variables related to individual differences in therapists' general ability to foster better (and poorer) outcomes, then it would be most strategic to investigate cases that represent more extreme psychological distress (e.g., clients who are scoring in and above the moderate to severe range on a reliable and valid clinical measure). Adopting this approach would provide researchers with the most likely route for identifying those factors that contribute to the phenomenon of therapist effects. For example, research indicates that a combination of resilience and mindfulness may be a distinguishing personal quality of more effective therapists working with more severe clients (Pereira, Barkham, Kellett, & Saxon, 2016). For practitioners, given that evidence suggests therapist effects operate with clients presenting with greater degrees of psychological distress, this would suggest that client severity be a major consideration in the assignment to therapists. Accordingly, it provides a practical way to assign clients to therapists.

Therapists as the Natural Focus of Psychotherapy Research

In terms of the wealth of published psychotherapy research literature, the majority of research evidence has been based on the assumption that clients are the unit of analysis (i.e., studies tend to provide relatively full descriptions of the client sample). By contrast, descriptions of the therapists delivering the interventions are often absent or described in relative summary format. It is often not possible to determine from such summary descriptions the actual frequency distribution of clients to therapists to determine how many clients each therapist saw in a study. Overall, there needs to be far greater attention given to reporting descriptors of the sample of therapists used in any study. For example, a minimum reporting schedule might comprise information on demographics, training, experience, and supervision. Reports might also include information that portrays a comprehensive account of the distribution of clients to therapists (e.g., box plot rather than minimum and maximum).

One implication of the failure to design and analyze therapist effects is that there will be areas of evidence in which claims have been made about the effectiveness of a particular therapeutic approach that may be overstated. This is especially problematic in clinical trials aimed at comparing different psychotherapies (the assumed gold standard for practice guidelines), where the number of therapists and number of clients are small. This is because any effects that might be attributable to therapists will have been assigned to the treatment and reported as part of the treatment effects and thereby elevating the treatment effects (see Owen, Drinane, Idigo, & Valentine, 2015). Logically, therefore, if there are therapist effects, they will be a portion of the treatment effects. Hence, the precise size of the treatment effects will be smaller than stated unless therapists offer both treatments in any comparison.

The study of psychological interventions, and in particular the role of therapists, parallels the study of education and the relative effectiveness of teachers and schools. For example, education comprises at least four main components: pupils, teachers, schools, and curricula. The study of pupil attainment has recognized the inherent hierarchical nature of data (i.e., pupils are nested within classes [teachers], which are nested within schools, which are nested within curricula, which are themselves nested within regions [states]). The parallel with psychological therapy services is clear: Clients are nested within therapists, who are themselves nested within a service, which is itself nested within a locality, etc. This recognition of the natural structure of the system, and hence the data, is a fundamental starting point for investigating and understanding therapist effects in the context of large systems of care and in routine practice settings.

Analytic methods that take this structure into account also enable us to control for other variables at all levels as well as estimating the effects at all levels. Hence, we can also investigate effects at the level of the clinic or organization. Ignoring this natural structure and the natural variability between therapists in the analysis of client outcomes may produce misleading rankings and unfair comparisons between therapists and between clinics or organizations. At the same time, in applied clinical research it is imperative to identify therapists, clinics, and systems of care that yield poorer client outcomes to be able to attempt to improve them. Imel, Sheng, Baldwin, and Atkins (2015) showed the long-term dramatic effects of dropping the lowest performing therapists in a Monte Carlo simulation. The challenge for practitioners is how they respond when becoming aware that their clients' outcomes are low in comparison with those of their peers' clients.

The Number of Therapists Matters

If therapists are at least an equal focus in research studies, there needs to be a sufficient number to ensure a robust test of their effect. Maas and Hox (2004) advised a sample size of 100+ group units (i.e., therapists), but less if fewer predictor variables are included. Hence, if only the presence, or not, of therapist effects is being investigated, then the sample size can be lower, although numbers below 50 will usually be problematic. Similarly, complex models, with many variables and interactions, may require a sample of over 200 therapists. Studies with a number of predictor variables require a large number of therapists but also have implications for the number of clients. Maas and Hox and others suggested that 10 clients to each therapist would be adequate for most models. But following the rules for single level regression, it would seem to be a fair assumption that having more predictors in the model would require a larger sample size.

Although the focus might be on obtaining the largest number of therapists, a key issue in applying this approach in routine practice is defining the lower limits of the number of therapists to make inclusion of therapist effects standard in the analyses of data from clinical settings. Schiefele et al. (2016) addressed this issue on the basis of a large sample of 48,648 clients treated by 1,800 therapists combined from eight naturalistic datasets from three countries. Results from this large naturalistic dataset yielded therapist effects of 6.7% with initial impairment as a significant predictor for the aggregated sample, with a range between 2.7% and 10.2% depending on the sample. The authors constructed sample size tables for use in future research studies. For example, a study with at least four clients per therapist would need about 300 therapists, whereas a study with 30 clients per therapist would only require 40 therapists to have a comparable probability of yielding a statistically significant therapist effect. However, such criteria should not detract from efforts to include the analyses of therapist effects as standard in routine clinical data, providing that we understand the reliability of the given estimates where the number of therapists is smaller.

APPLYING THERAPIST-FOCUSED RESEARCH IN PRACTICE SETTINGS

Extending therapist-focused research into practice settings is a huge undertaking and is addressed extensively in other chapters in this volume (see Chapters 2 and 16). However, we conclude by making a few suggestions concerning areas of application that we consider would benefit from this approach.

Engagement, Dropout, and Deterioration

In terms of where to look for therapist effects, there is an argument for placing a focus very early in service delivery systems, in particular, focusing on investigating the association of therapist effects, engagement, and client dropout (e.g., Saxon, Barkham, Foster, & Parry, 2016; Saxon, Firth, & Barkham, 2016). In the same way that therapists differ in their client outcomes, they are likely to differ in terms of their rate of client dropout. However, dropout has been defined in various ways, making it difficult to estimate rates and draw conclusions. In addition, the phenomenon of early dramatic response (e.g., Haas, Hill, Lambert, & Morrell, 2002) has shed light on the fact that a substantial percentage of clients respond very early (within the first three sessions) and also depart from treatment before expected. Swift and Greenberg (2014) suggested that therapist and client characteristics are the most likely predictors. However, a key question is the contribution made by therapists to very early client dropout. Early dramatic treatment response aside, in general, past literature suggests that clients who drop out very early tend to have poorer clinical outcomes.

Therapist Training

It might be expected that there would be greater variability for novice trainees. It could be argued that reduced variability within a therapist's caseload would be the goal of training, because it would happen if deterioration rates were reduced. To address this issue, we recommend that clients be assessed on a session-by-session basis, and that therapist effects could then be managed by providing feedback to therapists about their clients' outcomes relative to average outcomes within a clinic or to benchmarks (see Okiishi et al., 2003). In such a setting, therapists could get feedback and compare their outcomes on the basis of clients' pre- and posttreatment change; the percentage of their clients who have recovered, improved, experienced no change, or deteriorated as compared to center averages; and which class of therapist they are based on their effectiveness and efficiency using CIs as protection from simplistic rankings.

Exceptional Therapists

A further issue centers on therapists who are outliers in the sense that they are exceptional therapists (see Elkin et al., 2006; Lutz, Leon, Martinovich, Lyons, & Stiles, 2007). What does it mean if therapist effects are attributable to only a few outlying therapists? Are the less effective therapists the ones with less competence, whereas therapists with very good outcomes have the highest competence? Is it adherence to a manual or the skill of therapists to adapt to the needs of clients? Furthermore, not much is known as to whether therapists achieve greater success with certain groups of clients and whether this could explain the differences between therapists. Future studies need to focus on the analyses of such outlier therapists (e.g., video analyses) that might identify the predictors as well as moderating and mediating variables contributing to therapist effects. It appears at this time that much of the variability in therapist outcomes can be explained by therapist interpersonal skills (Anderson, Ogles, Patterson, Lambert, & Vermeersch, 2009; Hansen, Lambert, & Vlass, 2015; Pereira & Barkham, 2015).

CONCLUSION

We have drawn on research evidence spanning differing organizations and countries, using different measures, and differing durations of therapy and argued that there is a need to incorporate the study of therapist effects into research designs. This area of study would appear to be well suited to research carried out within the paradigm of practice-oriented research rather than clinical trials where clients are selected according to very specific criteria. In terms of research, it is not a question of arguing that therapist effects exist or not. Rather, it is a question concerning the conditions under which they are most apparent and then understanding what components or processes are contributing to such an effect. In terms of practice, it is a matter of using the available research evidence to improve clinical care to clients in everyday practice.

APPENDIX 1.1

The phenomenon of therapist effects can be represented visually. Figure 1A.1 comprises three representations using data from a published study (Saxon & Barkham, 2012). It shows how multilevel modeling extends single level regression analysis to take into account therapist variability and produces a more informative and accurate picture of data at the level of a clinical setting.

The top portion of Figure 1A.1, produced by a single level linear regression model, has a single regression line, or "line of best fit," through the clients'

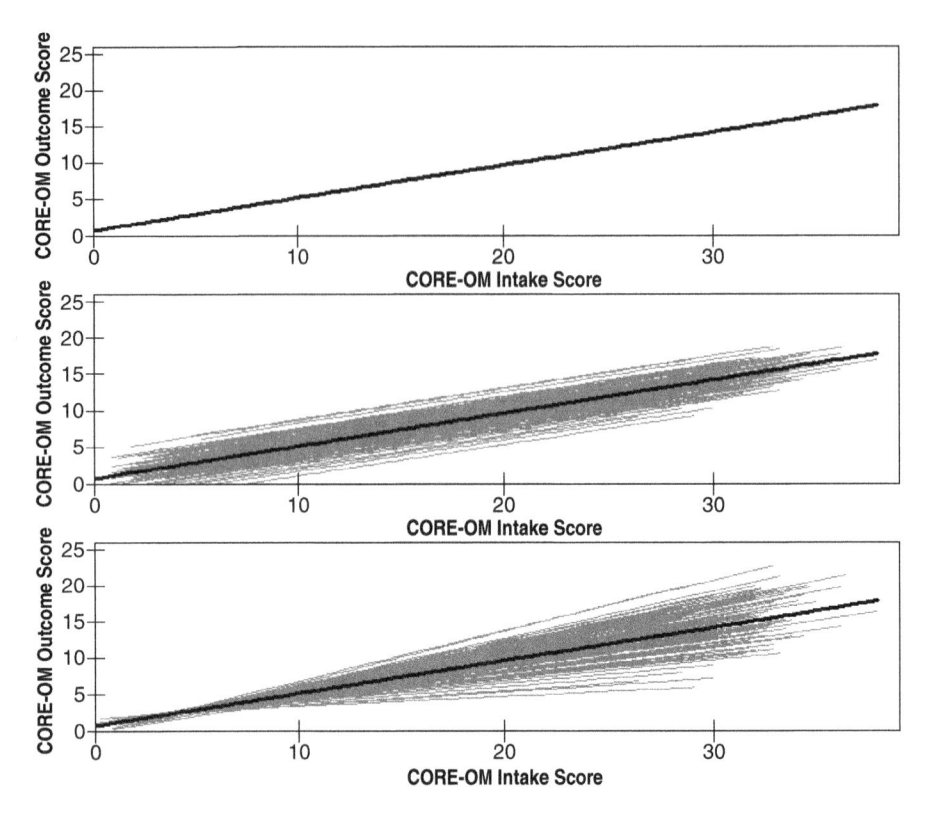

Figure 1A.1. Lines of "best fit" through client intake and outcome scores on the Clinical Outcomes in Routine Evaluation–Outcome Measure (CORE-OM). Data from Saxon and Barkham (2012).

($N = 10,786$) intake and outcome score data. For example, clients with an intake score of 20 (*x*-axis) would be predicted to have an outcome score of approximately 10 (*y*-axis). Although the slope indicates that higher clients' intake scores generally result in higher client outcome scores, its usefulness is limited and, as with a single service effect size, it may be masking variability between therapists.

In the middle portion of Figure 1A.1, produced by a multilevel model, the variability between the therapists ($N = 119$) is shown by the individual lines, each representing the best-fitting line through each therapist's client data. Here, each therapist has their own regression line through their data. The chart shows the variability between therapists with the distance between the uppermost and lowermost gray line indicating the extent of that variability. However, each therapist's line is parallel. That is, in this model it is assumed that client intake scores are impacting on therapists' outcomes to exactly the same degree and the therapist effects are the same across intake severity.

In contrast, the bottom portion of Figure 1A.1 allows the relationship between client intake and outcome scores to vary between therapists. Here, the therapist regression lines are not parallel but fan out as client severity increases. Those therapists' lines toward the bottom of the fan appear to have better outcomes generally and considerably better outcomes for more severe clients than those therapists toward the top of the fan. The distance between the uppermost and lowermost therapist lines at each client intake score reflects the degree of variability between therapists at each level of client severity. While there is little variability between therapists for lower intake scores, this variability increases as client intake severity increases. Therefore, unlike the middle portion, the therapist effects are not the same across levels of severity, but increase as severity increases.

REFERENCES

Adelson, J. L., & Owen, J. (2012). Bringing the psychotherapist back: Basic concepts for reading articles examining therapist effects using multilevel modeling. *Psychotherapy: Theory, Research, Practice, Training, 49*, 152–162. http://dx.doi.org/10.1037/a0023990

Anderson, T., Ogles, B. M., Patterson, C. L., Lambert, M. J., & Vermeersch, D. A. (2009). Therapist effects: Facilitative interpersonal skills as a predictor of therapist success. *Journal of Clinical Psychology, 65*, 755–768. http://dx.doi.org/10.1002/jclp.20583

Baldwin, S. A., & Imel, Z. E. (2013). Therapist effects: Findings and methods. In M. J. Lambert (Ed.), *Bergin and Garfield's handbook of psychotherapy and behavior change* (6th ed., pp. 258–297). New York, NY: Wiley.

Barkham, M., Margison, F., Leach, C., Lucock, M., Mellor-Clark, J., Evans, C., . . . McGrath, G. (2001). Service profiling and outcomes benchmarking using the CORE-OM: Toward practice-based evidence in the psychological therapies. *Journal of Consulting and Clinical Psychology, 69*, 184–196. http://dx.doi.org/10.1037/0022-006X.69.2.184

Brown, G. S., Lambert, M. J., Jones, E. R., & Minami, T. (2005). Identifying highly effective psychotherapists in a managed care environment. *The American Journal of Managed Care, 11*, 513–520.

Cella, M., Stahl, D., Reme, S. E., & Chalder, T. (2011). Therapist effects in routine psychotherapy practice: An account from chronic fatigue syndrome. *Psychotherapy Research, 21*, 168–178. http://dx.doi.org/10.1080/10503307.2010.535571

Crits-Christoph, P., Baranackie, K., Kurcias, J., Beck, A., Carroll, K., Perry, K., . . . Zitrin, C. (1991). Meta-analysis of therapist effects in psychotherapy outcome studies. *Psychotherapy Research, 1*, 81–91. http://dx.doi.org/10.1080/10503309112331335511

Derogatis, L. R. (1975). *Brief symptom inventory.* Baltimore, MD: Clinical Psychometric Research.

Dinger, U., Strack, M., Leichsenring, F., Wilmers, F., & Schauenburg, H. (2008). Therapist effects on outcome and alliance in inpatient psychotherapy. *Journal of Clinical Psychology, 64,* 344–354. http://dx.doi.org/10.1002/jclp.20443

Elkin, I., Falconnier, L., Martinovich, Z., & Mahoney, C. (2006). Therapist effects in the National Institute of Mental Health Treatment of Depression Collaborative Research Program. *Psychotherapy Research, 16,* 144–160. http://dx.doi.org/10.1080/10503300500268540

Haas, E., Hill, R. D., Lambert, M. J., & Morrell, B. (2002). Do early responders to psychotherapy maintain treatment gains? *Journal of Clinical Psychology, 58,* 1157–1172. http://dx.doi.org/10.1002/jclp.10044

Hansen, B. P., Lambert, M. J., & Vlass, E. N. (2015). Sudden gains and sudden losses in the clients of a "supershrink": 10 case studies. *Journal of Pragmatic Case Studies in Psychotherapy, 11,* 154–201. http://dx.doi.org/10.14713/pcsp.v11i3.1915

Horowitz, L. M., Rosenberg, S. E., Baer, B. A., Ureño, G., & Villaseñor, V. S. (1988). Inventory of interpersonal problems: Psychometric properties and clinical applications. *Journal of Consulting and Clinical Psychology, 56,* 885–892. http://dx.doi.org/10.1037/0022-006X.56.6.885

Imel, Z. E., Sheng, E., Baldwin, S. A., & Atkins, D. C. (2015). Removing very low-performing therapists: A simulation of performance-based retention in psychotherapy. *Psychotherapy: Theory, Research, Practice, Training, 52,* 329–336. http://dx.doi.org/10.1037/pst0000023

Jacobson, N. S., & Truax, P. (1991). Clinical significance: A statistical approach to defining meaningful change in psychotherapy research. *Journal of Consulting and Clinical Psychology, 59,* 12–19. http://dx.doi.org/10.1037/0022-006X.59.1.12

Kiesler, D. J. (1966). Some myths of psychotherapy research and the search for a paradigm. *Psychological Bulletin, 65,* 110–136. http://dx.doi.org/10.1037/h0022911

Kim, D.-M., Wampold, B. E., & Bolt, D. M. (2006). Therapist effects in psychotherapy: A random-effects modeling of the National Institute of Mental Health Treatment of Depression Collaborative Research Program data. *Psychotherapy Research, 16,* 161–172. http://dx.doi.org/10.1080/10503300500264911

Kraus, D. R., Castonguay, L., Boswell, J. F., Nordberg, S. S., & Hayes, J. A. (2011). Therapist effectiveness: Implications for accountability and patient care. *Psychotherapy Research, 21,* 267–276. http://dx.doi.org/10.1080/10503307.2011.563249

Lambert, M. J., Kahler, M., Harmon, C., Burlingame, G. M., & Shimokawa, K. (2011). *Administration & scoring manual for the Outcome Questionnaire-45.2.* Salt Lake City, UT: OQMeasures.

Lutz, W., & Barkham, M. (2015). Therapist effects. In R. Cautin & S. Lilienfeld (Eds.), *Encyclopedia of clinical psychology* (pp. 1–6). Hoboken, NJ: Wiley-Blackwell. http://dx.doi.org/10.1002/9781118625392.wbecp109

Lutz, W., Leon, S. C., Martinovich, Z., Lyons, J. S., & Stiles, W. B. (2007). Therapist effects in outpatient psychotherapy: A three-level growth curve approach. *Journal of Counseling Psychology, 54*, 32–39. http://dx.doi.org/10.1037/0022-0167.54.1.32

Lutz, W., Rubel, J., Schiefele, A.-K., Zimmermann, D., Böhnke, J. R., & Wittmann, W. W. (2015). Feedback and therapist effects in the context of treatment outcome and treatment length. *Psychotherapy Research, 25*, 647–660. http://dx.doi.org/10.1080/10503307.2015.1053553

Maas, C. J. M., & Hox, J. J. (2004). Robustness issues in multilevel regression analysis. *Statistica Neerlandica, 58*, 127–137. http://dx.doi.org/10.1046/j.0039-0402.2003.00252.x

Martindale, C. (1978). The therapist-as-fixed-effect fallacy in psychotherapy research. *Journal of Consulting and Clinical Psychology, 46*, 1526–1530. http://dx.doi.org/10.1037/0022-006X.46.6.1526

Najavits, L. M., & Strupp, H. H. (1994). Differences in the effectiveness of psychodynamic therapists: A process-outcome study. *Psychotherapy: Theory, Research, & Practice, 31*, 114–123. http://dx.doi.org/10.1037/0033-3204.31.1.114

Okiishi, J., Lambert, M. J., Nielsen, S. L., & Ogles, B. M. (2003). Waiting for supershrink: An empirical analysis of therapist effects. *Clinical Psychology & Psychotherapy, 10*, 361–373. http://dx.doi.org/10.1002/cpp.383

Okiishi, J. C., Lambert, M. J., Eggett, D., Nielsen, L., Dayton, D. D., & Vermeersch, D. A. (2006). An analysis of therapist treatment effects: Toward providing feedback to individual therapists on their clients' psychotherapy outcome. *Journal of Clinical Psychology, 62*, 1157–1172. http://dx.doi.org/10.1002/jclp.20272

Osler, W. (1904). *Aequanimitas, with other addresses to medical students, nurses and practitioners of medicine.* Philadelphia, PA: Blakiston's, Son, & Co.

Owen, J., Drinane, J. M., Idigo, K. C., & Valentine, J. C. (2015). Psychotherapist effects in meta-analyses: How accurate are treatment effects? *Psychotherapy: Theory, Research, Practice, Training, 52*, 321–328. http://dx.doi.org/10.1037/pst0000014

Pereira, J.-A., & Barkham, M. (2015). An exceptional, efficient, and resilient therapist: A case study in practice-based evidence. *Pragmatic Case Studies in Psychotherapy, 11*, 216–223.

Pereira, J.-A., Barkham, M., Kellett, S., & Saxon, D. (2016). The role of practitioner resilience and mindfulness in effective practice: A practice-based feasibility study. *Administration and Policy in Mental Health.* Advance online publication. http://dx.doi.org/10.1007/s10488-016-0747-0

Project MATCH Research Group. (1998). Therapist effects in three treatments for alcohol problems. *Psychotherapy Research, 8*, 455–474.

Raudenbush, S. W., & Bryk, A. S. (2002). *Hierarchical linear models: Applications and data analysis methods* (2nd ed.). Thousand Oaks, CA: Sage.

Ricks, D. F. (1974). Supershrink: Methods of a therapist judged successful on the basis of adult outcomes of adolescent patients. In D. F. Ricks, M. Roff, & A. Thomas (Eds.), *Life history research in psychopathology* (Vol. 3, pp. 275–297). Minneapolis: University of Minnesota Press.

Saxon, D., & Barkham, M. (2012). Patterns of therapist variability: Therapist effects and the contribution of patient severity and risk. *Journal of Consulting and Clinical Psychology, 80,* 535–546. http://dx.doi.org/10.1037/a0028898

Saxon, D., Barkham, M., Foster, A., & Parry, G. (2016). The contribution of therapist effects to patient dropout and deterioration in the psychological therapies. *Clinical Psychology & Psychotherapy.* Advance online publication. http://dx.doi.org/10.1002/cpp.2028

Saxon, D., Firth, N., & Barkham, M. (2016). The relationship between therapist effects and therapy delivery factors: Therapy modality, dosage, and non-completion. *Administration and Policy in Mental Health and Mental Health Services Research.* Advance online publication. http://dx.doi.org/10.1007/s10488-016-0750-5

Schiefele, A-K., Lutz, W., Barkham, M., Rubel, J., Saxon, D., Schulte, D., . . . Lambert, M. J. (2016). The extent of therapist effects in routine care—An investigation of contributing factors on 50,000 cases. *Administration and Policy in Mental Health.* Advance online publication. http://dx.doi.org/10.1007/s10488-016-0736-3

Snijders, T., & Bosker, R. (2004). *Multilevel analysis: An introduction to basic and advanced multilevel modeling.* London, England: Sage.

Swift, J. K., & Greenberg, R. P. (2014). A treatment by disorder meta-analysis of dropout from psychotherapy. *Journal of Psychotherapy Integration, 24,* 193–207. http://dx.doi.org/10.1037/a0037512

Wampold, B. E. (2001). *The great psychotherapy debate: Models, methods, and findings.* Mahwah, NJ: Routledge.

Wampold, B. E., & Brown, G. S. (2005). Estimating variability in outcomes attributable to therapists: A naturalistic study of outcomes in managed care. *Journal of Consulting and Clinical Psychology, 73,* 914–923. http://dx.doi.org/10.1037/0022-006X.73.5.914

2

WHAT CHARACTERIZES EFFECTIVE THERAPISTS?

BRUCE E. WAMPOLD, SCOTT A. BALDWIN,
MARTIN GROSSE HOLTFORTH, AND ZAC E. IMEL

There are therapist effects. That is, some therapists consistently achieve better outcomes with patients than other therapists—and these differences are not due to random error, patient characteristics, or other systematic sources of variation. These effects are well established, most systematically in a meta-analysis, and found to exist in clinical trials and general practice, as well as in specialty clinics (Baldwin & Imel, 2013; see also Wampold & Imel, 2015). Therapist effects are described and the evidence for these effects is reviewed in Chapter 1 of this volume.

The most apparent question—and an urgent one—is, what are the characteristics and actions of the more effective therapists? Who are they? What do they do? This chapter focuses on what has historically been the focus of research addressing these questions, the challenges for research in this area, and the emerging answers to these questions.

---

http://dx.doi.org/10.1037/0000034-003
How and Why Are Some Therapists Better Than Others? Understanding Therapist Effects, L. G. Castonguay and C. E. Hill (Eds.)
Copyright © 2017 by the American Psychological Association. All rights reserved.

HISTORY OF RESEARCH ON THERAPIST CONTRIBUTIONS TO THE OUTCOME OF PSYCHOTHERAPY

In 2004, Larry Beutler and colleagues (2004) reviewed the literature related to variables that characterize effective therapists—including age, race/ethnicity/culture, gender, training (e.g., psychology, social work, professional counselor), background, personality, attitudes, and experience—and found little evidence that any of the therapist variables examined were consistently related to outcome. Besides finding a lack of evidence for therapist variables, Beutler et al. also observed that research on therapist variables had been decreasing in the decade preceding their review:

> The strongest impression with which we are left at the conclusion of this review is that over the last two decades, there had been a precipitous decline of interest in researching areas that are not associated with specific effects of treatment and its implementation. (p. 289)

A historical perspective on this observation is informative and involves the history of medicine, education, statistics, and agriculture, as well as psychology.

The experimental design and the statistical methods for analyzing data from randomized experiments was developed in the 1920s, most prominently by Sir Ronald Fisher (1925, 1935) and applied in three areas. Most directly, Fisher's methods were used in agriculture, particularly genetics, but also in agricultural experiments (there is a reason the split-plot design refers to plots of land). The second area was in education, where experimental designs were used to identify the most effective educational programs, motivated by the American Psychological Association's desire to convince the American public that psychology could be used for the public good (Danziger, 1990). The third area was medicine, where the double-blind randomized placebo control group design became the standard for testing the efficacy and specificity of drugs and approving their use (Shapiro & Shapiro, 1997).

In each of these instances the provider was not considered a source of variation. Agriculturists studied seed variation, irrigation practices, and fertilizers, but ignored the farmer; psychologists studied whether one curriculum was superior to another, but ignored the teachers, who were thought to be interchangeable (the teachers were mostly female and were replaced when they married and became pregnant); and, of course, medicine privileged the substance (or procedure) provided to patients and not something about the characteristics of the physician (Wampold & Bhati, 2004; Wampold & Imel, 2015). In all three cases, the investigative focus was on the practice rather than the provider, and variability in outcomes because of the provider was ignored, even though the statistical machinery for modeling provider effects within clinical trials was developed in the 1920s (as discussed by Serlin, Wampold,

& Levin, 2003). The emphasis on treatments to the exclusion of therapists peaked with the availability of empirically supported treatments (Task Force on Promotion and Dissemination of Psychological Procedures, 1995).

Identifying the characteristics and actions of effective therapists can be challenging methodologically. Fortunately, since 2004, when Beutler et al. published their review, many of these challenges have been discussed in detail and methods for examining therapist effects have been developed and popularized. We now turn to examining the methodological issues involved in understanding what effective therapists do.

METHODOLOGICAL ISSUES INVOLVED IN IDENTIFYING THE CHARACTERISTICS AND ACTIONS OF EFFECTIVE THERAPISTS

The complicating factor involved in identifying the characteristics and actions of effective therapists is that patients are nested within therapists. That is, each patient is treated by one therapist, and each therapist treats multiple patients.[1] Nested data are often analyzed with multilevel models, in which patients would be one level and therapists would be another level.

Therapist Effects

Therapist effects can be described as *between-therapist variability*. That is, the average of the outcomes for Therapist A (i.e., the therapeutic benefit of psychotherapy averaged over all of the Therapist A's patients) may be greater than the average of the outcomes for Therapist B, which in turn is greater than the average of the outcomes for Therapist C. The greater the differences among the therapists, the greater the variability among the therapists. Because we are not interested in just these three particular therapists, the issue is whether the variability among the three therapists is greater than one would expect by chance had the therapists been selected from a broader population of therapists. As discussed in Chapter 1 of this volume, therapists do vary in their outcomes to a greater extent than would be expected by chance (Baldwin & Imel, 2013).

Therapist effects are typically indexed with an *intraclass correlation* (ICC), which can be defined as the proportion of total variability in outcomes that is associated with therapists. This definition of the ICC indicates how much of the variability in outcomes is due to the therapists. It is often expressed as a proportion or as a percentage. As reviewed in Chapter 1, the

---

[1]In cross-classified designs, some or all of patients see more than one therapist. Although cross-classification presents some additional challenges, largely with estimation, the general framework we discuss here generalizes to cross-classified data as well.

ICC for therapist effect is about 0.05, which actually is quite large, much larger than, for example, the differences between treatments (Wampold & Imel, 2015).

Identifying Characteristics and Actions of Effective Therapists

Next, we consider how to identify the characteristics and actions of effective therapists. Process research often involves correlating some variable derived from psychotherapy process with the outcome of psychotherapy. For example, one could assess empathy, either by ratings of observers of the psychotherapy or by ratings of the participants (patients or therapists), and correlate the empathy ratings with the outcome of psychotherapy across the cases. Many studies have done this and have found that empathy is indeed correlated with outcome (Elliott, Bohart, Watson, & Greenberg, 2011). Similarly, several other variables are correlated with outcome, including the alliance between patient and therapist (Flückiger, Del Re, Wampold, Symonds, & Horvath, 2012; Horvath, Del Re, Flückiger, & Symonds, 2011), goal consensus/collaboration (Tryon & Winograd, 2011), positive regard/affirmation (Farber & Doolin, 2011), and congruence/genuineness (Kolden, Klein, Wang, & Austin, 2011). It would be tempting to say that effective therapists are empathic, form good alliances with their patients, collaborate with their patients, and show positive regard and affirmation, but this is not necessarily the case.

The correlation between these variables and outcome, often called the *total correlation*, does not establish the importance of empathy as a characteristic of effective therapists because it ignores the levels of analysis (Baldwin, Wampold, & Imel, 2007). The problem can be illustrated with empathy. Empathy may well be a characteristic of therapists—some therapists may be characterologically more empathic than other therapists, and it shows in their work with patients. However, patients influence the process as well. It is more difficult to express empathy to an interpersonally aggressive patient, especially if the patient is dismissive of the therapist, than it is to a patient who is cooperative, motivated, and attached to the therapist. Clearly, some, if not much, of the variability in empathy is due to the patient. Thus, there are two sources of variability in empathy: the patient and the therapist. The question is, which level predicts outcome? Is it the therapist's contribution? That is, do therapists who generally express empathy across a range of patients produce better outcomes? Or is it the patient's contribution? Do cooperative, motivated, and attached patients elicit empathy from their therapists and also have better outcomes? Or is it both? Or maybe there is an interaction, in which some therapists can express empathy with some types of patients and this produces better outcomes.

The challenge is to isolate aspects of what the therapist brings to the therapy (characteristics of the therapist) and what the therapist does (actions) that leads to beneficial outcomes. Three methods have been used to identify some characteristics and actions of effective therapists.

Statistical Disaggregation Using Multilevel Models

The first way to identify the characteristics and actions of effective therapists is to disaggregate the total correlation into patient level and therapist level parts (Baldwin & Imel, 2013; Baldwin et al., 2007). The total correlation is composed of a within-therapist correlation (patient level) and a between-therapist correlation (therapist level). In the former, variability within each therapist is examined—this is the contribution that patients make because the therapist is held constant (the estimate of the patient contribution is actually the pooled estimate of all the within therapist coefficients). The between-therapist coefficient is derived by taking the average of a variable for each therapist (e.g., how empathic is a particular therapist, based on the average of the empathy scores for all his or her patients, compared with other therapists). Then the association with outcome of the within-patient and between-patient contributions can then be calculated, which provides an assessment of the relative contributions of each to outcome. This strategy has been used with the alliance, as discussed and illustrated next.

Measuring Therapist Responses to the Same Therapeutic Situation

The challenge is to isolate some characteristics or actions of therapists that are not elicited by differences among patients. In the previous strategy, the isolation is accomplished statistically. A second means to identify characteristics and actions of effective therapists is to have therapists respond to a challenging interpersonal situation, which remains constant from one therapist to the next, thus "equalizing" the patient contribution. These responses are an indication of a characteristic or action of each therapist. Statistically, the responses are a therapist-level variable directly measured instead of estimated by taking the average of some variable over all of the therapist's patients. Nevertheless, patients remain nested with therapists and this therapist-level variable must be considered in the context of multilevel models.

Assess Characteristics of Therapists Outside of Psychotherapy

Assessing nontherapy characteristics outside of psychotherapy is a variant of the previous strategy. In this strategy, some therapist characteristics are measured by self-report or report of others. Like the previous strategy, this directly yields a therapist-level variable that would be used in a multilevel model. Variables that could be measured in this way include those discussed by Beutler et al. (2004; e.g., age, gender). However, one could also assess characteristics more closely related to psychotherapy, such as the amount of time spent practicing therapeutic skills outside of psychotherapy and attitudes toward one's own practice, two variables discussed later in this chapter. Although many of the variables mentioned were reviewed by Beutler et al., it is important to note that multilevel models were not in use at the time and the analyses that were used violated assumptions of independence (i.e., ignored the fact that patients were nested within therapists).

IDENTIFIED CHARACTERISTICS AND ACTIONS OF EFFECTIVE THERAPISTS

We now turn to various characteristics and actions of effective therapists that have been identified through the methods previously described. Because this volume is devoted to many of these characteristics and actions, we mention them only briefly. Keep in mind that the exploration of therapist effects, despite a long history, is really only beginning.

The Ability to Form an Alliance Across a Range of Patients

The *alliance* is defined as a pantheoretical construct that reflects collaborative and purposeful work and is composed of three components: the bond between the patient and the therapist, an agreement about the goals of psychotherapy, and an agreement about the tasks of psychotherapy (Bordin, 1979; Hatcher & Barends, 2006; Horvath, 2006; Horvath & Luborsky, 1993). The alliance is the most researched construct in psychotherapy process research. Nearly 200 studies have investigated the correlation of alliance with outcome and found meta-analytically that there is a strong association of the alliance, measured early in psychotherapy, and the final outcome (Flückiger et al., 2012; Horvath et al., 2011). On the basis of this research, it would be tempting to say that a characteristic of effective therapists is that they form strong alliances with their patients, but it is unknown whether it is due to the patients' or the therapists' contribution.

Baldwin et al. (2007) statistically disaggregated the patient and therapist contribution to the alliance on the basis of data from counseling centers that measured alliance early in psychotherapy and outcome using the Outcome Questionnaire of 80 therapists and 331 patients. The total correlation was −.24, which is very close to the meta-analytic estimate, and 3% of the variability in outcomes was due to therapists (i.e., ICC = .03), which is smaller than estimates derived from other naturalistic settings (cf. Baldwin & Imel,

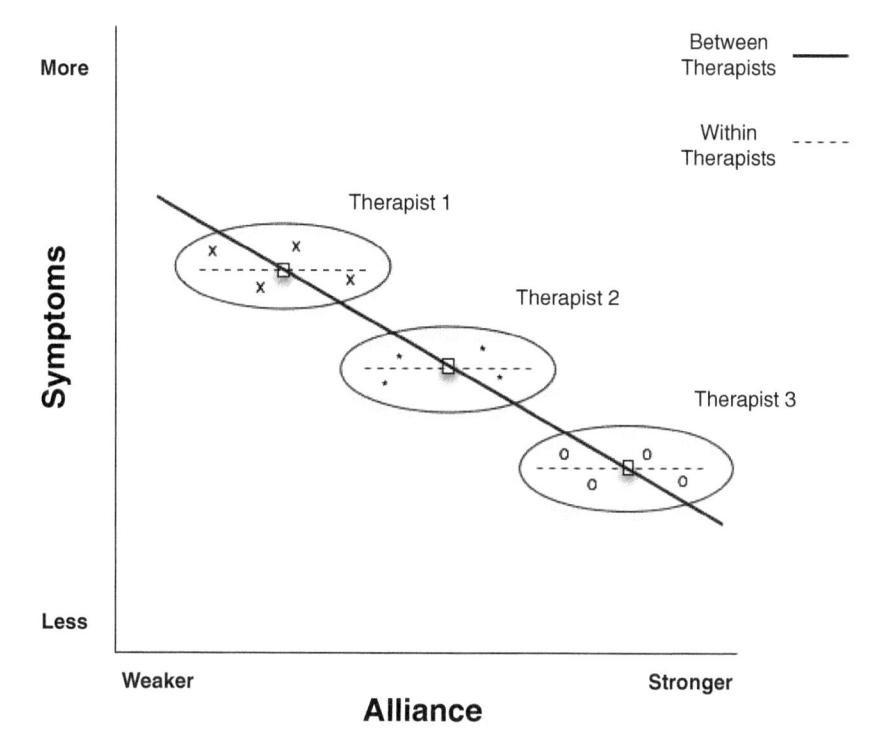

Figure 2.1. An illustration of the within- and between-therapist alliance–outcome correlations. Within- and between-therapist correlations are illustrated with only three therapists using simulated data to aid in the presentation of the correlations. The Xs refer to the alliance scores for Therapist 1's patients; the asterisks refer to the alliance scores of Therapist 2's patients; open circles refer to the alliance scores of Therapist 3's patients; open squares refer to each therapist's mean alliance score. From "Untangling the Alliance–Outcome Correlation: Exploring the Relative Importance of Therapist and Patient Variability in the Alliance," by S. A. Baldwin, B. E. Wampold, and Z. E. Imel, 2007, *Journal of Consulting and Clinical Psychology, 75,* p. 847. Copyright 2007 by the American Psychological Association.

2013). The between-therapist coefficient[2] was equal to −.33 ($p < .01$), indicating that the therapist contribution to the alliance was associated with outcome. However, the within-therapist coefficient was small (viz., −.08) and nonsignificant, indicating the patient contribution to the alliance was not associated with outcome. The results are presented graphically in Figure 2.1, which illustrates the results for five patients for each of three therapists. In this

---

[2]The model included the baseline values of outcome; thus, the between-therapist coefficient controlled for differences in the outcome prior to treatment.

figure, Therapist 3 is able to form stronger alliances with his or her patients than is Therapist 1 (i.e., the average alliance of Therapist 3 is greater than the average alliance of Therapist 1) and also has better outcomes (i.e., less distress, adjusted for pretreatment functioning). Therefore, one characteristic of effective therapists is that they are able to form alliances across a range of patients. Note that patients who have poorer alliances than other patients of the same therapist do not have poorer outcomes than these other patients (i.e., the within-therapist effect was nil). Think of it this way. A patient with a poor attachment history, an insecure attachment style, chaotic and impoverished interpersonal relationships, and features of borderline personality comes to psychotherapy with Therapist 3. Because of characteristics of the patient, the alliance with Therapist 3 will be relatively low compared with another patient who comes to psychotherapy with Therapist 3; however, the relationship that this patient has with Therapist 3 is better than it would have been had this patient seen Therapist 1 and possibly better than any relationship the patient has ever had—and this is therapeutic.

The importance of the therapist contribution to the alliance has been verified several times (Crits-Christoph et al., 2009; Dinger, Strack, Leichsenring, Wilmers, & Schauenburg, 2008; Zuroff, Kelly, Leybman, Blatt, & Wampold, 2010), although not always (Falkenström, Granström, & Holmqvist, 2014). Importantly, there is a meta-analytic result that supports Baldwin et al.'s (2007) conclusions, on the basis of primary studies that report only the total correlation of alliance and outcome. Del Re, Flückiger, Horvath, Symonds, and Wampold (2012) observed that the ratio of patients to therapists (PTR) varied greatly in these studies. When the PTR was large (i.e., many patients per therapist), then most of the variability in the alliance is due to the patient, whereas when PTR equals 1, the variability in the alliance is due entirely to the therapist. As expected, if Baldwin et al.'s results hold, then PTR should be associated with the size of the total correlation reported in each primary study: the larger the PTR, the smaller the total correlation. The expected association was found; it was not due to various other moderators that posed confounds, and quantitatively, the estimates produced by the meta-analysis were approximately equal to Baldwin et al.'s results.

Facilitative Interpersonal Skills

Characteristics of patients influence the therapeutic process, making it difficult to identify the characteristics and actions of effective therapists. One way around this problem is to use a standard stimulus, which is what Anderson, Ogles, Patterson, Lambert, and Vermeersch did in their 2009 study. They presented a video of a challenging patient to 25 therapists at a college counseling center, and the therapists recorded their responses to the patient at various instances. The responses were then coded for what the authors called *facilitative interpersonal skills* (FIS), which included verbal fluency, emotional expression, persuasiveness, hopefulness, warmth, empathy, alliance-bond capacity, and problem focus. In a multilevel model, FIS scores, at the therapist level, were used to predict the improvement of 1,141 patients seen by the therapists. The results showed that FIS was a strong predictor of patient improvement in psychotherapy, roughly equivalent to a correlation of .47 between FIS and outcome. This research suggested that effective therapists are verbally fluent, express emotion appropriately, are persuasive, communicate hopefulness, are warm and empathic, have the capacity to create a bond with patients, and focus on patients' problems.

Anderson et al.'s (2009) study was retrospective because they collected FIS after the therapists had seen the patients. A similar study used a prospective design, in which psychology trainees in their first weeks of training watched the psychotherapy video and their responses were recorded and coded for FIS (Anderson, McClintock, Himawan, Song, & Patterson, 2016). The FIS scores were then used to predict the outcomes of the therapists as they began to see patients in their training, at least a year after the FIS was assessed. The results were not as strong as those of the previous study, but the FIS of therapists did predict outcomes of patients who were seen for eight or fewer sessions. The importance of FIS of trainees was also established in a randomized clinical trial (Anderson, Crowley, Himawan, Holmberg, & Uhlin, 2016).

Recently, Schöttke, Flückiger, Goldberg, Eversmann, and Lange (2016) conducted a study that produced results complementary to those of Anderson and colleagues (2009). Postgraduate students in a 5-year psychotherapy training course in either cognitive–behavioral psychotherapy or psychodynamic training in Germany were assessed via a structured interview and by applicants' response in a group discussion with other applicants after viewing a provoking film. The interview was designed to assess interpersonally related competencies and personal strengths/capabilities, and trainees' responses were rated by experts. The trainees' responses in the group discussion were rated on the following dimensions: (a) clarity of communication, (b) empathy and communicative attunement, (c) respect and warmth, (d) management of criticism, and (e) willingness to cooperate. These actions overlap with FIS to a great extent. The scores of the interview and the group interaction were used to predict the outcomes of patients seen during training. In a multilevel model with patients nested within therapists, the performance of the trainees in the group interaction predicted outcomes of patients, whereas the responses to the structured interview did not predict outcomes.

Professional Self-Doubt

Nissen-Lie, Monsen, Ulleberg, and Rønnestad (2013) investigated the effects of therapists' self-reported difficulties in practice and interpersonal functioning in therapeutic work on the outcomes of their patients. The use of therapist self-report is interesting because such variables rely on the therapists' perceptions of themselves, rather than something that is assessed by their actual performance in psychotherapy or by response to a stimulus. The sample involved 70 therapists seeing patients in multiple outpatient clinics in Norway. This research focused on several factors, although the results revealed that one factor of the questionnaire that assessed professional self-doubt (PSD) was predictive of outcome. PSD contained items that measured the therapists' doubt about their skill in helping patients (e.g., "lacking confidence that you might have a beneficial effect on a patient" and "unsure about how best to deal effectively with a patient"). In the multilevel models, the more therapists expressed PSD, the better the outcomes, suggesting that effective therapists are reflective about their professional practice and question their ability to help patients.

Deliberate Practice

Deliberate practice is defined as "individualized training activities especially designed . . . to improve specific aspects of an individual's performance through repetition and successive refinement" (Ericsson & Lehmann, 1996, pp. 278–279). These training activities need to fall outside of engagement in performance (e.g., deliberate practice for an athlete would involve practicing skills outside of games played). In a number of areas, including music, chess, athletics, and surgery, engagement in deliberate practice improves performance (Ericsson & Lehmann, 1996). In a sense, deliberate practice involves a willingness and investment in professional improvement and quite likely is used by clinicians who indicate that they have PSD.

Chow et al. (2015) hypothesized that the amount of time therapists devote to deliberate practice of psychotherapy, as reported by the therapists, would be related to the outcomes they achieve. Chow et al. used multilevel models to study the outcomes of 1,632 patients seen by 17 therapists. The therapists were part of a practice network and were in independent practice in the United Kingdom. Chow et al. found that the amount of time therapists reported spending time on improving targeted therapeutic skills predicted therapist outcomes. This result suggests that a characteristic of effective therapists is that they engage (or at least report that they engage) in deliberate practice.

ARE CHARACTERISTICS AND ACTIONS OF EFFECTIVE THERAPISTS UNIFORM?

Up to this point, we have discussed characteristics and actions of effective therapists as if they were universal—the characteristics and actions of effective therapists identified previously would benefit all patients, regardless of the characteristics of patients. Most clinicians would agree that therapists work better with some types of patients over other types of patients. For example, some therapists may work more effectively with women, and some therapists may work more effectively with ethnic minorities. In addition, some therapists may have special skills to work with particular problems, such as sexual dysfunction or personality disorders, because of specialized training for the treatment of such problems. This conjecture, in terms of research, would be an interaction between therapist (or therapist characteristics and actions) and characteristics of the patients (in multilevel models, this would be tested as a cross-level interaction). The question is whether therapist effects are uniform or whether they vary depending on characteristics of the patient. If the latter is true, then who is an effective therapist depends on the patient and patients should be matched with therapists.

Wampold and Brown (2005) found evidence for uniformity of therapist effects as therapists' outcomes were not influenced by patients' age, gender, severity of distress, or diagnosis. For example, therapists who were more effective treating moderately distressed patients were also more effective treating more severely distressed patients. The results for diagnosis were supported by the finding that those therapists who successfully reduced depressive symptoms also successfully reduced anxiety symptoms (Green, Barkham, Kellett, & Saxon, 2014). On the other hand, Kraus, Castonguay, Boswell, Nordberg, and Hayes (2011) found that therapist effects were not uniform across problem domains, and they went so far as to say that "therapists skilled in one domain may be harmful in another" (p. 273). However, a replication of this study using the same outcome measure showed that therapists were relatively consistent in their performance across domains (Kraus et al., 2016), a result consistent with the research using two other outcome measures (the Outcome Questionnaire and the Clinical Outcomes in Routine Evaluation–Outcome Measure; Nissen-Lie et al., 2016). The uniformity of therapist effects is discussed in more detail in Chapter 3 of this volume, but is clearly an area of further inquiry.

There is emerging evidence for cultural competence. Some therapists in the United States seem to produce better outcomes with racial and ethnic minority patients than they do with European Americans, whereas others seem to produce better outcomes with European Americans than they do with racial and ethnic minorities (Hayes, Owen, & Bieschke, 2015; Imel et al., 2011). There is also evidence that some therapists have relatively better outcomes with female patients than male patients and that the opposite holds for other therapists (Owen, Wong, & Rodolfa, 2009; but see Huppert, Bufka, Barlow, Gorman, Shear, & Woods, 2001, who did not find therapist effects for gender matching). With regard to the cultural competence and gender competence, the size of the interaction is modest in comparison with therapist effects—that is, more effective therapists generally get better outcomes with all cultural groups and genders.

BACK TO THE FUTURE: WHAT THERAPIST CHARACTERISTICS AND ACTIONS ARE NOT PREDICTIVE OF OUTCOME?

We noted at the beginning of this chapter that Beutler et al. (2004) found that many therapist variables were unrelated to the outcome achieved by the therapists. Many of these variables were examined in the various studies reviewed in this chapter, and the researchers used the proper statistical methods—the conclusions from these studies are similar to those of Beutler et al.

Generally, the age of therapists has been found to be unrelated to outcome (e.g., Chow et al., 2015; Huppert et al., 2001; Wampold & Brown, 2005; but see Anderson et al., 2009, for an exception). Therapist gender also does not seem to predict outcome (Anderson et al., 2009; Chow et al., 2015; Owen et al., 2009; Schöttke et al., 2016; Wampold & Brown, 2005). Professional degree (e.g., psychology, psychiatry, social work, professional counselor) similarly appears to be unrelated to outcome (Chow et al., 2015; Kraus et al., 2016; Wampold & Brown, 2005).

An interesting null result was found in Anderson et al.'s (2009) investigation of the role of facilitative interpersonal skills. Beside the difficult patient stimulus, the social skills of the therapists were assessed using a widely used self-report instrument (the Social Skills Inventory). As mentioned previously, therapist facilitative interpersonal skills predicted outcomes, but self-reported social skills did not. Also, Schöttke et al. (2016) found that trainees' responses to a structured interview designed to assess interpersonal competence did not predict psychotherapy outcomes. It seems that particular interpersonal skills demonstrated in challenging situations (e.g., in response to a difficult patient or after watching a provoking film) are important but are not revealed by a self-report or responses to questions about interpersonal competence.

A somewhat controversial finding is that therapist experience appears to be unrelated to outcome (Tracey, Wampold, Lichtenberg, & Goodyear,

2014), a result that is replicated in several of the studies cited in this chapter (Chow et al., 2015; Kraus et al., 2016; Wampold & Brown, 2005; but see Huppert et al., 2001). Studies examining experience typically have relied on cross-sectional designs (i.e., do more experienced therapists at one point in time have better outcomes that less experienced therapists at the same point in time?). The first longitudinal study of therapist experience showed that over time (or number of cases treated), therapists' outcomes actually decrease, albeit by a very small amount (Goldberg et al., 2016). However, in this study, there was a random effect, which showed that some therapists did improve over time. It is necessary, then, to characterize those therapists who do improve with deliberate practice as one candidate to investigate.

Consistent with the more general literature on theoretical orientation (Wampold & Imel, 2015), the studies examining characteristics and actions of effective therapists have found that theoretical orientation did not predict therapists' outcomes (Anderson et al., 2009; Chow et al., 2015; Schöttke et al., 2016). It also appears that therapists' adherence to a treatment protocol and the rated competence of delivering a particular treatment does not predict the outcomes of psychotherapy (Boswell et al., 2013; Huppert et al., 2001; Webb, DeRubeis, & Barber, 2010), although more rigorous disaggregation studies are needed to corroborate this conclusion.

CONCLUSION

The identification of characteristics and actions of effective therapists has been hindered by a number of factors. First, methods able to disentangle the therapist and the patient contribution to psychotherapy process have only recently been developed and applied to psychotherapy research. Second, the variables examined traditionally have been limited to self-report measures. Third, research devoted to identifying more effective treatments with clinical trials has ignored therapist effects. Nevertheless, the application of innovative research designs and sophisticated statistical methods has revealed that effective therapists (a) form alliances across a range of patients, (b) have a sophisticated set of interpersonal skills that are revealed in challenging situations, (c) express professional self-doubt, and (d) practice psychotherapy skills outside of delivering treatment to patients. Whether therapists are uniformly effective or whether therapist effects depend on patients' characteristics or problem-type is not yet clear. Also, it seems that some characteristics of therapists do not predict outcomes, including demographics (e.g., age, gender), self-reported interpersonal skills, theoretical orientation, experience, adherence to a treatment protocol, and rated competence performing a particular treatment.

The effort to identify the characteristics and actions of effective therapists has increased in the past decade. Together with the application of more sophisticated methods, much about effective therapists is being revealed. However, there is much to be learned, and previous results need to be replicated.

REFERENCES

Anderson, T., Crowley, M. J., Himawan, L., Holmberg, J. K., & Uhlin, B. D. (2016). Therapist facilitative interpersonal skills and training status: A randomized clinical trial on alliance and outcome. *Psychotherapy Research*, 26, 511–529.

Anderson, T., McClintock, A. S., Himawan, L., Song, X., & Patterson, C. L. (2016). A prospective study of therapist facilitative interpersonal skills as a predictor of treatment outcome. *Journal of Consulting and Clinical Psychology*, 84, 57–66. http://dx.doi.org/10.1037/ccp0000060

Anderson, T., Ogles, B. M., Patterson, C. L., Lambert, M. J., & Vermeersch, D. A. (2009). Therapist effects: Facilitative interpersonal skills as a predictor of therapist success. *Journal of Clinical Psychology*, 65, 755–768. http://dx.doi.org/10.1002/jclp.20583

Baldwin, S. A., & Imel, Z. E. (2013). Therapist effects: Finding and methods. In M. J. Lambert (Ed.), *Bergin and Garfield's handbook of psychotherapy and behavior change* (6th ed., pp. 258–297). New York, NY: Wiley.

Baldwin, S. A., Wampold, B. E., & Imel, Z. E. (2007). Untangling the alliance-outcome correlation: Exploring the relative importance of therapist and patient variability in the alliance. *Journal of Consulting and Clinical Psychology*, 75, 842–852. http://dx.doi.org/10.1037/0022-006X.75.6.842

Beutler, L. E., Malik, M., Alimohamed, S., Harwood, T. M., Talebi, H., Noble, S., & Wong, E. (2004). Therapist variables. In M. J. Lambert (Ed.), *Bergin and Garfield's handbook of psychotherapy and behavior change* (5th ed., pp. 227–306). New York, NY: Wiley.

Bordin, E. S. (1979). The generalizability of the psychoanalytic concept of the working alliance. *Psychotherapy: Theory, Research & Practice*, 16, 252–260. http://dx.doi.org/10.1037/h0085885

Boswell, J. F., Gallagher, M. W., Sauer-Zavala, S. E., Bullis, J., Gorman, J. M., Shear, M. K., . . . Barlow, D. H. (2013). Patient characteristics and variability in adherence and competence in cognitive-behavioral therapy for panic disorder. *Journal of Consulting and Clinical Psychology*, 81, 443–454. http://dx.doi.org/10.1037/a0031437

Chow, D. L., Miller, S. D., Seidel, J. A., Kane, R. T., Thornton, J. A., & Andrews, W. P. (2015). The role of deliberate practice in the development of highly effective psychotherapists. *Psychotherapy*, 52, 337–345. http://dx.doi.org/10.1037/pst0000015

Crits-Christoph, P., Gallop, R., Temes, C. M., Woody, G., Ball, S. A., Martino, S., & Carroll, K. M. (2009). The alliance in motivational enhancement therapy and counseling as usual for substance use problems. *Journal of Consulting and Clinical Psychology, 77*, 1125–1135. http://dx.doi.org/10.1037/a0017045

Danziger, K. (1990). *Constructing the subject: Historical origins of psychological research.* Cambridge, England: Cambridge University Press. http://dx.doi.org/10.1017/CBO9780511524059

Del Re, A. C., Flückiger, C., Horvath, A. O., Symonds, D., & Wampold, B. E. (2012). Therapist effects in the therapeutic alliance-outcome relationship: A restricted-maximum likelihood meta-analysis. *Clinical Psychology Review, 32*, 642–649. http://dx.doi.org/10.1016/j.cpr.2012.07.002

Dinger, U., Strack, M., Leichsenring, F., Wilmers, F., & Schauenburg, H. (2008). Therapist effects on outcome and alliance in inpatient psychotherapy. *Journal of Clinical Psychology, 64*, 344–354. http://dx.doi.org/10.1002/jclp.20443

Elliott, R., Bohart, A. C., Watson, J. C., & Greenberg, L. S. (2011). Empathy. *Psychotherapy, 48*, 43–49. http://dx.doi.org/10.1037/a0022187

Ericsson, K. A., & Lehmann, A. C. (1996). Expert and exceptional performance: Evidence of maximal adaptation to task constraints. *Annual Review of Psychology, 47*, 273–305. http://dx.doi.org/10.1146/annurev.psych.47.1.273

Falkenström, F., Granström, F., & Holmqvist, R. (2014). Working alliance predicts psychotherapy outcome even while controlling for prior symptom improvement. *Psychotherapy Research, 24*, 146–159. http://dx.doi.org/10.1080/10503307.2013.847985

Farber, B. A., & Doolin, E. M. (2011). Positive regard and affirmation. In J. C. Norcross (Ed.), *Psychotherapy relationships that work: Evidence-based responsiveness* (2nd ed., pp. 168–186). New York, NY: Oxford University Press. http://dx.doi.org/10.1093/acprof:oso/9780199737208.003.0008

Fisher, R. A. (1925). *Statistical methods for research workers.* London, England: Oliver & Boyd.

Fisher, R. A. (1935). *The design of experiments.* Edinburgh, Scotland: Oliver & Boyd.

Flückiger, C., Del Re, A. C., Wampold, B. E., Symonds, D., & Horvath, A. O. (2012). How central is the alliance in psychotherapy? A multilevel longitudinal meta-analysis. *Journal of Counseling Psychology, 59*, 10–17. http://dx.doi.org/10.1037/a0025749

Goldberg, S. B., Rousmaniere, T., Miller, S. D., Whipple, J., Nielsen, S. L., Hoyt, W. T., & Wampold, B. E. (2016). Do psychotherapists improve with time and experience? A longitudinal analysis of outcomes in a clinical setting. *Journal of Counseling Psychology, 63*, 1–11. http://dx.doi.org/10.1037/cou0000131

Green, H., Barkham, M., Kellett, S., & Saxon, D. (2014). Therapist effects and IAPT psychological wellbeing practitioners (PWPs): A multilevel modelling and mixed methods analysis. *Behaviour Research and Therapy, 63*, 43–54. http://dx.doi.org/10.1016/j.brat.2014.08.009

Hatcher, R. L., & Barends, A. W. (2006). How a return to theory could help alliance research. *Psychotherapy: Theory, Research, Practice, Training, 43*, 292–299. http://dx.doi.org/10.1037/0033-3204.43.3.292

Hayes, J. A., Owen, J., & Bieschke, K. J. (2015). Therapist differences in symptom change with racial/ethnic minority clients. *Psychotherapy, 52*, 308–314. http://dx.doi.org/10.1037/a0037957

Horvath, A. O. (2006). The alliance in context: Accomplishments, challenges, and future directions. *Psychotherapy: Theory, Research, Practice, Training, 43*, 258–263. http://dx.doi.org/10.1037/0033-3204.43.3.258

Horvath, A. O., Del Re, A. C., Flückiger, C., & Symonds, D. (2011). Alliance in individual psychotherapy. In J. C. Norcross (Ed.), *Psychotherapy relationships that work: Evidence-based responsiveness* (2nd ed., pp. 25–69). New York, NY: Oxford University Press. http://dx.doi.org/10.1093/acprof:oso/9780199737208.003.0002

Horvath, A. O., & Luborsky, L. (1993). The role of the therapeutic alliance in psychotherapy. *Journal of Consulting and Clinical Psychology, 61*, 561–573. http://dx.doi.org/10.1037/0022-006X.61.4.561

Huppert, J. D., Bufka, L. F., Barlow, D. H., Gorman, J. M., Shear, M. K., & Woods, S. W. (2001). Therapists, therapist variables, and cognitive-behavioral therapy outcome in a multicenter trial for panic disorder. *Journal of Consulting and Clinical Psychology, 69*, 747–755. http://dx.doi.org/10.1037/0022-006X.69.5.747

Imel, Z. E., Baldwin, S., Atkins, D. C., Owen, J., Baardseth, T., & Wampold, B. E. (2011). Racial/ethnic disparities in therapist effectiveness: A conceptualization and initial study of cultural competence. *Journal of Counseling Psychology, 58*, 290–298. http://dx.doi.org/10.1037/a0023284

Kolden, G. G., Klein, M. H., Wang, C.-C., & Austin, S. B. (2011). Congruence/genuineness. *Psychotherapy, 48*, 65–71. http://dx.doi.org/10.1037/a0022064

Kraus, D. R., Bentley, J. H., Alexander, P. C., Boswell, J. F., Constantino, M. J., Baxter, E. E., & Castonguay, L. G. (2016). Predicting therapist effectiveness from their own practice-based evidence. *Journal of Consulting and Clinical Psychology, 84*, 473–483. http://dx.doi.org/10.1037/ccp0000083

Kraus, D. R., Castonguay, L., Boswell, J. F., Nordberg, S. S., & Hayes, J. A. (2011). Therapist effectiveness: Implications for accountability and patient care. *Psychotherapy Research, 21*, 267–276. http://dx.doi.org/10.1080/10503307.2011.563249

Nissen-Lie, H. A., Goldberg, S. B., Hoyt, W. T., Falkenström, F., Holmqvist, R., Nielsen, S. L., & Wampold, B. E. (2016). Are therapists uniformly effective across patient outcome domains? A study on therapist effectiveness in two different treatment contexts. *Journal of Counseling Psychology, 63*, 367–378. http://dx.doi.org/10.1037/cou0000151

Nissen-Lie, H. A., Monsen, J. T., Ulleberg, P., & Rønnestad, M. H. (2013). Psychotherapists' self-reports of their interpersonal functioning and difficulties in practice as predictors of patient outcome. *Psychotherapy Research, 23*, 86–104. http://dx.doi.org/10.1080/10503307.2012.735775

Owen, J., Wong, Y. J., & Rodolfa, E. (2009). Empirical search for psychotherapists' gender competence in psychotherapy. *Psychotherapy: Theory, Research, Practice, Training, 46*, 448–458. http://dx.doi.org/10.1037/a0017958

Schöttke, H., Flückiger, C., Goldberg, S. B., Eversmann, J., & Lange, J. (2016). Predicting psychotherapy outcome based on therapist interpersonal skills: A five-year longitudinal study of a therapist assessment protocol. *Psychotherapy Research.* Advance online publication. http://dx.doi.org/10.1080/10503307.2015.1125546

Serlin, R. C., Wampold, B. E., & Levin, J. R. (2003). Should providers of treatment be regarded as a random factor? If it ain't broke, don't "fix" it: A comment on Siemer and Joormann (2003). *Psychological Methods, 8,* 524–534. http://dx.doi.org/10.1037/1082-989X.8.4.524

Shapiro, A. K., & Shapiro, E. S. (1997). *The powerful placebo: From ancient priest to modern medicine.* Baltimore, MD: The Johns Hopkins University Press.

Task Force on Promotion and Dissemination of Psychological Procedures. (1995). Training in and dissemination of empirically-validated psychological treatment: Report and recommendations. *Clinical Psychologist, 48,* 2–23.

Tracey, T. J. G., Wampold, B. E., Lichtenberg, J. W., & Goodyear, R. K. (2014). Expertise in psychotherapy: An elusive goal? *American Psychologist, 69,* 218–229. http://dx.doi.org/10.1037/a0035099

Tryon, G. S., & Winograd, G. (2011). Goal consensus and collaboration. In J. C. Norcross (Ed.), *Psychotherapy relationships that work: Evidence-based responsiveness* (2nd ed., pp. 153–167). New York, NY: Oxford University Press. http://dx.doi.org/10.1093/acprof:oso/9780199737208.003.0007

Wampold, B. E., & Bhati, K. S. (2004). Attending to the omissions: A historical examination of the evidenced-based practice movement. *Professional Psychology: Research and Practice, 35,* 563–570. http://dx.doi.org/10.1037/0735-7028.35.6.563

Wampold, B. E., & Brown, G. S. (2005). Estimating variability in outcomes attributable to therapists: A naturalistic study of outcomes in managed care. *Journal of Consulting and Clinical Psychology, 73,* 914–923. http://dx.doi.org/10.1037/0022-006X.73.5.914

Wampold, B. E., & Imel, Z. E. (2015). *The great psychotherapy debate: The research evidence for what works in psychotherapy* (2nd ed.). New York, NY: Routledge.

Webb, C. A., DeRubeis, R. J., & Barber, J. P. (2010). Therapist adherence/competence and treatment outcome: A meta-analytic review. *Journal of Consulting and Clinical Psychology, 78,* 200–211. http://dx.doi.org/10.1037/a0018912

Zuroff, D. C., Kelly, A. C., Leybman, M. J., Blatt, S. J., & Wampold, B. E. (2010). Between-therapist and within-therapist differences in the quality of the therapeutic relationship: Effects on maladjustment and self-critical perfectionism. *Journal of Clinical Psychology, 66,* 681–697.

3

WHO WORKS FOR WHOM AND WHY? INTEGRATING THERAPIST EFFECTS ANALYSIS INTO PSYCHOTHERAPY OUTCOME AND PROCESS RESEARCH

MICHAEL J. CONSTANTINO, JAMES F. BOSWELL, ALICE E. COYNE, DAVID R. KRAUS, AND LOUIS G. CASTONGUAY

There is growing evidence that the individual psychotherapist can have a notable effect on clients' mental health treatment outcomes, with most research to date centered on the outcome of global symptom reduction and functional improvement (Baldwin & Imel, 2013; see also Chapters 2 and 3, this volume). Because the field has been somewhat slow to recognize the importance of these *therapist effects*, research is only beginning to address its complexity and determinants.

As one layer of complexity, symptom- and function-based outcomes can be conceptualized clinically and analyzed empirically at finer-grained multidimensional levels than the more typical global indices. In fact, a multidimensional approach to routine outcome assessment was recommended by the Society for Psychotherapy Research–American Psychological Association Core Battery Conference (Strupp, Horowitz, & Lambert, 1997). Consistent with this perspective, when therapist effects have been examined across

http://dx.doi.org/10.1037/0000034-004
How and Why Are Some Therapists Better Than Others? Understanding Therapist Effects, L. G. Castonguay and C. E. Hill (Eds.)
Copyright © 2017 by the American Psychological Association. All rights reserved.

multiple specific client outcome domains (e.g., depression, anxiety, substance use, sleep, quality of life, sexual functioning) with a measure like the Treatment Outcome Package (Kraus, Seligman, & Jordan, 2005), two main findings have emerged.

First, in large naturalistic samples, therapist effects are evident on specific outcomes; the individual psychotherapist can have a notable effect on clients' depression, substance use, and so forth (Kraus et al., 2016; Kraus, Castonguay, Boswell, Nordberg, & Hayes, 2011). Practically, when assessing a specific outcome domain such as depression, some therapists' clients (on average) achieve consistently better depression reduction than other therapists' clients (on average), with this same notion holding for other specific outcome domains. Although, which therapists are more effective could, and likely would, differ depending on the domain. Interestingly, the degree to which variability in a specific outcome is explained by therapists varies by domain. For example, in the Kraus et al. (2016) study, when accounting for initial severity and other risk factors (e.g., unemployment, divorce), the therapist had a more pronounced effect on outcome domains, like substance abuse (18.28% variance explained) and quality of life (18.72%) than other domains, like psychosis (3.71%) and mania (1.56%). Practically, it appears that the person of the therapist may have a greater influence when treating clients with substance abuse problems than when treating clients with psychosis (for the latter, other factors will explain a greater portion of the outcome variance pie). Others have replicated this finding of differential therapist effects across quality of life, functional, and symptom domains (e.g., Owen, Adelson, Budge, Kopta, & Reese, 2016).

The second finding that has emerged from multidimensional outcome studies focused on the therapists is a pattern of relative strengths and weaknesses within therapists' own practice. In the Kraus et al. (2011) study, results demonstrated a differential pattern of individual therapist performance depending on their clients' problem domain; for example, some therapists demonstrated substantial effectiveness in depression reduction but ineffectiveness or even harm in other domains. Many therapists demonstrated effectiveness over multiple domains, yet no therapists demonstrated reliable effectiveness across all domains. A small but notable 4% of therapists failed to demonstrate positive outcomes on any domain. These findings were replicated in the Kraus et al. (2016) study; even after controlling for significant variance at the client level, therapists demonstrated differential patterns of relative strengths and weaknesses within their caseload. Additionally, hierarchical linear modeling-based correlations demonstrated stability in therapists' domain-specific performance across subsequent clients. As one concrete example, therapists who were particularly effective in facilitating depression reduction in one wave of 30 clients within their caseload remained above average in facilitating depression reduction with a subsequent wave of 30 clients within their caseload.

Therefore, these studies suggest that globally focused outcome assessment may not capture all of the nuances of therapist effects. Rather, the potency of therapist effects in general may differ depending on the outcome domain, and therapists are differentially (and stably) effective within their own practices depending on the outcome domain. It is important to note, however, that although the outcome instruments in the studies mentioned previously were multidimensional in focus, other potentially important outcome domains were not investigated. For example, from a psychodynamic perspective, it may also be important to assess changes in personality organization or the development of more adaptive defenses. We assume that significant therapist effects would also be observed on such variables; however, we are unaware of therapist effects research that has focused on these constructs. These different types of outcomes (beyond symptoms and functioning assessed globally and specifically) would reflect yet another layer of complexity of the therapist effects.

The studies revealing that there are therapist effects on broad and domain-specific outcomes have far-reaching implications for clients, therapists, administrators, trainers, and policy makers, examples of which are discussed in depth in other chapters in this volume (e.g., Chapter 16). However, therapist effects research has yet to reach its full potential. It remains largely unknown (a) why or how some therapists are more effective than others, or largely comparable to others, in producing *global* client outcomes (e.g., general distress); (b) why or how some therapists are more effective than others, or largely comparable to others, in producing *specific* client outcomes (e.g., anxiety); and (c) why or how therapists are good at treating some conditions within their own caseloads, but not others (i.e., therapists' personal strengths and weaknesses).

To satisfy all stakeholders, especially therapists and those who train them, there is a pressing need for the field to turn its attention to uncovering such determinants of therapist effects, drawing on "big" (e.g., large-scale naturalistic studies), "medium" (e.g., single clinical trials), and "small" (e.g., microprocess comparisons of known good versus poor clinicians) data. To this effect, the remainder of this chapter discusses two main categories of the most promising determinants: individual characteristics of therapists and characteristics of the during-therapy process. More specifically, and expanding on issues covered in Chapter 2 of this volume, our main goals are to identify the determinants that have received empirical support, to suggest potential candidate determinants for future investigation, and to delineate statistical and methodological considerations that are relevant for such future research. For this last goal, we spotlight conceptually how the use of multilevel statistical modeling can be, and should be, used to assess therapist characteristics and characteristics of the during-therapy process that may promote a better understanding of why and how the individual therapist affects client improvement, lack thereof, or deterioration during psychotherapy. Using examples that reflect complex clinical realities, including different domains of functioning and the interaction between several variables, we also demonstrate that the failure to use multilevel modeling can lead to false empirical and clinical conclusions.

INDIVIDUAL CHARACTERISTICS OF THE THERAPIST

Individual therapist characteristics that might explain the therapist effect could involve a myriad of variables such as personality, attachment style, interpersonal history, history with own psychotherapy, training background, and experience, among others. The keys are to measure such therapist variables (historically a challenging task) and, assuming therapist willingness to be measured, to analyze the data in a way that can reveal determinants (predictors) of therapist effects. As Wampold et al. noted in Chapter 2 of this volume, this involves multilevel modeling to account for inherently nested data and to reveal between-therapist variability and within-therapist (or between-client) variability. Although an in-depth discussion of the statistical details is beyond the scope of this chapter, it may prove useful to outline the levels of a model and the steps to testing determinants of therapist effects with a concrete example in mind.

Consider that we were interested in testing whether therapist attachment anxiety explains between-therapist variability in an outcome (in this case, depression) that was discovered in the data. The first step would be to show that there is variability in clients' depression outcome that needs to be explained. If we had measured depression levels over time, these repeated measures (one form of nesting—measurement occasions within clients) would represent the first level of data in the model. Then, assuming between-client variability in depression change over treatment, at the second level of data we could add client level predictors of depression change. For this discussion, the most important element of this multilevel model is to investigate possible influences of the therapist on client depression change at the third level (another form of nesting—clients within therapists). Setting up this model allows for the proportion of variability in depression change accounted for by clients and therapists to be decomposed. It might be, for example, that the therapist explained 10% of the variability in client depression change, as revealed by an intraclass correlation (see Adelson & Owen, 2012; Chapter 2, this volume). As this is likely a clinically relevant proportion of variance explained by the person of the therapist, true therapist level predictors (such as therapist attachment anxiety) could be added to try to explain these therapist differences (i.e., reduce unexplained variance in the between-therapist effect). Like any regression model, the goal would be to reduce the unexplained variance (in this case, between-therapist variance) to zero (although, variables will at best decrease only some of the unexplained variance). In this example, it could be that therapists with less attachment anxiety have significantly better average outcomes across the clients on their caseload, implicating attachment anxiety as one, at least partial, determinant of the therapist effect.

We should reiterate that to do this kind of work effectively, researchers should design their studies and analyses with the possibility (or even likelihood) that therapist effects on outcome will exist. With such forethought, they can assess well-conceived putative (therapist-level) predictors of these effects. To date, studies including true therapist level predictors are limited; however, the limited work has revealed at least two promising individual therapist characteristics that likely explain at least part of therapist effects. As reviewed by Wampold et al. (Chapter 2, this volume), these characteristics are facilitative interpersonal skill (FIS) and deliberative practice (DP). FIS encompasses various features of clinical interaction, such as therapist verbal fluency, emotional expression, hope inspiration, and accurate empathy. In one study, therapist FIS (as assessed when each therapist simulated a response to the same video stimulus of a challenging client) predicted between-therapist differences in their *actual* clients' outcomes; that is, part of what made some therapists more effective on average (across their cases) than other therapists was possessing FIS vis-à-vis a standardized challenging therapeutic scenario (Anderson, Ogles, Patterson, Lambert, & Vermeersch, 2009).

DP encompasses an intentional effort to improve performance through methodical practice (Ericsson & Lehmann, 1996). In one study, the amount of time that therapists spent in DP predicted between-therapist differences in outcome; part of what made some therapists more effective on average than others was spending more time per week (by their own report) engaging in DP (Chow et al., 2015). Although promising, it is important to point out that research on FIS and DP as determinants of therapist effects requires replication.

In the Anderson et al. (2009) and Chow et al. (2015) studies, client outcome was assessed with a global outcome index. Thus, in addition to uncovering other individual therapist characteristics that predict between-therapist effects on global outcomes, future research also will need to assess what predicts therapists being especially good (or not), compared with others or themselves, at treating specific outcome domains as per multidimensional measures like the Treatment Outcome Package. As a speculative example, "wounded" therapists (clinicians who have experienced a similar mental health problem to the one that they are now treating) could be particularly effective at treating substance use compared with "nonwounded" therapists; however, these wounded therapists may be less effective at treating depression compared with their nonwounded counterparts who might be effective at treating depression because of interpersonal skill, which in turn might be less important for the most expert practitioners treating anxiety.

CHARACTERISTICS OF DURING-THERAPY PROCESS

Given that processes that occur during a course of psychotherapy can come in many guises, we are adopting a broad definition of a during-therapy process variable as any variable that might help explain how treatment works, whether measured in a moment during a session, following a session, or at some other time after treatment starts but before it ends (Castonguay, Nordberg, Schut, & Constantino, 2010). With this broad definition in mind, during-therapy process characteristics that might explain therapist effects could be explicit dyadic processes such as client–therapist bond, goal agreement, or collaboration. Alternatively, they could be therapist behaviors or attitudes that happen within the context of a treatment dyad (when considering individual therapy, which is our focus here), such as techniques delivered, during-session immediacy, or belief in the treatment. In fact, such variables could even be clients' behaviors or attitudes, such as homework compliance, emotional expression, or expectation for improvement. Implicit in investigating client process factors is the idea that different therapists may have different abilities to facilitate such processes (e.g., certain therapists may evoke more client emotion in session or inspire greater expectation of treatment success), which could then explain between-therapist differences in outcome. Like the individual characteristics of the therapists reviewed in the previous section, there are many possible dyadic process variables and during-therapy process variables (e.g., therapist or client behaviors and attitudes) that could explain some amount of the therapist effect on client outcomes. The keys, again, are to measure such variables and to analyze the data in a way that can reveal determinants of therapist effects (i.e., multilevel modeling).

To date, there is much research that does measure process variables; however, there is, relatively speaking, limited research that has used multilevel modeling, which has implications for how the extant literature is interpreted, empirically and clinically. For example, there is voluminous research on the total correlation between psychotherapy process variables and client outcomes (Crits-Christoph, Connolly Gibbons, & Mukherjee, 2013)—a correlation that does not disaggregate the association into therapist and client contributions. Such process variables include dyadic factors like the quality of the client–therapist alliance, a variable that has been frequently analyzed as a correlate of client treatment success. In a meta-analysis, the alliance has been shown to be significantly and positively correlated with client improvement ($r = .28, p < .0001$; Horvath, Del Re, Flückiger, & Symonds, 2011). Other process variables include therapist behaviors, like adherence to a treatment protocol, which was unrelated to outcome in a meta-analysis ($r = .02$; Webb, DeRubeis, & Barber, 2010). Still other process variables, like client attitudes, can correlate with outcome; for example, clients' early expectation for their treatment's success has been shown to be positively correlated with improvement ($r = .12$, $p < .001$; Constantino, Arnkoff, Glass, Ametrano, & Smith, 2011). These findings suggest that different process variables explain (in total) different amounts of variability between clients' outcomes during or after therapy.

Although these findings provide global information on correlates of client improvement, they say nothing about the therapist's *specific* contributions to the processes or to the role of these processes in explaining between-therapist differences in client outcomes. Without partitioning, or untangling, these between-therapist or within-therapist effects, our understanding of process-outcome correlational analyses will be incomplete at best, and possibly misleading at worst. As noted, to fully understand therapist effects, we need to move beyond a total correlation; even a total correlation between a therapist behavior and an outcome is not a therapist effect (at least not before the untangling occurs). For example, although therapist in-session expressions of hostility may be predictive of client outcomes, this correlation is not, in itself, a therapist effect. It could be that therapists vary within their own caseloads in the amount of hostility they express with clients (i.e., within-therapist variability), and/or different therapists vary in the amount of hostility they express across all of their clients (i.e., between-therapist variability). Either, or both, of these hostility variables could be predictive of client outcomes. This parsing of therapist–client processes into the unique contribution of each dyad member is what differentiates process variables from the individual characteristics fully "owned" by the therapist as possible determinants of between-therapist effects on client outcome. After this initial step, though, the models testing these two general categories of variables as possible predictors of therapist effects on client outcome are largely similar.

To illustrate this point, we continue with the previous example of therapist hostility using depression as the outcome variable, with therapists explaining 10% of the variability in client depression change (as revealed by an intraclass correlation). We can model within-client depression change at Level 1 and add any client level predictors of depression change at Level 2, including the client's contribution to a process predictor (e.g., the within-therapist hostility). Then, at Level 3, we would add therapists' contribution to the process predictor (e.g., the between-therapist hostility). As with any regression model, we can see how much of the unexplained between-therapist variability in client depression change is explained by between-therapist hostility. In this example, it could be that therapists with higher average hostility expressions across their caseload also tend to have clients with worse average outcomes. This is different from interpreting the within-therapist (or between-client) effect of therapist hostility on outcome, which might suggest that a client whose therapist expressed more hostility toward him or her relative to other clients treated by that therapist would have a worse outcome compared to that therapist's other clients. It is possible that the client in this example might be especially likely to elicit therapist hostility compared to other clients because of his or her personality style. Note from the interpretation of these two effects, that only between-therapist hostility could account for between-therapist differences in depression outcomes. This example of using a process variable (that inherently involves both therapist and client) is another step toward answering the vital question of what accounts for between-therapist differences in client outcomes. This type of work is just emerging, and it remains unclear what will be the best process variables to explain the therapist outcome effect.

However, the limited work to date is compelling. There is some evidence that the between-therapist alliance–outcome correlation is significant, whereas the within-therapist alliance–outcome correlation is not; that is, clients treated by therapists with higher average alliances (among clients in their caseload) had better outcomes than clients treated by therapists with lower average alliances among their clients (e.g., Baldwin, Wampold, & Imel, 2007; Crits-Christoph et al., 2009). This tells us that one reason why some therapists achieve better average outcomes with their clients seems to be that these therapists also achieve better average alliances across all of their clients. Beyond the well-established total correlation between alliance and outcome, this finding says something about the person of the therapist. In other words, having a higher alliance is therapeutic (the typical, yet incomplete implication); however, most important with this finding is that clients are more likely to achieve said alliance quality (no matter who they are) with Therapist A compared with Therapist B. This distinction has important implications. The typical interpretation states that fostering better alliances should be a goal of practitioners; however, the more refined interpretation is that it is important for the field to find out what it is about Therapist A that allows him or her to foster alliances so competently, or what is it about Therapist B that does not allow him or her to foster alliances as competently as Therapist A. It could be, for example, that FIS, and/or DP, actually predict better alliance formation, which then predicts better outcomes. This would reflect a therapist level mediational model, which we see as a next, and essential, wave of therapist effects research.

As researchers continue to search for determinants of the therapist effect, they might draw on research that explores influences on processes serving as dependent variables in themselves. Process variables that consistently reveal between-therapist differences in their level or development are prime candidates to predict between therapist differences on client outcomes. In fact, there is such variability between-therapists on alliance quality that it made it a logical place to start as a determinant of between-therapist outcomes. On the basis of a meta-analysis of the effects of 15 samples that isolated therapist contributions to the alliance, the person of the therapist accounted for approximately 9% of the variability in alliance ratings (Baldwin & Imel, 2013). With this aggregated result, one might be tempted to conclude that the alliance has the most promise as a determinant of therapist outcome effects. However, Baldwin and Imel (2013) cautioned against this notion given that therapists' contribution to the alliance is extremely variable across studies, meaning that it may not be a very good (or at least consistently good) indicator of how the more versus less effective therapists attain their status. Thus, researchers will need to continue to search for process variables that not only predict between-therapist differences in client outcomes, but also consistently indicate therapists' contribution to the process variable.

Examples of other variables that fit the bill (on the basis of very limited research to date) include client outcome expectation and therapist treatment adherence. In one study that examined between-therapist differences in their clients' outcome expectation (Vîslă, Flückiger, Krieger, Constantino, & grosse Holtforth, 2015), the authors found that the person of the therapist accounted for approximately 9% of the variability in the client outcome expectancy slope over time. In one of the few studies examining between-therapist differences in their adherence to treatment, the person of the therapist accounted for 19% of the variability in adherence ratings (Boswell et al., 2013; see also Imel, Baer, Martino, Ball, & Carroll, 2011). If such works are replicated, consistently revealing between-therapist differences on these processes, it will be important to test therapist-level mediational models like the one proposed previously. For example, is there a characteristic that Therapist A possesses (e.g., persuasiveness) that relates to his or her ability to foster positive outcome expectations in his or her clients (relative to Therapist B) that in turn relates to better outcomes for Therapist A relative to Therapist B? And, in light of the research reviewed previously on therapists' relative strengths and weaknesses, will this mediational path differ depending on the problem domain being treated?

It is important to keep in mind when considering variability in process and outcome variables that between-therapist effects generally explain less than within-therapist (between-client) effects. In other words, although therapist differences are meaningful, client differences are often stronger determinants of treatment outcome. Thus, an ongoing, simultaneous effort is also required to understand between-client effects on process and outcome, and the multilevel model affords us one opportunity to do this consistently and effectively. Of course, there are challenges to being able to capitalize on multilevel modeling for therapist effects. For example, researchers need to have an interest in the topic and the forethought to measure true therapist level predictors, which has been historically difficult. In addition, a process variable needs to vary across therapists (i.e., therapists need to differ in their average level of the variable); otherwise, the variable could not explain between-therapist differences in outcome.

OTHER COMPLEX CONSIDERATIONS

As noted, there are other complexities as the field searches for determinants of therapist effects on client outcomes. For example, there could be even more nesting than measurement occasions within clients and clients within therapists. It could be that therapists are nested within treatment sites or training locations, which would call for a fourth level in the model. If significant variability existed between such sites/organizations, researchers would then need to search for predictors of such variability (e.g., climate, supervisor quality, training model). This represents even more partitioning of possible determinants of why some therapists' clients outperform, on average, other therapists' clients.

Researchers also need to be aware of a different type of therapist effect, whereby the person of the therapist moderates/changes the nature of a process–outcome correlation. Although not directly explaining a therapist effect on an outcome, there can still exist between-therapist differences on a process–outcome correlation; for example, the extent to which the alliance is associated with outcome may be different for different therapists. If the relation between alliance and outcome varies on the basis of therapists who are in that relationship, then researchers would need to examine why some therapists foster and/or use the relationship to create a therapeutic effect where others do not (Adelson & Owen, 2012). In this case, one implication is not simply to teach everyone how to foster adaptive alliances generically; rather, providers need to learn how to use alliances in the way that effective therapists use alliances to promote client gain. A second implication could be that different therapists use different processes to be effective; Therapist A might use the alliance to promote client gain, although Therapist B's alliance might not relate to his or her clients' outcomes, but use of directive strategies might. This implies that our search is not only what works best for whom with regard to clients and their outcome, but also what works best for whom in terms of therapists and their means to fostering those client outcomes.

CONCLUSION

As Chow et al. (2015) astutely noted, "no longer treated as a nuisance variable, therapist effects have become a serious focus of clinical trials and naturalistic research" (p. 343). Helping to bring therapist variability into focus is the application of multilevel modeling. With this method, and others, the field is evolving to better reveal psychotherapy nuance. Attempting to appreciate this nuance is exciting. Although it may challenge long-standing interpretations of data, or at least reveal incompleteness, we can take comfort in the fact that our field has gone through such evolutions before, and such evolutions are often ultimately embraced and perfected, before giving way to yet other evolutions later. There are certainly things that we are not anticipating now about the psychotherapy endeavor that may seem so apparent 20 years later with newer minds, methods, and milieus. With that in mind, the pursuit of understanding what therapists have the best outcomes when working with which clients in which dyads or contexts and through which processes continues. Once research tells us which process variables, and especially those for which therapists makes a clear and consistent contribution, explain between-therapist effects on outcome, it will be important to be responsive to them in some way to foster success and avoid harm (Castonguay, Boswell, Constantino, Goldfried, & Hill, 2010).

As Boswell et al. (Chapter 16, this volume) noted, one type of responsiveness could involve changing health care systems to match clients to therapists who have a proven track record of success in treating clients with a particular type of presenting problem (and to avoid referring clients to therapists with track records of "unsuccess" in a relevant outcome domain). FIS research also suggests, at least preliminarily, the importance of engaging an individual characteristic at the right time. As a field, we need to find the markers of these right times and therapist and process characteristics that predict therapist variability in responding to them in a way that facilitates improvement. Perhaps these will be in the form of modular trainings built around discovered determinants of therapist effects (Constantino, Boswell, Bernecker, & Castonguay, 2013). For example, therapists could learn to engage in effective DP when they are experiencing an "outcome slump" among their clients. Or therapists could learn to expertly use motivational interviewing when their clients show resistance. Or therapists can learn to be persuasive when their clients' hope for improvement wanes. The key for such "right time" applications, though, is that therapist effects research shows that these applications characterize the most effective therapists and are therapeutic. Of course, these are just a few of the many ways that therapist responsiveness manifests most usefully; others await more discoveries and testing.

In closing, we view the concepts discussed here as being relevant for all psychotherapy researchers, not just those explicitly interested in the therapist effect that typically gets associated with fancy statistics and big data (see Chapter 16, this volume). As we have shown, even those interested in more traditional process–outcome correlations in smaller data cannot simply turn a blind eye to the ambiguity in a total correlation. Given that psychotherapy is an inherently dyadic construct (and in some cases even more complex), it is incomplete to examine the influence of a process variable on an outcome variable without disaggregating the client and therapist contributions. This entire volume pushes us to do so and to be more complete as a field.

REFERENCES

Adelson, J. L., & Owen, J. (2012). Bringing the psychotherapist back: Basic concepts for reading articles examining therapist effects using multilevel modeling. *Psychotherapy, 49*, 152–162. http://dx.doi.org/10.1037/a0023990

Anderson, T., Ogles, B. M., Patterson, C. L., Lambert, M. J., & Vermeersch, D. A. (2009). Therapist effects: Facilitative interpersonal skills as a predictor of therapist success. *Journal of Clinical Psychology, 65*, 755–768. http://dx.doi.org/10.1002/jclp.20583

Baldwin, S. A., & Imel, Z. E. (2013). Therapist effects: Findings and methods. In M. J. Lambert (Ed.), *Bergin and Garfield's handbook of psychotherapy and behavior change* (6th ed., pp. 258–297). Hoboken, NJ: Wiley.

Baldwin, S. A., Wampold, B. E., & Imel, Z. E. (2007). Untangling the alliance-outcome correlation: Exploring the relative importance of therapist and patient variability in the alliance. *Journal of Consulting and Clinical Psychology, 75*, 842–852. http://dx.doi.org/10.1037/0022-006X.75.6.842

Boswell, J. F., Gallagher, M. W., Sauer-Zavala, S. E., Bullis, J., Gorman, J. M., Shear, M. K., . . . Barlow, D. H. (2013). Patient characteristics and variability in adherence and competence in cognitive-behavioral therapy for panic disorder. *Journal of Consulting and Clinical Psychology, 81*, 443–454. http://dx.doi.org/10.1037/a0031437

Castonguay, L. G., Boswell, J. F., Constantino, M. J., Goldfried, M. R., & Hill, C. E. (2010). Training implications of harmful effects of psychological treatments. *American Psychologist, 65*, 34–49. http://dx.doi.org/10.1037/a0017330

Castonguay, L. G., Nordberg, S. S., Schut, A. J., & Constantino, M. J. (2010). Psychotherapy research. In I. Weiner & W. E. Craighead (Eds.), *The Corsini encyclopedia of psychology* (Vol. 3, 4th ed., pp. 1389–1392). New York, NY: Wiley.

Chow, D. L., Miller, S. D., Seidel, J. A., Kane, R. T., Thornton, J. A., & Andrews, W. P. (2015). The role of deliberate practice in the development of highly effective psychotherapists. *Psychotherapy, 52,* 337–345. http://dx.doi.org/10.1037/pst0000015

Constantino, M. J., Arnkoff, D. B., Glass, C. R., Ametrano, R. M., & Smith, J. Z. (2011). Expectations. *Journal of Clinical Psychology, 67,* 184–192. http://dx.doi.org/10.1002/jclp.20754

Constantino, M. J., Boswell, J. F., Bernecker, S. L., & Castonguay, L. G. (2013). Context-responsive integration as a framework for unified psychotherapy and clinical science: Conceptual and empirical considerations. *Journal of Unified Psychotherapy and Clinical Science, 2,* 1–20.

Crits-Christoph, P., Connolly Gibbons, M. B., & Mukherjee, D. (2013). Psychotherapy process-outcome research. In M. J. Lambert (Ed.), *Bergin and Garfield's handbook of psychotherapy and behavior change* (6th ed., pp. 298–340). Hoboken, NJ: Wiley.

Crits-Christoph, P., Gallop, R., Temes, C. M., Woody, G., Ball, S. A., Martino, S., & Carroll, K. M. (2009). The alliance in motivational enhancement therapy and counseling as usual for substance use problems. *Journal of Consulting and Clinical Psychology, 77,* 1125–1135. http://dx.doi.org/10.1037/a0017045

Ericsson, K. A., & Lehmann, A. C. (1996). Expert and exceptional performance: Evidence of maximal adaptation to task constraints. *Annual Review of Psychology, 47,* 273–305. http://dx.doi.org/10.1146/annurev.psych.47.1.273

Horvath, A. O., Del Re, A. C., Flückiger, C., & Symonds, D. (2011). Alliance in individual psychotherapy. *Psychotherapy, 48,* 9–16. http://dx.doi.org/10.1037/a0022186

Imel, Z. E., Baer, J. S., Martino, S., Ball, S. A., & Carroll, K. M. (2011). Mutual influence in therapist competence and adherence to motivational enhancement therapy. *Drug and Alcohol Dependence, 115,* 229–236. http://dx.doi.org/10.1016/j.drugalcdep.2010.11.010

Kraus, D. R., Bentley, J. H., Alexander, P. C., Boswell, J. F., Constantino, M. J., Baxter, E. E., & Castonguay, L. G. (2016). Predicting therapist effectiveness from their own practice-based evidence. *Journal of Consulting and Clinical Psychology, 84,* 473–483. http://dx.doi.org/10.1037/ccp0000083

Kraus, D. R., Castonguay, L., Boswell, J. F., Nordberg, S. S., & Hayes, J. A. (2011). Therapist effectiveness: Implications for accountability and patient care. *Psychotherapy Research, 21,* 267–276. http://dx.doi.org/10.1080/10503307.2011.563249

Kraus, D. R., Seligman, D. A., & Jordan, J. R. (2005). Validation of a behavioral health treatment outcome and assessment tool designed for naturalistic settings: The treatment outcome package. *Journal of Clinical Psychology, 61,* 285–314. http://dx.doi.org/10.1002/jclp.20084

Owen, J. J., Adelson, J., Budge, S., Kopta, S. M., & Reese, R. J. (2016). Good-enough level and dose-effect models: Variation among outcomes and therapists. *Psychotherapy Research, 26,* 22–30. http://dx.doi.org/10.1080/10503307.2014.966346

Strupp, H. H., Horowitz, L. M., & Lambert, M. J. (Eds.). (1997). *Measuring patient changes in mood, anxiety, and personality disorders: Toward a core battery*. Washington, DC: American Psychological Association. http://dx.doi.org/10.1037/10232-000

Vîslă, A., Flückiger, C., Krieger, T., Constantino, M. J., & grosse Holtforth, M. (2015). *Depressed patients' outcome expectations: Are there any differences between therapists?* Manuscript in preparation.

Webb, C. A., DeRubeis, R. J., & Barber, J. P. (2010). Therapist adherence/competence and treatment outcome: A meta-analytic review. *Journal of Consulting and Clinical Psychology, 78*, 200–211. http://dx.doi.org/10.1037/a0018912

II
CONCEPTUAL CONTRIBUTIONS

4

APPROPRIATE RESPONSIVENESS AS A CONTRIBUTION TO THERAPIST EFFECTS

WILLIAM B. STILES AND ADAM O. HORVATH

In this chapter, we address the question of why certain therapists are more effective than others from a different perspective. We do not propose that particular actions or strategies produce such therapist effects. Instead, we argue that a therapist is effective because he or she is appropriately responsive, that is, because he or she consistently does the right thing, which may be different each time, providing each client with a different, individually tailored treatment. Our argument hinges on the broad psychological concept of *responsiveness*, which refers to behavior as being influenced by emerging context.

RESPONSIVENESS AND APPROPRIATE RESPONSIVENESS

Responsiveness is ubiquitous: People are responsive to each other and their context on time scales from milliseconds to months (Stiles, Honos-Webb, & Surko, 1998). The concept of responsiveness by itself does not

http://dx.doi.org/10.1037/0000034-005
How and Why Are Some Therapists Better Than Others? Understanding Therapist Effects, L. G. Castonguay and C. E. Hill (Eds.)
Copyright © 2017 by the American Psychological Association. All rights reserved.

specify that the goal of the behavior is to benefit others, and people may be responsive to others with uncaring or harmful intent. However, psychotherapists generally respond to benefit their clients, seeking to be aware of their behavior and to adjust it in response to clients' needs. We call this *appropriate responsiveness*. Thus, to be appropriately responsive means to do the right thing.

Examples of therapist responsiveness include choosing treatments on the basis of presenting problems, planning treatments on the basis of how a client is progressing, actively listening, using the client's evolving response to treatment to guide interventions, and adjusting interventions already in progress in light of subtle signs of uptake. For example, as a therapist engages in conversation with a client, the therapist is attuned to verbal and nonverbal clues and uses these to adjust, emphasize, or mitigate interventions (Muntigl, Bänninger-Huber, & Horvath, 2015).

Appropriate responsiveness—doing the right thing in any particular instance—yields different behaviors depending on the unique and evolving circumstances of each situation. Sometimes the right thing for a therapist to do is to nod and smile, and sometimes the right thing is to do nothing. The right thing depends on such factors as a client's diagnosis, intelligence, education, personality, social situation, stage of life, values, personal history, stage of therapy, and momentary requirements. The right thing to do is also likely to vary depending on the therapist's, skills, personality, personal characteristics, and theoretical approach; different therapists cannot and should not respond exactly alike. For example, the right response for a psychoanalytic therapist may be different from the right response for a cognitive therapist; the right response for a young female therapist may be different from the right response for an old male therapist. The right thing also depends on the history of this particular therapeutic relationship, the immediately preceding events, the circumstances of the session, and many other factors in each instance. In brief, the right thing is not always the same thing.

Appropriate responsiveness is central to practicing all psychotherapeutic approaches, including manualized treatments. Each form of therapy offers certain ways of understanding the client's predicament and the therapist's techniques for intervening therapeutically. An appropriately responsive therapist skillfully adapts these techniques to the client's requirements and circumstances. In treatment descriptions and manuals, therapists are enjoined to establish rapport, to frame and time interventions to fit the client's immediate need, and to pursue interventions that seem to be working. Such injunctions can be understood as telling therapists to respond appropriately within the framework they are using.

This chapter's central conjecture, in concert with Hatcher (2015), is that therapist differences in appropriate responsiveness can help explain therapist effects, the observed differences in therapist effectiveness that are the focus of this book (see Chapter 1, this volume). A therapist who more often does the right thing will tend to have better outcomes. This hypothesized relation between appropriate responsiveness and outcome is mediated by good process. A therapist promotes good process, such as developing strong alliances, by appropriately optimizing the choice, dose, and timing of his or her actions in therapy. And good process begets good outcome. Therapists who are consistently better or worse at doing the right thing will have better or worse process and better or worse outcomes, respectively, resulting in statistical therapist effects.

HOW TO MEASURE APPROPRIATE RESPONSIVENESS

We suggest that if a therapist is appropriately responsive, then the process will go well and the outcome will be positive. This may look like circular reasoning (if a response did not contribute to positive outcomes, then by definition it was not the right thing to do), but we suggest that it helpfully focuses attention on the question of what is the right therapist behavior. How do we know what response is appropriate? How do we measure appropriate responsiveness?

Appropriate responsiveness is not just a matter of choosing approved techniques from lists in a manual. A particular technique may be a key element of an effective approach, but to be effective, it must be used appropriately, depending on all of the characteristics of the client, the therapist, the approach, and the emerging circumstances, as listed in the previous section. A therapist can do too much of the technique as well as too little of it, do it with the wrong client, or at the wrong time, in the wrong way, and so forth. This holds for common techniques, like minimal encouragers ("mm-hm") or eye contact, as well as treatment-specific techniques, like homework, relaxation exercises, two-chair dialogue, interpretation of the transference, or reflection of feeling.

In some therapeutic approaches, appropriate therapist responsiveness may entail interventions that seem impolite or that cause the client short-term discomfort. For example, a psychoanalytic or nondirective therapist may not answer some questions directly. Behavior therapists may prescribe exposure to distressing situations. The right thing depends in part on the long-term goals and the therapeutic strategy for attaining those goals.

It is sometimes possible to specify contingencies—moments or markers when particular interventions are more likely or less likely to be appropriate. Supervisors may advise, for example, not to interpret too early, to use empty chair dialogue for self-evaluative splits, or not to engage in confrontation. However, even these rules must be used appropriately; that is, appropriate use of such contingencies is itself contingent on the state of the client–therapist rapport, the timing within the session, the level of the therapist's technical skills, the tolerance of the client for challenge, and other specific contextual factors.

There is a paradox embedded in the notion that we can prescribe appropriate responsiveness: We know that an intervention was appropriate because it has produced good results (or vice versa). A particular behavior may or may not be appropriately responsive depending on the context of the situation. Strictly speaking, we do not know whether a therapist was appropriately responsive until we measure the outcome of the treatment. However, our conjecture that the responsiveness–outcome relation is mediated by good process gives us a partial way around the paradox.

Participants and observers can often recognize aspects of good process. Experienced clinicians, supervisors, or trained raters can usually evaluate whether an intervention (or nonintervention) at a particular juncture was an appropriate or inappropriate thing to do, taking into account context, timing, and delivery, even if they cannot specify the appropriate behaviors in advance. Likewise, a client can rate his or her experiences globally, implicitly taking into account how the therapist was able to respond to the client's need in the moment. In making such judgments, judges and clients implicitly take into account that different behaviors are effective at different times. They may not be able to specify the right behaviors in advance, but when they see them, they know they are good. We call such ratings *evaluative measures*, in contrast with descriptive measures, which include categories of techniques. Evaluative measures are, in substantial part, judgments about quality—whether the target processes or events were good, right, competent, skillful, or appropriate in the context. As Persig (1974) pointed out, people can recognize quality even though they cannot always specify in advance exactly of what quality consists. Perhaps this ability to recognize quality is related to what Rogers (1959) described as the organismic valuing process and what Zajonc (1980) meant in saying "preferences need no inferences" (p. 151). Participant and observer evaluations of psychotherapy process incorporate judgments of appropriate responsiveness, and we suggest that these evaluative assessments are a good way to measure appropriate responsiveness.

THERAPIST RESPONSIVENESS AND PROCESS–OUTCOME RESEARCH

As the foregoing reasoning suggests, attempts to measure responsiveness using descriptive categories of therapist behaviors have fared poorly; one cannot specify the right thing ahead of the event. These issues have made it difficult for researchers to document the relation between therapists' behavior and treatment outcome using traditional research methods. Nonetheless, research on process–outcome relations has yielded a pattern of evidence consistent with the conjecture outlined in the preceding section. In this section, we review some of this research.[1]

Effective Therapists Use Techniques Responsively

There is evidence that therapists vary their techniques systematically in response to clients' differential requirements, even though such variation sometimes results in lower adherence to formal treatment protocols (Boswell et al., 2013; Imel, Baer, Martino, Ball, & Carroll, 2011). For example, Hardy, Stiles, Barkham, and Startup (1998) found that therapists offered more affective interventions for relationally overinvolved patients but more cognitive and behavioral interventions to relationally underinvolved patients, and both types of patients had similar favorable outcomes. Owen and Hilsenroth (2014) showed that greater adherence flexibility—deviations from adherence to psychodynamic technique—was associated with better outcomes.

Sometimes appropriate responsiveness entails apparent inconsistencies between short-term effects and long-term outcomes. For example, a client may feel worse before he or she gets better. Ruptures in the alliance are distressing, but they can be opportunities for productive work on interpersonal problems (e.g., Safran et al., 2014). Castonguay, Pincus, Agras, and Hines (1998) reported that in a study of clients in cognitive–behavioral therapy (CBT) for eating disorders, negative feelings at mid-treatment were associated with positive outcomes; clients remained engaged despite difficult therapeutic processes if they perceived that therapy was responsive to their long-term needs. Conversely, treatments that are pleasant but do not facilitate change will not yield good outcomes. For example, in an intensive analysis of cases conducted by effective and less effective therapists, Youn et al. (Chapter 14, this volume) found that although the less effective therapist validated the client's experience, he failed to foster the emotional deepening prescribed by the treatment but instead provided intellectual insight. The client appeared to feel understood and rated the sessions as helpful, but she did not get what she needed.

Horvath and Goheen (1990), in effect, manipulated responsiveness by randomly assigning clients who were either high or low in defiance, a trait-like tendency to resist commands or instructions, to one of two treatments

---

[1]Additional efforts to engage with the responsiveness problem by researchers and clinicians have been reviewed elsewhere (Kramer & Stiles, 2015).

for sleep onset insomnia. Half of the clients received stimulus control therapy (SC), and half of the clients received symptom prescription therapy (SP). The SP treatment was a defiance-based intervention in which clients were paradoxically instructed to stay alert and observe how they keep themselves awake. Both treatments had been shown to be effective, and a rationale was provided for each. Both trait groups experienced sleep improvements, and the treatments appeared equally effective at the end of treatment. However, at follow-up, the more defiant clients maintained and increased their gains if they had received the defiance-based SP intervention, whereas the more compliant clients who received SP treatment regressed to baseline. Conversely, the more compliant clients who received SC treatment maintained or increased their gains at follow-up, whereas the more defiant clients who received the SC treatment went back to baseline within a week. Of course, in this study, treatment assignment was random rather than responsive, but it illustrates how the right thing does not depend on whether an intervention is effective per se but on how well it responds to the client's capacities and needs.

Process–Outcome Correlations Fail to Reflect the Importance of Therapist Techniques

Responsiveness poses a major challenge for researchers seeking to empirically identify the effective technical ingredients in any particular treatment. For example, in data drawn from a clinical trial comparing psychodynamic–interpersonal therapy with CBT, Stiles and Shapiro (1994) found negligible, nonsignificant correlations between improvement on standard outcome measures and therapists' use of verbal techniques that were theoretically important in the respective treatments (e.g., reflections, interpretations, directives, questions). The lack of statistical association was not a failure of measurement. The techniques were frequently used and reliably coded, and the outcome measures detected large, clinically and statistically significant improvement in these treatments. These null results were consistent with the generally modest, inconsistent yields of process–outcome comparisons involving therapist techniques (Orlinsky, Grawe, & Parks, 1994).

The responsiveness account can explain this inconsistency between theoretical importance and statistical associations. The correlational model tests whether more is better. It ignores a client's differing requirements; each application of the technique is treated as equivalent, regardless of whether it was appropriate to what the client needed or could use at that moment. To understand this, consider that if a therapist uses interpretations appropriately, then each of his or her clients will receive the right number and kind of interpretations. Each client will receive a different number of interpretations, but all clients will get enough and therefore, will have outcomes that are optimal with respect to interpretations. As a result, interpretations will be uncorrelated with outcome (Stiles, 2013; Stiles & Shapiro, 1994; Stiles et al., 1998). Clinically, to infer that techniques (e.g., interpretations) do not matter would miss this point. Techniques may matter a great deal, but they must be used appropriately.

Evaluative Measures Capture Responsiveness Better Than Descriptive Measures Do

Using data drawn from a large collaborative clinical trial of treatments for depression, Elkin et al. (2014) developed a three-part instrument intended to measure therapist responsiveness. Part I consisted of 11 specific behaviors (e.g., makes eye contact, uses minimal encouragers, focuses on and demonstrates interest in the patient). Part II consisted of items rated globally on the basis of the entire session (e.g., compatible level of discourse, appropriate level of emotional quality and intensity). Part III was a one-item global rating of therapist responsiveness. Indexes based on these ratings were all compared with several measures of subsequent patient engagement in therapy. Factors based on the descriptive categories in Part I did not predict engagement. The global evaluative items from Part II and the single item responsiveness rating from Part III, however, did predict engagement.

Similarly, Aviram (2015; Aviram, Westra, Constantino, & Antony, 2016) hypothesized that appropriate responsiveness to client resistance in CBT may entail a switch from CBT's usual directive approach to the empathic, collaborative stance that characterizes motivational interviewing (MI). To test this hypothesis, Aviram measured adherence to the MI approach during selected episodes of active client resistance using coding of specific MI techniques (i.e., descriptive categories similar to those in Part I of Elkin et al., 2014) and global ratings. Results showed that global ratings of MI adherence, but not the coding of specific techniques, predicted better outcome (less worry) on a posttreatment measure and less resistance in the subsequent session. Paralleling the results of the Elkin et al. (2014) study, the global evaluative indexes predicted improvement but those based on counts of the specific behaviors did not.

Elkin et al.'s (2014) and Aviram's (2015) descriptive measures failed to predict desirable consequences because even though these behaviors are valuable techniques, more of them is not always better. Even simple attentive behaviors like eye contact and minimal encouragers can be overdone as well as underdone (cf. Bachelor, 1988).

Consistently with this argument, most, perhaps all, of the process variables that consistently predict outcome are evaluative variables. For example, all of the elements of "evidence-based therapy relationships" (Norcross & Lambert, 2011, p. 3) assembled by Norcross (2002, 2011) are substantially evaluative: alliance, group cohesion, empathy, goal consensus and collaboration, and positive regard, among others. Such evaluative process variables incorporate judgments of appropriate responsiveness; that is, they reflect whether the observed behaviors were appropriate to the circumstances rather than describing specific behaviors. The behaviors that yield high ratings on alliance, group cohesion, empathy, and so forth, differ across cases and times, as therapists do the right thing in response to clients' emerging needs and circumstances (Stiles & Wolfe, 2006).

RESPONSIVENESS AT WORK: THE ALLIANCE

To illustrate how responsiveness underlies evidence-based effective elements of therapy relationships, we focus on the most studied element, the client–therapist alliance (Horvath & Bedi, 2002; Horvath, Del Re, Flückiger, & Symonds, 2011).

Alliance Is an Evaluative Variable That Predicts Outcome

The alliance is the quintessential evaluative variable. It reflects an evaluation by whoever completes the measure (participants or observers) of relevant aspects of the therapeutic relationship and the therapeutic process—whether these are going well or not. A strong alliance is not a technique but an achievement, one that requires doing the right thing over a period of time. The evaluative nature of alliance assessments is clearly illustrated by items on alliance rating scales, like "My therapist and I collaborate on setting goals for my therapy" or "I feel I am working together with my therapist in a joint effort." They reflect judgments that the right thing is happening.

The positive relationship between the quality of the alliance and therapy outcome—across varied treatments and outcome measures—is one of the most robust findings in the therapy process literature (Flückiger, Del Re, Wampold, Symonds, & Horvath, 2012; Horvath et al., 2011; Martin, Garske, & Davis, 2000). The alliance is measured in a variety of ways but, at their core, these assessments indicate that a client who reports having a strong alliance with his or her therapist feels a sense of shared goals for therapy and strongly endorse the kinds of activities in which they engage during their sessions. As a result, this client enthusiastically participates in the work of therapy (Hatcher & Barends, 2006; Hatcher, Barends, Hansell, & Gutfreund, 1995).[2] Alliance assessments

---

[2]Bordin (1975) suggested three components: tasks, goals, and bonds. However of these three, when considered separately, the two former have stronger correlation with outcome than the latter (Horvath & Bedi, 2002; Horvath & Symonds, 1991; Martin, Garske, & Davis, 2000; Webb et al., 2011).

are consistently linked to indicators of therapy outcome because they are evaluative. They tell us that the therapist did the right thing; that is, they selected interventions that were appropriate for the client, introduced them at the appropriate time, and administered them in the appropriate dose. A therapist who can develop good alliances is described as attentive, flexible, and showing high levels of interest in their clients (Ackerman & Hilsenroth, 2003).

Alliance–Outcome Correlations Are Therapist Effects

Even if we have made a convincing case for our conjecture that appropriate responsiveness promotes a strong alliance and a strong alliance promotes a positive therapy outcome, we need to ask whether the quality of the alliance is responsible for therapist effects. Recent research evidence indeed suggests that the alliance–outcome correlations, to a large degree, depend on differences among therapists. Baldwin, Wampold, and Imel (2007) directly compared therapists' and clients' contributions to the alliance with the proportion of variance in outcome each source accounted for in a large-scale study. They found that the therapist's contribution to the alliance (between-therapists), but not the client's contribution (within therapists), predicted a significant portion of outcome (see also Chapter 2, this volume). That is, the robust correlation between alliance and outcome reflects primarily a correlation between therapists' means on alliance and outcome rather than correlations between alliance and outcome within each therapist's practice.

Similarly, Crits-Christoph et al. (2009) examined the relative contributions of clients and therapists to the quality of the alliance and associations with outcomes in a population of clients receiving therapy for drug dependence. Between-therapist variation in alliance rating was a significant predictor of substance abuse outcome, whereas the within-therapists (between-clients) variation in alliance was not significant.[3]

Finally, in a meta-analysis of studies of alliance–outcome associations Del Re, Flückiger, Horvath, Symonds, and Wampold (2012) corroborated these reports, showing that therapist variability in the alliance was more important than patient variability in predicting improved patient outcomes, even when simultaneously controlling for potential confounding variables. Together, these studies support the contention that therapist effects may, at least in large part, reflect differences in the therapist's characteristic alliance with their clients, which, we have argued, are substantially traceable to therapist differences in appropriate responsiveness.

---

[3]Studies that can partition the variance due to clients and therapists, of necessity, are large scale and must have each therapist treating multiple clients. A smaller scale investigation by Huppert et al. (2014; n = 19) did not replicate these findings.

IMPLICATIONS OF APPROPRIATE RESPONSIVENESS

Research Implications

Responsiveness poses a challenge for psychotherapy research. Comparisons of descriptive variables with outcomes using linear statistical techniques—the main statistical tools of the trade—do not take appropriate responsiveness into account and so fail to properly assess the value of the techniques and interventions that a therapist uses. On the other hand, evaluative variables fail to specify which behaviors and techniques are responsible for a treatment's effectiveness.

Successful therapists responsively adapt their treatment approach's resources and strategies specifically for each client and session, so the brand of treatment is variable rather than constant across clients. Because appropriate responsiveness is an integral part of the treatment, this client-to-client and moment-to-moment variability in the treatment cannot be eliminated by more careful specification. And the appropriateness of each technique varies with too many conditions to specify. Conclusions linked to particular brands of therapies are therefore somewhat illusory. Furthermore, because of the difficulty in specifying the right thing before the event, research on the proposition that a therapist is more successful if he or she does the right thing has to face concerns about tautology or empty abstracting.

But our framework does suggest paths for moving forward. It points toward a need to investigate in greater detail how therapists (particularly successful therapists) make appropriate choices of interventions (or refraining from intervention) in specific circumstances. What kinds of signals are they tuned to, and how do they use this information to make the intervention better fit the client and the circumstances? For example, research on the accuracy and timing of interpretations in relation to alliance strength and outcome (e.g., Crits-Christoph & Gibbons, 2001) begins to unpack therapist responsiveness. Ribeiro, Ribeiro, Gonçalves, Horvath, and Stiles (2013) investigated when it was safe and productive to challenge a client and when offering more support was needed.

Clinical Implications

Responsiveness may be a challenge for research, but it is at the core of psychotherapy practice. Much of treatment training and supervision emphasizes appropriate responsiveness (Friedlander, 2015; Hatcher, 2015). Many treatment approaches make responsiveness an explicit goal (see review by Kramer & Stiles, 2015). A few examples include pluralistic therapy (Cooper & McLeod, 2011), plan analysis (Caspar, 2007), marker-guided interventions in emotion-focused therapy (Elliott, Watson, Goldman, & Greenberg, 2004), and alliance-focused training (Safran, Muran, Demaria, Boutwell, Eubanks-Carter, & Winston, 2014).

Appropriate responsiveness is common sense, but how can a therapist become more appropriately responsive? We think most psychotherapy training and supervision has been designed for precisely this purpose. Elements include attending to client requirements and circumstances, becoming sensitive to the range and depth of human experience, and mastering a framework to guide the use of a repertoire of techniques. Supervised experience can be valuable, especially if it is accompanied by feedback. Knowledge of personality, psychopathology, culture, and the rich diversity of human experience can sensitize therapists to their clients' changing requirements and how interventions address those requirements.

To put it another way, we think the clinical take-home message is easy to say, if not easy to do. Build strong alliances and repair ruptures. Work for goal consensus and collaboration. Manage the countertransference. Be empathic, courageous, wise, skillful, creative, and psychologically present. Do the right thing!

REFERENCES

Ackerman, S. J., & Hilsenroth, M. J. (2003). A review of therapist characteristics and techniques positively impacting the therapeutic alliance. *Clinical Psychology Review, 23*, 1–33. http://dx.doi.org/10.1016/S0272-7358(02)00146-0

Aviram, A. (2015). *Testing the context responsivity hypothesis: Managing resistance in cognitive behavioural therapy*. Unpublished doctoral dissertation, York University, Toronto, Ontario, Canada.

Aviram, A., Westra, H. A., Constantino, M. J., & Antony, M. M. (2016). Responsive management of early resistance in cognitive behavioral therapy for generalized anxiety disorder. *Journal of Consulting and Clinical Psychology, 84*, 783–794.

Bachelor, A. (1988). How clients perceive therapist empathy: A content analysis of "received" empathy. *Psychotherapy: Theory, Research, Practice, Training, 25*, 227–240. http://dx.doi.org/10.1037/h0085337

Baldwin, S. A., Wampold, B. E., & Imel, Z. E. (2007). Untangling the alliance–outcome correlation: Exploring the relative importance of therapist and patient variability in the alliance. *Journal of Consulting and Clinical Psychology, 75*, 842–852. http://dx.doi.org/10.1037/0022-006X.75.6.842

Bordin, E. S. (1975, September). *The working alliance: Basis for a general theory of psychotherapy*. Paper presented at the Society for Psychotherapy Research, Washington, DC.

Boswell, J. F., Gallagher, M. W., Sauer-Zavala, S. E., Bullis, J., Gorman, J. M., Shear, M. K., . . . Barlow, D. H. (2013). Patient characteristics and variability in adherence and competence in cognitive-behavioral therapy for panic disorder. *Journal of Consulting and Clinical Psychology, 81,* 443–454. http://dx.doi.org/10.1037/a0031437

Caspar, F. (2007). Plan analysis. In T. D. Eells (Ed.), *Handbook of psychotherapy case formulations* (2nd ed., pp. 251–289). New York, NY: Guilford Press.

Castonguay, L. G., Pincus, A. L., Agras, W. S., & Hines, C. E., III. (1998). The role of emotion in cognitive-behavior therapy for binge eating disorder: When things have to feel worse before they get better. *Psychotherapy Research, 8,* 225–238. http://dx.doi.org/10.1080/10503309812331332327

Cooper, M., & McLeod, J. (2011). *Pluralistic counselling and psychotherapy.* London, England: Sage.

Crits-Christoph, P., Gallop, R., Temes, C. M., Woody, G., Ball, S. A., Martino, S., & Carroll, K. M. (2009). The alliance in motivational enhancement therapy and counseling as usual for substance use problems. *Journal of Consulting and Clinical Psychology, 77,* 1125–1135. http://dx.doi.org/10.1037/a0017045

Crits-Christoph, P., & Gibbons, M. B. C. (2001). Relational interpretations. *Psychotherapy: Theory, Research, Practice, Training, 38,* 423–428. http://dx.doi.org/10.1037/0033-3204.38.4.423

Del Re, A. C., Flückiger, C., Horvath, A. O., Symonds, D., & Wampold, B. E. (2012). Therapist effects in the therapeutic alliance–outcome relationship: A restricted-maximum likelihood meta-analysis. *Clinical Psychology Review, 32,* 642–649. http://dx.doi.org/10.1016/j.cpr.2012.07.002

Elkin, I., Falconnier, L., Smith, Y., Canada, K. E., Henderson, E., Brown, E. R., & McKay, B. M. (2014). Therapist responsiveness and patient engagement in therapy. *Psychotherapy Research, 24,* 52–66. http://dx.doi.org/10.1080/10503307.2013.820855

Elliott, R., Watson, J. C., Goldman, R. N., & Greenberg, L. S. (2004). *Learning emotion-focused therapy: The process-experiential approach to change.* Washington, DC: American Psychological Association. http://dx.doi.org/10.1037/10725-000

Flückiger, C., Del Re, A. C., Wampold, B. E., Symonds, D., & Horvath, A. O. (2012). How central is the alliance in psychotherapy? A multilevel longitudinal meta-analysis. *Journal of Counseling Psychology, 59,* 10–17. http://dx.doi.org/10.1037/a0025749

Friedlander, M. L. (2015). Use of relational strategies to repair alliance ruptures: How responsive supervisors train responsive psychotherapists. *Psychotherapy, 52,* 174–179. http://dx.doi.org/10.1037/a0037044

Hardy, G. E., Stiles, W. B., Barkham, M., & Startup, M. (1998). Therapist responsiveness to client interpersonal styles during time-limited treatments for depression. *Journal of Consulting and Clinical Psychology, 66,* 304–312. http://dx.doi.org/10.1037/0022-006X.66.2.304

Hatcher, R. L. (2015). Interpersonal competencies: Responsiveness, technique, and training in psychotherapy. *American Psychologist, 70,* 747–757. http://dx.doi.org/10.1037/a0039803

Hatcher, R. L., Barends, A., Hansell, J., & Gutfreund, M. J. (1995). Patients' and therapists' shared and unique views of the therapeutic alliance: An investigation using confirmatory factor analysis in a nested design. *Journal of Consulting and Clinical Psychology, 63,* 636–643. http://dx.doi.org/10.1037/0022-006X.63.4.636

Hatcher, R. L., & Barends, A. W. (2006). How a return to theory could help alliance research. *Psychotherapy: Theory, Research, Practice, Training, 43,* 292–299. http://dx.doi.org/10.1037/0033-3204.43.3.292

Horvath, A. O., & Bedi, R. P. (2002). The alliance. In J. C. Norcross (Ed.), *Psychotherapy relationships that work: Therapist contributions responsiveness to patients* (pp. 37–70). New York, NY: Oxford University Press.

Horvath, A. O., Del Re, A., Flückiger, C., & Symonds, D. B. (2011). Alliance in individual psychotherapy. In J. C. Norcross (Ed.), *Psychotherapy relationships that work* (2nd ed., pp. 25–69). New York, NY: Oxford University Press. http://dx.doi.org/10.1093/acprof:oso/9780199737208.003.0002

Horvath, A. O., & Goheen, M. D. (1990). Factors mediating the success of defiance and compliance based interventions. *Journal of Counseling Psychology, 37,* 363–371. http://dx.doi.org/10.1037/0022-0167.37.4.363

Horvath, A. O., & Symonds, B. D. (1991). Relation between working alliance and outcome in psychotherapy: A meta-analysis. *Journal of Counseling Psychology, 38,* 139–149.

Huppert, J. D., Kivity, Y., Barlow, D. H., Gorman, J. M., Shear, M. K., & Woods, S. W. (2014). Therapist effects and the outcome-alliance correlation in cognitive behavioral therapy for panic disorder with agoraphobia. *Behaviour Research and Therapy, 52,* 26–34. http://dx.doi.org/10.1016/j.brat.2013.11.001

Imel, Z. E., Baer, J. S., Martino, S., Ball, S. A., & Carroll, K. M. (2011). Mutual influence in therapist competence and adherence to motivational enhancement therapy. *Drug and Alcohol Dependence, 115,* 229–236. http://dx.doi.org/10.1016/j.drugalcdep.2010.11.010

Kramer, U., & Stiles, W. B. (2015). The responsiveness problem in psychotherapy: A review of proposed solutions. *Clinical Psychology: Science and Practice, 22,* 277–295. http://dx.doi.org/10.1111/cpsp.12107

Martin, D. J., Garske, J. P., & Davis, M. K. (2000). Relation of the therapeutic alliance with outcome and other variables: A meta-analytic review. *Journal of Consulting and Clinical Psychology, 68,* 438–450. http://dx.doi.org/10.1037/0022-006X.68.3.438

Muntigl, P., Bänninger-Huber, E., & Horvath, A. O. (2015, September). *Affiliation in psychoanalytic psychotherapy: Interactional sequences that maintain a balance between conflicting tension and security.* Paper presented at the European Congress of the Society for Psychotherapy Research Conference, Klagenfurt, Austria.

Norcross, J. C. (Ed.). (2002). *Psychotherapy relationships that work: Therapist contributions and responsiveness to patient needs.* New York, NY: Oxford University Press.

Norcross, J. C. (Ed.). (2011). *Psychotherapy relationships that work* (2nd ed.). New York, NY: Oxford University Press. http://dx.doi.org/10.1093/acprof:oso/9780199737208.001.0001

Norcross, J. C. & Lambert, M. J. (2011). Evidence-based therapy relationships. In J. C. Norcross (Ed.), *Psychotherapy relationships that work* (2nd ed., pp. 3–21). New York, NY: Oxford University Press.

Orlinsky, D. E., Grawe, K., & Parks, B. K. (1994). Process and outcome in psychotherapy—Noch einmal. In A. E. Bergin & S. L. Garfield (Eds.), *Handbook of psychotherapy and behavior change* (4th ed., pp. 270–376). New York, NY: Wiley.

Owen, J., & Hilsenroth, M. J. (2014). Treatment adherence: The importance of therapist flexibility in relation to therapy outcomes. *Journal of Counseling Psychology, 61*, 280–288. http://dx.doi.org/10.1037/a0035753

Persig, R. M. (1974). *Zen and the art of motorcycle maintenance.* New York, NY: William Morrow.

Ribeiro, E., Ribeiro, A. P., Gonçalves, M. M., Horvath, A. O., & Stiles, W. B. (2013). How collaboration in therapy becomes therapeutic: The therapeutic collaboration coding system. *Psychology and Psychotherapy, 86*, 294–314. http://dx.doi.org/10.1111/j.2044-8341.2012.02066.x

Rogers, C. R. (1959). A theory of therapy, personality, and interpersonal relationships as developed by the client-centered framework. In S. Koch (Ed.), *Psychology: A study of a science: Vol. III. Formulations of a person and the social context* (pp. 184–256). New York, NY: McGraw-Hill.

Safran, J., Muran, J. C., Demaria, A., Boutwell, C., Eubanks-Carter, C., & Winston, A. (2014). Investigating the impact of alliance-focused training on interpersonal process and therapists' capacity for experiential reflection. *Psychotherapy Research, 24*, 269–285. http://dx.doi.org/10.1080/10503307.2013.874054

Stiles, W. B. (2013). The variables problem and progress in psychotherapy research. *Psychotherapy, 50*, 33–41. http://dx.doi.org/10.1037/a0030569

Stiles, W. B., Honos-Webb, L., & Surko, M. (1998). Responsiveness in psychotherapy. *Clinical Psychology: Science and Practice, 5*, 439–458. http://dx.doi.org/10.1111/j.1468-2850.1998.tb00166.x

Stiles, W. B., & Shapiro, D. A. (1994). Disabuse of the drug metaphor: Psychotherapy process-outcome correlations. *Journal of Consulting and Clinical Psychology, 62*, 942–948. http://dx.doi.org/10.1037/0022-006X.62.5.942

Stiles, W. B., & Wolfe, B. E. (2006). Relationship factors in treating anxiety disorders. In L. G. Castonguay & L. E. Beutler (Eds.), *Principles of therapeutic change that work* (pp. 155–165). New York, NY: Oxford University Press.

Webb, C. A., De Rubeis, R. J., Amsterdam, J. D., Shelton, R. C., Hollon, S. D., & Dimidjian, S. (2011). Two aspects of the therapeutic alliance: Differential relations with depressive symptom change. *Journal of Consulting and Clinical Psychology, 79*, 279–283. http://dx.doi.org/10.1037/a0023252

Zajonc, R. B. (1980). Feeling and thinking: Preferences need no inferences. *American Psychologist, 35*, 151–175. http://dx.doi.org/10.1037/0003-066X.35.2.151

5

THERAPIST PRESENCE, ABSENCE, AND EXTRAORDINARY PRESENCE

JEFFREY A. HAYES AND MARIA VINCA

Therapists face a considerable number of challenging situations in their day-to-day work. Clients present with troubled moods, poor relationships, pessimistic outlooks, disordered personalities, self-hatred, crises, and traumatic memories. The negative, almost toxic, client material that therapists must contend with can be compounded by problems in the therapists' workplace, including bothersome coworkers, poor staff morale, and an excessively high demand for services. In addition, difficulties in therapists' personal lives can further affect their work with clients. In a single day, a therapist might be exposed to all sorts of noxious affect, images, words, and behaviors, from a variety of sources. How do therapists stay present to clients in the face of such negativity? In other words, how do therapists overcome these distractions to fully engage with their clients and attune to their needs?

The truth is, therapists are not always present. They occasionally become overwhelmed by clients' emotions, histories, actions, or lack of progress. They

---

http://dx.doi.org/10.1037/0000034-006
How and Why Are Some Therapists Better Than Others? Understanding Therapist Effects, L. G. Castonguay and C. E. Hill (Eds.)
Copyright © 2017 by the American Psychological Association. All rights reserved.

can lose perspective and identify with clients' pessimism and negative moods. Therapists get bored, occasionally, with clients' stories. They sometimes pull away from clients to protect themselves psychologically (Gelso & Hayes, 2007). And, because they are human, therapists can become distracted, whether as a self-protective strategy or unintentionally. While sitting with a client, a therapist may be preoccupied with something another client said an hour ago, or ruminate about an interaction they had with a colleague in the hallway, or be reminded of an argument with a spouse over breakfast. Colosimo and Pos (2015) suggested that there are

> five possible sources of therapists' nonpresent behavior, including (a) hyperintellectualization; (b) fear; (c) fatigue; (d) reactivity (interpersonal or intrapersonal); and (e) distractibility. All of these processes may cause therapists to "leave" or be "pulled away" from being in good current contact with the environment and the client. (p. 102)

Therapists do not like to admit that they become distracted in session, and they certainly do not publicize it to their clients or colleagues, but it happens. For therapy to be successful, we assume that therapists should be present and attend to clients in a focused and relaxed way, compared with distracted or absent therapists. A therapist who lacks sufficient presence by missing what clients say entirely is unlikely to be helpful. But what, exactly, is presence? To what extent do therapists need to be present to clients, and in what ways, for therapy to be effective? In what ways does presence, or absence, affect therapy? How can presence be conveyed most effectively? How can presence be cultivated?

These are the questions that drive this chapter, all with the aim of examining the larger question about the possibility that presence is one factor that distinguishes more effective from less effective therapists. We draw from theory, professional and personal experience, and empirical findings to develop and explore these questions. We also suggest toward the end of the chapter that there is a rare form of presence, perhaps best thought of as *extraordinary presence*, that may be a hallmark of some exceptional therapists. We begin by defining and describing ordinary presence.

ORDINARY PRESENCE

Presence is a state of being aware of and centered in oneself while maintaining attunement to and engagement with another person. Geller and Greenberg (2002) described presence as containing an openness to experience on emotional, cognitive, and visceral levels that often is accompanied by a subjective sense of enhanced awareness. Colosimo and Pos (2015) referred to presence as a state in which the therapist is aware of "being here," "being open," "being now," and "being with and for the client." Schneider (2015) contended that presence is a core therapeutic factor, germane to the working alliance, the provision of hope, and installation of meaning in therapy. It seems that a starting place for presence in therapy is that therapists' attention be directed outwardly, toward clients, and inwardly, toward themselves. This is more difficult than it might seem at first glance, in part because bifurcated attention is not one's typical mode. This idea is reflected in the following excerpt from de Salzmann (2010):

> In my usual state my attention is undivided. When I open to the outside, I am naturally interested in it. My attention goes there. I cannot prevent myself. If my force of attention is entirely taken, I am lost . . . identified, asleep. All my capacity to be present is lost . . . so the first step is a separation in which my attention is divided. . . . With the attention divided, I am present in two directions, as present as I can be. My attention is engaged in two opposite directions, and I am at the center. (p. 16)

On the basis of our clinical and supervisory experience, we consider therapist presence to be a prerequisite for successful therapy. Absent or preoccupied therapists are likely to be less effective than other therapists, and they are likely to be less effective than times when they are more fully present. In addition, we view presence to be a central element of effective therapy for clinicians of all persuasions. May (1983) shared this perspective, noting that the construct of presence "is found in therapists of various schools and differing beliefs" (p. 158).

Even among the more technically oriented approaches to therapy, determining which interventions are likely to be most effective at a given moment requires that therapists understand clients' current experience, and this understanding hinges on therapists being present to clients. Therapists who are not present will necessarily have a limited understanding. Carl Rogers, toward the end of his career, went so far as to say that he may have overemphasized the role of empathy, unconditional regard, and congruence in therapy, neglecting the importance of therapist presence. "In my writing I have stressed too much the three basic conditions. . . . Perhaps it is something around the edges of those conditions that is really the most important element of therapy—when my self is very clearly, obviously present" (Baldwin, 1986, p. 30).

Research on the Role of Therapist Presence

There is a small body of empirical literature on therapist presence and its role in therapy. This body of research is reviewed next, followed by a summary of how these findings inform our understanding of therapist effects; suggestions for future research are also offered.

In one of the first studies on therapeutic presence, Geller and Greenberg (2002) interviewed seven experienced therapists from a variety of theoretical orientations (four humanistic, one cognitive–behavioral, and two psychodynamic). Therapists were asked to discuss their thoughts about and experiences of presence in their work with clients. Analyses of the interview data yielded three interrelated themes: preparing to be present to clients, in life generally and before sessions specifically; the in-session experience of presence; and activities therapists are engaged in when present to clients. These findings gave rise to the development of an instrument known as the Therapist Presence Inventory (TPI). The TPI contains 21 items rated by therapists on a 7-point scale to measure their perceptions of how present they were to clients in a session (e.g., "I felt fully immersed in my experience and yet still centered within myself;" "I was fully in the moment in this session"). Factor analyses and examination of the scale's internal consistency in clinical trials involving cognitive–behavioral, person-centered, and process-experiential therapy provided evidence indicating that the TPI measures a unitary construct (Geller & Greenberg, 2012). In addition, support for the construct validity of the TPI has been found in terms of correlations with therapists' ratings of their warmth, empathy, and unconditional regard; however, therapists' ratings of their presence were unrelated to clients' perceptions of the working alliance, counter to what one might expect from a valid measure of therapist presence (Geller & Greenberg, 2012).

Vinca (2009) used the TPI in a mixed-methods case study to investigate how therapist presence was related to therapist empathy, session quality, and client improvement. The therapist was a 32-year-old male doctoral student, and the client was a 22-year-old woman with depression, which included symptoms of low energy, pessimism, social isolation, alcohol and drug abuse, and irritability.

The client and therapist met for eight sessions, each of which was observed live by a researcher who then interviewed the therapist immediately after every session. In the interview, the therapist was asked to discuss moments when he felt especially present to the client while remaining aware of his inner experience in the session, as well as when he perceived himself to be distracted or less present. He was also asked if there was anything that happened before or during the session that helped him to be present to the client or interfered with his being present. In addition, the therapist completed the TPI after each session. For the client's part, she filled out an adapted form of the TPI (the TPI-C) after each session, which contains 18 items that measure the client's perception of how present the therapist was during a session. The client also completed postsession measures of therapist empathy and session quality. Finally, the client completed the Outcome Questionnaire-45

(OQ-45; Lambert, Gregersen, & Burlingame, 2004) before each session to measure progress in therapy.

On the whole, the client perceived the therapist to be moderately present during sessions. On the 7-point TPI-C, average scores ranged between 5 and 6. The therapist's self-perceptions of his presence varied more widely, from a low score on the TPI of 4.5 to a high score of 6.4. Interestingly, the client's distress did not ameliorate during the course of therapy. She began and ended therapy with OQ-45 scores in the clinical range, and in fact, scores were slightly elevated at termination relative to intake. Although causal inferences certainly cannot be drawn from the study, it is worth observing that the therapist thought, on average, he displayed only moderate amounts of presence to the client and the client did not improve.

In terms of process variables, the client's perception of the therapist's presence was strongly related to her perceptions of the quality of the session ($r = .85$) and the therapist's empathy ($r = .81$). On one hand, the fact that the ratings were coming from the same source (i.e., the client) likely contributed to these high correlations. On the other hand, perhaps it is the subjective perception of presence—as with so many therapy variables—that is critically important. Furthermore, it makes sound theoretical and clinical sense that these constructs would be strongly related, particularly presence and empathy.

We consider presence to be a prerequisite for empathy. As Geller and Greenberg (2012) stated, "Being fully present . . . allows for an attuned responsiveness that is based on a kinesthetic and emotional sensing of the other's affect and experience" (p. 7). When therapists are distracted, preoccupied, or otherwise not present to their clients, to themselves, and/or to the therapeutic relationship, their understanding of the client's experience is necessarily limited. Because meta-analyses indicate that empathy is a demonstrably effective element of successful therapy, accounting for about 9% of the variability in outcome (Elliott, Bohart, Watson, & Greenberg, 2011; Norcross & Wampold, 2011), if presence is a prerequisite for empathy, it may also distinguish more and less effective therapists. In other words, therapists who are not present enough to empathize with their clients will probably suffer worse outcomes than other therapists, and presence is likely to facilitate empathy. This would apply to therapists of all persuasions, because an empathic understanding of the client is necessary, regardless of whether a therapist adheres to a cognitive–behavioral, humanistic, systems, psychodynamic, or other approach.

Returning to the case study conducted by Vinca (2009), results indicated that the more present to the client the therapist perceived himself to be, the better the client's ratings were of the quality of the session ($r = .65$). These findings cannot be attributed to mono-source bias because the ratings came from two different entities. The client had no way of knowing how present the therapist perceived himself to be, and similarly, the therapist did not have access to client scores derived from the measure of session quality. Therefore, this high correlation points to the theoretically plausible conclusion that therapist presence enhances the quality of sessions. Still further, the therapist's ratings of his presence were directly related to the client's perceptions of his empathy ($r = .30$). Again, this finding supports the notion that presence may be a prerequisite for empathy.

The idea that presence is a necessary condition for empathy, and thus a predictor of outcome, has been supported in other studies as well. Pos, Geller, and Oghene (2011) investigated the relationship of therapist presence to empathy and the working alliance in a sample of 17 therapists and 52 depressed clients. They found that clients' ratings of their therapists' presence at Session 3 predicted their perceptions of therapist empathy at Sessions 9 ($r = .37$) and 12 ($r = .33$), and clients' perceptions of therapist presence at Session 9 continued to be related to their perceptions of therapist empathy at Session 12 ($r = .45$). What is particularly interesting about this study is that, although presence and empathy were related to one another, they were differentially related to the working alliance. Therapist presence, as rated by clients during Session 3, predicted strength of the alliance at Session 15; empathy did not. In fact, client ratings of therapist presence at Session 3 predicted about 5% of the alliance ratings at Session 15 above and beyond any variance accounted for by ratings of therapist empathy. Therefore, it seems that although presence and empathy are theoretically related constructs, they are sufficiently discrete that they can be distinguished empirically.

In another quantitative study that examined the relationship between therapist presence and empathy, Hayes and Vinca (2011) investigated a sample of 42 therapist–trainees and 88 clients seen for an average of eight sessions at a university training clinic. Approximately 2 weeks prior to the end of treatment, clients and therapists completed the TPI-C and TPI, respectively, and clients also completed a measure of therapist empathy. Because of the nested nature of the data, multilevel modeling analyses were conducted. Client ratings of therapist presence were once again positively associated with client ratings of therapist empathy (beta = .32). Even more strikingly, however, this relationship was stronger when the ratings were made by different sources. That is, when therapists perceived themselves to be more present, clients perceived therapists to be more empathic (beta = .62). These findings lend additional support to the notion that therapist presence may distinguish therapists who have better and worse outcomes in that presence may facilitate empathy, which is directly related to outcome (Elliott et al., 2011).

Presession Factors That Affect Therapeutic Presence

Geller and Greenberg (2012) suggested that preparing to be present to a client before a session

> involves taking the time to clear one's self of personal issues, self-needs and concerns, judgments, preconceptions, plans, and conceptualizations so that the therapist can create room inside to take in the experience of the client. It involves emptying out from the self unwanted distractions so that the therapist can enter freely into the session with the client. (pp. 84–85)

In the mixed-methods study conducted by Vinca (2009), the postsession interview data yielded themes that provide empirical support and guidance for therapists about how to prepare to be present in sessions. In this study, the therapist described his presence being facilitated by being intentional and mindful in the time leading up to a session (i.e., embodying and maintaining a warm, relaxed, nonjudgmental awareness of moment-to-moment experience); instilling feelings of confidence in himself, which may be particularly important among trainees and novice therapists; and planning for sessions (e.g., reading case notes, which helped him feel less preoccupied with trying to recall information from previous sessions). A more recent study by Dunn, Callahan, Swift, and Ivanovic (2013) challenged the idea that preparing oneself to be present before a session is useful, at least in clients' eyes. This study found that clients tended to perceive therapists as manifesting high amounts of presence during sessions, whether therapists intentionally prepared themselves to be present prior to a session or not. These conflicting data between the studies provide us with a question involving how much the intentional practice of trying to develop a sense of presence prior to a session is necessary. We wonder if the therapists in Dunn et al.'s study were already skilled in their ability to be present during therapy sessions (through which means we are not sure), such that an intentional practice prior to any given session would not be necessary.

Vinca (2009) also found that the therapist's presession anxiety interfered with his feeling present to the client in session. He stated that he was having stress and anxiety about things that were unrelated to his work with the client. The therapist perceived that his anxiety prior to session was "taking up space" inside of him, diminishing his ability to be present to the client during session. This finding is consistent with research indicating that anxiety that is unmanaged is associated with poor therapy outcomes (Hayes, Gelso, & Hummel, 2011). It stands to reason that therapists who are better at managing their anxiety are better able to maintain a sense of presence to their clients, and this process may differentiate more and less effective therapists.

Another presession factor that interfered with the therapist's sense of presence was his occasional feelings of general discouragement about his life. According to the therapist, the heaviness of feeling discouraged took away from his being as present to the client as he could have been otherwise. The therapist thought that when he overidentified with stressors in his life, it took away from the overall energy and attention that he could devote to therapy. These data speak to the need for therapists to attend to their own mental health and monitor its impact on their work with clients. Although data on this subject are sparse, it does seem reasonable to posit that therapists who are more psychologically healthy produce better outcomes, on the whole, than therapists who struggle with their mental health. A prototype of therapists who chronically seem psychologically worse off than their clients can be imagined. Such therapists, although relatively few in number, probably account for a disproportionately large number of cases in which clients deteriorate, or at least do not improve, in therapy. And it is not hard to fathom that these therapists, who often seem to have narcissistic or grandiose personalities, would have difficulty being present to clients for any length of time.

In-Session Factors Perceived to Affect Presence

One factor that seems to facilitate presence is therapists' inward attention to themselves. This might seem paradoxical in that therapists who are attending to themselves are better able to be present to their clients, and yet, the necessity to attend to oneself seems to facilitate presence to another. Geller and Greenberg (2012) explained this by noting, "In the process of presence, the therapist uses his or her *self as an instrument* to understand the client" (p. 101). In Vinca's (2009) study, when the therapist was asked if there was anything that happened during session that helped him to be present, the therapist described numerous instances in which paying attention to himself facilitated his presence to the client. For example, the therapist discussed the process by which he "watched my reactions" and "paid attention to by breathing, my body, my experiences." Focusing in the present helped him maintain a dual attention toward himself and his client. To be clear, therapists' attention is not to be understood as a dichotomy (i.e., either focusing on clients or on themselves), and the ability to maintain a bifurcated attention in session may differentiate better therapists from less effective therapists. One experienced therapist who was quoted by Geller and Greenberg (2012) put it this way:

> In those moments of presence, I do have some sense of what Rogers was talking about . . . the "as if" in which that what the client is experiencing I seem to be experiencing in some way . . . and often it's a bodily sensa-

tion for me.... But I'm not aware of doing any particular cognitive sort of processing. It just seems to rise out of my experience with them. (p. 101)

Why would it be necessary to maintain presence to the client and simultaneously to oneself? Clients necessarily evoke reactions in therapists—emotional, cognitive, behavioral, and visceral—and attending to these reactions can provide important information about the client and the nature of the work at hand (Gelso & Hayes, 2007). Disregarding these reactions, either because therapists are not conscious of them or because they are viewed as unimportant to the work at hand, can have deleterious effects on the process and outcome of therapy, especially when the working alliance is weak (Hayes et al., 2011). Novice therapists often experience an unhelpful self-preoccupation (e.g., "What will my supervisor think of what I am doing?" "Does my client like me?") and a lack of self-awareness about how clients are affecting them (Fauth & Williams, 2005). Effective therapists are able to be self-aware without becoming self-absorbed and are simultaneously able to be attuned to clients without identifying with them.

Another therapist factor that seems to facilitate presence is trust. Geller and Greenberg (2012) proposed that more experienced, and presumably more effective, therapists

> will take more risks and will trust and respond from an intuitive sense.... In contrast, when not in [a state of] presence, therapists may deliberate about their insights and responses as well as experience self-doubt about their own inner understanding of images, words, and responses. (p. 102)

They quoted an experienced therapist who said, "I always have intuitions, but I don't always trust them. I think in the present mode I don't even stop to think about whether I trust it. I just do because I just go with it" (Geller & Greenberg, 2012, pp. 102–103). This same sentiment was echoed by the therapist in Vinca's (2009) case study, who described his attempts to maintain presence by "trusting myself," "dissipating tensions and purposefully relaxing myself using the breath," and "moving out of my head and away from too much thinking" (p. 123). In contrast, there were times when the therapist felt critical of the client and not accepting her for who she was and where she was in the process of therapy. He noted that his expectations of the client interrupted his ability to be present in session.

Furthermore, the therapist in Vinca's (2009) case study described feeling more present to the client when there was validation that therapy was working. For example, when the client expressed emotion and insight, this seemed to relieve the therapist of the question of whether he was doing good work and helped him to be present to the client. At the same time, when therapy was not going well—and it is worth remembering that the client's symptoms increased on the OQ-45 over the course of therapy—the therapist felt less present to the client and was more occupied with self-doubt. Although it may be tempting to view these reactions as specific to a therapist in training, it is worth noting that lack of progress in therapy has been found to provoke problematic reactions among experienced therapists as well (Hayes, Nelson, & Fauth, 2015). In any case, one can readily envision a vicious cycle in which therapy is not going well and so the therapist becomes less present, which diminishes the quality of therapy, which reinforces the therapist's lack of presence, and on and on (see Figure 5.1).

Therapists' countertransference reactions also can inhibit a sense of presence (see Chapter 6, this volume). For example, the therapist in Vinca's (2009) case study struggled with his attraction to the client. He said in one postsession interview, "She's attractive and I was trying not to focus on her attractiveness" (p. 111). He also discussed his difficulties with feeling powerless to help the

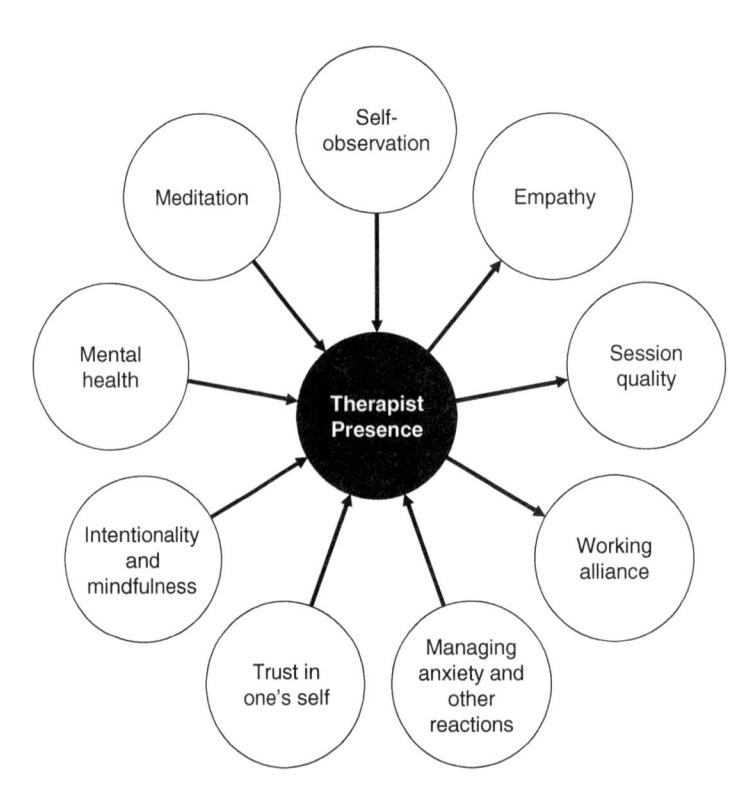

Figure 5.1. Facilitators and consequences of therapist presence. The variables of mental health and meditation denote presession factors that facilitate presence. The variable of self-observation denotes an in-session factor that facilitates presence. The variables of empathy, session quality, and working alliance denote consequences of presence. The variables of intentionality and mindfulness, trust in one's self, and managing anxiety and other reactions denote presession and in-session factors that facilitate presence.

client ("She's in pain and I really can't stand not being of help to her; I want to help" [p. 99]). In addition, the similarities between the therapist's current client and a former client evoked internal reactions that interfered with his sense of presence ("I had feelings that I'm going to have to pull teeth to get her to talk because I was remembering a similar client from before" [p. 102]). Finally, termination provoked preoccupying reactions for the therapist ("I didn't want to end our therapy; I wanted to continue with her" [p. 101]), as it does for many therapists (Hayes et al., 2015). The therapist experienced himself at times as being heavily identified with these feelings and reported that this overinvolvement took away from his capacity to be present to her. Again, the take home message here is that therapists need to attend to and manage their internal reactions so they are able to maintain a therapeutic presence in sessions. Failure to do so is likely to contribute to differential therapist outcomes that have been reported in meta-analyses (Hayes et al., 2011) and elsewhere in this book (see Chapter 10, this volume).

EXTRAORDINARY PRESENCE

There is yet another quality that can be embodied by therapists, further down the spectrum from ordinary presence. Although we believe it is a rare state, it is nonetheless easier to experience than to describe. Words serve only as symbols for experience, and once an experience is symbolized, it inevitably becomes distorted; the symbol is not the experience. And so how do we accurately convey the experience of extraordinary presence? It is a bit like describing Zanzibar to someone who has never left their own neighborhood; understanding is likely to be limited.

Extraordinary presence is a state in which one feels fully and deeply collected, relaxed, open, and watchful. Unlike ordinary presence, which may be experienced by clients—especially those who do not want to be seen—as unwelcome and even intrusive unless conveyed sensitively, therapists who are in a state of extraordinary presence are fully contained within themselves and do not risk overstepping boundaries with clients. Extraordinary presence involves a deep state of connection to oneself and a connection to a source of fine energy of which one is typically unaware (de Salzmann, 2010). One feels energized without a sense of excitement, alert without hyperarousal, sensitive without being identified, calm without being removed. To the contrary, in a state of extraordinary presence, one is interested in one's inner and outer experience without having one's attention taken. We have found that the ability to direct and sustain one's attention is exceptionally challenging and unusual, although most people would say they are able to do so with little difficulty. If one pays attention to the data from everyday life—especially one's own—as impartially as possible, one notices how attention is constantly taken: by mental associations, by emotional reactions, by daydreams, by sensations, by imagination, by fleeting thoughts. In a state of extraordinary presence, attention is directed, inwardly and outwardly.

How can a state of extraordinary presence be cultivated? Our own experience suggests that a regular practice in one's daily life may be required, a practice that sharpens the attention, such as meditation. Along these lines, Fatter and Hayes (2013) found that, in a sample of therapists in training, the amount of time they spent meditating each week was directly related to supervisors' ratings of therapists' ability to manage their adverse reactions to clients. Attaining a state of extraordinary presence seems to require that

> the sensation, the thinking and the feeling have to turn inward, trying to find a common tempo, an accord in which they do not diverge and disconnect so easily. . . . I let go, not in order to relax but because the more I let go, the stronger the movement of collecting becomes, the movement of coming together. I let go in order to feel contained in myself. I concentrate on the point where my thoughts arrive and disappear, and I go beyond. (de Salzmann, 2010, pp. 188–190)

Carl Rogers (1986) was perhaps speaking of extraordinary presence when he described a similar, atypical state of consciousness:

> I find that when I am closest to my inner, intuitive self, when I am somehow in touch with the unknown in me, when perhaps I am in a slightly altered state of consciousness in the relationship, then whatever I do seems to be full of healing. Then simply my presence is releasing and helpful. . . . When I can relax and be close to the transcendental core of me, then. . . . it seems that my inner spirit has reached out and touched the inner spirit of the other. Our relationship transcends itself and becomes a part of something larger. Profound growth and healing and energy are present. (p. 129)

In other words, in a state of extraordinary presence, the therapist is likely to facilitate change, irrespective of theoretical orientation or specific interventions; the quality of extraordinary presence is therapeutic in and of itself.

It would be exceptionally difficult to do quantitative research on extraordinary presence because operationalizing the construct and measuring it accurately would present a formidable, though perhaps not impossible, challenge. Observer ratings would prove almost useless because the inner experience of extraordinary presence would not be readily accessible to anyone but the therapist. At the same time, many therapists who have never experienced this remarkable state would probably insist that they have, just as a sleeping person who is dreaming has difficulty distinguishing between states of consciousness. Qualitative research would be challenging as well, because it would require locating therapists—or perhaps nontherapists—who have experienced extraordinary presence and who would be willing to talk about a phenomenon that may be considered deeply personal, and which could be subjected to skepticism and misunderstanding from others. Nonetheless, should a qualitative study manage to overcome such obstacles, it would likely make a valuable contribution to the field, in terms of expanding our knowledge base and by potentially identifying master therapists from whom other therapists could learn. The results of qualitative research could then serve as the foundation for the creation of an instrument that could be used to measure extraordinary therapist presence.

CONCLUSION

One may conceive of a bell-shaped curve with therapist absence on one end, ordinary presence occupying the middle ground and bulk of the curve, and extraordinary presence at the other end. The two extremes occur, in our estimation, relatively infrequently and have the most pronounced effects on clients. For a variety of reasons, therapists' attention occasionally wanders during sessions so that they are momentarily absent, but most of the time, therapists are able to maintain a presence that is a necessary prerequisite for virtually any other aspect of therapy. It would seem to us that less effective therapists are absent more of the time, and with more clients, than are therapists whose outcomes are generally superior. Conversely, more effective therapists would be better able to sustain a sense of presence with most of their clients through the majority of a session. By extension, therapists with generally better outcomes are capable of conveying their presence in ways that are helpful to clients, so that clients do not perceive the therapist as intrusive or invasive. This may require, depending on a client's cultural composition, diagnosis, interpersonal style, and other characteristics, that the therapist "titrate" the amount of presence that is communicated to the client and sensitively adjust the manner in which it is conveyed. A rare few therapists have the capacity, seemingly through long work on themselves (through their own psychotherapy, through meditation, and other self-work practices), to manifest an extraordinary presence that is transformative, in and of itself. In our estimation, these therapists would consistently produce outcomes that differentiated them favorably from other therapists. Although these conclusions are based on existing theory, our own clinical observations, reason, and a scant amount of research, much more empirical scholarship is needed to advance the field's understanding of therapist presence and its role in differentiating more and less effective therapists.

REFERENCES

Baldwin, M. (1986). *The use of the self in therapy*. Binghamton, NY: Haworth.

Colosimo, K. A., & Pos, A. E. (2015). A rational model of expressed therapeutic presence. *Journal of Psychotherapy Integration, 25*, 100–114. http://dx.doi.org/10.1037/a0038879

de Salzmann, J. (2010). *The reality of being*. Boston, MA: Shambhala.

Dunn, R., Callahan, J. L., Swift, J. K., & Ivanovic, M. (2013). Effects of pre-session centering for therapists on session presence and effectiveness. *Psychotherapy Research, 23*, 78–85. http://dx.doi.org/10.1080/10503307.2012.731713

Elliott, R., Bohart, A. C., Watson, J. C., & Greenberg, L. S. (2011). Empathy. In J. C. Norcross (Ed.), *Psychotherapy relationships that work* (2nd ed., pp. 132–152). New York, NY: Oxford University Press.

Fatter, D. M., & Hayes, J. A. (2013). What facilitates countertransference management? The roles of therapist meditation, mindfulness, and self-differentiation. *Psychotherapy Research, 23*, 502–513. http://dx.doi.org/10.1080/10503307.2013.797124

Fauth, J., & Williams, E. N. (2005). The in-session self-awareness of therapist-trainees: Hindering or helpful? *Journal of Counseling Psychology, 52*, 443–447. http://dx.doi.org/10.1037/0022-0167.52.3.443

Geller, S. M., & Greenberg, L. S. (2002). Therapeutic presence: Therapists' experience of presence in the psychotherapy encounter. *Person-Centered and Experiential Psychotherapies, 1*, 71–86. http://dx.doi.org/10.1080/14779757.2002.9688279

Geller, S. M., & Greenberg, L. S. (2012). *Therapeutic presence: A mindful approach to effective therapy*. Washington, DC: American Psychological Association. http://dx.doi.org/10.1037/13485-000

Gelso, C. J., & Hayes, J. A. (2007). *Countertransference and the therapist's inner experience: Perils and possibilities*. Mahwah, NJ: Erlbaum.

Hayes, J. A., Gelso, C. J., & Hummel, A. M. (2011). Managing countertransference. *Psychotherapy, 48*, 88–97. http://dx.doi.org/10.1037/a0022182

Hayes, J. A., Nelson, D. L., & Fauth, J. (2015). Countertransference in successful and unsuccessful cases of psychotherapy. *Psychotherapy, 52*, 127–133. http://dx.doi.org/10.1037/a0038827

Hayes, J. A., & Vinca, M. A. (2011, June). *Therapist presence and its relationship to empathy, session depth, and symptom reduction*. Paper presented at the meeting of the Society for Psychotherapy Research, Bern, Switzerland.

Lambert, M. J., Gregersen, A. T., & Burlingame, G. M. (2004). The Outcome Questionnaire-45. In M. E. Maruish (Ed.), *The use of psychological testing for treatment planning and outcomes assessment: Instruments for adults* (3rd ed., pp. 191–234). Mahwah, NJ: Erlbaum.

May, R. (1983). *The discovery of being*. New York, NY: Norton.

Norcross, J. C., & Wampold, B. E. (2011). Evidence-based therapy relationships: Research conclusions and clinical practices. In J. C. Norcross (Ed.), *Psychotherapy relationships that work* (2nd ed., pp. 423–430). New York, NY: Oxford University Press.

Pos, A., Geller, S., & Oghene, J. (2011). *Therapist presence, empathy, and the working alliance in experiential treatment for depression.* Paper presented at the meeting of the Society for Psychotherapy Research, Bern, Switzerland.

Rogers, C. R. (1986). Client-centered therapy. In I. L. Jutash & A. Wolf (Eds.), *Psychotherapist's casebook* (pp. 197–208). San Francisco, CA: Jossey-Bass.

Schneider, K. (2015). Presence: The core contextual factor of effective psychotherapy. *Existential Analysis, 26,* 304–312.

Vinca, M. A. (2009). *Mindfulness and psychotherapy: A mixed methods investigation.* Unpublished doctoral dissertation, Pennsylvania State University.

6

INNER EXPERIENCE AND THE GOOD THERAPIST

CHARLES J. GELSO AND ANDRES E. PEREZ-ROJAS

The premise of this chapter is that the therapist's inner experience matters considerably when providing psychotherapy. It has a major and far-reaching effect on what transpires in psychotherapy, how the work goes, and the extent to which the treatment is successful. Similarly, effective therapy of all persuasions is not simply a matter of the skilled application of techniques (e.g., reflection of the patient's feelings, interpretations, systematic desensitization) but also the therapist's inner experience, which impacts not only what techniques are chosen but also how they are applied. To use the technique of interpretation as an example, the tone, duration, content, depth, timing, and ultimately, the effectiveness of an interpretation will depend importantly on what the therapist is feeling and thinking about a patient and himself or herself at the moment of that interpretation, and probably at other moments, as well.

Our focus in this chapter is twofold. First, we explore the inner experience of the good (i.e., effective) psychotherapist. The current wealth of

http://dx.doi.org/10.1037/0000034-007
How and Why Are Some Therapists Better Than Others? Understanding Therapist Effects, L. G. Castonguay and C. E. Hill (Eds.)
Copyright © 2017 by the American Psychological Association. All rights reserved.

multilevel modeling studies in which therapist and patient factors are partitioned into independent levels clearly underscores that some therapists are more effective than others on the whole, and also that a given therapist will be more effective with some of his or her patients than others. Our conceptualization of the effective therapist includes therapists who are more effective overall and effective with given patients. Do more effective therapists have different inner experiences than less effective therapists? Are inner experiences different when a therapist is being more effective than when that therapist is being less effective? Second, we focus on how the good therapist handles, uses, and manages his or her inner experience. This focal point is based on the premise that what a therapist does with his her inner experience is as important as what that therapist experiences.

What do we mean by *inner experience*? This refers to the thoughts, feelings, images, fantasies, and inner physical sensations of the therapist during the times when the patient and the work are on the therapist's mind, including during the therapy hour. All of these inner experiences naturally matter. However, in this chapter we focus more on the affective side of things than the cognitive side, although admittedly both are important and both are probably synergistically related. When initially developing this chapter, we intended to emphasize inner experience in therapists who practiced psychodynamic and experiential treatments, and to exclude cognitive–behavioral therapists. However, when presenting this to participants at the Penn State Conference on Therapist Effects, we were persuaded to include cognitive–behavioral therapy (CBT), as most felt the topic may be even more important in CBT because of the lack of attention it typically receives in CBT training. The conference participants who spoke most strongly to this point were themselves CBT therapists!

We consider three key areas that have much to do with the inner experience of the effective therapist and its effects on treatment. First, we briefly review the three therapist-offered conditions that are a central element of Carl Rogers's (1957) statement of the necessary and sufficient conditions for therapeutic personality change. Second, we examine inner states in the therapist that are perhaps the most difficult to experience and work with: hate and love. Third, we discuss the ingredients that allow therapists to deal effectively with inner experience. These ingredients come under the heading of countertransference (CT) management.

INNER EXPERIENCE AND THE FACILITATIVE CONDITIONS

Arguably, the most powerful and heuristic theoretical proposition ever made in psychotherapy was C. R. Rogers' (1957) statement of the necessary and sufficient conditions in psychotherapy for effective patient personality change. More than half a century after its presentation, it had and is still having a wide impact on therapeutic thought and research. Rogers audaciously suggested six conditions that were necessary for effective change and sufficient, in and of themselves, to create such change in psychotherapies of all theoretical persuasions: (a) two persons are in psychological contact; (b) the patient is in a state of incongruence, being vulnerable and anxious; (c) the therapist is congruent or integrated in the relationship; (d) the therapist experiences unconditional positive regard for the patient; (e) the therapist experiences empathic understanding of the patient's internal frame of reference and seeks to communicate this to the patient; and (f) the communication to the patient of empathy and unconditional positive regard is achieved, at least to a minimal degree.

We focus here on the three widely known and studied therapist-offered conditions that pertain to the therapist's role: congruence, unconditional positive regard, and empathy. Decades of research have indeed supported the importance of the conditions, particularly when assessed from the patient's vantage point as Rogers suggested, even though the conditions have not been found to be fully sufficient (see meta-analytic reviews on empathic understanding—Elliott, Bohart, Watson, & Greenberg, 2011; positive regard—Farber & Doolin, 2011; congruence or genuineness—Kolden, Klein, Wang, & Austin, 2011).

The key point for this chapter is that the three therapist-offered conditions are, to an important extent, inner experiences in the therapist that matter for the success of the work, depending on how they are expressed. C. R. Rogers (1957) accentuated this point when he stated that the conditions are therapist attitudes, not techniques. In what sense do the therapist-offered conditions tap inner experiences?

In the case of *empathy*, it is first and foremost an experience of identification with the patient's inner world—an affective and a cognitive identification. Therefore, empathy involves the therapist's partaking of the patient's inner experience, feeling what the patient feels to an extent, and cognitively seeking to grasp the patient's experience. It is important that this identification be partial, so that the therapist maintains his or her sense of self, but it is generally agreed that empathy cannot exist without a degree of inner identification. The importance of empathy as a kind of vicarious identification is also prominent in current relational theories of psychoanalysis, and was given great impetus by the theoretical work of the psychoanalytic self-psychologist, Heinz Kohut (1971). Kohut conceptualized empathy as what he termed *vicarious introspection*, by which he meant the analyst's dwelling in the patient's inner world as if he or she were the patient (while also maintaining separateness).

In recent years, there has been a tendency to conceptualize empathy as a kind of technique or helping skill (most often a reflection of feeling). In contrast, we underscore that empathy may be expressed in many ways, and at times, accurate reflections of feeling may even be experienced as a lack of empathy (see Elliott et al., 2011, for a discussion of ways of exhibiting empathy). We suggest that in therapist training, the focus needs to be on the trainee's actually experiencing empathy rather than on teaching trainees to exhibit behaviors that are theoretically linked to empathy (i.e., acting empathically). It is hard to imagine an effective psychotherapy in the absence of therapist-experienced empathy.

Unconditional positive regard (UPR) has a more controversial history than the other therapist-offered conditions. How can a therapist feel unconditionally positive toward a patient? Indeed, can anyone other than a parent be unconditionally positive? Is being unconditionally positive actually negatively related to another therapist-offered condition, congruence, as some early studies found (Mills & Abeles, 1965)? These are knotty theoretical and clinical questions that we do not have space to explore. We do underscore, however, that C. R. Rogers (1957) himself noted that UPR was more of a principle that therapists should strive to achieve, and he well understood that therapists could not be completely unconditional. As an inner experience, Rogers conceived of UPR as follows:

> To the extent that the therapist finds himself experiencing a warm acceptance of each aspect of the client's experience as being a part of the client, he is experiencing unconditional positive regard. . . . It means prizing the person. . . . It is at the opposite pole from a selective evaluating attitude. . . . It involves as much feeling of acceptance for the client's expression of negative, "bad," painful, fearful, defensive, abnormal feelings, as much as his expression of "good," positive, mature, confident, social feelings. . . . It means caring for the client as a *separate* person, with permission to have his own feelings, his own experiences. (p. 98)

This conception does not mean that the therapist approves of everything the patient does; only, fundamentally, of who the patient is. It leaves room for the therapist's negative reactions to the patient, even very strong negative reactions, as we discuss in the next section. UPR aside, it is hard to imagine a successful treatment of any duration in the absence of this fundamental regard for the patient's inner being. As Farber and Doolin (2011) concluded, at a minimum, positive regard sets the stage for other change-inducing interventions and in some cases has a profound effect in itself. They added, "To many, if not most clients, the conviction that 'my therapist really cares about me' likely serves as a critical function, especially during times of stress" (p. 184).

The final therapist-offered condition, *congruence* (or genuineness), is the most fundamental to C. R. Rogers (1957) because empathy and UPR cannot have the desired effect in the absence of congruence. As an inner experience, congruence means that within the therapeutic relationship, the therapist is able to be aware of his or her feelings. Indeed, such awareness is possible because there is congruence between inner experience and the therapist's self-concept. Congruence, like the other two conditions, also implies action: The therapist is able to be himself or herself in the relationship and does not hide behind a professional façade. Research during the past decade on the real relationship in psychotherapy (Gelso, 2011, 2014), of which genuineness is a key element, also strongly supports the importance of this condition.

We have focused mostly on the three therapist-offered conditions as inner experiences and on how these experiences are enacted within the therapeutic relationship. Such enactments may be straightforward, or they may be remarkably subtle (e.g., facial expressions, tone of voice), but the enactments are informed by the therapist's inner experiences, and those that reflect C. R. Rogers's (1957) facilitative conditions are highly robust therapist factors (see Chapter 5, this volume, for a discussion of therapeutic presence, which bears similarity to Rogers' conditions).

INADMISSIBLE THERAPIST AFFECTIVE STATES: HATE AND LOVE

The therapist-offered condition of congruence highlights the importance of allowing into awareness the therapist's organismic experiencing with the patient—the positive and the negative. However, doing so may be particularly difficult when the states are "inadmissible" by ordinary therapeutic standards. By inadmissible states, we mean inner experiences of the therapist that are typically unwanted, uncomfortable, shameful, and incongruent with what is generally thought of as helpful (i.e., a benevolent attitude). These are inner experiences that therapists may prefer to suppress, repress, or otherwise disavow. Feelings such as hate, rage, love, and sexual arousal (tantamount to Freud's sex and aggression) are perhaps the most commonly denied ones, and these are the focus of this section. There are, however, other states that may come under this umbrella (e.g., boredom, fear, pity; see Wolf, Goldfried, & Muran, 2013).

Why are feelings of love and hate, and more generally the therapist's emotional frailties, so difficult to admit? Freud ironically may have paved the road to such suppression/repression with his attitude toward the analyst's CT. He believed that analysts needed to recognize and overcome their CT, and that "anyone who cannot succeed in this self-analysis may without more ado regard himself as unable to treat neurotics by analysis" (Freud, 1910/1959a, p. 289).

Additionally, in his famous surgeon's analogy, Freud (1912/1959b) stated,

> I cannot recommend my colleagues emphatically enough to take as a model in psycho-analytic treatment the surgeon who puts aside all of his own feelings, including that of human sympathy, and concentrates his mind on one single purpose, that of performing the operation as skillfully as possible. (p. 327)

In these two passages, Freud communicates that CT feelings need to be analyzed out of the therapeutic equation. To be unable to work them through makes one unsuitable for the work of analysis. It would appear that nothing good comes from CT, and that being the case, certainly nothing good can come from intense states such as love and hate.

Although psychoanalysis and psychotherapy have moved well beyond the belief that therapists should put their feelings aside, Freud's statements have taken their toll (Gelso & Hayes, 2007). They have tended to make the study and admission (to oneself and others) of a therapist's love and hate extremely difficult, instead driving them into the therapeutic underground. The thesis of this chapter, however, is that it is important and ultimately helpful for a therapist to allow himself or herself to accept his or her intense feelings, such as love and hate. The good therapist allows intense affects such as hate and love into the relationship and is able to experience these feelings.

Hate in the Countertransference

As psychoanalysts and therapists of all persuasions began treating more deeply disturbed patients, such as those with borderline personality disorder (BPD) and other severe personality disorders, it became clear that it was nearly impossible for therapists to avoid intense affects. It is generally understood that patients with BPD behave in ways that stir very negative feelings in their therapists, feelings that may be called hateful or rageful (see Lingiardi, Tanzilli, & Colli, 2015, for empirical support). Such reactions have been examined extensively from a CBT perspective (see Linehan, 1993; McMain & Wiebe, 2013), as well as from psychodynamic vantage points (cf. Chapter 10, this volume).

The seminal conceptualization of the psychoanalyst Winnicott (1949) had a major impact on the field. For Winnicott, when working with severely disturbed patients, such as those with BPD, hateful feelings on the part of the therapist are not only inevitable but could be helpful to the treatment. Such feelings provide a window into the inner world of the patient, and a telescope into what the patient experienced in childhood. Winnicott famously likened the therapist's hateful feelings to those of a mother with her infant, and he listed 18 reasons why a mother hates (as well as loves) her infant. Like a mother, the therapist must contain his or her hateful feelings when they occur. The therapist must let himself or herself know these feelings and where they come from if he or she is not to act them out on the patient, either through subtle and corrosive aggressive reactions or defensively giving too much and being overly kind.

The great difficulties therapists have in facing hateful feelings toward their patients and revealing them to others are beautifully captured by Carter (2006):

> As I have thought about my own experiences of hateful countertransference, I feel a depth of shame. Those hateful feelings are unacceptable to one's self.... They are unacceptable because they threaten our own self-concept and self-esteem. They bring up our own sense of failure, the ways in which we are deficient and disappointing to ourselves.... We want to avoid those feelings because they are the feelings of shame, and shame leads to a wish to conceal, to hide, to remain blind to our own shameful experiences.

As we have said, when working with more severely disturbed patients, such as those with BPD, reactions such as hate and rage seem almost inevitable. Within the psychoanalytic literature, such patients are typically seen as using a defense mechanism labeled projective identification. Here, as a way of avoiding facing their own hateful feelings, patients create them within the therapist. In some descriptions, this process of transporting feelings into the therapist seems almost magical. A belief in such a magical process might make things easier for the therapist in that he or she does not have to accept responsibility for feelings that are transported into him or her. Missed, however, is the realization that, although precipitated by the patient, the therapist's feelings and inner experiences are also connected to his or her unresolved conflicts and vulnerabilities. Although more taxing for the therapist, we believe it important to examine how the therapist's hate (its particular content, frequency, intensity, and duration), while stimulated by the patient, is also shaped by the therapist's own issues.

A case example[1] from the work of the first author early in his career exemplifies this approach (discussed in first person for ease of reading). At the time of treatment, which occurred over a period of 20 months, David was a 19-year-old university student. He was an emotionally young patient who yearned to be cared for and loved. In a needy way, he pulled loving and sympathetic feelings from others, even when they did not experience those feelings. He behaved in relationships in a way that friends had to either come

---

[1]This case example has been disguised to protect patient confidentiality.

through with loving feelings or feel guilty for not caring enough. As a result, David's friendships did not last long.

Although these patterns were being explored over the course of many weeks, I did not see the extent to which they were invading the therapeutic relationship. These patterns were most notably enacted during one session in which David asked me to hug him. I did so, while at the same time experiencing discomfort and not having the feelings that were congruent with hugging another person. Just what I was feeling for David was unclear to me, even though I was aware that I was feeling a lot. However, things became very clear to me one night in the form of a dream. In this dream, I had the patient pinned to the ground and was choking him. It felt good to be doing so. Needless to say, when I awoke, I was unsettled. The realization came through to me very clearly that I was angry with this patient, in fact, furious. I had felt manipulated into caring for him over many weeks. As this awareness emerged, I also became aware that on the mornings of our 9 a.m. sessions, I always seemed to feel grouchy, at times snapping at my wife and kids.

As all of this became clear to me, I was able to be more in touch with my feelings in the moment with David, and to get in touch with the deeper fears that caused him to pull for love and affection. This awareness in me served to modulate my feelings toward David, and to use them to frame helpful interpretations to him about what he was doing with me and with others, as well as the needs underlying his interpersonal patterns and others' reactions to him. It was also more possible to refrain from falsely sympathizing with David and acting like I felt more positively than I did. My ability to modulate my feelings was aided by an understanding of my own personal conflicts around giving and receiving, and a tendency toward guilt about not giving enough. The intensity of my reactions was fueled by my revulsion of my own neediness, a conflict of which I was only dimly aware at the time. These conflicts made me both an easy target for David's affective yearnings and pull for affection, and they also fueled the intensity of my unconscious hateful reaction. Although I never told David of my dream, the feelings that I came to grasp in myself became a key part of this successful therapy. What a therapist does with hateful affects depends a great deal on his or her theoretical inclinations. However, for all therapists, there is agreement that it is first important to admit and grasp these feelings, to try to understand them in terms of what the patient is doing along with the therapist's vulnerabilities, and to devise responses that take this understanding into account (see separate chapters in Wolf et al., 2013, for suggestions both across and within varied theoretical orientations).

Winnicott (1949) believed it useful for therapists to communicate what patients stirred in them when patients had overcome many of their problems and were mature enough to hear these painful affective realities. Others (e.g., Mehlman & Glickauf-Hughes, 1994) have recommended that the therapist communicate a metabolized (transformed into a more manageable, less intense form) version of his or her feelings that are stimulated by the patient's attacks (Green, 2006). Most agree that it is unhelpful to react with total kindness or neutrality to aggressive onslaughts, as this deepens the patient's sense of helplessness and emotional impotence.

Love and Sexuality in the Therapeutic Relationship

The topic of the therapist's love for his or her patient may be even more avoided, more "inadmissible," than the feeling of hate. Perhaps this is because love conjures images of boundary violations in the form of sexual acting out. The avoidance also may reflect ambivalence about how close we should be getting to our patients and letting them get to us. For example, a colleague noted that the topic of love in therapy made her think about "how we both seek and fear intimacy with our patients, and how we long for closeness as human beings with our patients, but shy away from it" (K. Aafjes-Van Doorn, personal communication, July 22, 2015).

Our view, as recently described in some depth (Gelso, Perez-Rojas, & Marmarosh, 2014), is that the therapist's loving feelings can have an important, healing effect on the patient, particularly in longer term therapies where the dyad has spent many hours together and the patient has communicated very deep feelings and thoughts that may have been shared with no other person. Here the therapist gets to know the patient in a profound way, and especially as the latter's barriers to his or her inner world have been lifted, feelings that go beyond positive regard are likely to emerge.

When we discuss the therapist's love in psychotherapy, it is important to ask what kind of love, and how it relates to sexual feelings. The existential psychoanalyst Rollo May (1969) had much to say about this topic. He believed that

> there are four kinds of love in Western tradition. One is *sex*, or what we call lust, libido. The second is *eros*, the drive of love to procreate—the urge, as the Greeks put it, toward higher forms of being and relationship. A third is *philia*, or friendship, brotherly love. The fourth is *agape* or *caritas* as the Latins called it, the love that is devoted to the welfare of the other, the prototype of which is the love of God for man. Every human experience of authentic love is a blending, in varying proportions, of these four. (p. 38)

We have proposed that this blending also occurs in the therapeutic relationship. For the therapist, *philia* and *agape* can have a healing effect on the patient. Therefore, when the therapist cares deeply for his or her patient, as in *philia* or *agape*, this likely will shift how the patient perceives, interprets, and behaves in relationships, as well as how the patient feels about himself or herself. Within the context of this kind of love, there may also be a healthy sexual element, similar to May's (1969) *eros*, a kind of affectionate caring combined with attraction (see Blum's, 1973, landmark paper on healthy erotic transferences). As we have elsewhere stated,

> Because the therapist is experiencing these feelings toward a person that he or she has come to or is coming to know deeply, the feelings and attraction can be mostly reality-based and genuine and thus, be part of the real relationship. It may be of greater concern when such feelings are absent in the therapist than when they are present, given the intimate nature of the therapeutic relationship. (Gelso et al., 2014, p. 319)

Annie Rogers got at the depth of affect, including love, in *A Shining Affliction* (1996), when she stated, "The psychotherapy relationship is two-sided, whether we acknowledge it or not. . . . [It] is an interchange of love, longing, frustration, and anger in the vicissitudes of a real relationship" (p. 319).

Although *agape* may be indicative of a strong and healthy real relationship, we should not ignore the likelihood that it also at times may reflect CT conflicts in the therapist. Gelso et al. (2014) used as an example of such conflicts the therapist who suffers from unresolved dependency issues and who feels loving toward a patient who compulsively takes charge. In addition, more purely lustful or sexual feelings, depending on their frequency, intensity, and duration, may also be indicative of unresolved issues within the therapist. It is crucial that the therapist seek to understand these so as not to act them out on or with the patient.

We do not believe that loving feelings generally need to be shared explicitly with patients. These feelings are likely to form the backdrop of effective therapies, particularly long-term therapies. They have their effect through the therapist's abiding concern for doing what is best for the patient, the therapist's abiding attempt to empathically climb into the patient's world, and the therapist's abiding efforts to stay in tune with his or her own feelings in the relationship, to "look deeply into his or her own inner world to admit sexual and loving feelings to him/herself, and to seek to understand, however imperfectly, their sources, especially the extent to which these feelings are countertransference based" (Gelso et al., 2014, p 135). Not doing so is likely to result in the therapist acting out, usually indirectly (e.g., through being detached, seductive, aggressive), but at times directly, with deeply damaging effects.

Because of the taboos that have existed around strong therapist affects such as hate and love, and the resulting shame that a therapist often experiences around these affects, little empirical research exists on such feelings. If research is to move forward, perhaps the first step that is needed is to normalize such affects—to understand and communicate that they are usually a natural part of many therapeutic relationships; that some of them are an almost inevitable part of working with certain patients; and that all therapists are, above all, human beings with many warts and frailties, wounded healers so to speak (see Gelso & Hayes, 2007; Yalom, 2002), even though most of the wounds are sufficiently healed to allow him or her to do effective therapy. Researchers need to be sensitive and respectful toward the therapists they are studying, and ideally the researchers would themselves be experienced therapists who know firsthand these difficult and threatening feelings.

WHAT IS A THERAPIST TO DO? THE MANAGEMENT OF INNER EXPERIENCE

What should a therapist do about inner experience? More to the point of this chapter, what does a good therapist do about his or her inner experience? The most fundamental and overarching answer pertains to awareness. As Wolf et al. (2013) proposed, first the therapist needs to be aware of his or her own moment-to-moment reactions to patients. He or she then must regulate and contain his or her expression of powerful affects. Third, particularly when the therapist's affects toward the patient are highly negative, it is important that the therapist seek to empathically grasp where the patient is coming from in his or her inner world. This grasping will not rid the therapist of his or her feelings, but it will tend to make them more tolerable and understandable, and at times even transform them.

The area of CT management (Gelso & Hayes, 2007; Hayes, Gelso, & Hummel, 2011) points to certain ingredients that are central to the therapist's successful management of his or her inner experiences with patients. Whether focusing on conflict-based experience or non-conflictual, healthy, and positive responses, the ingredients of CT management are likely to apply. In the first of a series of studies and conceptual papers, Van Wagoner, Gelso, Hayes, and Diemer (1991) posited five such ingredients, which are seen as constituents or manifestations of CT management (Gelso & Hayes, 2007). We should note that by *CT management*, Gelso, Hayes, and their collaborators did not mean simply controlling CT. Management also includes actually using one's inner experience to better understand the patient and the patient's impact on others. In this sense, CT management is theorized to advance psychotherapy rather than simply help therapists control their feelings.

THE FIVE-FACTOR THEORY . . . OR IS IT TWO?

The first of the five ingredients or factors of CT management is labeled *self-insight*. Understanding oneself within the therapeutic relationship, cognitively and emotionally, may be the most fundamental element of managing one's CT. Self-insight does not stop internal experiencing, but it is key to the therapist's being aware of this experiencing, understanding its triggers and sources, and refraining from acting out feelings that would be injurious to the therapeutic process. It is also key to using internal experience in a way that benefits the work.

The second factor is termed *self-integration*. The integrated therapist possesses a sound sense of self within the therapeutic relationship, even though at times this sense is threatened, for example, by patients who themselves are poorly integrated. In addition, the therapist has sound boundaries between himself or herself and the patient, without those boundaries being too strong or impermeable. In essence, the therapist knows where he or she stops and the patient starts. To the extent that the therapist is integrated or whole in the relationship, he or she is less likely to feel overly conflicted, and even more so, is unlikely to act out such conflicts on or against the patient.

Empathy is the third element of CT management. This may be the most potent of C. R. Rogers's (1957) facilitative conditions, and it reflects the therapist's willingness and ability to climb into the patient's inner world and intellectually grasp that world, and also to some extent, feel what the patient is feeling. The ability to be empathic with a patient certainly works against what might otherwise be the poisonous effects of negative feelings, and in fact is likely to help the therapist feel less negatively. That is, if a therapist really grasps where the patient is coming from, hateful feelings, for example, may be transformed into less hateful affects.

The fourth constituent of CT management is labeled *anxiety management*. Effective CT management does not entail eliminating anxiety in the therapist. Indeed, anxiety may be quite important as a signal, and its absence may itself reflect a CT problem. Anxiety management instead refers to the therapist's skill in grasping and controlling his or her anxiety with patients so that it does not bleed into the work and adversely affect the therapist's behavior.

The fifth and final element of CT management is theorized to be *conceptualizing ability*. Effective CT management is aided by the therapist's ability to have a theory of the therapeutic relationship, a theoretical conceptualization of the patient, the therapist, and their interactions. Having such an understanding adds rhyme and reason to what at times may seem like incomprehensible feelings and actions on the part of the patient, and the therapist, as well. For example, because the therapist has a sound conceptualization of his or her BPD patient's underlying rage and where it comes from, the edge is likely taken off the therapist's hateful affect, and the probability of damaging acting out is diminished.

A range of empirical studies have supported the value of these five factors combined in fostering successful psychotherapy, and meta-analyses of such studies have revealed a large effect size in positive outcomes (Hayes et al., 2011). To return to our original framework, the good therapist is likely to excel at managing CT. The initial study of CT management, in fact, found that therapists who were nominated by other therapists as excellent scored substantially higher on a CT management measure than average therapists (Van Wagoner, Gelso, Hayes, & Diemer, 1991).

Despite the promising findings around CT management, nagging measurement problems remained. In addressing these problems, preliminary data gathered on an improved version of the most commonly used measure of CT management have suggested that the five existing factors may be grouped into two overarching factors (Perez-Rojas et al., 2016): (a) understanding self and others and (b) personal security. This is a statistically cleaner division than the five factors, and it does include all of the ingredients of the five.

One of the deficiencies in CT management theory and research to date has been the lack of work on how to strengthen CT management skills. However, two studies in New Zealand (Cartwright & Read, 2011; Cartwright, Rhodes, King, & Shires, 2015) suggest that a two-day workshop incorporating a systematic five-step approach to CT identification and management can help trainees and practicing psychologists who were largely oriented toward cognitive and CBT therapy strengthen their recognition and management of CT. These studies used correlational and qualitative methods, and controlled experimental research would be useful at this point. Clearly, we are at the earliest stages of understanding how to help therapists and trainees manage their CT reactions.

SUMMARY

We have suggested that the inner experience of a good therapist typically includes the Rogerian conditions of empathy, positive regard for the patient, and inner congruence. The good therapist also is able to be in touch with what we have called inadmissible inner experiences, those that are emotionally threatening and often experienced as shameful. As an example, we discussed the experience of hate and love in the therapeutic relationship and how the effective therapist is able to admit these states to awareness and work with them in treatment. Finally, and more generally, the good therapist tends to be aware of and manage his or her inner experience. We described a theory of CT management as an example of the qualities within the therapist that facilitate the management of inner experience, including CT and non-CT experience, so that these benefit the work and the patient rather than adversely affect treatment.

REFERENCES

Blum, H. P. (1973). The concept of erotized transference. *Journal of the American Psychoanalytic Association, 21,* 61–76. http://dx.doi.org/10.1177/000306517302100104

Carter, J. A. (2006, August). *The eye can't see itself because the eye hides in shame.* Paper presented at the Annual Convention of the American Psychological Association, Washington, DC.

Cartwright, C., & Read, J. (2011). An exploratory investigation of psychologists' responses to a method for considering "objective" countertransference. *New Zealand Journal of Psychology, 40,* 46–54.

Cartwright, C., Rhodes, P., King, R., & Shires, A. (2015). A pilot study of a method for teaching clinical psychology trainees to conceptualize and manage countertransference. *Australian Psychologist, 50,* 148–156. http://dx.doi.org/10.1111/ap.12092

Elliott, R., Bohart, A. C., Watson, J. C., & Greenberg, L. S. (2011). Empathy. *Psychotherapy, 48,* 43–49. http://dx.doi.org/10.1037/a0022187

Farber, B. A., & Doolin, E. M. (2011). Positive regard. *Psychotherapy, 48,* 58–64. http://dx.doi.org/10.1037/a0022141

Freud, S. (1959a). The future prospects of psycho-analytic therapy. In J. Strachey (Ed.) & J. Riviere (Trans.), *Collected papers* (Vol. 2, pp. 285–296). New York, NY: Basic Books. (Original work published 1910)

Freud, S. (1959b). Recommendations for physicians on the psychoanalytic method of treatment. In J. Strachey (Ed.) & J. Riviere (Trans.), *Collected papers* (Vol. 2, pp. 323–333). New York, NY: Basic Books. (Original work published 1912)

Gelso, C. (2014). A tripartite model of the therapeutic relationship: Theory, research, and practice. *Psychotherapy Research, 24,* 117–131. http://dx.doi.org/10.1080/10503307.2013.845920

Gelso, C. J. (2011). *The real relationship in psychotherapy: The hidden foundation of change.* Washington, DC: American Psychological Association. http://dx.doi.org/10.1037/12349-000

Gelso, C. J., & Hayes, J. A. (2007). *Countertransference and the therapist's inner experience: perils and possibilities.* Mahwah, NJ: Erlbaum.

Gelso, C. J., Perez-Rojas, A. E., & Marmarosh, C. (2014). Love and sexuality in the therapeutic relationship. *Journal of Clinical Psychology/In Session, 70,* 123–134. http://dx.doi.org/10.1002/jclp.22064

Green, L. B. (2006). The value of hate in the countertransference. *Clinical Social Work Journal, 34,* 187–199. http://dx.doi.org/10.1007/s10615-005-0008-2

Hayes, J. A., Gelso, C. J., & Hummel, A. M. (2011). Managing countertransference. *Psychotherapy, 48,* 88–97. http://dx.doi.org/10.1037/a0022182

Kohut, H. (1971). *The analysis of the self.* New York, NY: International Universities Press.

Kolden, G. G., Klein, M. H., Wang, C., & Austin, S. B. (2011). Congruence/genuineness. *Psychotherapy, 48*, 65–71. http://dx.doi.org/10.1037/a0022064

Linehan, M. (1993). *Cognitive-behavioral treatment of BPD*. New York, NY: Guilford.

Lingiardi, V., Tanzilli, A., & Colli, A. (2015). Does the severity of psychopathological symptoms mediate the relationship between patient personality and therapist response? *Psychotherapy, 52*, 228–237. http://dx.doi.org/10.1037/a0037919

May, R. (1969). *Love and will*. Oxford, UK: Norton & Co.

McMain, S., & Wiebe, C. (2013). Therapist compassion: A dialectical behavior therapy perspective. In A. W. Wolf, M. R. Goldfried, & C. J. Muran (Eds.), *Transforming negative reactions to clients* (pp. 163–173). Washington, DC: American Psychological Association. http://dx.doi.org/10.1037/13940-007

Mehlman, E., & Glickauf-Hughes, C. (1994). The underside of psychotherapy: Confronting hateful feelings toward clients. *Psychotherapy: Theory, Research, Practice, Training, 31*, 434–439. http://dx.doi.org/10.1037/0033-3204.31.3.434

Mills, D. H., & Abeles, N. (1965). Counselor needs for affiliation and nurturance as related to liking for clients and counseling process. *Journal of Counseling Psychology, 12*, 353–358. http://dx.doi.org/10.1037/h0022767

Perez-Rojas, A., Palma, B., Bhatia, A., Jackson, J., Norwood, E., Rodgers, K., . . . Gelso, C. (2016, November). *Development and initial validation of the Countertransference Management Scale*. Paper presented at the 2016 conference of the North American Society for Psychotherapy Research, Berkeley, CA.

Rogers, A. G. (1996). *A shining affliction: Harm and healing in psychotherapy*. New York, NY: Penguin.

Rogers, C. R. (1957). The necessary and sufficient conditions of therapeutic personality change. *Journal of Consulting Psychology, 21*, 95–103. http://dx.doi.org/10.1037/h0045357

Van Wagoner, S. L., Gelso, C. J., Hayes, J. A., & Diemer, R. A. (1991). Countertransference and the reputedly excellent therapist. *Psychotherapy: Theory, Research, Practice, Training, 28*, 411–421. http://dx.doi.org/10.1037/0033-3204.28.3.411

Winnicott, D. W. (1949). Hate in the counter-transference. *The International Journal of Psychoanalysis, 30*, 69–74.

Wolf, A. W., Goldfried, M. R., & Muran, J. C. (Eds.). (2013). *Transforming negative reactions to clients: From frustration to compassion*. Washington, DC: American Psychological Association. http://dx.doi.org/10.1037/13940-000

Yalom, I. D. (2002). *The gift of therapy: An open letter to a new generation of therapists and their patients*. New York, NY: HarperCollins.

7

THE ROLE OF THE THERAPIST'S ATTACHMENT IN THE PROCESS AND OUTCOME OF PSYCHOTHERAPY

BERNHARD M. STRAUSS AND KATJA PETROWSKI

Attachment theory provides a model to explain individual differences in experience and behavior related to interpersonal proximity and distance, as well as the regulation of affect and stress (Bowlby, 1988). Whereas Bowlby's (1988) original intention was to develop a theory for the assessment and treatment of emotional disorders, his ideas were primarily assimilated in developmental psychology, leading to numerous studies validating the concepts of attachment theory, such as maternal sensitivity or patterns of attachment behavior (Ainsworth, Blehar, Waters, & Wall, 1978). These studies provided a solid basis for the extension of our knowledge of human development, its influence on personality, psychopathology, and psychotherapy.

Primary attachment relationships with sensitive adult attachment figures contribute to a person's ability to explore his or her environment from a base of felt security. Bowlby (1988) assumed that early attachment experiences are internalized, forming an inner working model of attachment that

http://dx.doi.org/10.1037/0000034-008
How and Why Are Some Therapists Better Than Others? Understanding Therapist Effects, L. G. Castonguay and C. E. Hill (Eds.)
Copyright © 2017 by the American Psychological Association. All rights reserved.

comprises expectations toward the self and others on the basis of former experiences. Disruptions of early attachment and the experience of insensitive attachment figures can contribute to the formation of insecure inner working models or attachment representations in later life, which, in turn, increase the vulnerability for the development of psychopathological symptoms (e.g., Strauss, 2008). The interpersonal expectations and emotional regulation in psychotherapeutic sessions related to patients' or therapists' attachment might explain a part of the psychotherapeutic outcome. Hentschel (2005) described a model in which early attachment experiences as a part of the inner working model might influence a patient's perception of others as well as his or her transference patterns. For the therapist, the inner working model might explain which patient needs a therapist perceives during a psychotherapeutic session. Both a patient's perception and a therapist's perception could influence therapeutic alliance and outcome. This would be in line with Orlinsky and Howard's (1987) assumption that "the working alliance is determined jointly by the patient's and the therapist's personal role-investment" (p. 11). Therefore, therapists' attachment and its relationship to the therapeutic alliance and outcome should be considered.

Before describing research evidence pertaining to this question, we offer an overview of the conceptual model of psychotherapy that has been derived from attachment theory, as well as a summary of psychotherapy research on patient attachment. We believe that a brief review of this literature provides a necessary context for understanding the constructs and empirical studies that have been conducted so far on therapist attachment.

ATTACHMENT THEORY AS A THEORETICAL MODEL IN PSYCHOTHERAPY

Although attachment theory has been rejected for a long time by the psychoanalytical community, psychoanalytically oriented authors in the United Kingdom (e.g., Holmes, 1994) and Germany (e.g., Köhler, 1991) nevertheless deserve the merit for having reintegrated attachment theory into the clinical field. Since the early 1990s, a huge number of studies based on attachment theory have been conducted in psychotherapy research.

Bowlby (1988) conceptualized attachment theory as a guiding clinical principle by describing implications of attachment for conducting and adapting psychotherapy. Attachment states of mind are thought to represent conscious and unconscious strategies adults develop for organizing attachment-related information. These strategies might influence ways in which individuals approach interpersonal relationships and how individuals manage emotions in the context of relationships (Dozier & Lee, 1995). Individuals with a more deactivating attachment system remain more distanced in relationships to stay emotionally organized (Kobak, Cole, Ferenz-Gillies, Fleming, & Gamble, 1993; Kobak & Sceery, 1988). In contrast, more hyperactivating individuals experience more emotional distress and engage in greater self-disclosure with others.

Attachment research in the fields of developmental and clinical psychology has promoted theoretical work providing an important basis for a better understanding of psychotherapy. In a model provided by Hentschel (2005), early attachment experiences as part of the inner working model are supposed to influence patients' perception of others and, accordingly, their transference patterns. The model of Hentschel (2005) demonstrates how the early attachment experiences of patients might affect the complex relationships in psychotherapy (see Figure 7.1). This model can be extended by including therapists' inner working models, which, in turn, might explain how therapists act on the basis of their own inner working models of attachment.

On the basis of the construct of sensitivity used in attachment research as a behavioral indicator of an attachment figure, Fonagy, Luyten, Campbell, and Allison (2014) introduced the concepts of metacognitive regulation and reflective functioning as important parts of mentalization, which, in turn, is seen as a complex interpersonal function developing on the basis of a secure attachment. According to Fonagy et al.'s model, attachment security and a related "agentic self" provide the basis for the development of an adequate and coherent representation of affect, the development of selective attention and mentalization, which together form an "interpersonal interpretative mechanism" (Fonagy & Allison, 2014). The development of this mechanism largely relies on interpersonal experiences with attachment figures who are stronger and wiser than oneself, provide sensitivity and have the potential to show sensitivity and support the development of self-reflective functions.

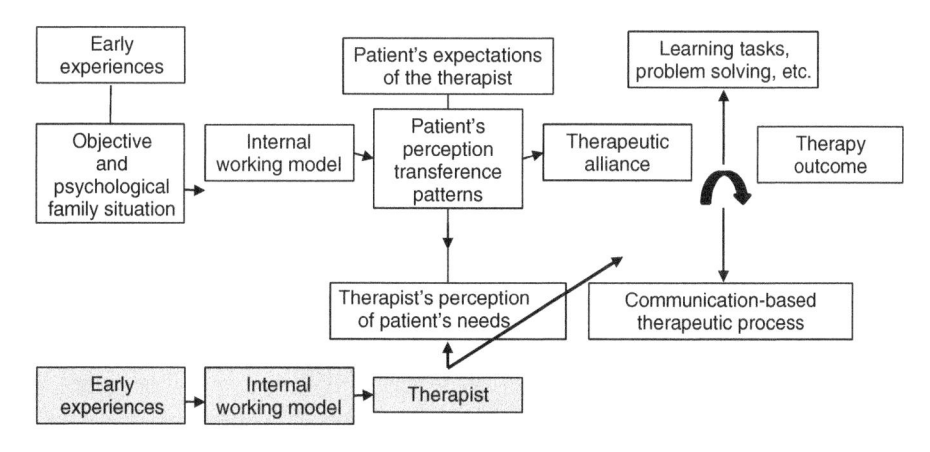

Figure 7.1. The relationship between the attachment experiences of the patient and the inner working models of the therapist.

Accordingly, Fonagy et al. described parallels between developmental processes and the process of psychotherapy and considered the enhancement of metacognition and the bringing about of integration of unmentalized internal working models as an almost generic aspects of therapy. At least in the studies of mentalization-based treatment of patients with personality disorders, it has been shown that an increase in mentalizing capacities is generally connected with better outcome (e.g., Bateman & Fonagy, 2008). Within this treatment model, change is assumed to take place when therapists successfully enhance mentalization while simultaneously activating patients' attachment.

PATIENTS' ATTACHMENT AS AN ISSUE IN PSYCHOTHERAPY RESEARCH

Empirical studies related to attachment and psychotherapy so far have mainly focused on *patients' attachment characteristics* (i.e., attachment representation or style) and their role in psychotherapy. We know that among patients with different psychological disorders who are in psychotherapy—in contrast to the general population—secure attachment is rather an exception than the rule (Strauss, 2008). In addition, Mallinckrodt (2000, 2001), who developed the Client Attachment to Therapist Scale (CATS; Mallinckrodt, Gantt, & Coble, 1995), demonstrated that attachment-related expectations directed toward therapists are rather similar to general attachment styles, also indicating a dominance of insecure attachment expectations toward therapists (anxious-dismissing, preoccupied-merger in the CATS terminology).

Numerous studies with different patient populations, treatment modalities, and therapeutic approaches have shown that attachment characteristics and attachment-related interpersonal expectations predict treatment outcome in psychotherapy (Levy, Ellison, Scott, & Bernecker, 2011; Liotti, 1991). Securely attached patients, overall, have a better prognosis (reflected by a positive effect size) than preoccupied patients, whereas there is no systematic relationship between dismissing attachment and treatment outcome. Other psychotherapy studies dealing with attachment have focused on the change of attachment security during psychotherapy, indicating an increase in security and a decrease in anxiety (Taylor, Rietzschel, Danquah, & Berry, 2015).

With regard to the psychotherapeutic process, Diener and Monroe (2011) and Bernecker, Levy, and Ellison (2014) showed that patients' attachment characteristics are related to the therapeutic/working alliance. Diener and Monroe summarized 17 studies in a meta-analysis and found a significant relationship between secure attachment and a positive alliance. They also showed a higher rate of ruptures in the therapeutic alliance among insecurely attached patients. Bernecker et al., on the basis of 24 primary studies, showed that attachment anxiety and avoidance were slightly negatively correlated with the quality of the alliance. More recently, Mallinckrodt and Jeong (2015) summarized studies using the CATS and reported that a secure attachment to the therapist was positively correlated ($r = .76$), whereas dismissing attachment was negatively correlated with alliance ratings ($r = -.63$). Surprisingly, preoccupied-merger attachment was uncorrelated with the quality of the helping alliance. The secure factor of the CATS shares a common core with the helping alliance construct and might represent enduring and affectionate ties between patient and therapist (Robbins, 1995).

Interestingly, a wide variety of features associated with secure, dismissing, and preoccupied attachment (related to the patient as well as the therapist) potentially explain the reported results related to alliance and outcome. Securely attached individuals are described as being cooperative, optimistic, and confident; as showing flexible coping strategies during stress; and as being able to assess realistically personal resources and needs. These ways of being and relating contrast sharply with those of insecurely attached individuals. Dismissing attachment is indeed associated with more interpersonal distance or control, distrust, and negative expectations within relationships, whereas preoccupied attachment is commonly associated with an excessive and vigorous seeking of social support, or a more demanding, dependent, and diffuse attitude in close relationships (for details, see Strauss & Brenk-Franz, 2016). Accordingly, it can be assumed that insecure attachment affects patients' ability for self-disclosure (e.g., Wei, Russell, & Zakalik, 2005), the depth of their self-exploration (e.g., Mohr, Gelso, & Hill, 2005; Romano, Fitzpatrick, & Janzen, 2008), and their ability to seek closeness with therapists (e.g., Talia et al., 2014).

Several studies have explored whether the different interpersonal characteristics associated with patients' attachment might have an influence on transference and on the countertransference reactions of their therapists. Although there are only a few studies dealing with these constructs, it seems that the attachment to the therapist has an impact on the patient's transference of earlier relationships to the therapist (Woodhouse, Schlosser, Crook, Ligiéro, & Gelso, 2003). Marmarosh et al. (2009) reported a correlation of attachment anxiety and positive transference, whereas avoidance was not related to the quality of transference. Some studies focusing on countertransference have shown that patients' attachment can have an impact on countertransference reactions (Ligiéro & Gelso, 2002; Martin, Buchheim, Berger, & Strauss, 2007; Mohr et al., 2005) even on a neurobiological level (Krause et al., 2016).

In sum, patients' attachment characteristics seem to be highly important to the process and outcome of psychotherapy. Assuming that the psychotherapeutic process shows parallels with the developmental process aimed at incrementing trust and security, one could argue that the attachment of the therapist may have a role in facilitating or hindering the process and outcome of psychotherapy. Framed more specifically toward the topic of this book, one could well ask whether attachment-related variables might help to explain therapist effects (i.e., the observation that some therapists are more effective then others; see Chapters 1 and 2, this volume).

To address this question, we address the potential role of the therapist as an attachment figure. We then report results of studies investigating attachment characteristics of therapists, as well as findings of research on the relationship of therapists' attachment to outcome and alliance. Moreover, studies dealing with a matching of the therapist–patient attachment representations and its influence on the therapeutic process and outcome are described. Finally, we offer some speculations regarding what therapists could do to improve their effectiveness (in some circumstances, with some patients) on the basis of what these studies are suggesting regarding therapist effects.

THE THERAPIST AS AN ATTACHMENT FIGURE

To understand which role the attachment of the therapist plays in the process and outcome of psychotherapy, the potential role of the therapist in a psychotherapeutic process must be discussed.

Besides primary parental attachment figures, Bowlby (1988) suggested that the person of a psychotherapist may become an attachment figure, at least temporarily. The psychotherapist should, according to Bowlby, represent a reliable and trustworthy person during the patient's exploration of his or her experiences and emotions. In line with this theoretical position, a substantial body of evidence shows that therapists have the potential to act as an attachment figure by providing patients with a "secure base" and a "safe haven" (Borelli & David, 2003). Dozier and Bates (2004) noted that "the client finds in the therapist someone who seems stronger and wiser than him- or herself. Therefore, the client may interact with the clinician in ways that reflect expectations from other relationships" (p. 167). From the patient's perspective, secure attachment behavior in psychotherapy would include accepting the therapist as a secure base from which the patient can freely think about his or her experiences; reflect on intentions, beliefs, and feelings of significant others; explore new experiences; and engage in novel behaviors.

Several researchers have critically discussed Bowlby's conception of the therapist as an attachment figure and noted that there are differences between private and professional relationships (e.g., Farber, Lippert, & Nevas, 1995), and that it is important to consider that the attachment system is only temporarily activated during psychotherapy. On the other hand, it can be assumed that themes and situations related to attachment experiences frequently arise during treatment, activated within therapy (e.g., when separation, loss, or treatment termination is discussed) and by events outside psychotherapy (cf. Ehrenthal, Tomanek, Schauenburg, & Dinger, 2013). Bowlby (1988) stated that the attachment system is activated, not only when individuals are frightened or exhausted but also when they are sick or ill, resulting in attachment behavior which aims at eliciting caregiving behavior in others. Empirically, the activation of the attachment system during psychotherapeutic sessions has not yet been clearly established. There are indications for the activation of such a system (reflected in language as well as psychophysiological responses) during procedures meant to measure attachment style, such as the Adult Attachment Interview (AAI) and the Strange Situation.

If (and when) the attachment system is activated during treatment, it is very likely that the therapist would serve, consciously or not, as an attachment figure. As we know from numerous studies in developmental psychology, when the attachment system is activated, the management of attachment relevant situations is a result of an interactive process between the child's attachment needs and the sensitivity of the attachment figure. As we mentioned when describing Fonagy's conception (Fonagy & Allison, 2014; Fonagy et al., 2014), this might be a model for the psychotherapeutic process. Only recently, Holmes (2013) argued that partial contingent mirroring, a construct from interactive research with babies (cf. Beebe & Lachmann, 2005), might be a model for the therapist's task in helping patients dealing with emotionally stressful activations of the attachment system. Partial contingent mirroring implies that the parent's facial and vocal expressions correspond with the child's emotional experiences but are displayed "in a jazz-like improvisational manner" (Holmes, 2013, p. 211).

THERAPISTS' ATTACHMENT

To properly address the question of whether the attachment of the therapist might explain, at least in part, why some of them are better than others, the basic distribution of attachment characteristics among therapists has to be clarified.

Studies that have investigated people's motives for choosing to be therapists have indicated that therapists often report their own adverse developmental experiences ("wounded healers"; Farber, Manevich, Metzger, & Saypol, 2005). Such findings raise the possibility that many therapists are at risk of having developed insecure attachment characteristics. In one of the first studies on therapists' attachment, Nord, Höger, and Eckert (2000) reported that almost half of the therapists revealed a "conditionally secure" partner-related attachment, which is characterized by reduced needs for closeness in relationships and is commonly interpreted as a form of dismissing attachment (on the Bielefeld Questionnaire on Partner Expectations; cf. Nord et al., 2000). In contrast, the proportion of secure and preoccupied therapists was low (10% & 12%). In another study using a partner-related attachment questionnaire, Martin et al. (2007) described 56% of therapists in training as securely attached. Yusof and Carpenter (2013) studied British family therapists and found discrepant results. Using the Relationship Questionnaire, 61 of 82 therapists classified themselves as securely attached, nine as preoccupied, six as fearful, and six as dismissing. In contrast, the self-ratings from the Experience in Close Relationship Questionnaire indicated only 24 of 82 therapists to be securely attached, 16 preoccupied, 15 dismissing, and 27 fearful. The authors explained this discrepancy as being the result of the transparency of the Relationship Questionnaire; because it rates the extent to which prototypical descriptions of the four attachment styles apply to oneself, Yusof and Carpenter suggested that this might have invited socially desirable answers.

Studies using the AAI as a measure of attachment states of mind revealed distributions of attachment patterns similar to those reported for nonclinical samples (i.e., around 60% of autonomous/secure individuals; see van IJzendoorn & Bakermans-Kranenburg, 1996). Although Petrowski, Pokorny, Nowacki, and Buchheim (2013) found a slightly higher proportion of dismissing therapists in their sample, Schauenburg et al. (2010) found more enmeshed therapists on the basis of the AAI. Schauenburg, Dinger, and Buchheim (2006) analyzed the same sample using the interview-based Adult Attachment Prototype Rating and reported a different distribution of attachment styles: 45.2% secure, 12.9% ambivalent, and 22.6% dismissing. The remaining therapists were classified as "mixed insecure."

In a subsample of a study focusing on psychotherapy trainees, Taubner et al. (2014) found some indications for a higher rate of adverse childhood experiences among therapists. However, compared with the general population, a higher proportion of securely attached trainees (78%) was also found. Among the insecurely attached trainees, preoccupied attachment was more common than dismissing attachment. Taken as a whole, these studies suggest that there is no evidence for an extensive accumulation of insecure attachment among populations of therapists.

THERAPISTS' ATTACHMENT AND THE HELPING ALLIANCE

Although there is no accumulation of insecure attachment among therapists, the variance of secure and insecure attachment observed in this population allows us to test whether therapists' different attachment styles relate to common indicators of the process of change (e.g., the alliance).

Responses to questionnaires that assess attachment and helping alliance indicate that therapists with more trust and more comfort with closeness developed a stronger therapeutic alliance with their patients (Black, Hardy, Turpin, & Parry, 2005; Dunkle & Friedlander, 1996). As an explanation of such findings, it may be that securely attached therapists have a variety of relevant skills, such as maintaining appropriate eye contact (Mallinckrodt, 2000, 2001) or constructive strategies for conflict resolution that might facilitate the handling of alliance ruptures and restoration of the quality of alliance (Martin et al., 2007; Mohr et al., 2005). In contrast, therapists with higher attachment anxiety had a positive effect on the early alliance but significant negative effects over time (Sauer, Lopez, & Gormley, 2003). Attachment anxiety may render therapists more vulnerable with regard to a reactivation of their own attachment-related worries and defenses. In such cases, therapists may lack the skills needed to regulate their own distress and remain fairly accurate in their perception of patients' signals.

Similarly, on the basis of interviews (e.g., AAI), securely attached therapists were associated with a better helping alliance (Schauenburg et al., 2010). In patients with a high level of distress and a higher number of interpersonal problems, attachment security of the therapists was associated with a better helping alliance and a better outcome, whereas the helping alliance was more impaired in treatments of therapists with preoccupied attachment (Dinger, Strack, Sachsse, & Schauenburg, 2009). Concerning insecurely attached therapists, Rubino, Barker, Roth, and Fearon (2000) showed that therapists with an insecure attachment status responded less empathically in therapy.

THERAPIST ATTACHMENT AND PATIENT ATTACHMENT TO THE THERAPIST

Only a few studies so far have investigated the relationship between the therapist's attachment and the patient's attachment to the therapist (measured with the CATS; Petrowski et al., 2013; Romano et al., 2008). Romano and colleagues (2008) first showed that therapists' global attachment moderates the relationship between patients' global attachment and session exploration (i.e., patients' session exploration appeared to be a function of their global attachment and their attachment to the counselor). Contrary to expectation, therapists' secure, as well as insecure, attachment style did not influence patients' attachment to the therapists. The second study (Petrowski et al., 2013) also observed that patients treated by therapists with a secure attachment representation did not report more secure attachment to their therapist.

Patients of therapists with a more insecure (dismissing) attachment representation (as measured by the AAI) described their attachment to the therapist as more insecure avoidant/fearful in the CATS (Petrowski et al., 2013). This is in line with the literature linking attachment avoidance (dismissing attachment) to a more rejecting interpersonal deportment (Bartholomew & Horowitz, 1991) and more distance in relationships (Kobak et al., 1993; Kobak & Sceery, 1988). In addition, for therapists with an insecure preoccupied attachment representation, patients perceived the relationship as preoccupied/merger in the CATS (Petrowski et al., 2013). The preoccupied therapists were likely to focus on emotional distress and maintain a high degree of involvement in their relationships (Tyrrell et al., 1999), which might be negatively experienced by patients. These therapists might show loose boundaries with their patients and difficulties in emotion regulation, which might interfere with empathic sensitivity as well as responsiveness to patients' needs (Slade, 1999). This could explain why preoccupied/anxiously attached therapists reported more therapy-related problems (Black et al., 2005). In addition, therapists with an insecure attachment status in the AAI show more defensive processes, such as idealization (deactivation of negative attachment-related feelings) and derogation, and they directly expressed anger when talking about their attachment history. These defensive processes might be transferred into the current interaction with patients (e.g., by not restoring alliance after ruptures properly; Rubino et al., 2000), or by staying more distant and less empathic (Kobak et al., 1993; Kobak & Sceery, 1988).

In a very recent study, Robinson, Hill, and Kivlighan (2015) investigated the influence of patients' and therapists' attachment and patients' attachment to therapists on the amount and type of crying (which could be an expression of attachment behavior). They described specific patterns, for example, therapists who established a secure attachment, according to their patients, elicited more crying and a higher intensity of protest. On the other hand, patients cried less if their therapists were not perceived as establishing a secure attachment. This study shows that even specific patient behavior seems to depend on the therapist's attachment.

Overall, studies combining therapists' attachment and patients' experiences of attachment to their therapist indicate that insecure attachment representations of the therapists are partially reflected in the subjective attachment experiences of the patients. Direct comparison of patients' self-reported attachment and the therapists' representational attachment status reveal that therapists showing emotional defensive strategies when confronted with their own attachment history are commonly linked with patients' experiencing insecure attachment to these therapists. From a clinical point of view, attachment insecurity may render therapists more vulnerable for a reactivation of their own attachment-related worries and defenses during psychotherapy, which might interfere with their countertransference reactions.

In a study of 46 therapy dyads, Marmarosh and colleagues (2014) used the actor-partner interdependence model to determine the influence of patient and therapist attachment styles on early alliance ratings. The study showed no direct effects of patient or therapist attachment styles on alliance. However, they reported a significant interaction between patients' perceived alliance and attachment anxiety (of therapist and patient): Alliance ratings were higher when more anxious therapists treated patients with decreasing anxiety; ratings were also higher when less anxious therapists treated patients with an increasing anxiety, indicating a specific match being related to the patients' perception of early alliance. This study by Marmarosh et al., together with other studies focusing on the correlation between therapists' and patients' attachment, suggests that more explicit attention should be given to the match between therapists' and patients' attachment and its effect on process and outcome.

THE MATCH BETWEEN THERAPISTS' AND PATIENTS' ATTACHMENT REPRESENTATIONS AND THE THERAPEUTIC PROCESS

Regarding the matching of therapist and patient, only a few studies have assessed attachment representations with the AAI (Dozier, Cue, & Barnett, 1994). Dozier et al. (1994) compared case managers with secure and insecure attachment representation with respect to the depth of interventions using the Kobak Q-Set analysis from the AAI. They showed that insecure case managers intervened in greater depth with preoccupied patients than they did with dismissing patients. Using the same AAI method as Dozier et al. (1994) and Tyrrell, Dozier, Teague, and Fallot (1999) found that therapists with a preoccupied attachment status obtained a stronger alliance with a dismissing patient and that therapists with a dismissing attachment status achieved a stronger working alliance with preoccupied patients.

In another study, this one of 67 patients undergoing psychodynamic psychotherapy provided by 27 different therapists, Wiseman and Tishby (2014) measured patients' and therapists' attachment (using the ECR), patients' attachment to therapist (using the CATS), and outcome (using the OQ-45) at intake and four times during the 2-year period of the treatment. Basically, the results showed that (a) patients (most with mild depression and/or anxiety depressive disorders) with avoidant attachment, including an avoidant attachment to their therapist, showed least improvement, and (b) the match of a low-avoidant patient and a low-avoidant therapist led to a greater decrease in symptoms than did the combination of a low-avoidant therapist with a high-avoidant patient.

ATTACHMENT MATCH AND SPECIFIC DISORDERS

The studies mentioned so far were all related to mixed patient samples (e.g., patients with severe psychiatric disorders, including schizophrenia, schizoaffective disorder, and bipolar disorder). Because one can assume that specific disorders have partly specific attachment-related characteristics (cf. Strauss, 2008), it would be interesting to see how the match of therapists' and patients' attachment might work in more specific samples.

Specific early attachment experiences are characteristic of the development of different disorders (Dozier, Stovall-McClough, & Albus, 2008). Anxious patients predominantly show insecure attachment representations (Buchheim & Benecke, 2007; Fonagy et al., 1996; Manassis, Bradley, Goldberg, Hood, & Swinson, 1994) and/or an unresolved trauma attachment representation (Adam, Sheldon-Keller, & West, 1996; Fonagy et al., 1996; Manassis et al., 1994). However, there are also clear differences in attachment representations between the different anxiety disorders. For panic disorder, 85% of the patients predominantly show disorganized unresolved trauma attachment representation (Dozier, 1990; Petrowski, Nowacki, Pokorny, & Buchheim, 2011). In contrast, patients with social phobia rather show dismissing attachment (Eng, Heimberg, Hart, Schneier, & Liebowitz, 2001).

In a study focusing on patients with panic disorders with and without agoraphobia, therapists' attachment representations, as well as their matching with patient attachment, had an influence on the alliance only in highly insecure patients (cf. Petrowski et al., 2013). Patients showing a more insecure attachment representation evaluated their relationship with highly dismissing therapists as more satisfying than with the highly preoccupied therapists. In addition, patients with a more insecure attachment representation showed a better outcome when treated by a highly dismissing therapist than by a highly preoccupied therapist. Accordingly, depending on patients' attachment insecurity, therapists' attachment representation appeared to have had an influence on the therapeutic outcome. In contrast to the expectation, therapists' attachment security had no influence on the therapeutic alliance in this study.

Nevertheless, the interaction effect of the patients' insecure attachment and the therapists' dismissing attachment representation on the helping alliance might be explicable by the homogeneous sample of the anxiety patients (Petrowski et al., 2013). Because specific early attachment experiences are characteristic for the development of the disorder (Dozier et al.,

2008), it is not surprising that patients with anxiety have been shown to experience significantly more separation from one of the caregivers, as well as strong neglect compared with controls (Faravelli, 1985). These early attachment experiences might influence the individuals' capacities for reciprocal interactions as well as the formation of the helping alliance (Bowlby, 1988). One can assume that anxiety patients with predominantly insecure attachment representations (Fonagy et al., 1996; Manassis et al., 1994) need a specific attachment representation of the therapist to develop a strong alliance, as they did not experience a reliable sensitive caregiver in their childhood and therefore, do not believe in a strong, trustworthy alliance with the therapist.

In sum, a stronger alliance can be expected if the patient is dissimilar to the therapist in terms of deactivating versus hyperactivating dimensions of attachment. This finding is consistent with Bowlby's (1988) view of therapeutic change. He suggested that an important role of the therapist is to disconfirm the patient's usual interpersonal and emotional strategies and expectations. By disconfirming patients' usual strategies, therapists are able to facilitate patients' emotional change and growth. This might explain why attachment representation of the patient or the therapist by itself does not influence the alliance (Dunkle & Friedlander, 1996; Ligiéro & Gelso, 2002; Sauer et al., 2003), but the matching of attachment representations in the dyad does influence the alliance.

We tried to replicate the finding of attachment matching in a subsample of the SOPHO-Net study (Leichsenring et al., 2008), a large randomized controlled trial comparing short-term cognitive and psychodynamic psychotherapy for patients with social anxiety disorders. A subsample of 36 patients with a primary social phobia diagnosis (22 women, mean age = 35.64 years, $SD = 12.16$) was included in an analysis of matching therapists' and patients' attachment study. Fourteen therapists treated these patients. Therapists were between 25 and 60 years old at the beginning of this study. With respect to attachment patterns assessed with the Bielefeld Questionnaire of Partner Expectations, 78.6% ($n = 11$) were assessed as securely attached, 14.3% ($n = 2$) showed an anxious-avoidant insecure attachment, and 7.1% ($n = 1$) showed an anxious-resistant insecure attachment. The data show that the patients', as well as the therapists', need for care concerning attachment had a significant influence on the symptom change from admission to discharge on the Liebowitz Social Anxiety Scale (Heimberg et al., 1999). In addition, the matching of the intensities of patients' and therapists' needs for care influenced the symptom intensity at discharge. A patient with high need for care reached better outcome in combination with a therapist with low need for care. A therapist with high scores in this subscale reached better outcome in patients showing lower scores.

CONCLUSION

Attachment theory and related constructs have had a substantial impact on psychotherapeutic theories, as well as psychotherapy research. Numerous studies have shown that patients' attachment characteristics are important for a variety of process factors in psychotherapy, predominantly the working alliance, and that patients with different attachment experiences show specific characteristics, which, in turn, might have an influence on the interactive processes between patient and therapist, including transference and countertransference processes. We also know that attachment is a predictor of outcome, although the percentage of outcome variance explained by attachment measures is not larger than that of other common patient-related predictors.

As Bowlby (1988) noted, attachment theory has been primarily integrated and investigated within developmental psychology. From developmental studies, we know that the attachment system is activated within specific situations related mostly to separation. We also know that how attachment figures (i.e., parental figures in early development, other individuals representing close relationships in later development) respond to a person's signals and needs is of crucial importance. It is not surprising that developmental processes have been considered as a model for the therapeutic process, especially when issues that take place in this process are relevant to the human attachment system, such as when separation has been experienced by the patient outside therapy or termination is discussed in session. Within such contexts, the role that therapists' attachment might play in the process of therapy appears to be highly relevant, and it seems justified to ask whether attachment characteristics of the therapist might explain therapist effects, or a unique part of its variance.

As we can see from the literature, therapists' attachment characteristics seem to be similarly distributed as attachment characteristics within the general population (i.e., there is no indication of a higher prevalence of insecure attachment among therapists, which could have been expected on the basis of studies related to the biographical background of therapists and their motives to seek this profession). Nevertheless, a considerable percentage of therapists show insecure attachment, which provides justification for investigations of how therapists' attachment might be of influence. At this point in time, however, the evidence is limited. With respect to outcome (i.e., whether some therapists are more effective than others), one study has shown evidence that secure attachment of the therapist might be associated with better outcome for patients with more impairment (Schauenburg et al., 2010). Although only tentative statements can be made on the basis of a single study, it is noteworthy that this finding is consistent with one of the main conclusions that have been derived from therapists' effects research: For most patients, who their therapist is does not appear to matter, outcome wise. Put in another way, across a majority of patients, most therapists have similar effect. For the most distressed patients, however, who they see in therapy can have a major impact on whether they will improve or get worse (see Chapter 1, this volume). Therefore, research on therapist attachment offers possible pathways of explanation for one aspect of the therapist effects: It is plausible that therapists' attachment is of specific importance among patients with a significant amount of distress, interpersonal problems, and functional and/or structural impairment because these patients have the most potential to activate defensive strategies and negative countertransference reactions leading to hasty actions by confronting the therapists emotionally with their own attachment history. Accordingly, it is feasible that, especially in those patients, therapists' secure attachment is associated with a better outcome and working alliance.

Studies assessing therapists' attachment representations and patients' attachment to their therapists indicate that there might be a specific interplay between patients' and therapists' attachment. It might be a promising task to continue studying the matching between therapists' and patients' attachment and how different matches affect process and outcome in psychotherapy. Unfortunately, only a few studies have dealt with this question so far, showing contradicting results. Three studies found that some form of complementarity was associated with positive alliance and outcome (Petrowski et al., 2013; Tyrrell et al., 1999; Wiseman & Tishby, 2014). In contrast, a more recent, though very small, study showed no clear complementary interaction between patients' and therapists' attachment in patients with social phobia (Petrowski & Strauss, 2016).

Although much more research would be desirable, it might be a good working hypothesis to assume that there are similarities between therapist–patient interaction and parent–infant interaction. On the basis of the studies reviewed in this chapter, we must further test whether therapists' attachment is of special importance as a complementary form of working with attachment related features, especially in the sphere of insecure attachment. We believe that future studies investigating the complexity of such development and interpersonal complementarity might help us better understand therapist effects (i.e., why some therapists are better and others are not as effective).

Related to the question of therapist effects, we also believe that the attachment literature can provide hypotheses about what therapists can do to improve their effectiveness. As an ending point to our chapter, we would like to offer a few ways for therapists to reflect on their own and their patients' attachment. Bowlby (1988) postulated that the important role of the therapist is to disconfirm the patient's usual interpersonal and emotional strategy during the psychotherapeutic process and to continuously provide the secure base from which patients can explore and hope to revise their interpersonal experiences. Results showing that dissimilar attachment constellations between therapists' and patients' attachment might lead to a better alliance and outcome can be seen as some support for Bowlby's postulation. From these empirical and theoretical points of convergence, one might suggest that therapists could improve their effectiveness by skillfully challenging common attachment-related strategies of emotion regulation and by helping to modify these strategies. For example, because dismissingly attached patients often show cool, remote, smooth, seemingly friendly exterior attributes during the process of psychotherapy (see Slade, 1999), therapists might intentionally present emotional attributes toward their patients. The therapist should be prepared for upcoming resistant behavior to treatment and the denial for help. The common strategy of avoidant patients to divert attention from emotional issues can be challenged by sticking to emotional topics, provided that therapists are able to self-reflect on their own ways of dealing with emotions.

In contrast, anxiously attached patients tend to intensively express theirs needs, appear needy, dependent, and demanding. To challenge these interpersonal patterns, a therapist might present a more cool and controlled behavior, helping the patient to structure his or her emotions and thoughts. If therapists intentionally chose such a complementary behavior, common attachment-related strategies of emotion regulation can be challenged, explored, and modified by the corrective experiences.

Above all, a general clinical implication of attachment theory is that the therapist should provide a secure base for the exploration of the actual relationship in the therapeutic setting. These here-and-now experiences have to be compared with attachment experiences from early childhood to facilitate building trust, integrate contradicting emotions, develop self-reflective functioning, and analyze transfer processes (cf. Bowlby, 1988). Therapists might be characterized as competently applying attachment theory when they are aware of their own attachment experiences and are playing the role of a sensitive caregiver with the goal of developing mutual interactive and reflective skills that can be internalized by their patients (cf. Holmes, 2013).

REFERENCES

Adam, K. S., Sheldon-Keller, A. E., & West, M. (1996). Attachment organization and history of suicidal behavior in clinical adolescents. *Journal of Consulting and Clinical Psychology, 64,* 264–272. http://dx.doi.org/10.1037/0022-006X.64.2.264

Ainsworth, M. D. S., Blehar, M. C., Waters, E., & Wall, S. (1978). *Patterns of attachment: A psychological study of the strange situation.* Hillsdale, NJ: Erlbaum.

Bartholomew, K., & Horowitz, L. M. (1991). Attachment styles among young adults: A test of a four-category model. *Journal of Personality and Social Psychology, 61*, 226–244. http://dx.doi.org/10.1037/0022-3514.61.2.226

Bateman, A., & Fonagy, P. (2008). 8-year follow-up of patients treated for borderline personality disorder: Mentalization-based treatment versus treatment as usual. *The American Journal of Psychiatry, 165*, 631–638. http://dx.doi.org/10.1176/appi.ajp.2007.07040636

Beebe, B., & Lachmann, F. M. (2005). *Infant research and adult attachment: Co-constructing interactions.* New York, NY: Routledge.

Bernecker, S. L., Levy, K. N., & Ellison, W. D. (2014). A meta-analysis of the relation between patient adult attachment style and the working alliance. *Psychotherapy Research, 24*, 12–24. http://dx.doi.org/10.1080/10503307.2013.809561

Black, S., Hardy, G., Turpin, G., & Parry, G. (2005). Self-reported attachment styles and therapeutic orientation of therapists and their relationship with reported general alliance quality and problems in therapy. *Psychology and Psychotherapy, 78*, 363–377. http://dx.doi.org/10.1348/147608305X43784

Borelli, J. L., & David, D. H. (2003). Attachment theory and research as a guide to psychotherapy practice. *Journal of Imagination, Cognition, and Personality, 23*, 257–287. http://dx.doi.org/10.2190/KQYE-P3EN-XATC-PWB7

Bowlby, J. (1988). *A secure base: Parent-child attachment and healthy human development.* New York, NY: Basic Books.

Buchheim, A., & Benecke, C. (2007). Mimisch-affektives verhalten bei patientinnen mit angststörungen während des adult-attachment-interviews: Eine pilotstudie [Affective facial behavior of patients with anxiety disorders during the adult attachment interview: A pilot study]. *Psychotherapie, Psychosomatik, Medizinische Psychologie, 57*, 343–347. http://dx.doi.org/10.1055/s-2006-952030

Diener, M. J., & Monroe, J. M. (2011). The relationship between adult attachment style and therapeutic alliance in individual psychotherapy: A meta-analytic review. *Psychotherapy, 48*, 237–248. http://dx.doi.org/10.1037/a0022425

Dinger, U., Strack, M., Sachsse, T., & Schauenburg, H. (2009). Therapists' attachment, patients' interpersonal problems and alliance development over time in inpatient psychotherapy. *Psychotherapy: Theory, Research, Practice, Training, 46*, 277–290. http://dx.doi.org/10.1037/a0016913

Dozier, M. (1990). Attachment organization and treatment use for adults with serious psychopathological disorders. *Development and Psychopathology, 2*, 47–60. http://dx.doi.org/10.1017/S0954579400000584

Dozier, M., & Bates, B. (2004). Attachment state of mind and the treatment relationship. In L. Attkinson & S. Goldberg (Eds.), *Attachment issues in psychopathology and intervention* (pp. 167–180). Mahwah, NJ: Erlbaum.

Dozier, M., Cue, K. L., & Barnett, L. (1994). Clinicians as caregivers: Role of attachment organization in treatment. *Journal of Consulting and Clinical Psychology, 62*, 793–800. http://dx.doi.org/10.1037/0022-006X.62.4.793

Dozier, M., & Lee, S. (1995). Discrepancies between self- and other-report of psychiatric symptomatology: Effects of dismissing attachment strategies. *Development and Psychopathology, 7,* 217–226. http://dx.doi.org/10.1017/S095457940000643X

Dozier, M., Stovall-McClough, K. C., & Albus, K. (2008). Attachment and psychopathology in adulthood. In J. Cassidy & P. R. Shaver (Eds.), *Handbook of attachment: Theory, research, and clinical applications* (pp. 718–744). New York, NY: Guilford Press.

Dunkle, J. H., & Friedlander, M. L. (1996). Contribution of therapist experience and personal characteristics to the working alliance. *Journal of Counseling Psychology, 43,* 456–460. http://dx.doi.org/10.1037/0022-0167.43.4.456

Ehrenthal, J. C., Tomanek, J., Schauenburg, H., & Dinger, U. (2013). Bindungsrelevante Situationen in der Psychotherapie [Attachment-related situations in psychotherapy]. *Psychotherapeut, 58,* 474–479. http://dx.doi.org/10.1007/s00278-012-0912-1

Eng, W., Heimberg, R. G., Hart, T. A., Schneier, F. R., & Liebowitz, M. R. (2001). Attachment in individuals with social anxiety disorder: The relationship among adult attachment styles, social anxiety, and depression. *Emotion, 1,* 365–380. http://dx.doi.org/10.1037/1528-3542.1.4.365

Faravelli, C. (1985). Life events preceding the onset of panic disorder. *Journal of Affective Disorders, 9,* 103–105.

Farber, B. A., Lippert, R. A., & Nevas, D. B. (1995). The therapist as attachment figure. *Psychotherapy: Theory, Research, Practice, Training, 32,* 204–212. http://dx.doi.org/10.1037/0033-3204.32.2.204

Farber, B. A., Manevich, I., Metzger, J., & Saypol, E. (2005). Choosing psychotherapy as a career: Why did we cross that road? *Journal of Clinical Psychology, 61,* 1009–1031. http://dx.doi.org/10.1002/jclp.20174

Fonagy, P., & Allison, E. (2014). The role of mentalizing and epistemic trust in the therapeutic relationship. *Psychotherapy, 51,* 372–380. http://dx.doi.org/10.1037/a0036505

Fonagy, P., Leigh, T., Steele, M., Steele, H., Kennedy, R., Mattoon, G., . . . Gerber, A. (1996). The relation of attachment status, psychiatric classification, and response to psychotherapy. *Journal of Consulting and Clinical Psychology, 64,* 22–31. http://dx.doi.org/10.1037/0022-006X.64.1.22

Fonagy, P., Luyten, P., Campbell, C., & Allison, L. (2014, December). *Epistemic trust, psychopathology and the great psychotherapy debate.* Retrieved from http://www.societyforpsychotherapy.org/epistemic-trust-psychopathology-and-the-great-psychotherapy-debate

Heimberg, R. G., Horner, K. J., Juster, H. R., Safren, S. A., Brown, E. J., Schneier, F. R., & Liebowitz, M. R. (1999). Psychometric properties of the Liebowitz Social Anxiety Scale. *Psychological Medicine, 29,* 199–212. http://dx.doi.org/10.1017/S0033291798007879

Hentschel, U. (2005). Therapeutic alliance: The best synthesizer of social influences on the therapeutic situation? On links to other constructs, determinants of its effectiveness, and its role for research in psychotherapy in general. *Psychotherapy Research, 15*(1–2), 9–23. http://dx.doi.org/10.1080/10503300512331327001

Holmes, J. (1994). The clinical implications of attachment theory. *British Journal of Psychotherapy, 11*, 62–76. http://dx.doi.org/10.1111/j.1752-0118.1994.tb00702.x

Holmes, J. (2013). *Exploring in security: Towards an attachment-informed psychoanalytic.* New York, NY: Wiley.

Kobak, R. R., Cole, H. E., Ferenz-Gillies, R., Fleming, W. S., & Gamble, W. (1993). Attachment and emotion regulation during mother-teen problem solving: A control theory analysis. *Child Development, 64*, 231–245. http://dx.doi.org/10.2307/1131448

Kobak, R. R., & Sceery, A. (1988). Attachment in late adolescence: Working models, affect regulation, and representations of self and others. *Child Development, 59*(1), 135–146. http://dx.doi.org/10.2307/1130395

Köhler, L. (1991). Neuere ergebnisse der kleinkindforschung. Ihre bedeutung für die psychoanalyse erwachsener [Recent results of infant research. Their importance for the psychoanalysis of adults]. *Forum der Psychoanalyse, 6*, 32–35.

Krause, A. L., Borchardt, V., Li, M., van Tol, M.-J., Demenescu, L. R., Strauss, B., . . . Walter, M. (2016). Dismissing attachment characteristics dynamically modulate brain networks subserving social aversion. *Frontiers in Neuroscience, 10*, 77. http://dx.doi.org/10.3389/fnhum.2016.00077

Leichsenring, F., Hoyer, J., Beutel, M., Herpertz, S., Hiller, W., Irle, E., . . . Leibing, E. (2008). The social phobia psychotherapy research network. The first multicenter randomized controlled trial of psychotherapy for social phobia: Rationale, methods and patient characteristics. *Psychotherapy and Psychosomatics, 78*, 35–41. http://dx.doi.org/10.1159/000162299

Levy, K. N., Ellison, W. D., Scott, L. N., & Bernecker, S. L. (2011). Attachment style. *Journal of Clinical Psychology, 67*, 193–203. http://dx.doi.org/10.1002/jclp.20756

Ligiéro, D. P., & Gelso, C. J. (2002). Countertransference, attachment, and the working alliance: The therapist's contribution. *Psychotherapy: Theory, Research, Practice, Training, 39*, 3–11. http://dx.doi.org/10.1037/0033-3204.39.1.3

Liotti, G. (1991). Patterns of attachment and the assessment of interpersonal schemata: Understanding and changing difficult patient therapist relationships in cognitive psychotherapy. *Journal of Cognitive Psychotherapy, 5*, 105–114.

Mallinckrodt, B. (2000). Attachment, social competencies, social support and interpersonal process in psychotherapy. *Psychotherapy Research, 10*, 239–266. http://dx.doi.org/10.1093/ptr/10.3.239

Mallinckrodt, B. (2001). Interpersonal processes, attachment, and development of social competencies in individual and group psychotherapy. In R. Sarason & S. Duck (Eds.), *Personal relationships: Implications for clinical and community psychology* (pp. 89–117). New York, NY: John Wiley & Sons.

Mallinckrodt, B., Gantt, D. L., & Coble, H. M. (1995). Attachment patterns in the psychotherapy relationship: Development of the client attachment therapist scale. *Journal of Counseling Psychology, 42,* 307–317. http://dx.doi.org/10.1037/0022-0167.42.3.307

Mallinckrodt, B. & Jeong, J. (2015). Meta-analysis of client attachment to therapist: associations with working alliance and client pretherapy attachment. *Psychotherapy, 52,* 134–139. http://dx.doi.org/10.1037/a0036890

Manassis, K., Bradley, S., Goldberg, S., Hood, J., & Swinson, R. P. (1994). Attachment in mothers with anxiety disorders and their children. *Journal of the American Academy of Child & Adolescent Psychiatry, 33,* 1106–1113. http://dx.doi.org/10.1097/00004583-199410000-00006

Marmarosh, C. L., Gelso, C. J., Markin, R. D., Majors, R., Mallery, C., & Choi, J. (2009). The real relationship in psychotherapy: Relationships to adult attachments, working alliance, transference, and therapy outcome. *Journal of Counseling Psychology, 56,* 337–350. http://dx.doi.org/10.1037/a0015169

Marmarosh, C. L., Kivlighan, D. M., Jr., Bieri, K., LaFauci Schutt, J. M., Barone, C., & Choi, J. (2014). The insecure psychotherapy base: Using client and therapist attachment styles to understand the early alliance. *Psychotherapy, 51,* 404–412. http://dx.doi.org/10.1037/a0031989

Martin, A., Buchheim, A., Berger, E., & Strauss, B. (2007). The impact of attachment organization on potential countertransference reactions. *Psychotherapy Research, 17,* 46–58. http://dx.doi.org/10.1080/10503300500485565

Mohr, J. J., Gelso, C. J., & Hill, C. E. (2005). Client and counselor trainee attachment as predictors of session evaluation and countertransference behavior in first counseling sessions. *Journal of Counseling Psychology, 52,* 298–309. http://dx.doi.org/10.1037/0022-0167.52.3.298

Nord, C., Höger, D., & Eckert, J. (2000). Bindungsmuster von psychotherapeuten. Persönlichkeitsstörungen [Binding pattern of psychotherapists: Personality disorders]. *Theorie und Therapie, 4,* 76–86.

Orlinsky, D. & Howard, K. (1987). A generic model of psychotherapy. *Journal of Integrative & Eclectic Psychotherapy, 6*(1), 6–27.

Petrowski, K., Nowacki, K., Pokorny, D., & Buchheim, A. (2011). Matching the patient to the therapist: The roles of the attachment status and the helping alliance. *Journal of Nervous and Mental Disease, 199,* 839–844. http://dx.doi.org/10.1097/NMD.0b013e3182349cce

Petrowski, K., Pokorny, D., Nowacki, K., & Buchheim, A. (2013). The therapist's attachment representation and the patient's attachment to the therapist. *Psychotherapy Research, 23*(1), 25–34. http://dx.doi.org/10.1080/10503307.2012.717307

Petrowski, K., & Strauss, B. (2016). *Complementarity between therapists' and patients' attachment in social phobia.* Manuscript in preparation.

Robbins, S. (1995). Attachment perspectives on the counseling relationship. Comment on Mallinckrodt, Gantt, and Coble (1995). *Journal of Counseling Psychology, 42,* 318–319. http://dx.doi.org/10.1037/0022-0167.42.3.318

Robinson, N., Hill, C. E., & Kivlighan, D. M. (2015). Crying as communication in psychotherapy: The influence of client and therapist attachment dimensions and client attachment to therapist on amount and type of crying. *Journal of Counseling Psychology, 62,* 379–392.

Romano, V., Fitzpatrick, M., & Janzen, J. (2008). The secure-base hypothesis: Global attachment, attachment to counselor, and session exploration in psychotherapy. *Journal of Counseling Psychology, 55,* 495–504. http://dx.doi.org/10.1037/a0013721

Rubino, G., Barker, C., Roth, T., & Fearon, P. (2000). Therapist empathy and depth of interpretation in response to potential alliance ruptures: The role of therapist and patient attachment styles. *Psychotherapy Research, 10,* 408–420. http://dx.doi.org/10.1093/ptr/10.4.408

Sauer, E. M., Lopez, F. G., & Gormley, B. (2003). Respective contributions of therapist and client adult attachment orientations to the development of the early working alliance: A preliminary growth modeling study. *Psychotherapy Research, 13,* 371–382. http://dx.doi.org/10.1093/ptr/kpg027

Schauenburg, H., Buchheim, A., Beckh, K., Nolte, T., Brenk-Franz, K., Leichsenring, F., ... Dinger, U. (2010). The influence of psychodynamically oriented therapists' attachment representations on outcome and alliance in inpatient psychotherapy [corrected]. *Psychotherapy Research, 20,* 193–202. http://dx.doi.org/10.1080/10503300903204043

Schauenburg, H., Dinger, U., & Buchheim, A. (2006). Bindungsmuster von psychotherapeuten [Attachment patterns in psychotherapists]. *Zeitschrift für Psychosomatische Medizin, 52,* 358–372. http://dx.doi.org/10.13109/zptm.2006.52.4.358

Slade, A. (1999). Attachment theory and research: Implications for the theory and practice of individual psychotherapy with adults. In J. Cassidy & P. Shaver (Eds.), *Handbook of attachment: Theory, research, and clinical applications* (pp. 575–594). New York, NY: Guilford Press.

Strauss, B. (Ed.). (2008). *Bindung und psychopathologie* [Attachment and psychopathology]. Stuttgart, Germany: Klett-Cotta.

Strauss, B., & Brenk-Franz, K. (2016). The relevance of attachment theory in medical care. In J. Hunter & R. Maunder (Eds.), *Improving patient treatment with attachment theory* (pp. 39–52). New York, NY: Springer. http://dx.doi.org/10.1007/978-3-319-23300-0_4

Talia, A., Daniel, S. I. F., Miller-Bottome, M., Brambilla, D., Miccoli, D., Safran, J. D., & Lingiardi, V. (2014). AAI predicts patients' in-session interpersonal behavior and discourse: A "move to the level of the relation" for attachment-informed psychotherapy research. *Attachment & Human Development, 16,* 192–209. http://dx.doi.org/10.1080/14616734.2013.859161

Taubner, S., Ulrich-Manns, S., Klasen, J., Curth, C., Möller, H., & Wolter, S. (2014). Innere arbeitsmodelle von bindung und aversive kindheitserfahrungen bei psychotherapeuten in ausbildung [Inner working models of attachment and aversive childhood experiences of psychotherapists in training]. *Psychotherapie Forum, 19*, 2–12. http://dx.doi.org/10.1007/s00729-014-0005-4

Taylor, P., Rietzschel, J., Danquah, A. & Berry, K. (2015). Changes in attachment representations during psychological therapy. *Psychotherapy Research, 25*, 222–238. http://dx.doi.org/10.1080/10503307.2014.886791

Tyrrell, C. L., Dozier, M., Teague, G. B., & Fallot, R. D. (1999). Effective treatment relationships for persons with serious psychiatric disorders: The importance of attachment states of mind. *Journal of Consulting and Clinical Psychology, 67*, 725–733. http://dx.doi.org/10.1037/0022-006X.67.5.725

van IJzendoorn, M. H., & Bakermans-Kranenburg, M. J. (1996). Attachment representations in mothers, fathers, adolescents, and clinical groups: A meta-analytic search for normative data. *Journal of Consulting and Clinical Psychology, 64*, 8–21. http://dx.doi.org/10.1037/0022-006X.64.1.8

Wei, M., Russell, D. W., & Zakalik, R. A. (2005). Adult attachment, social self-efficacy, self-disclosure, loneliness, and subsequent depression for freshman college students: A longitudinal study. *Journal of Counseling Psychology, 52*, 602–614. http://dx.doi.org/10.1037/0022-0167.52.4.602

Wiseman, H., & Tishby, O. (2014). Client attachment, attachment to the therapist and client-therapist attachment match: How do they relate to change in psychodynamic psychotherapy? *Psychotherapy Research, 24*, 392–406.

Woodhouse, S. S., Schlosser, L. Z., Crook, R. E., Ligiéro, D. P., & Gelso, C. J. (2003). Client attachment to therapist: Relations to transference and client recollections of parental caregiving. *Journal of Counseling Psychology, 50*, 395–408. http://dx.doi.org/10.1037/0022-0167.50.4.395

Yusof, Y., & Carpenter, J. S. W. (2013). A survey of family therapists' adult attachment styles in the UK. *Contemporary Family Therapy: An International Journal, 35*, 452–464. http://dx.doi.org/10.1007/s10591-012-9230-6

8

THE ROLE OF THERAPIST SKILLS IN THERAPIST EFFECTIVENESS

TIMOTHY ANDERSON AND CLARA E. HILL

The English word *skill* is derived from Old Norse *skilja*, meaning, "to separate, divide." In this chapter, we separate or divide therapist skills into technical, relational, conceptualization, and cultural aspects.

- *Technical skills* are defined by the delivery of interventions, specific strategies, and techniques.
- *Relational skills* refer to emotional and interpersonal communication.
- *Conceptual skills* refer to cognitive and organizational ability to understand the client.
- *Cultural skills* are defined by the therapist's awareness of cultural context.

After discussing each of these skills separately, we integrate them into a contextual model for explaining therapist effectiveness. Our overarching goal is

http://dx.doi.org/10.1037/0000034-009
How and Why Are Some Therapists Better Than Others? Understanding Therapist Effects, L. G. Castonguay and C. E. Hill (Eds.)
Copyright © 2017 by the American Psychological Association. All rights reserved.

to derive an explanation for the finding that some therapists are better (or worse) than others.

TECHNICAL SKILLS

Technical skills are the interventions the therapist uses to help clients. In other words, these skills refer to *what* the therapist does in sessions. In this section, we describe the three levels at which techniques can be conceptualized and assessed, according to Stiles, Hill, and Elliott (2015): treatment, session, and sentence.

Techniques Conceptualized and Assessed at the Treatment Level

At the treatment level, techniques are most often thought of as the treatment itself (e.g., psychodynamic, cognitive–behavioral). They are measured either by judgments of adherence to and competence with a particular treatment manual or by naturalistically observing behaviors and determining the approach with which the therapist is most closely aligned.

Therapists differ in how much they adhere to manuals (Webb, DeRubeis, & Barber, 2010), although most studies have found that this variance among therapist adherence does not predict treatment outcomes (see also Chapter 3, this volume). Furthermore, it is not clear whether therapist differences in adherence to technical skills are due to the techniques themselves, to individual therapist or client characteristics, or even perhaps to the processes by which techniques unfold. It is possible that competent delivery of techniques ultimately predicts outcomes (e.g., Barber, Crits-Christoph, & Luborsky, 1996; Sharpless & Barber, 2009) and that therapist characteristics influence how techniques are differentially expressed among therapists; one therapist may adhere to using techniques as appropriated, whereas another may use them with expertise or mastery. Therapists may also differ in their identification, enthusiasm, and beliefs in the treatment approach. For example, therapist adherence has been found to be conflated with therapist allegiance effects (Hollon, 1999), and there is reason to believe that therapist allegiance, enthusiasm, and involvement may be implicated in client outcomes. Further complicating matters, there is evidence that treatment adherence is irrelevant to outcomes when the therapeutic alliance is high, but is relevant when the therapeutic alliance is low (Barber et al., 2006). Although a good argument can be made for the lack of a direct relationship between technical adherence and therapist effects, it may be that there is an indirect effect with a mediating variable that links therapist technical adherence with outcome. For example, findings that therapists who were higher in adherence were also higher in internalized hostility (Henry, Schacht, Strupp, Butler, & Binder, 1993) suggest that other therapist variables need to be controlled to understand the relationship between technical adherence and therapist effects.

Techniques Conceptualized and Assessed at the Session Level

At the session level, skills may involve such things as analyzing transference or addressing cultural issues. Judges typically observe an entire research or training session and determine how much of each skill is used.

Ackerman and Hilsenroth (2001, 2003) reviewed the literature on in-session activities and techniques associated with good and poor therapeutic alliance. Their reviews indicated that the quality of specific techniques or technical activity matters most. Sometimes the overuse of certain techniques (e.g., interpretation of client resistance, therapist silence, disclosure of personal conflicts) had deleterious effects. In contrast, several studies found positive influences for the accuracy and appropriateness of several techniques (e.g., reflection, exploration, other techniques designed to encourage client expression of emotion, and transference interpretations).

Techniques Conceptualized and Assessed at the Sentence Level

At the sentence level, the therapist delivers verbal response modes (VRMs), which include techniques such as reflections of feelings and interpretations (e.g., Hill, 1978; Stiles, 1992).

Considerable controversy exists over how to best examine the effects of specific VRMs. Stiles and Horvath (see Chapter 4) argue compellingly that the traditional paradigm of correlating the proportion of VRMs with session and treatment outcomes is inadequate because it does not account for therapist responsiveness to client needs (e.g., one well-timed interpretation will have more effect than 10 poorly timed interpretations). However, when they investigated the immediate effects of VRMS (e.g., client reactions and behaviors in the subsequent speaking turn), Hill et al. (1988) found minimal effects. Relationships among techniques, timing, quality, and client involvement all seem to be important moderators of therapist techniques.

Furthermore, examining the influence of all therapist techniques seems too global when individual techniques can have very different outcomes depending on the context. More recent research, investigating specific well-defined techniques (e.g., therapist self-disclosure, therapist immediacy) within the context of specific sessions within cases using a qualitative methodology has proven to be a more effective way of examining the influence of therapist techniques (e.g., Hill et al., 2014; Pinto-Coelho, Hill, & Kivlighan, 2016).

Excellent examples of how skills can be investigated and linked with outcome are provided elsewhere in this volume (see Chapters 13, 14, and 15).

RELATIONAL SKILLS

Relational skills involve the therapist's ability to express, receive, and interpret emotional and interpersonal exchanges with the client. These skills focus on how the therapist interacts with the client and responds to the client's needs (see Chapter 4). Relational skills have been defined as using internal experiences to process interpersonal information, including emotional and personality characteristics of others (Ackerman & Hilsenroth, 2003; Anderson & Strupp, 2015).

Therapist inner experiences of empathy, positive regard (warmth), and genuineness have been found to be strong predictors of therapy outcome (Elliott, Bohart, Watson, & Greenberg, 2011; Farber & Doolin, 2011; Kolden, Klein, Wang, & Austin, 2011). Some research has even shown a causal influence for empathy on outcome (e.g., Burns & Nolen-Hoeksema, 1992). Empathy, positive regard, and genuineness variables have theoretical roots in Rogers (1957), who considered them to be necessary and sufficient conditions, although later research found them to be necessary but not sufficient in terms of client outcomes (Elliott et al., 2011; Farber & Doolin, 2011). Part of what defines empathy (and also positive regard and genuineness) as relational is that it involves the therapist feeling the empathy and then communicating the empathy, and the client perceiving the empathy (Barrett-Lennard, 1962, 1981).

Although relational skills are usually assessed at the session level, these skills can also be conceptualized as occurring in the therapist's momentary reactions and internal processes. Benjamin's (1979) Structural Analysis of Social Behavior, where each therapist's unit of speech is rated within circular interpersonal space (e.g., friendliness, agency, focus), is one example of how a therapist's momentary reactions to a client can be empirically judged. For example, the presence of subtle expressions of interpersonal hostility using Structural Analysis of Social Behavior was associated with communication patterns in which therapists were "telling" versus "listening" to their clients (Anderson, Knobloch-Fedders, Stiles, Ordoñez, & Heckman, 2012).

CONCEPTUALIZATION SKILLS

Conceptualization skills involve cognitive processes whereby the therapist uses an organizing scheme (i.e., theory) to understand the client's problems or dynamics (Eells, 2010; see also Chapter 11, this volume). As a profession, therapists believe that good theory explains the client's suffering as well as suggests appropriate therapeutic actions in the form of techniques and/or relational engagement.

Mostly, we think of conceptualization skills as occurring at the treatment level. For example, an entire case tends to be understood using a cognitive–behavioral, humanistic, or psychodynamic approach. But we can also think of conceptualization at a session level in that therapists develop general strategies of intervention for how to approach sessions (Goldfried, 1980), and at a sentence level in that therapists develop intentions for how to intervene in specific instances (Fuller & Hill, 1985). We suggest that the following conceptualization skills are important at the session/sentence level: (a) awareness of what the client is experiencing and needs in the moment, (b) awareness of the therapist's own experience (e.g., feelings, thoughts), and (c) awareness of goals for the next intervention within the context of goals and for treatment more globally. Therefore, case conceptualization is not only an overall understanding of the client's dynamics but also a moment-to-moment skill.

It should be noted that, other than formal intake or assessment reports, it is not easy to observe conceptualization skills because they mostly occur within the therapist's head (see Chapter 11). Attention to the therapist's more momentary mentation of the client, however, may facilitate understanding about how theoretical thinking can be integrated with in-session therapeutic processes. It is important to note that conceptual skills are not traits or something that a therapist possesses in the abstract, but rather they are situational expressions. A therapist might generally be able to conceptualize cases, but she or he might have difficulty with a particular case in a particular moment because clients are complex or because the therapist's own personal issues get triggered.

CULTURAL SKILLS

The therapist's cultural skills involve an understanding of research about cultural identity and how mental disorders might be differentially expressed cross-culturally. Use of cultural skills is related to conceptualization skills in that heightened awareness is involved. However, cultural skills involve an awareness of the cultural context for both the client and the therapist.

Frank and Frank's (1993) contextual model of psychotherapy was groundbreaking by describing how psychological practices vary across cultures. In addition to techniques, the therapeutic relationship, and theory, Frank and Frank focused on the healing power of the setting as one of four common factors. Not only is the setting a recognition of a protected space, but it was specifically emphasized as the cultural influences of this distinctive use of space, "Both secular and religious healing sites are distinguished from the rest of the patients' surroundings by special attributes, including sharply delineated spatial and temporal boundaries" (Frank & Frank, 1993, p. 41). Although cross-cultural differences exist in the setting of those designated to provide therapy or religious healing, the meanings attributed to these socially sanctioned spaces lend psychological power to the therapist's role as a healer.

Whereas the setting may provide healing power to the roles of therapist and client, it does not speak to the rich history of cultural identities that each participant brings when entering a healing setting. Sue, Arredondo, and McDavis (1992) suggested that therapists take a multicultural perspective by becoming adept in cultural competencies needed to practice in a complex, diversified society: "Although all of us are racial, ethnic, and cultural beings, belonging to a particular group does not endow a person with the competencies and skills necessary to be a cultural skilled counselor" (p. 478).

Ivey, D'Andrea, Ivey, and Simek-Morgan (2002) described the awareness of the client's and the therapist's cultural contexts in multicultural counseling as more of a "meta-theory" than the conventional use of theory in psychological treatments. However, we believe that it is important not to relegate cultural skills as another layer of abstraction to the treatment level. Cultural skill involves the therapist's well-attuned awareness of his or her own cultural identity and that of his or her client, as well as how these identities are (or are not) dynamically intertwined within the cultural context.

Ideally, cultural skills at the treatment level also influence the session and sentence levels. However, it is one thing to have attained awareness and cross-cultural experiences about cultures, systems, and families, but it is another skill to be able to implement this awareness as a session-relevant focus or within a momentary interaction. For example, when conducting emotion-focused therapy, cultural skill involves having not only the awareness of how different cultures process emotional experience but also a practical and even visceral experience of how culture might influence emotional schemes and problem-solving. Given that many Asian cultures rely on subtle forms of emotional expression, therapists might explore these modes of expression within the session before assuming that more evocative exploration of client emotions is warranted. Furthermore, when cultural differences exist, they are likely to be complex, and there is danger in oversimplification. For example, although emotional expression may be subtler within some Asian cultures (relative to many Western cultures), there also tends to be a greater emphasis on internal experiencing in which identifying separate entities of experience (e.g., cognitions) might be more unfamiliar (relative to Western cultures; Tseng, Chang, & Nishozono, 2005). The discussion and use of discrete and separate aspects of a client's experience within a "clinical" context might have marked implications for cultural adaptation of many Western psychotherapies.

Similarly, cultural skill involves an ability to understand that men and women may have different modes of understanding that may link to the therapist's (and client's) cultural identity and personhood (e.g., Belenky, Clinchy, Goldberger, & Tarule, 1997). For example, a culturally skilled older male therapist would understand that a younger female client might remain silent because of the interpersonal power dynamic. This female client may not believe that her subjective knowledge will be acknowledged as valid and legitimate, especially if the male therapist emphasizes objectivity and rationality within the treatment. Therefore, a culturally aware therapist remains attuned to how a client expresses self-knowledge in unique and gendered ways.

More recently, greater attention has been given to how therapist cultural skills are expressed at a sentence/momentary level. Sue et al. (2007) introduced the notion of microaggressions, in which subtle expressions of interpersonal hostility are expressed that involve an individual's cultural identity. Microaggressions can have a profound and long-lasting effect on the client. As Owen et al. (2014) demonstrated, the amount of microaggressions in therapy is negatively associated with the alliance, and the failure to address microaggressions is associated with an even lower alliance.

Hayes, Owen, and Nissen-Lie (Chapter 9, this volume) effectively point out the perils for "therapists who become 'culturally encapsulated,' defining reality according to one set of cultural assumptions, acting insensitively toward cultural variations, and judging others from their own self-referent criteria" (p. 165). Hence, failure to gain cultural competency can wreak havoc across a therapist's set of technical, relational, and conceptual skills. It is easy to imagine how the unaddressed microaggression would contribute to an alliance rupture.

A CONTEXTUAL MODEL FOR INTEGRATING THE SKILLS

Prior attempts to isolate effective therapist skills have yielded disappointing results or have been limited in generalizability across therapists and therapies (Wampold & Imel, 2015). The most effective therapist skills are likely to be identified by taking a broader approach that integrates across the four skills that have been identified in this chapter (technical, relational, conceptualization, and cultural).

The Contextual Model

Anderson, Lunnen, and Ogles's (2010) contextual model integrated several similar models and processes, including Frank and Frank's (1993) original contextual model of psychotherapy, Orlinsky and Howard's (1986) sequentially arranged generic model of psychotherapy, Goldfried's (1980) psychotherapy principles, and Castonguay and Beutler's (2006) empirically supported principles of change. Anderson et al. clarified the use of the treatment setting as a common factor that extends beyond the therapist's office to include broader cultural influences such as the client's and the therapist's cultural identity.

Our visual representation of this model is presented in Figure 8.1. The four common factors are in the boxes on the outer perimeter of the figure. However, the factors have been replaced by the skills reviewed in this chapter. Examples of more specific therapist skills are provided within the circles of the figures. This figure illustrates that skills are interrelated. The linking of these skills can be thought of as integrative skills, or skill sets, analogous to Goldfried's (1980) principles of change. In fact, it would be rationally consistent to assume that consistently integrated skill sets would be effective in the same way that empirically supported techniques and relationship factors have

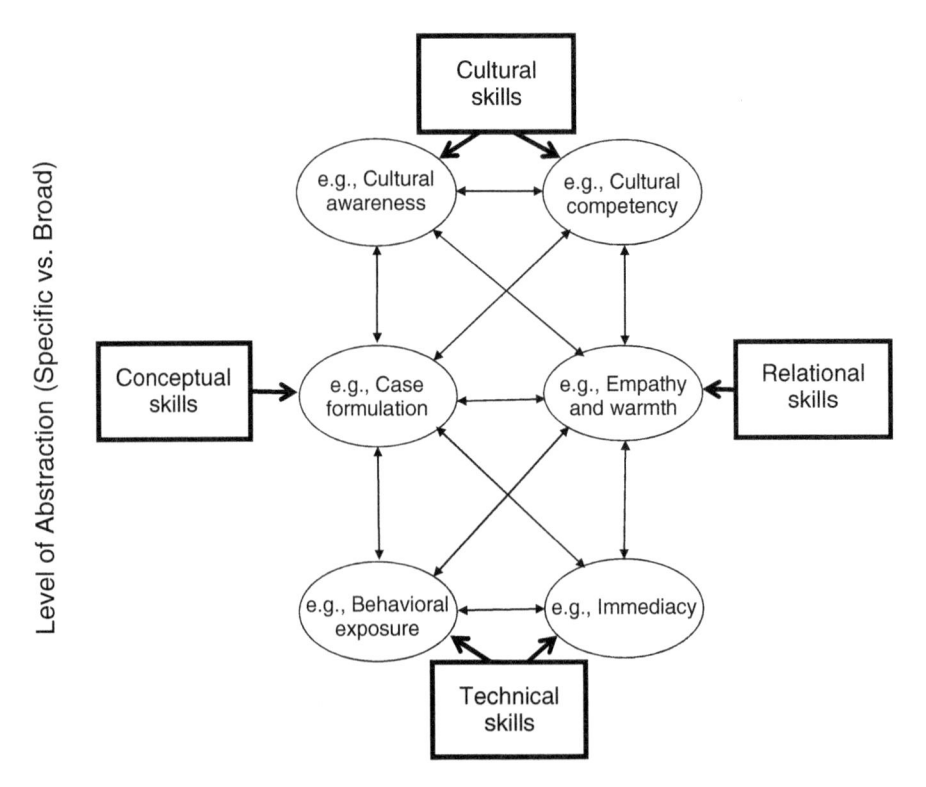

Figure 8.1. An integrated contextual model of therapist skill. Each of the boxes represents one of the four skill sets described in this chapter. Circles provide examples of skills (many other examples are possible). Arrows illustrate that the optimal use of any specific skill involves integration with skills from other skill sets.

been linked (Castonguay & Beutler, 2006). Using behavioral exposure in anxiety provides an example of this point. As seen in Figure 8.1, behavioral exposure can be implemented within a fairly narrow and somewhat mechanical manner, but the same behavioral intervention can be integrated with other common skills as a part of a sophisticated and broad set of skills. The technical skill of behavioral exposure can be linked to the therapist's consistent overarching cultural beliefs, psychological theory (behavior change induces psychological changes), and relationships (therapist immediacy with the client, which might convey that the therapist is earnest and genuinely believes the theory).

One value in integrating technical, relational, conceptual, and cultural skills is that it allows for recognition of how a therapist adapts treatments to be responsive to multiple factors. For example, it is now commonly recognized that competent practice involves deviations from treatment manuals because of the emergence of various "real life" events and that a therapist makes cultural adaptations to treatments as needed (Wampold & Imel, 2015; Whaley & Davis, 2007). It is sometimes easy for a therapist to fall into focusing on just one of these factors (e.g., implementing techniques) and lose sight of the fact that a client and his or her problems are experientially multifaceted. It is also sometimes easy for a therapist to become absorbed in maintaining a warm relationship, lost in theoretical abstractions, or focused on cultural contributions without considering how all of these factors can be integrated.

Coming from a slightly different model, Hill (2014) described how some of these components work together. She suggested that at any given moment in the therapy session, a therapist must have a conceptual awareness of the client dynamics, including some treatment-level knowledge of the client history, attachment style, psychodynamics, and culture, as well as an understanding of the therapeutic relationship (the dynamics between client and therapist). The therapist also needs to have a very specific sense of what the client is thinking and feeling in the current moment. In addition, the therapist needs to be aware of his or her own issues and reactions in the moment, and how these reactions might help or hinder the therapeutic work. Because of the therapist's conceptualization of the client, awareness of the client's dynamics, sense of what the client is thinking and feeling at the moment, and awareness of own motives, the therapist formulates intentions for what she or he wants to accomplish in the next intervention. These intentions are determined by the therapist's theoretical orientation, and might include such things as wanting the client to explore, to gain insight, or to act in some way. The therapist then selects an intervention that seems likely to accomplish the goals for the client in the moment. With empathy, respect, and genuineness, the therapist delivers the intervention and carefully observes how the client responds, modifying subsequent responses accordingly. Obviously, the therapist must have these skills in his or her repertoire, and it is hoped that these skills were acquired after practicing them extensively until they were simply part of his or her being and could be called forth when needed. Typically, several skills can be used to accomplish the same goals depending on how they are implemented, whereas other skills might be very unlikely to accomplish the goals.

Case Example[1]

The following clinical example illustrates how the integration of these four contextual skill sets likely contributes to therapist effects. Alice, a 62-year-old office worker, had a successful treatment outcome after 25 sessions of psychotherapy. Her therapist, Dr. A, was a highly regarded therapist with extensive clinical experience; she had demonstrated positive outcomes in a small sample of previous cases. Alice presented with depression and complicated grief, which included loss of appetite, sleep, and a persistent gloomy outlook. Dr. A's early interventions were exploratory reflections and restatements that focused on Alice's continued despair about the death of her husband 2 years before the beginning of therapy. In addition, Dr. A's use of technical skills involved cognitive restructuring around Alice's beliefs that she could not recover from her loss because she perceived herself as empty and worthless without the presence of her husband. Dr. A's early use of cognitive interventions quickly became integrated with a conceptualization of Alice on the basis of interpersonal and psychodynamic theory. Dr. A's cultural skills were apparent as she carefully asked Alice about her family of origin. They were ardent members of a fundamentalist Christian religion and believed in strict discipline and corporal punishment enforced by a demanding father, whom Alice described as mean-spirited. Dr. A connected Alice's cognitive beliefs about low self-regard to Alice's perception of not being valued as a woman within this fundamentalist culture. Alice was already aware of her negative feelings around fundamentalism and her family, given that as a teenager she had bolted from her family after meeting her husband, a man of a markedly different faith whom she viewed as her "savior." Her family and religious community severed social ties with her for having married a perceived infidel to her faith, so she was adrift.

As therapy progressed, Dr. A increasingly communicated to Alice that her beliefs about her lack of value were linked to cultural origins. Alice's dominating and cruel father came to represent what she had escaped from,

---

[1]Client identifiers have been disguised to protect patient confidentiality.

interpersonally and culturally. As a dynamic conceptualization, these early experiences were less easy to leave behind. Alice presented in a highly controlled and emotionally constricted manner; however, she became tearful as Dr. A increasingly focused on her self-hatred, which then developed into attention toward her anger at her father and all that this larger fundamentalist culture had meant to her, including a devalued identity as a woman. For example, Dr. A had noticed that Alice had been nervously swinging her leg when describing the dominance and discipline of her father, which included how Alice believed that he ultimately despised his daughters because they were a burden on him. At one point, Dr. A interrupted Alice in mid-sentence and disclosed that she had noticed Alice's foot "kicking" and that Dr. A had a fantasy that it was Alice's father's kicking, but really, Alice had been kicking herself throughout her life. The kicking foot became an emotionally infused metaphor for future sessions, and Alice frequently commented on how much she felt that Dr. A understood her as a person.

The relationship was highly positive as these technical, conceptual, and cultural elements appeared to merge. For example, a discussion about Dr. A's and Alice's clothing, which started as a seemingly simple woman-to-woman aside about fashion, led to a series of rich, transference-based interventions about the socioeconomic and class differences between them. Dr. A was persistent in asking about the differences, which Alice initially attributed merely to financial differences. Dr. A persisted and asked what Alice thought Dr. A had thought about her, because she had noticed Alice withdrawing during the initial discussion about the cost of their apparel (which had been brought up by Alice). Alice became more forthcoming, however, as Dr. A continued to ask her how she (Dr A) would be able to know if Alice had negative feelings toward her. Dr. A was particularly attentive to Alice's silence about vocalizing her experiences that involved such differences, especially those that might evoke judgments. The cultural attentiveness of Dr. A was integrated within a conceptual framework; her technical interventions (this time for transference exploration) were grounded within a highly positive, emotionally charged therapeutic relationship. Her skill sets of technical, relational, conceptual, and cultural skills were seamlessly integrated.

Implications of the Contextual Model

We propose that the use of any one of the therapy skills discussed here will be more effective when consistently combined with the other three therapy skills. Using the example of the therapist who implements behavioral exposure to treat social anxiety, it is important that this technical skill be integrated with relational, conceptual, and cultural skills. In other words, to be effective, this therapist must responsively apply behavioral exposure in an interpersonally warm manner, on the basis of a good conceptualization of the client, which is integrated into an understanding of the client's cultural identity and background. A therapist may unwittingly express a lack of understanding of the client's distress when using behavioral exposure in the context of a weak therapeutic bond, when the client has other more pressing problems than social anxiety, or when the client does not understand the rationale for the behavioral exposure because it conflicts with his or her cultural beliefs.

A second implication is that the contextual integration of skills has additive benefits that extend beyond the skills themselves. Similar to the notion that the gestalt is greater than the sum of its parts, it could also be said that contextual skills are greater than the sum of the four skills. Therefore, the use of any skill is strengthened when combined with other contextual skills in a competent manner.

Third, therapists who are attuned to the full context of skills might be more likely to have their skill set extend into a more advanced and personalized development of novel nuanced skills, leading to the attainment of therapeutic mastery. It has been said that therapists often begin practice by following skills from a particular theory, but by the time they attain expertise, the expression of theory is personalized and automatic and becomes indistinguishable from the person of the therapist (Hill, 2014). Recent research on expertise and mastery has addressed how masters of a discipline can appear to have natural talents of intuition (see Chapter 11, this volume); however, what may not be apparent to the casual observer is that this effortless talent may be the effects of considerable practice of more basic skills (Gladwell, 2007).

Using a lifetime of decision-making research, Kahneman (2011) described how many master firefighters, for example, can skillfully identify dangerous zones within a building through what might, at first glance, appear to be natural and intuitive talent. However, as Kahneman described, these abilities may be best characterized as complex sets of skills, developed through extensive practice of more primordial skills, which serve as building blocks for more complex and advanced skill sets. Similarly, master therapists have a capacity for intuitive understanding of others ("mind reading"), which may appear to the casual observer as something of a natural, inborn talent (see also Hill, Spiegel, Hoffman, Kivlighan, & Gelso, in press).

Future research may facilitate our understanding of how therapists develop these advanced skills. Psychotherapy may benefit from recent observations in other fields of sociology about how advanced skills develop, or what Coyle (2009) referred to as "talent hotbeds." Models for identifying broader skill sets are needed so that we can begin to understand how basic skill sets develop into more advanced expertise (Kahneman, 2011).

THE CONTEXTUAL MODEL AND THERAPIST EFFECTS

How might a more contextual approach to skills advance the effort to identify the source of therapist effects? Both authors of this chapter have conducted studies of therapist skills that, although different, shared an integrative theme.

Hill's Research on Helping Skills

Hill's (2014) helping skills model serves as a good example for understanding how specifically defined interventions can be conceived narrowly (as specific techniques that can be operationalized at the sentence level) and applied broadly at session and treatment levels. Helping skills integrate these operationalized techniques by organizing them within sequenced sets via which many treatments are commonly organized: (a) exploratory skills (e.g., reflections), (b) insight skills (e.g., interpretations), and (c) action skills (e.g., giving homework). Helping skills have clear definitions, but are not taught in a cookbook approach or with an orthodoxy about which skills must always be used. Skills are specifically taught within the context that they must be implemented with empathy, compassion, self-awareness, and cultural awareness.

Furthermore, part of what makes helping skills useful within the contextual model is that the skills can be combined in nearly unlimited combinations and can be practically implemented within a wide variety of contexts. For example, it is recognized that not all clients respond to empathy in the same way, and, furthermore, clients have different needs (e.g., some like to focus on feelings, others do not). This flexibility provides the building blocks for therapists to gain expertise by flexibly combining helping skills in the integrative manner that we have recommended in this chapter. As Ridley, Kelly, and Mollen (2011) stated, Hill's (2014) helping skills model, relative to other models, has the most comprehensive coverage of skills, culture, theory, relationship of skills to therapeutic change, and integration of skills.

Research has shown that helping skills can be effectively taught (Hill & Kellems, 2002; Hill et al., 2008; Hill, Spangler, Jackson, & Chui, 2014). Use of helping skills not only increased after helping skills training, but were judged as being associated with higher posttraining ratings of the therapeutic relationship, and higher evaluations of the session quality (Hill et al., 2008). Hill, Sullivan, Knox, and Schlosser (2007) found that as a result of training, master's level trainees were better able to use exploration and insight skills, felt better about themselves as therapists, were less anxious, had more self-efficacy, were more comfortable in the role of therapist, were less self-critical, and felt themselves better able to connect with clients. Furthermore, self-efficacy ratings in application of helping skills progressively increased throughout training until completion (Hill et al., 2008). Hill et al. (2015) recently reported that advanced doctoral students continued learning and applying the more advanced skills as a result of increased practice and experience.

Anderson's Research on Facilitative Interpersonal Skills

Another research program that is compatible with a contextual model is Anderson's research on facilitative interpersonal skills (FIS; Anderson, Ogles, Patterson, Lambert, & Vermeersch, 2009). FIS is based on a broader definition of skills and is grounded by assessing therapist responses to a standard set of realistic therapy situations. Observational ratings of responses are built from therapist relational abilities, inferred from therapy processes that have been strongly linked to outcome (e.g., empathy, alliance, warmth/positive regard) and items inspired by Frank and Frank's (1993) contextual model (e.g., persuasiveness, hope). On the basis of these contextual items, raters are encouraged to not weigh assumptions about technical models and assumptions, and to consider psychological healing principles that may appear unorthodox. For example, it is possible that therapists can have successful outcomes but appear unorthodox and even somewhat questionable in terms of contemporary standards of psychotherapy (Anderson & Strupp, 2015).

FIS and outcome have been evaluated in various settings using different research designs. First, in a randomized controlled trial that categorized "therapists" (master's level therapists and novices) by interpersonal skills, Anderson, Crowley, Himawan, Holmberg, and Uhlin (2016) found that clients treated by therapists with high interpersonal skills had better outcomes and alliances than did clients whose therapists had low interpersonal skills. Anderson et al. (2009) assessed therapist FIS at the Brigham Young Counseling Center, where prior analysis had identified the presence of therapist effects in a large sample of clients. Using hierarchical linear modeling, they found that therapists with higher FIS had clients who reported better outcomes (on a symptom measure) relative to therapists with lower FIS. Most recently, when FIS was administered to entering graduate students at Ohio University, Anderson, McClintock, Himawan, Song, and Patterson (2016) found that FIS predicted therapist effectiveness when trainees began seeing clients within an in-house clinic. In contrast, FIS was not correlated with measures of empathy and helping skills in undergraduate students prior to or after training in helping skills (Hill et al., 2016). Although training was effective and trait empathy was correlated with helping skills near the beginning of training, FIS was not correlated with helping skills. Interestingly, FIS predicted posttraining gains in the student's reported self-efficacy in providing helping skills even though none of the variables (including FIS) were significant in predicting the implementation of actual helping skills. Apparently, FIS predicted helpers who gained confidence in their helping skills without being able to predict demonstrated learning of helping skills.

CONCLUSION

We suggest that the contextual model could be used to investigate whether therapist skills help to explain therapist effects. We argue that skills should have the greatest efficacy when combined and used in context.

Our research programs in helping skills and FIS provide examples of how this model can be investigated. Specific skill sets from within these approaches (e.g., empathy, alliance building, friendly forms of persuasiveness, insight, building hope and positive expectations, and finally, skillful use of homework and other action-oriented skills) seem to be effective when used appropriately (i.e., within the context of a good relationship and with cultural awareness). We hope that future research, using newer methods, will allow empirical investigation of whether such integration can account for therapist effects. Stiles et al. (2015) described how examining technical skills can be examined within context by using qualitative and case study approaches. At the other extreme, recent advances in statistical methodology (see Chapter 3, this volume) have been developed for analyzing large, nested data sets making it possible to investigate which of these skills independently explains outcome variance because of the therapist (although we must be careful because often this research relies on quantity rather than quality of interventions).

REFERENCES

Ackerman, S. J., & Hilsenroth, M. J. (2001). A review of therapist characteristics and techniques negatively impacting the therapist alliance. *Psychotherapy: Theory, Research, Practice, Training, 38*, 171–185. http://dx.doi.org/10.1037/0033-3204.38.2.171

Ackerman, S. J., & Hilsenroth, M. J. (2003). A review of therapist characteristics and techniques positively impacting the therapeutic alliance. *Clinical Psychology Review, 23*, 1–33. http://dx.doi.org/10.1016/S0272-7358(02)00146-0

Anderson, T., Crowley, M. J., Himawan, L., Holmberg, J., & Uhlin, B. (2016). Therapist facilitative interpersonal skills and training status: A randomized clinical trial on alliance and outcome. *Psychotherapy Research, 26*, 511–529. http://dx.doi.org/10.1080/10503307.2015.1049671

Anderson, T., Knobloch-Fedders, L. M., Stiles, W. B., Ordoñez, T., & Heckman, B. D. (2012). The power of subtle interpersonal hostility in psychodynamic psychotherapy: A speech acts analysis. *Psychotherapy Research, 22*, 348–362. http://dx.doi.org/10.1080/10503307.2012.658097

Anderson, T., Lunnen, K. M., & Ogles, B. (2010). Putting models and techniques in context. In B. Duncan, S. Miller, & B. Wampold (Eds.), *The heart and soul of change* (pp. 143–166). Washington, DC: American Psychological Association. http://dx.doi.org/10.1037/12075-005

Anderson, T., McClintock, A. S., Himawan, L., Song, X., & Patterson, C. L. (2016). A prospective study of therapist facilitative interpersonal skills as a predictor of treatment outcome. *Journal of Consulting and Clinical Psychology, 84*, 57–66. http://dx.doi.org/10.1037/ccp0000060

Anderson, T., Ogles, B. M., Patterson, C. L., Lambert, M. J., & Vermeersch, D. A. (2009). Therapist effects: Facilitative interpersonal skills as a predictor of therapist success. *Journal of Clinical Psychology, 65*, 755–768. http://dx.doi.org/10.1002/jclp.20583

Anderson, T., & Strupp, H. H. (2015). Training in time-limited dynamic psychotherapy: A systematic comparison of pre- and post-training cases treated by one therapist. *Psychotherapy Research, 25*, 595–611. http://dx.doi.org/10.1080/10503307.2014.935517

Barber, J. P., Crits-Christoph, P., & Luborsky, L. (1996). Effects of therapist adherence and competence on patient outcome in brief dynamic therapy. *Journal of Consulting and Clinical Psychology, 64*, 619–622. http://dx.doi.org/10.1037/0022-006X.64.3.619

Barber, J. P., Gallop, R., Crits-Christoph, P., Frank, A., Thase, M. E., Weiss, R. D., & Gibbons, M. B. C. (2006). The role of therapist adherence, therapist competence, and alliance in predicting outcome of individual drug counseling: Results from the National Institute Drug Abuse Collaborative Cocaine Treatment Study. *Psychotherapy Research, 16*, 229–240. http://dx.doi.org/10.1080/10503300500288951

Barrett-Lennard, G. T. (1962). Dimensions of therapist response as causal factors in therapeutic change. *Psychological Monographs: General and Applied, 76*(43), 1–36. http://dx.doi.org/10.1037/h0093918

Barrett-Lennard, G. T. (1981). The empathy cycle: Refinement of a nuclear concept. *Journal of Counseling Psychology, 28*, 91–100. http://dx.doi.org/10.1037/0022-0167.28.2.91

Belenky, M. F., Clinchy, B. M., Goldberger, N. R., & Tarule, J. M. (1997). *Women's ways of knowing: The development of self, voice, and mind* (10th ed.). New York, NY: Basic Books.

Benjamin, L. S. (1979). Structural analysis of differentiation failure. *Psychiatry: Journal for the Study of Interpersonal Processes, 42*, 1–23. http://dx.doi.org/10.1080/00332747.1979.11024003

Burns, D. D., & Nolen-Hoeksema, S. (1992). Therapeutic empathy and recovery from depression in cognitive–behavioral therapy: A structural equation model.

Journal of Consulting and Clinical Psychology, 60, 441–449. http://dx.doi.org/10.1037/0022-006X.60.3.441

Castonguay, L. G., & Beutler, L. E. (2006). *Principles of therapeutic change that work.* Oxford, England: Oxford University Press.

Coyle, D. (2009). *The talent code: Greatness isn't born. It's grown. Here's how.* New York, NY: Bantam Books.

Eells, T. D. (2010). *Handbook of psychotherapy case formulation* (2nd ed.). New York, NY: Guilford Press.

Elliott, R., Bohart, A. G., Watson, J. C., & Greenberg, L. S. (2011). Empathy. In J. C. Norcross (Ed.), *Psychotherapy relationships that work: Evidence-based responsiveness* (2nd ed., pp. 132–152). Oxford, England: Oxford University Press. http://dx.doi.org/10.1093/acprof:oso/9780199737208.003.0006

Farber, B. A., & Doolin, E. M. (2011). Positive regard and affirmation. In J. C. Norcross (Ed.), *Psychotherapy relationships that work: Evidence-based responsiveness* (2nd ed., pp. 168–186). Oxford, England: Oxford University Press. http://dx.doi.org/10.1093/acprof:oso/9780199737208.003.0008

Frank, J. D., & Frank, J. B. (1993). *Persuasion and healing: A comparative study of psychotherapy* (3rd ed.). Baltimore, MD: Johns Hopkins University Press.

Fuller, F., & Hill, C. E. (1985). Counselor and helpee perceptions of counselor intentions in relation to outcome in a single counseling session. *Journal of Counseling Psychology, 32*, 329–338. http://dx.doi.org/10.1037/0022-0167.32.3.329

Gladwell, M. (2007). *Blink: The power of thinking without thinking.* New York, NY: Little, Brown and Company.

Goldfried, M. R. (1980). Toward the delineation of therapeutic change principles. *American Psychologist, 35*, 991–999. http://dx.doi.org/10.1037/0003-066X.35.11.991

Henry, W. P., Schacht, T. E., Strupp, H. H., Butler, S. F., & Binder, J. L. (1993). Effects of training in time-limited dynamic psychotherapy: Mediators of therapists' responses to training. *Journal of Consulting and Clinical Psychology, 61*, 441–447. http://dx.doi.org/10.1037/0022-006X.61.3.441

Hill, C. E. (1978). Development of a counselor verbal response category. *Journal of Counseling Psychology, 25*, 461–468. http://dx.doi.org/10.1037/0022-0167.25.5.461

Hill, C. E. (2014). *Helping skills: Facilitating exploration, insight, and action* (4th ed.). Washington, DC: American Psychological Association. http://dx.doi.org/10.1037/14345-000

Hill, C. E., Anderson, T., Kline, K., McClintock, A. S., Cranston, S. M., McCarrick, S. M., . . . Gregor, M. (2016). Helping skills training for undergraduate students: Who should we select and train? *The Counseling Psychologist, 44*, 50–77. http://dx.doi.org/10.1177/0011000015613142

Hill, C. E., Baumann, E., Shafran, N., Gupta, S., Morrison, A., Rojas, A. E., . . . Gelso, C. J. (2015). Is training effective? A study of counseling psychology doctoral trainees in a psychodynamic/interpersonal training clinic. *Journal of Counseling Psychology, 62,* 184–201. http://dx.doi.org/10.1037/cou0000053

Hill, C. E., Helms, J. E., Tichenor, V., Spiegel, S. B., O'Grady, K. E., & Perry, E. S. (1988). The effects of therapist response modes in brief psychotherapy. *Journal of Counseling Psychology, 35,* 222–233. http://dx.doi.org/10.1037/0022-0167.35.3.222

Hill, C. E., & Kellems, I. S. (2002). Development and use of the Helping Skills Measure to assess client perceptions of the effects of training and of helping skills in sessions. *Journal of Counseling Psychology, 49,* 264–272. http://dx.doi.org/10.1037/0022-0167.49.2.264

Hill, C. E., Roffman, M., Stahl, J., Friedman, S., Hummel, A., & Wallace, C. (2008). Helping skills training for undergraduates: Outcomes and predictors of outcomes. *Journal of Counseling Psychology, 55,* 359–370. http://dx.doi.org/10.1037/0022-0167.55.3.359

Hill, C. E., Spangler, P. T., Jackson, J., & Chui, H. (2014). Training undergraduate students to use insight skills: Integrating results across three studies. *The Counseling Psychologist, 42,* 800–820. http://dx.doi.org/10.1177/0011000014542602

Hill, C. E., Spiegel, S. B., Hoffman, M. A., Kivlighan, D. M., Jr., & Gelso, C. J. (in press). Therapist expertise in psychotherapy revisited. *The Counseling Psychologist.*

Hill, C. E., Sullivan, C., Knox, S., & Schlosser, L. (2007). Becoming therapists: Experiences of novice trainees in a beginning graduate class. *Psychotherapy: Theory, Research, Practice, Training, 44,* 434–449. http://dx.doi.org/10.1037/0033-3204.44.4.434

Hollon, S. D. (1999). Allegiance effects in treatment research: A commentary. *Clinical Psychology: Science and Practice, 6,* 107–112. http://dx.doi.org/10.1093/clipsy.6.1.107

Ivey, A. E., D'Andrea, M. Ivey, M. B., & Simek-Morgan, L. (2002). *Theories of counseling and psychotherapy: A multicultural perspective* (5th ed.). Boston, MA: Allyn and Bacon.

Kahneman, D. (2011). *Thinking, fast and slow.* New York: Farrar, Straus and Giroux.

Kolden, G. G., Klein, M. H., Wang, C., & Austin, S. B. (2011). Congruence/Genuineness. In J. C. Norcross (Ed.), *Psychotherapy relationships that work: Evidence-Based Responsiveness* (2nd ed., pp. 187–202). Oxford, England: Oxford University Press.

Orlinsky, D. E., & Howard, K. I. (1986). Process and outcome in psychotherapy. In S. L. Garfield & A. E. Bergin (Eds.), *Handbook of psychotherapy and behavior change* (3rd ed., pp. 311–381). New York, NY: Wiley.

Owen, J., Tao, K. W., Imel, Z., Wampold, B. E., & Rodolfa, E. (2014). Addressing racial and ethnic micro-aggressions in therapy. *Professional Psychology: Research and Practice, 45,* 283–290. http://dx.doi.org/10.1037/a0037420

Pinto-Coelho, K., Hill, C. E., & Kivlighan, D. M. (2016). Therapist self-disclosure in psychodynamic psychotherapy: A mixed-methods investigation. *Counselling Psychology Quarterly, 29,* 29–52. http://dx.doi.org/10.1080/09515070.2015.1072496

Ridley, C. R., Kelly, S. M., & Mollen, D. (2011). Microskills training: Evolution, reexamination, and call for reform. *The Counseling Psychologist, 39,* 800–824. http://dx.doi.org/10.1177/0011000010378438

Rogers, C. R. (1957). The necessary and sufficient conditions of therapeutic personality change. *Journal of Consulting Psychology, 21,* 95–103. http://dx.doi.org/10.1037/h0045357

Sharpless, B. A., & Barber, J. P. (2009). A conceptual and empirical review of the meaning, measurement, development, and teaching of intervention competence in clinical psychology. *Clinical Psychology Review, 29,* 47–56. http://dx.doi.org/10.1016/j.cpr.2008.09.008

Stiles, W. B. (1992). *Describing talk.* Newbury Park, CA: Sage.

Stiles, W. B., Hill, C. E., & Elliott, R. (2015). Looking both ways. *Psychotherapy Research, 25,* 282–293. http://dx.doi.org/10.1080/10503307.2014.981681

Sue, D. W., Arredondo, P., & McDavis, R. (1992). Multicultural counseling competencies and standards: A call to the profession. *Journal of Counseling & Development, 70,* 477–486. http://dx.doi.org/10.1002/j.1556-6676.1992.tb01642.x

Sue, D. W., Capodilupo, C. M., Torino, G. C., Bucceri, J. M., Holder, A. M., Nadal, K. L., & Esquilin, M. (2007). Racial microaggressions in everyday life: Implications for clinical practice. *American Psychologist, 62,* 271–286. http://dx.doi.org/10.1037/0003-066X.62.4.271

Tseng, W., Chang, S. C., & Nishozono, M. (2005). *Asian culture and psychotherapy: Implications for East and West.* Honolulu: University of Hawaii Press.

Wampold, B. E., & Imel, Z. E. (2015). *The great psychotherapy debate: The evidence for what makes psychotherapy work.* New York, NY: Routledge.

Webb, C. A., DeRubeis, R. J., & Barber, J. P. (2010). Therapist adherence/competence and treatment outcome: A meta-analytic review. *Journal of Consulting and Clinical Psychology, 78,* 200–211. http://dx.doi.org/10.1037/a0018912

Whaley, A. L., & Davis, K. E. (2007). Cultural competence and evidence-based practice in mental health services. *American Psychologist, 62,* 563–574.

9

THE CONTRIBUTIONS OF CLIENT CULTURE TO DIFFERENTIAL THERAPIST EFFECTIVENESS

JEFFREY A. HAYES, JESSE OWEN, AND HELENE A. NISSEN-LIE

Some therapists produce better outcomes than others because they are more adept at working effectively with various aspects of clients' culture. The central premise of this chapter is that a culturally effective therapist has developed a multicultural orientation (MCO; i.e., a humble, respectful, and open approach to addressing culture in therapy) rather than a specific set of multicultural competencies (MCCs). We elaborate on this concept further by noting at the outset that we believe this premise to be true for every theoretical approach to therapy, because culture is interwoven into all clients' views of themselves, their presenting problems, and what they consider to be therapeutic. Given the space limitations and the intentional focus on therapist effectiveness in this chapter, we will not delve into a broad discussion around the role of culture in therapy. Indeed, a great deal already has been written about this topic. This literature suggests that culture influences one's identity, communication style, values, and norms (Matsumoto, 2007). In the

http://dx.doi.org/10.1037/0000034-010
How and Why Are Some Therapists Better Than Others? Understanding Therapist Effects, L. G. Castonguay and C. E. Hill (Eds.)
Copyright © 2017 by the American Psychological Association. All rights reserved.

context of psychotherapy, clients' and therapists' culturally influenced beliefs about mental health and psychopathology, treatment goals, and useful interventions can be challenging, even delicate, topics to address, and therefore, they are frequently avoided or not explicitly discussed. Existing literature on culturally competent therapy offers suggestions for how to effectively address these topics, as we discuss subsequently.

At the same time, much of the existing literature on culture and therapy suffers from three significant and related problems. First, the literature is largely ethnocentric, in that a high percentage of authors are from the United States and their writing reflects issues that are most salient in the United States. Second, and by extension, scholarly discussions of culture and therapy typically are cast in a framework characterized by factors related to power, discrimination, prejudice, and oppression. These issues are particularly problematic in the United States, as they are in other countries that share similar sociohistorical features, but the role of culture in psychotherapy need not be understood solely within this context, as we hope to make clear. Third, among the many different components of culture, race and ethnicity often are privileged in terms of the attention they receive in the psychotherapy literature. Again, this is a natural consequence of historical and current sociopolitical factors in the United States, and elsewhere, pertaining to race and ethnicity and their effects on psychological well-being. Given that groups of people are marginalized, disempowered, and otherwise ill-treated because of their culture, we necessarily address these issues in this chapter but do restrict not our focus to them. Culture affects a multitude of therapy-relevant factors, even under circumstances where an individual is not suffering because of their culture.

In this chapter, we consider *culture* broadly, as referring to a group of people who share common history, values, beliefs, symbols, and rituals. The cultural groups to which one belongs include (but are not limited to) gender, religion, ethnicity, disability status, sexual orientation, race, and age. We address the influence of culture on differential therapist effectiveness in a manner that we hope will elucidate understanding of this important phenomenon and ultimately facilitate the practice of psychotherapy.

CULTURE AND EVIDENCE-BASED PSYCHOTHERAPY

Evidence-based psychotherapy represents "the integration of the best available research with clinical expertise in the context of patient characteristics, *culture* [emphasis added], and preferences" (APA Presidential Task Force on Evidence-Based Practice, 2006, p. 271). Developed in a European context, conventional psychotherapy includes certain underlying cultural assumptions that may better fit White people from Europe or North America than people of other continents. Being closely situated within an individualistic worldview, psychotherapy, as a specific form of healing, may need a fundamental reorientation to better serve people with a more collectivist orientation. Indeed, research suggests that culturally adapted psychotherapy may be more effective with racial and ethnic minority clients than unadapted, conventional therapies (Benish, Quintana, & Wampold, 2011). This cultural adaptation may take place in how therapists address clients' "illness myth." That is, more effective therapists seem to explain clients' mental health problems and provide a rationale for specific therapy interventions in a manner that is congruent with the client's beliefs about psychological suffering and its remedy (Wampold & Imel, 2015). Our own sense is that research in this area is in its infancy, but it holds tremendous promise and awaits further development before more specific statements can be made with confidence.

RECENT RESEARCH ON THERAPIST EFFECTS AND CLIENT CULTURE

Research has begun to emerge that examines therapists' cultural competence directly as a function of client outcomes rather than relying on therapist, client, or observer estimates. The assumption underlying these studies is that therapists who are more culturally competent will produce better outcomes across culturally diverse clients than will less culturally competent therapists. For example, Imel et al. (2011) found that, of the 13 therapists they studied, some were more effective with racial and ethnic minority clients and others were more effective with racial and ethnic majority clients, where effectiveness was defined in terms of clients' reduced cannabis use. Similar results were obtained in a study of 36 therapists and 228 clients at a university training clinic (Hayes, Owen, & Bieschke, 2015). Outcome in this study was defined in terms of reduction in client distress as measured by the Outcome Questionnaire-45. Larrison, Schoppelrey, Hack-Ritzo, and Korr (2011) studied a larger sample of therapists ($n = 62$) and clients ($n = 551$; 25% minorities) from 13 community mental health centers. They found evidence of differential therapist effectiveness with racial and ethnic majority and minority clients. Based on a measure of psychological symptoms and functioning, 12 therapists had better outcomes for racial and ethnic majority clients, 24 therapists had better outcomes for racial and ethnic minority clients, and 26 therapists had comparable outcomes for majority and minority clients. Of the many demographic and psychological predictors that were examined (e.g., therapist race, burnout), only therapists' ratings of the quality of their relationships with clients who were not of their race significantly predicted outcome. Unfortunately, in this study, some therapists saw as few as one minority client, and the median number of minority clients per therapist was only two, undermining the robustness of the study's findings. In a larger study of 3,825 clients seen by 251 therapists at 45 university counseling centers, evidence was found for disparities within therapists' caseloads in their effectiveness with racial and ethnic minority and majority clients, though effect sizes were small (Hayes, McAleavey, Castonguay, & Locke, 2016). Disparities within therapists' caseloads were not a function of any therapist variable that was studied, such as gender, years of experience, theoretical orientation, or—as was true in the other studies reviewed previously—race or ethnicity. These null effects are important as they highlight that no therapist is immune to having outcome disparities in their caseload. That is, cultural disparities within therapists' caseloads are not problematic only for therapists who belong to a majority culture. The findings also suggested that it is possible to identify therapists who demonstrate competence with racial and ethnic majority and minority clients and who might serve as models from whom other therapists could learn. The characteristics that these therapists share is an important issue for empirical investigation.

PREVAILING MYTHS ABOUT THE CULTURALLY COMPETENT THERAPIST

In general, the practice of psychotherapy has been criticized for overemphasizing intrapsychic phenomena and underemphasizing the role of social and environmental factors in the development and relief of mental health problems (Orlinsky, 2009). This same concern may be levied at therapists who become "culturally encapsulated," defining reality according to one set of cultural assumptions, acting insensitively toward cultural variations, and judging others from their own self-referent criteria.

At the other extreme, literature exists concerning characteristics of the culturally competent therapist. In early writings on the topic, the culturally competent therapist was championed as someone who was culturally aware, sensitive, and knowledgeable (Pedersen & Lefley, 1986), but rigorous empirical support for these claims has been lacking. Initial studies tended to rely on clients', therapists', and observers' perceptions of therapists' cultural competence rather than directly testing the assumption that more culturally competent therapists would produce better outcomes. In fact, therapists' self-perceived cultural competence has been found to be unrelated to client ratings of therapists' cultural competence (Worthington, Mobley, Franks, & Tan, 2000), as well as to actual client improvement in therapy (Larrison et al., 2011). Still further, a recent meta-analysis found wide variability in the extent to which client ratings of therapists' cultural competence are associated with actual outcomes (Tao, Owen, Pace, & Imel, 2015).

As a result of the burgeoning theoretical literature toward the end of the 20th century, coupled with the lack of corresponding empirical support, we believe that a number of unsubstantiated beliefs about culturally competent therapists have been promulgated. Among them are the following:

- Culturally competent therapists have a high degree of knowledge about many different cultures.
- There is a therapy-specific language required to conduct effective therapy with cultural minority clients.
- When working with cultural majority clients, therapists do not need to concern themselves with matters of culture.

As we will demonstrate subsequently, evidence suggests that therapists with cultural expertise acknowledge when they do not have specific knowledge about a culture and have a high tolerance for not knowing, and at the same time recognize that cultural socialization processes effect the mental health of all individuals. Culturally competent therapists strive toward an attitude of openness and humility when actively addressing issues of culture, and other kinds of issues relevant to clients' mental health, with both cultural majority and minority clients.

The myths mentioned previously, especially that therapists need particular knowledge or skills about cultural phenomena to address them in therapy, have influenced the training of a new generation of psychotherapists and have unnecessarily caused many promising therapists-in-training to doubt their natural abilities when addressing issues of culture in therapy. At other times, these myths have caused therapists-in-training to miss opportunities to work productively with clients' cultural characteristics when this would be useful or even essential. Integration of cultural aspects, such as a client's religious beliefs, is necessary for therapeutic effectiveness, as illustrated in the following example:[1]

A newly graduated clinical psychologist working in a public outpatient clinic met with a 25-year-old woman with severe depression, which included long-lasting suicidal ideation and hopelessness. The therapist tried to understand the client's despair using existential perspectives on human development, attuning to important choices of the client's life stage (e.g., finding the right profession, commitment in a romantic relationship), as well as addressing here-and-now stressors, combined with psychodynamic concepts of early relationship experiences and transference dynamics. Nothing happened.

---

[1]Client identifiers have been changed to maintain patient confidentiality.

The client reported a steady wish to die; no intervention seemed to make any difference. Gradually the therapist also went into a state of despair, and decided that seeking consultation from a more senior therapist would be wise. A highly experienced psychiatrist joined one of the sessions, also to assess whether the client needed hospitalization. Having read through the client's record beforehand and learning that she came from a region in which Christianity has a central place, the psychiatrist asked if the client believed in God. The patient nodded, looking down. The psychiatrist asked where God was for the client, and she looked up, in tears: "He has abandoned me, I am not even worthy of God's love." This turned out to constitute a shift in the therapeutic dialogue and one the therapist explored in more depth in the following sessions. The therapist finally had a place from which to connect with the patient, which helped the process move forward.

The therapist had not seen this as an opportunity, before the session with the psychiatrist. This may have been because of the assumption that therapists do not need to focus on cultural aspects with a cultural majority client, that the issue of religious beliefs is not relevant in a psychotherapeutic process, or perhaps more important, that addressing it requires specific skills. The therapist had not intervened in a way that brought to the foreground how important the client's faith was to her and had missed an opportunity to connect with her on a topic that truly mattered. After the session with the psychiatrist, the therapist felt more at ease addressing how the patient felt about God, and indirectly, about herself and the state of her hopelessness. The therapy could now also work on how the client saw God, and whether she could perceive God as a more benevolent figure to turn to for hope rather than a condemning entity who had given up on her, and on how the client could find her own, autonomous way in the religious community to which she belonged. By tying this focus in with other therapeutic focuses, the therapist helped the client move on in her development toward a healthier self-state. This learning experience countered some myths about cultural competence that were unconsciously present in the therapist, and contributed to broadening the therapist's understanding of therapeutic effectiveness with cultural majority and minority clients.

THEORETICAL IMPLICATIONS OF THE EMPIRICAL LITERATURE

It is becoming evident that therapists differ in their ability to treat patients on the basis of patient cultural demographics. What is less clear is why such disparities exist. Although it may be tempting to look toward therapists' MCCs as a potential source of this variation, we would like to offer an alternative, though related, perspective of MCO. To distinguish between the two, we first briefly review and critique literature on MCCs and then describe what is meant by MCO.

As mentioned previously, therapists' MCCs are commonly defined by their knowledge of various cultural groups; the skills to navigate cultural processes within therapy; and the self-awareness of personal biases, cultural identity, and various worldviews (Sue, 2003). This theory has had quite an impact on the landscape of multicultural training, research, and practice (Tao et al., 2015). It is important to consider what is being professed through this model. The concept of *competencies* would seem to suggest that there are sets of competencies that can be acquired (e.g., knowledge structures, skills) and that predict therapy outcomes. Additionally, there is an implied demarcation where one can reliably differentiate competent therapists and incompetent therapists (e.g., can a supervisor determine and assign a grade reflecting that a supervisee is not competent?). Relatedly, those competencies are assumed to be judged or assessed in a manner that is characteristic of the therapist and not idiosyncratic to any given client–therapist dyadic interaction (Owen, Leach, Wampold, & Rodolfa, 2011). In our estimation, these criteria have not been fully tested, established, or supported in the psychotherapy literature— even though MCCs were proposed more than 3 decades ago (Pedersen & Lefley, 1986).

The MCC model implicitly describes what we will call *common cultural processes* and *specific cultural processes*. For example, Budge (2015) described the processes needed to conduct a psychological evaluation and write a corresponding report for transgender individuals to meet the requirements for medical procedures related to changes in gender identity. There is no question that this specific knowledge is necessary to provide ethical care for transgender clients. At the same time, the idea of specific cultural processes becomes a bit more difficult to identify in some cases. For example, how much specific knowledge do therapists need to demonstrate to be competent to treat a Black male client? How much more specific knowledge would be needed if the client also identified as gay? Are there different skills that should be used with a White, Protestant, middle class, lesbian client with depression as compared with a Mexican American, Catholic, upper middle class, heterosexual male also with depression? If so, what empirical support do we have to answer these questions? As illustrated here, the possible combinations of clients' intersecting cultural identities, coupled with diagnostic presentation, interacting with therapists' multiple cultural identities, makes the pursuit of understanding specific cultural processes very challenging. Even worse, the focus on specific cultural processes may promote stereotyping without accounting for within-group cultural differences (e.g., should therapists use interpretations with Asian American clients, or only with East Asian American clients, or only with East Asian American clients with low levels of acculturation?).

In response to these difficulties, Owen (2013) explicated a framework of common cultural processes in therapy, known as *therapists'* MCO, which describes a way of being with clients versus a way of doing therapy (Owen, Tao, Leach, & Rodolfa, 2011). There are three pillars to the MCO framework: (a) therapists' cultural humility, (b) therapists' ability to attend to cultural issues within sessions (i.e., cultural opportunities), and (c) therapists' cultural comfort. Simply put, the MCO framework proposes that therapists need to approach interactions with clients surrounding their cultural identities in a culturally humble manner, by being curious, nonassuming, open, and respectful. Therapists should also listen for cultural markers and create opportunities to weave discussion of clients' cultural identities into the treatment process, when doing so is responsive to and in the best interests of clients (see Chapter 4, this volume). Therapists also need to engage clients in cultural discussions with comfort and ease. Importantly, the MCO framework is intended to help bolster and enhance therapists' current therapeutic practices. The MCO framework is not intended to provide an alternative, stand-alone therapeutic approach, and it is designed to be flexible such that therapists from various therapeutic approaches could integrate it into their work. Moreover, as discussed next, each aspect of the MCO framework has been associated with better client outcomes or reduced ethnic disparities in therapists' caseloads.

In contrast to competencies, the MCO framework emphasizes the degree to which therapists have an MCO. Therapists' MCO can be thought of as a way in which they see, interact with, and understand the world via cultural identities, cultural interactions, and varying worldviews. Just as some therapists tend to enact more cognitive–behavioral therapy techniques in sessions than others, there are also therapists who are more oriented than others to understand, engage, and be responsive to cultural dynamics in session. In this way, therapists' MCO shapes how they conceptualize their clients' presenting concerns, select, and/or modify treatment approaches, as well as how they relate to their clients. For example, therapists may recognize that they need to better understand clients' cultural heritage prior to deciding if challenging a deeply held core belief related to the clients' cultural upbringing is wise. Moreover, the MCO framework asserts that the degree to which cultural aspects need to be explicitly addressed in session is likely to vary from session to session as well as from client to client, even those from cultural minority statuses. For example, some clients may not need homework assignments for cognitive–behavioral therapy to be effective, or at least not after every session. Expert cognitive–behavioral therapists skillfully integrate homework in a manner that is responsive to individual clients (see Chapter 4, this volume). Similarly, culturally oriented therapists recognize the ways in which attending to cultural considerations is in clients' best interest.

Therapists whose practice is guided by an orientation (whether an MCO, a theoretical orientation, or both) ideally ought to be motivated to learn more about their orientation and be deliberate in enacting it. Rather than seeking to acquire competencies, according to the MCO framework, therapists should be motivated to view cultural dynamics as an evolving process, with some aspects unique to the client–therapist dyad and other aspects being part of the therapist's personal and professional development. In doing so, therapists should develop metacognitive processes to monitor their own development when working with clients who have varying cultural identities. For example, if a therapist is not feeling comfortable in session with a financially impoverished client, can he or she recognize these feelings and seek consultation to better understand his or her reactions? Additionally, the therapist should be able to determine if this reaction is unique to this one client or to multiple, similar clients. The highly effective therapist is able to recognize and manage her or his culturally based reactions to clients (see Gelso & Mohr, 2001). In summary, the MCO framework provides therapists a way to understand common cultural processes in psychotherapy.

RESEARCH SUPPORT FOR THERAPISTS' MULTICULTURAL ORIENTATION

In recent research, clients' perceptions of their therapists' cultural humility, missed opportunities, and cultural comfort have been linked to better therapy outcomes and/or helped explain racial and ethnic disparities within therapists' caseloads. For example, clients' perceptions of their therapists' cultural humility have been positively associated with therapy outcomes in four studies, including more than 3,000 clients (Hook, Davis, Owen, Worthington, & Utsey, 2013; Owen et al., 2014, 2015, 2016). Interestingly, Owen et al. (2014) found that clients' perceptions of their therapists' cultural humility was only positively associated with therapy outcomes for clients whose cultural identity (in this case, religious identity) was particularly salient. Additionally, Owen et al. (2016) found that clients who perceived that their therapist missed opportunities to discuss cultural issues in session had worse therapy outcomes, and this was more pronounced for those clients who rated their therapist as lower in cultural humility. Moreover, Owen et al. (2015) examined how therapists' cultural comfort might account for culture-related disparities in client dropout within therapists' caseloads. Racial and ethnic majority and minority clients rated their therapists on the Counselor Comfort Scale (e.g., "My therapist appeared calm, at ease, comfortable in session."), and a discrepancy variable was created for each therapist between their majority and minority clients' ratings. Dropout was predicted by therapists' cultural comfort, controlling for client ratings of therapist comfort. The researchers found that therapists' cultural comfort accounted for 6.1% of the variance in client outcomes and that client ratings of therapist comfort did not predict outcome.

Although these studies are an important step forward, there is relatively little research that directly examines differential therapist effectiveness and culture-related variables. In one of the few studies in this area, Owen, Leach, et al. (2011) gathered data from 143 clients and 31 therapists and found that therapists accounted for approximately 8.5% of the variance in client outcomes. Therapists' aggregate ratings of MCCs accounted for less than 1% of this variance. Given that client ratings of MCCs within therapists' caseloads were significantly associated with better outcomes, it may be that the processes attended to by culturally expert therapists are not generalizable from client to client, but rather a natural and unfolding process occurs that is unique to each client–therapist dyad. Alternatively, Owen et al. (2015, 2016) found that therapists accounted for the variance in their client ratings of cultural humility (22%), cultural comfort (11%), and missed opportunities (5%). Collectively, these studies suggest that there may, in fact, be specific characteristics that culturally expert therapists possess, and processes that they attend to in session, that distinguish them from less expert therapists.

IMPLICATIONS FOR PRACTICE

There are many practical ways to be culturally oriented with clients. Starting with the intake process, it is important to explore and assess clients' cultural identities. To do so, we encourage therapists to use open-ended questions for clients to discuss their cultural identities. Of the many different aspects of clients' culture (e.g., gender, sexual orientation, race, age, ethnicity, religion, disability, socioeconomic status), some will be more central to their identities and others will be less salient. For example, some therapists routinely ask clients in an initial session the extent to which religion and spirituality play an important role in their lives. Doing so creates an opening for clients to talk about a part of their culture that may not be evident to the therapists. Additionally, for clients who are religious, the question allows for subsequent exploration of the client's religious orientation and whether religion plays a role in either helping the client cope with problems or exacerbating her or his problems, as shown in the previous case example (Pargament, 1997). Third, initiating discussion of religion and spirituality in an inviting, nonjudgmental manner communicates to clients that the therapist is not likely to ignore, minimize, or pathologize their beliefs.

During the intake process, standardized forms also could include multiple, open-ended questions for clients to describe their cultural identities. This would allow therapists to learn how clients identify themselves in their own words. Moreover, doing so could avoid problems that can arise when therapists rely on limited categories and labels, such as "White" (which is an inexact descriptor for most people of European ancestry) and "male" and "female" (which may not be inclusive for transgender and gender nonconforming clients). Additionally, it might be useful to have a set of single items on an intake form for clients to rate the salience of various aspects of their culture. By doing so, therapists can avoid assuming that a particular aspect of a client's culture is important to them, as is often assumed of cultural minority clients.

Therapists can also take advantage of opportunities to attend to culture using what we call *cultural session markers*, where a deeper discussion of cultural issues may be warranted. Consider the following example in which the therapist attends to a cultural session maker:

Client: The loss of my husband has really taken a toll on me. I feel like I can't trust anything in my life anymore. I used to go church, but now my faith in God is gone. . . . Actually my reason for getting up, going on, living is all gone. I mean I feel so helpless, like I don't know what to do.

Therapist: I really get that this loss has hit at the core of your life. . . . I can see you are feeling really crushed right now, with little hope.

Client: Yes (crying).

Therapist: I wonder what it means for you that you have lost your faith?

Here the therapist had an opportunity to follow the client's sense of loss, depression, and suicide ideation. However, the therapist took the opportunity to explore the client's faith in God. Later in the session the therapist went back to address the client's suicide ideation. The therapist also could have addressed the suicide ideation first and then the client's faith in God. Ultimately, it was important that the faith in God was addressed, as this may have provided information about how the client copes with stress, finds social support, and reintegrates her sense of self.

Of course, clients do not always introduce cultural opportunities, which may necessitate that the therapist check in or create them. Consider a different version of the previous exchange:

Client: The loss of my husband has really taken a toll on me. I feel like I can't trust anything in my life anymore. I used to go church, but now my faith in God is gone. . . . Actually my

	reason for getting up, going on, living is all gone. I mean I feel so helpless, like I don't know what to do.
Therapist:	I really get that this loss has hit at the core of your life.... I can see you are feeling really crushed right now, with little hope.
Client:	Yes (crying).
Therapist:	I am not sure if this fits for you, but sometimes when people lose a loved one, they turn to faith or spirituality to cope or even question their faith. Does that fit for you?

In this case the therapist uses general knowledge about how individuals cope with grief and loss and creates an opportunity to discuss the client's faith and spirituality, if it is important to the client.

Although the previous examples highlight cultural opportunities, it is also true that therapists can feel uncomfortable with clients, which at times can lead to statements that are offensive and/or invalidating. In particular, microaggressions—subtle, often indirect, messages that are invalidating or insulting to clients regarding their cultural heritage—have been shown to negatively influence the therapeutic relationship and therapy outcomes (Tao et al., 2015). Consider the following example of a microaggression committed by a White therapist to a Mexican American client:

Client:	Over this past week, I've been trying to stay upbeat and to keep myself motivated. These past few months have just sucked—I can't kick these negative feelings. Even when I'm really putting in the effort, I go to work, push through the day, and (sigh) when I get home, I just have to unwind and reboot, and it doesn't feel like enough. It takes everything I've got just to tolerate my day and then I just settle in front of the TV, which makes my girlfriend upset.
Therapist:	Hmm, yeah, it sounds like you are spending so much energy at work, that you aren't able to take care of yourself when you get home. Does that sound right to you?
Client:	Exactly, work takes it out of me, and I don't have the motivation to put forth to work on my relationship or to spend time with my family and that's what I really want to do. I miss them and I miss feeling like myself.
Therapist:	So, you are in survival mode, just trying to make it through? Sounds hard to keep this up. What do you think is contributing to that?
Client:	I think in part it has to do with my being the only Mexican man in my office. Like I feel so on edge without a feeling of community and connection with my colleagues, and it

>   wears on me all the time. I'm on my own and people aren't really reaching out. It's exhausting trying to make it all come together and being by myself.
>
> *Therapist:* (feeling frustrated with the client) Well, after listening to you these past few sessions, I'm not really sure if you being Mexican has anything to do with it. . . . A lot of people experiencing depression like you are, feel lonely and isolated.
>
> *Client:* I mean, maybe, I guess so.

In this exchange, the therapist is feeling frustrated with the client's conveying his experience as an ethnic minority, and does not attempt to join with him in this session. In turn, the therapist minimizes the client's cultural identity, essentially invalidating the client's sense of how he understands his world and makes attributions about his distress. Following this exchange, a skilled therapist would read the client's tempered response and address the misstep. In doing so, it is important for the therapist to take a culturally humble approach—assuming an "other-oriented" perspective, and seek to better understand the client's cultural background. A clear mistake for the therapist would be to continue to provide explanations for why her intervention makes sense to the client. Outside of the session, the therapist might want to seek consultation to learn more about why this statement was a microaggression and how best to avoid committing similar mistakes in the future. We suspect that one of the factors that differentiates more and less effective therapists is the extent to which they seek and make use of supervision in which issues of culture are explored. Although this is an empirical question, therapists who do not engage in meaningful supervision run the risk of isolating themselves professionally and curtailing their own effectiveness. On the other hand, therapists who are motivated to regularly seek consultation and feedback from other therapists tend to have excellent, and likely well-deserved, reputations. This is what is entailed in the concept of *deliberate practice*, which is discussed in more depth in Chapter 2.

At the graduate-student level, helping trainees become more adept at addressing cultural issues is a challenging task. Graduate training programs must decide the extent to which to infuse courses with a cultural emphasis versus having a stand-alone course in a curriculum. In addition, when cultural issues are raised in the classroom, emotions can run strong, and it takes a skilled instructor to effectively facilitate discussion around cultural topics. Furthermore, instructors who decide to use experiential learning to teach about cultural issues in therapy must be particularly aware of the potential for planned exercises to generate strong reactions. Whereas straight didactic instruction may be a safer alternative, we have doubts about the effectiveness of such a pedagogical approach, especially one that takes a "cookbook" or "silo" approach to cultural issues, as is too often the case. In other words, textbooks and courses often are arranged so that one week students are supposed to learn about sexual orientation, the next week about socioeconomic status, the next week about disability, and so on, as if people with disabilities don't have a sexual orientation or a socioeconomic status. The focus on only one aspect at a time of a person's culture simplifies reality, runs the risk of promoting stereotypes, and does not sufficiently prepare students to work with real people who have complex, intersecting cultural identities. And, of course, the problem is not restricted to graduate training but also extends to the professional development of practicing therapists who may be required to attend expensive and time-consuming continuing education workshops, the value of which is unsubstantiated. We believe that supervision is perhaps the most useful venue where graduate students and practicing therapists can develop their cultural expertise. Within the context of a safe, supportive relationship (which may not characterize the classroom or the continuing education workshop auditorium), graduate students and therapists can make themselves vulnerable, seek guidance on problematic issues related to culture, and receive constructive feedback from a faculty member or, in the case of practicing therapists, peers whom they trust.

CONCLUSION

There is a growing body of empirical evidence to suggest that differential therapist effectiveness may be a function of clients' cultural characteristics. One model for explaining why some therapists are more effective than others at addressing cultural issues in therapy centers on therapists' MCO, and this model has begun to garner empirical support. In particular, factors such as therapists' humility, cultural comfort, and attention to opportunities to work productively with cultural issues in therapy may differentiate more and less effective therapists, although more research needs to be done in this realm. We also see promising ways in which these concepts tie in with characteristics that are becoming demonstrated as generally effective therapist characteristics (see Chapter 2). A shift away from emphasizing cultural competence and toward the development of therapists' MCO may represent a valuable transition in the training of future therapists.

REFERENCES

APA Presidential Task Force on Evidence-Based Practice. (2006). Evidence-based practice in psychology. *American Psychologist, 61,* 271–285. http://dx.doi.org/10.1037/0003-066X.61.4.271

Benish, S. G., Quintana, S., & Wampold, B. E. (2011). Culturally adapted psychotherapy and the legitimacy of myth: A direct-comparison meta-analysis. *Journal of Counseling Psychology, 58,* 279–289. http://dx.doi.org/10.1037/a0023626

Budge, S. L. (2015). Psychotherapists as gatekeepers: An evidence-based case study highlighting the role and process of letter writing for transgender clients. *Psychotherapy, 52,* 287–297. http://dx.doi.org/10.1037/pst0000034

Gelso, C. J., & Mohr, J. J. (2001). The working alliance and transference/countertransference relationship: Their manifestation with racial/ethnic and sexual orientation minority clients and therapists. *Applied & Preventive Psychology, 10,* 51–68. http://dx.doi.org/10.1016/S0962-1849(05)80032-0

Hayes, J. A., McAleavey, A. A., Castonguay, L. G., & Locke, B. D. (2016). Psychotherapists' outcomes with White and racial/ethnic minority clients: First, the good news. *Journal of Counseling Psychology, 63,* 261–268. http://dx.doi.org/10.1037/cou0000098

Hayes, J. A., Owen, J., & Bieschke, K. J. (2015). Therapist differences in symptom change with racial/ethnic minority clients. *Psychotherapy, 52,* 308–314. http://dx.doi.org/10.1037/a0037957

Hook, J. N., Davis, D. E., Owen, J., Worthington, E. L., & Utsey, S. O. (2013). Cultural humility: Measuring openness to culturally diverse clients. *Journal of Counseling Psychology, 60,* 353–366. http://dx.doi.org/10.1037/a0032595

Imel, Z. E., Baldwin, S., Atkins, D. C., Owen, J., Baardseth, T., & Wampold, B. E. (2011). Racial/ethnic disparities in therapist effectiveness: A conceptualization and initial study of cultural competence. *Journal of Counseling Psychology, 58,* 290–298. http://dx.doi.org/10.1037/a0023284

Larrison, C. R., Schoppelrey, S. L., Hack-Ritzo, S., & Korr, W. S. (2011). Clinician factors related to outcome differences between Black and White patients at CMHCs. *Psychiatric Services, 62,* 525–531. http://dx.doi.org/10.1176/ps.62.5.pss6205_0525

Matsumoto, D. (2007). Culture, context, and behavior. *Journal of Personality, 75,* 1285–1320. http://dx.doi.org/10.1111/j.1467-6494.2007.00476.x

Orlinsky, D. E. (2009). Research on psychotherapy and the psychotherapeutic profession(s). *European Journal of Psychotherapy and Counselling, 11,* 183–190. http://dx.doi.org/10.1080/13642530902927345

Owen, J. (2013). Early career perspectives on psychotherapy research and practice: Psychotherapist effects, multicultural orientation, and couple interventions. *Psychotherapy, 50,* 496–502. http://dx.doi.org/10.1037/a0034617

Owen, J., Drinane, J., Tao, K., Adelson, J., Hook, J., Davis, D., & Foo Kune, N. (2015). Racial/ethnic disparities in client unilateral termination: The role of therapists' cultural comfort. *Psychotherapy Research.* Advance online publication. http://dx.doi.org/10.1080/10503307.2015.1078517

Owen, J., Jordan, T., Turner, D., Davis, D., Hook, J., & Leach, M. (2014). Therapists' multicultural orientation. *Journal of Psychology and Theology, 42,* 91–99.

Owen, J., Leach, M. M., Wampold, B., & Rodolfa, E. (2011). Client and therapist variability in clients' perceptions of their therapists' multicultural competencies. *Journal of Counseling Psychology, 58*, 1–9. http://dx.doi.org/10.1037/a0021496

Owen, J., Tao, K., Drinane, J., Hook, J., Davis, D., & Foo Kune, N. (2016). Client perceptions of therapists' multicultural orientation: Cultural (missed) opportunities and cultural humility. *Professional Psychology, Research and Practice, 47*, 30–37.

Owen, J. J., Tao, K., Leach, M. M., & Rodolfa, E. (2011). Clients' perceptions of their psychotherapists' multicultural orientation. *Psychotherapy, 48*, 274–282. http://dx.doi.org/10.1037/a0022065

Pargament, K. I. (1997). *The psychology of religion and coping.* New York, NY: Guilford Press.

Pedersen, P. B., & Lefley, H. P. (1986). Introduction to cross-cultural training. *Cross-cultural training for mental health professionals* (pp. 5–10). Springfield, IL: Charles C. Thomas.

Sue, S. (2003). In defense of cultural competency in psychotherapy and treatment. *American Psychologist, 58*, 964–970. http://dx.doi.org/10.1037/0003-066X.58.11.964

Tao, K. W., Owen, J., Pace, B. T., & Imel, Z. E. (2015). A meta-analysis of multicultural competencies and psychotherapy process and outcome. *Journal of Counseling Psychology, 62*, 337–350. http://dx.doi.org/10.1037/cou0000086

Wampold, B. E., & Imel, Z. E. (2015). *The great psychotherapy debate* (2nd ed.). New York, NY: Routledge/Taylor and Francis.

Worthington, R. L., Mobley, M., Franks, R. P., & Tan, J. A. (2000). Multicultural counseling competencies: Verbal content, therapist attributions, and social desirability. *Journal of Counseling Psychology, 47*, 460–468. http://dx.doi.org/10.1037/0022-0167.47.4.460

10

THERAPIST NEGATIVE REACTIONS: HOW TO TRANSFORM TOXIC EXPERIENCES

ABRAHAM W. WOLF, MARVIN R. GOLDFRIED,
AND J. CHRISTOPHER MURAN

One of the psychotherapist's greatest challenges is maintaining a balance between professional standards and managing a range of personal emotional responses when working with clients. As therapists were people before they were professionals, they frequently struggle with feelings of anger, frustration, hatred, boredom, cynicism, indifference, blaming, power struggles, withdrawal, burnout, and other intense and unstable feelings. During the clinical hour, these very private feelings are unwanted, unpredictable, and run counter to their identity as professional and competent clinicians. As Freud (1933) confessed, "No one, who like me, conjures up the most evil of those half-tamed demons that inhabit the human beast, and seeks to wrestle with them, can expect to come through the struggle unscathed" (p. 109). We argue in this chapter, however, that these negative feelings can be important

---

Portions of this chapter were adapted from *Transforming Negative Reactions to Clients: From Frustration to Compassion*, by A. W. Wolf, M. R. Goldfried, and J. Christopher Muran (Eds.), 2013, Washington, DC: American Psychological Association. Copyright 2013 by the American Psychological Association.
http://dx.doi.org/10.1037/0000034-011
How and Why Are Some Therapists Better Than Others? Understanding Therapist Effects, L. G. Castonguay and C. E. Hill (Eds.)
Copyright © 2017 by the American Psychological Association. All rights reserved.

sources of clinical information. Effective therapists are able to manage these feelings and use them to understand clients' behaviors and personalities, strengthen the therapeutic alliance, and improve outcomes.

The premise of this chapter is that successful psychotherapy relies on relational and technical interventions to alleviate psychological pain and that the therapist's experience of negative reactions to his or her clients represents a serious, perhaps the most serious, source of interference in the practice of those interventions. As such, we believe that these experiences and the ways they are dealt with during psychotherapy explain, in least in part, therapist effects—the fact that some therapists are better and, perhaps more particularly in this case, worse than others (see Chapter 1, this volume). It may well be that negative and inappropriately handled reactions may be a potent avenue to help us understand the findings showing that some therapists are harmful to their clients (see Chapter 1). The chapter is also built on the assumption that the ways therapists mind their own experience and mine negative emotions from it affect the process and outcome of treatment by the creation and maintenance of the therapeutic alliance, as well as the competent implementation of techniques specified by various schools of psychotherapy. The importance of the therapist's inner life, the role of inadmissible therapist affect, and the management of countertransference reactions in psychotherapy are discussed further in Chapter 6 of this volume.

We propose that understanding and managing the range of negative therapeutic reactions, from mild irritation to overt expressions of contempt, are necessary but not sufficient conditions for effective psychotherapy. Effective therapists understand (a) how the creation of a therapeutic relationship may, in and of itself, lead to the alleviation of psychological distress, and how their negative reactions impede the creation and maintenance of a healing environment, but they also recognize (b) how to use their experience of their negative reactions as a source of data regarding clients' maladaptive interpersonal relationships and to differentiate these from their own unresolved problems. For therapists who adhere to the use of specific interventions, client resistance to the implementation of those techniques, whether transference interpretations or skills to regulate intense affect, the effective use of interventions depends on how therapists approach the experience and expression of their own frustration. When we speak of the "inner life of the therapist," we are referring to a special form of presence, self-awareness, and immediacy, in which therapists are participant–observers: participants in the interaction but also observers of that interaction, of what is happening moment-to-moment with the client (for a discussion how the concept of presence applies to therapist effects in general, see Chapter 5). We contend that effective therapists balance relational and technical factors and use an awareness of their inner life in the service of this ability, especially the understanding and use of their own negative affect as a significant factor in the successful implementation of those relational and technical interventions.

In this chapter, we first consider the empirical literature on therapists' negative reactions, reviewing survey studies of professional psychologists and research studies on the effects therapists' negative reactions have on the process and outcome of psychotherapy. Next, we present an integrative model for effectively managing negative reactions that is based on a consensus of experienced practitioners who describe their own challenges in this area. Finally, we discuss the implications of managing therapists' negative reactions in psychotherapy training and problems in researching this topic.

The ideas presented in this chapter are based on the contributions of experienced clinicians in the book *Transforming Negative Reactions to Clients: From Frustration to Compassion* (Wolf, Goldfried, & Muran, 2013). That work originated from a series of symposia organized for two annual conventions of the American Psychological Association (APA) dealing with therapists' anger and frustration toward clients. That book focused on a universal, but rarely discussed, experience among therapists: negative feelings toward the very individuals that they trying are to help. By *negative feelings* we refer to a range of challenging affective responses that therapists experience in their practice, including anxiety and panic, hopelessness and despair, shame and humiliation, boredom and neglect, and anger and seduction. Although these responses have typically been discussed in the psychoanalytic literature as *countertransference*, they are increasingly being raised in the behavioral literature as *therapy interfering behaviors*. In the spirit of facilitating discussion across different psychotherapy orientations, we use the term *negative emotions*, focusing specifically on feelings of anger and frustration therapists experience when working with clients.

RESEARCH ON THERAPISTS' NEGATIVE EMOTIONS

Survey Studies

Therapists and researchers have long been aware of the importance of therapists' emotional reactions to clients and how these reactions affect the process and outcome of treatment. In their survey of 285 psychologists, Pope and Tabachnick (1993) found that over 80% reported experiencing feelings of fear, anger, and sexual feelings toward clients in treatment; 90% of them experienced anger at clients for being uncooperative; and more than 50% admitted to raising their voice in anger to clients or having felt so emotionally concerned about clients that it affected their eating, sleeping, or concentration. Clients are aware of when therapists get angry at them. In a sample of 132 clients who completed long-term trauma psychotherapy (Dalenberg, 2004), 64% reported that their therapist had been "illegitimately" angry at them at least once. Of even greater significance is that of the 64% of clients who felt anger from the therapists, over half stated that the episode had temporarily or permanently damaged the therapeutic alliance.

Personal distress, burnout, and negative experiences with clients can impair therapists' functioning to the point that it adversely impacts the process and outcome of treatment. Pope, Tabachnick, and Keith-Spiegel (1987) reported that even though 85% of members of APA Division 29 (Society for the Advancement of Psychotherapy) believed that it was unethical to work when too distressed, 60% admitted that they had done so in the past. In a sample of members of APA practice divisions, Guy, Poelstra, and Stark (1989) reported that 74% admitted to experiencing personal distress during the previous 3 years, and of those, 36.7% indicated that it decreased the quality of client care, with 4.6% admitting that it resulted in inadequate care.

Research Studies

The seminal research on how therapists' negative emotions affect the process and outcome of psychotherapy came from the Vanderbilt I and II studies. In their systematic review of these studies, Binder and Strupp (1997) referred to a *negative process*, overt and covert hostile behaviors between therapists and clients that are related to poor outcome. Early in his program of research, Strupp (1980) noted therapists' vulnerability to client's negative emotions and their harmful, even permanent effect on the treatment:

> The plain fact is that any therapist—indeed any human being—cannot remain immune from negative reactions to the suppressed and repressed rage regularly encountered in clients with moderate to severe disturbances. (p. 953)

He went on to add,

> In our study, we failed to encounter a single instance in which a difficult client's hostility and negativism were successfully confronted or resolved . . . therapists' negative responses to difficult clients are far more common and far more intractable than has been generally recognized. (p. 954)

The Vanderbilt studies (Binder & Strupp, 1997) indicated that poor outcomes were associated with a poor or deteriorating alliance in the first three sessions and that the alliance was impacted in these early sessions by therapists' overt and covert hostile reactions to clients' provocative behaviors that were associated with clients' enactments of their problems within the therapeutic relationship. Subsequent research has supported the association of negative process early in treatment and poor treatment outcome

(Henry, Schacht, & Strupp, 1990; Tasca & McMullen, 1992). Even in studies designed to train therapists to detect and manage the maladaptive interpersonal patterns that clients enact in the treatment, negative reactions by therapists were difficult to control (Henry, Schacht, Strupp, Butler, & Binder, 1993). In a study designed to examine the effectiveness of specific therapeutic approaches, Najavits and Strupp (1994) noted that more effective therapists were less blaming, belittling, ignoring, and rejecting. Furthermore, effective therapists tended to be more self-critical, suggesting that more effective therapists were more self-reflective and engaged in greater self-monitoring.

As a whole, the Vanderbilt studies (Binder & Strupp, 1997) on negative process indicate that although the absence of therapists' negative emotions may not directly lead to a positive therapeutic outcome, the presence of therapists' negative reactions is associated with poor treatment outcome. This body of research suggests that ineffective psychotherapy is characterized by therapists' emotional reactivity, which leads to hostile interactions that corrode the therapeutic alliance and lead to poor outcome. This is why we suggest that the negative and inappropriately handled reactions might shed particularly helpful light on one aspect of the therapist effects: the harmful aspect.

Two current research programs that focus on the effect of therapists' negative reactions are the work of Gelso and Hayes on countertransference (Gelso & Hayes, 2007; Hayes, Gelso, & Hummel, 2011) and Safran and Muran on ruptures in the therapeutic alliance (Safran & Muran, 2000; Safran, Muran, & Eubanks-Carter, 2011). Gelso and Hayes emphasized the role of therapists' internal life when they defined *countertransference* as reactions because of therapists' unresolved conflicts. They operationalize countertransference and how therapists manage their responses through the Countertransference Factors Inventory which taps five dimensions of therapist attributes: self-insight, self-integration, anxiety management, empathy, and conceptualizing ability. In a series of meta-analyses, they examined the associations of countertransference, countertransference management, and psychotherapy outcome. Increased countertransference reactions were modestly related to psychotherapy outcome ($r = -.16$), although studies that assessed outcome at the end of treatment showed a stronger association ($r = -.36$) when compared to studies that assess outcome in a given session or series of sessions ($r = -.09$). Therapists who managed their countertransference had fewer reactions ($r = -.14$) and countertransference management resulted in improved psychotherapy outcomes ($r = .45$). Gelso and Hayes's research program on understanding the therapist's inner world, especially their discussion of therapists as wounded healers, provides empirical support for the association between (a) therapists' negative reactions and (b) management of these reactions in relation to treatment process and outcome.

In contrast to Gelso and Hayes (2007; Hayes et al., 2011), who focused on the inner world of therapists, Safran and Muran (2000; Safran et al., 2011) focused on the psychotherapy relationship, specifically, ruptures in the therapeutic alliance. Defined as tension or breakdown in the collaborative relationship between client and therapist, ruptures have two general forms: *withdrawal*, in which clients disengage, and *confrontational*, in which clients express anger or dissatisfaction. In studies that assessed the frequency of client-reported ruptures, results ranged from 19% to 42%; reports of therapists' attempts at rupture repair ranged 22% to 56%. The rupture repair model is a four-stage process of (a) attending to the rupture marker, (b) exploring the rupture experience, (c) exploring the avoidance, and (d) emergence of a wish or need. Meta-analyses indicated that the presence of rupture repair was positively associated with good psychotherapy outcome ($r = .24$) and that training and supervision in rupture resolution are associated with client improvement when compared to therapists who received no training ($r = .11$). Their training program includes mindfulness experiential exercises to enhance self-awareness, affect regulation and interpersonal sensitivity (see Muran, Safran, & Eubanks-Carter, 2010, for details).

A Convergence of Orientations

Although psychodynamic and humanistic–experiential therapists have long acknowledged the importance of therapists' negative emotional reactions to clients, cognitive and behavioral orientations have increasingly emphasized the clinical value of therapists' monitoring and managing their affective responses. Although schools of psychotherapy as diverse as humanistic–experiential, psychoanalysis, and cognitive–behavioral therapy (CBT) are grounded in differing philosophical and methodological assumptions, these theories are beginning to recognize common ground in a constructivist perspective that focuses on the immediate situational context. Humanistic and experiential schools of psychotherapy emphasize therapists' authenticity in the therapeutic relationship and value self-disclosure as evidence of the congruence of inner experience and outer expression. Intersubjective and relational schools of psychoanalysis (Stern, 2010; Stolorow, Brandchaft, & Atwood, 1987) understand the therapist's subjective world and personal responses not as contaminants to a therapeutic sterile field but part of a coconstructed reality. The therapist's experiences of frustration, boredom, and anger are not intrusive distracters that need to be contained and ignored, but emergent qualities of a uniquely constructed reality. Cognitive and cognitive–behavioral therapies are increasingly giving attention to therapists' subjective reactions as responses elicited by client behaviors. For example, a key component of McCullough's (2006) Cognitive Behavioral

Analysis System of Psychotherapy, for the treatment of chronic depression, is the therapist's "disciplined personal involvement" (p. 188). Kohlenberg and Tsai (1991), using a framework of radical behaviorism, similarly included therapists' expression of personal reactions as a form of natural reinforcers that identify problematic clinically relevant behaviors. They advocated for the judicious disclosure of therapists' negative reactions to clients' problematic behaviors that need to change and genuine expressions of caring to reinforce desirable client behaviors.

Different psychotherapeutic orientations understand therapists' negative reactions not just as therapy interfering behaviors but as a source of clinical information. In addition to "observable" sources of data, these personal reactions are essential in understanding and formulating a client's personality and how to manage the process of psychotherapy. The previously cited research emphasizes how containing negative affect is a factor in effective psychotherapy. The challenge for effective therapists, therefore, is how to use their affective reactions—positive and negative—in ways that facilitate process and outcome. How therapists' self-awareness is used in the service of understanding the therapeutic process and how that understanding is used in the service of furthering the psychotherapy are the focuses of metacommunication (Kiesler, 1996) and resolving ruptures in the therapeutic alliance (Safran & Muran, 2000). More important, the management of negative reactions points to how effective psychotherapy reflects a complex interaction of relational and technical factors that all therapists, regardless of orientation, need to manage.

The example of transference interpretations is particularly relevant. *Transference interpretations* are psychodynamic techniques intended to provide a client insight into how interactions with significant others in the past influence current relationships, especially in the moment-to-moment interactions with the therapist. Therapists' negative reactions can be understood as their responses to clients' reenactment of those past relationships, and provides an immediate experiential understanding of how clients impact others in their lives. The transference interpretation is a form of metacommunication in which, ideally, therapists invite clients to examine the interaction. The successful use of this technique is dependent on relational factors, and research findings indicate that it may even have a detrimental effect on psychotherapy process and outcome. As noted by Crits-Christoph and Gibbons (2002), research findings on "transference interpretations have recently converged toward the conclusion that high rates of transference interpretations can lead to poor outcome" (p. 294). Indeed, as a response to a therapist's negative emotional reaction to a client, a transference interpretation can be used in a blaming and belittling manner. Piper, McCallum, Joyce, Azim, and Ogrodniczuk (1999) suggested that even experienced therapists get caught up in a negative cycle of client resistance and transference interpretation. Schut et al. (2005) observed "that therapists who persisted with interpretations had more hostile interactions with clients and had clients who reacted with less warmth than [did] therapists who used interpretations more judiciously" (p. 494).

The interaction of increased adherence to technique as a manifestation of problems in the therapeutic alliance is also found in cognitive therapy. Castonguay, Goldfried, Wiser, Raue, and Hayes (1996) found that cognitive therapists who were confronted with clients' resistance to cognitive interventions persisted in their adherence to the therapeutic interventions. In their review of potentially harmful effects of psychological treatments, Castonguay, Boswell, Constantino, Goldfried, and Hill (2010) emphasized this complex interaction of relational and technical factors, suggesting that therapists' inability to repair toxic relational and technical processes might be mediating factors that link impaired therapist behaviors with poor outcomes. These conclusions were supported by Westra, Aviram, Connors, Kertes, and Ahmed (2012), who reported on the effects of therapists' emotional reactions to client resistance in cognitive–behavioral therapy. They found that greater displays of therapist positive reactions to clients were associated with lower levels of client resistance, an association independent of therapist competence in delivering CBT. Power struggles and feeling drained, helpless, guilty, and frustrated over the absence of client progress were related to higher levels of client resistance. Westra and colleagues suggested that therapist negative responses may influence client engagement by interfering with therapists' ability to competently deliver treatment.

The survey and research studies described in this section clearly indicate that therapists frequently have negative emotional responses to clients, and that these negative responses adversely affect the process and outcome of psychotherapy. The therapist's overt and covert expression of these emotions affect relational factors by compromising the therapeutic alliance and technical factors by compromising the competent delivery of specific techniques. Effective therapists are aware of how their emotional responses affect their clients and impair their ability to maintain an alliance and effectively implement techniques. The even greater challenge for them is how to transform those toxic experiences to facilitate a therapeutic process.

TRANSFORMING NEGATIVE REACTIONS TO CLIENTS: FROM FRUSTRATION TO COMPASSION

The experiences of skilled therapists in dealing with their negative reactions to clients are discussed in *Transforming Negative Reactions to Clients: From Frustration to Compassion* (Wolf et al., 2013). The contributors to that book—representing different theoretical orientations and areas of clinical specialization—offered recommendations on how they have managed experiences of frustration, anger, and other negative emotions experienced while conducting psychotherapy. Their recommendations to therapists converge on three main points: (a) to remain self-aware of their moment-to-moment reactions toward clients, (b) to regulate and contain the expression of frequently powerful emotions that can be experienced when working with difficult clients, and (c) to transform anger and frustration into empathy and compassion by reframing how they think about clients. Although coming from a different theoretical starting point, the consensus of these contributors is consistent with the model for managing countertransference as proposed by Gelso and Hayes (2007) and the three-factor model proposed by Gelso and Perez-Rojas (see Chapter 6, this volume).

Self-Awareness

All the contributors to *Transforming Negative Reactions to Clients: From Frustration to Compassion* (Wolf et al., 2013) emphasized the need for therapists to monitor their emotional responses to clients in treatment, characterizing therapists' self-awareness. Williams and Fauth (2005) defined this self-awareness as the "therapist's momentary recognition and attention to their immediate thoughts, emotions, physiological responses and behaviors during a therapy session" (p. 374). The contributors suggested that this self-awareness monitors and manages multiple channels, including the goals, tasks, and emotional bond of the therapeutic relationship. Therapists also need to monitor overt and covert emotional responses between clients and therapists. Clients scrutinize our affective reactions toward them as closely as we observe our clients. Especially in early sessions, clients will test us to see how we respond, waiting for a negative reaction. They know when we like them and when we are frustrated with them. Clients who have been treated badly by previous therapists are particularly sensitive to a new therapist. As therapists, we are participant–observers who need to simultaneously monitor our client's actions and emotions, our own affective responses to clients, and how clients respond to us both as professionals and people.

Most therapists are (reluctantly) aware of the strong frustration and anger they experience when working with difficult clients. More frequently, feelings of annoyance or boredom manifest themselves in subtle ways, such as deviations from the customary way therapists manage sessions. Distractions (e.g., not remembering what a client said, frequently looking at the clock) and changes in session starting and stopping times are all are signals that therapists are not present. During the course of a day, a therapist's attention may fluctuate from absorption and compassion with one client to boredom and impatience with another, only to again revert to an attentive stance with a third client. Even the most insightful of therapists, who are sensitive to the association of their experience to their clients' moods and intentions, can be challenged to make sense of how their experience relates, even tangentially, to the dynamics of a specific client.

In the same way that clients resist awareness of painful feelings, therapists resist awareness of negative reactions to clients. When clients do not do what "they are supposed to do" (i.e., what therapists want them to do), therapists are at risk of reacting negatively. When confronted with resistant clients, therapists may react negatively by adhering to specific techniques in an automatic and rigid manner that can unfortunately compromise the therapeutic alliance (Castonguay et al., 2010; Safran et al., 2011). As difficult as these hurdles are to experienced therapists, they can be devastating to novices, who may be reluctant to recognize their experience of negative emotions entirely. All therapists have blind spots and are never beyond the need for supervision and consultation to increase self-awareness.

Affect Regulation

The case studies of contributors to *Transforming Negative Reactions to Clients: From Frustration to Compassion* (Wolf et al., 2013) described clients who aroused intense and powerful reactions in the authors. Psychotherapy involves work with clients who live in crisis mode and who bring their world to the therapist's office. Clients can communicate in an immediate manner what it is like to live with sudden and powerful affective storms. In our attempts to identify with and be empathic about these states, therapists are vulnerable to experiencing these feelings as well. Even cognitive–behavioral therapists who treat phobias need to tolerate clients' fear during exposure sessions and not interrupt these procedures to rescue clients from their distress. To be empathic and compassionate requires that therapists be open to the pain of others, bear witness to their traumas, and tolerate the frequently intense feelings of helplessness that accompany clients' depressive episodes. Containing, tolerating, processing, and expressing their feelings are among the challenges of managing the therapeutic relationship.

Therapists are at increased risk of crossing and even violating ethical and professional boundaries when responding to desperate pleas for help. Peer consultation or supervision is critical for therapists who experience difficulty in containing expressions of anxiety and other behaviors that threaten the therapeutic relationship. In their discussion on the management of countertransference, Gelso and Hayes (2007) recognized the need for affect regulation when they discussed the importance of anxiety management. Mindfulness training has also been shown to facilitate affect regulation, as well as empathic understanding (Kelm, Womer, Walter, & Feudtner, 2014; Safran et al., 2011).

Staying focused for extended periods of time is hard work, and therapist self-care is a prerequisite for the practicing clinician. Failure to attend to their own person can compromise their effectiveness and lead to burnout.

Reframing

Effective therapists not only are aware of and tolerate their emotional responses without automatically acting on those impulses and feelings, but they also need to be able to transform those states into more empathic and compassionate responses. In the same way that self-awareness is fundamental to affect regulation, affect regulation is facilitated by reframing emotional responses. Attribution theory is one example of an approach for understanding the genesis of aggressive responses. As elaborated by Weiner (1986), attribution theory explains interpersonal conflict, whereby an individual interprets the motive of another person in a given way and then reacts emotionally in light of the attributed motive. The key to a negative emotional reaction toward the behavior of another is a function not so much of the behavior that is being observed but of whether one perceives the actor as being capable of doing something differently. As an example, effective therapists transform frustration to compassion by recognizing that clients' failure to comply with treatment is not due to their intentionally trying to be difficult or ungrateful about therapists' efforts to help, but rather because of distress and resistance that need to be empathically understood.

Contributors to *Transforming Negative Reactions to Clients: From Frustration to Compassion* (Wolf et al., 2013) consistently noted the need to work from a specific theoretical framework and to compassionately understand client behavior in terms of that framework. Effective therapists work from a clinical formulation that allows them to make sense of the interaction in the service of the therapeutic process. The need for supervision or consultation to assist in making this clinical formulation cannot be sufficiently emphasized.

In a qualitative study of compassionate psychotherapists, Vivino, Thompson, Hill, and Ladany (2009) distinguished between empathy and compassion. *Empathy* is characterized as a way in which therapists understand clients. *Compassion* goes beyond empathy and involves a deeper engagement with clients: "a process or state of being that connects to the client's overall suffering or struggle and provides the rationale or the impetus to help the client find relief from his or her suffering" (Vivino et al., 2009, p. 11). Empathy and compassion enjoin therapists to "get out of themselves," to challenge automatic tendencies to perceive a difficult client as the "other." A compassionate response poses a deeper challenge to therapists of making difficult clients' behavior more understandable and less blameworthy, and of stepping out of our usual modes of understanding to identify with and enter into our client's world, to understand what it is like to live in a world of psychological pain and cyclic dysfunction, where some form of self-destruction is seen as the only response to despair.

The relationship between compassion and mindfulness offers another perspective on the three factors of self-awareness, affect regulation, and reframing. The current emphasis on mindfulness and compassion blurs the boundary of psychotherapy with the practices of spirituality, an inevitable consequence when one is confronted with another's intense suffering and one's own helplessness to alleviate that pain. An understanding of mindfulness on the basis of openness to and acceptance of one's own experience and that of another may help therapists achieve a compassionate openness to and acceptance of the suffering of another. Indeed, when presented with the intense suffering of clients who have experienced trauma, being respectful witnesses to that pain and not feeling compelled to rescue (i.e., not be "a therapist") can be a tremendous challenge. When dealing with confusion about what is going on with clients, an openness to and curiosity about that confusion can help therapists communicate to clients that their experience is validated, if not deeply understood.

IMPLICATIONS FOR TRAINING AND RESEARCH

A number of guidelines on what therapists should and should not do when they are experiencing negative reactions toward their clients have been provided. We discuss a few implications of this empirical and clinical knowledge with regard to the training of future therapists and to future directions of research.

A major goal of *Transforming Negative Reactions to Clients: From Frustration to Compassion* (Wolf et al., 2013) was to emphasize how those experiences are common, perhaps unavoidable, and not a source of shame or inadequacy. How therapists learn to attend to their thoughts and feelings and use their affective responses should be a central factor in professional development. Novice therapists, even more than experienced practitioners, are uncomfortable with negative feelings toward clients (Brody & Farber, 1996), and respond differently to their negative reactions (Williams, Judge, Hill, & Hoffman, 1997; Williams, Polster, Grizzard, Rockenbaugh, & Judge, 2003). The need to destigmatize therapists' negative feelings toward clients should be addressed early in training.

Research findings here are mixed. The Vanderbilt (Binder & Strupp, 1997) studies found that even when therapists were trained to deal with negative emotions, their feelings continued to adversely affect the process and outcome of treatment. Yet, Strupp (1989) suggested that this may be due to the time-limited nature of his study, such that therapists increased the use of interpretations that led to a negative process. As reviewed previously, results from Gelso and Hayes and from Safran and Muran are more promising in training therapists, and their models are consistent with the factors of therapist self-awareness, affect regulation, and reframing proposed in this chapter (see Muran, Safran, Eubanks, & Winston, 2014, for recent findings from an NIMH-funded study demonstrating the positive impact of training designed to recognize and resolve ruptures). In the spirit of facilitating a career scientist–practitioner model, Castonguay and colleagues (2010) suggested that students be encouraged early in training to use measures of process and outcome to help them and their supervisors identify vulnerabilities to specific clinical situations that interfere with client progress. Data on the basis of such measures would prove invaluable not just in comparing therapists for effectiveness but identifying developmental trajectories and especially obstacles in professional development for individual therapists. Findings from this ongoing monitoring can result in more systematic training, intensive supervision, or personal psychotherapy.

The clinical and empirical literature on therapists' negative reactions to clients supports the association between (a) therapists' experience of anger and frustration and (b) adverse effects on the process and outcome of psychotherapy (e.g., Henry et al., 1993). The challenge of future research is to identify how these negative reactions moderate and/or mediate the effective implementation of relational and technical interventions, and how therapists can overcome these adverse experiences to facilitate the therapeutic process. Although the collection of data using the instruments suggested by Castonguay and colleagues (2010) provides an important macroperspective, research that establishes a causal connection will need to use more specific instruments and designs. This need is reflected in the work of Westra and colleagues (2012) on how therapists' emotional reactions to client resistance affect adherence to techniques in CBT, and that of Piper and colleagues (1999) on how the persistence of transference interpretations can have an adverse impact on clients.

Najavits (2000) listed the methodological challenges of research on therapists' negative emotions, such as their willingness to honestly identify and report those feelings, the range of instrumentation from relatively quick self-report checklist measures to labor-intensive ratings of recorded sessions, and sensitivity to therapist confidentiality when they are asked about embarrassing personal experiences as therapists. Furthermore, a comprehensive account of the effects therapists' experience of frustration and anger on process and outcome, and how these experiences are managed, requires a grounding in basic research on attentional and affective processes, and the effect of overt and covert communication of such reactions on interpersonal processes. Finally, although this chapter has focused on therapists' experiences of anger and frustration, clinical observation and research findings are needed on how the wider range of negative affect influences therapy process and outcome, such as feelings of anxiety and panic, hopelessness and despair, shame and humiliation, boredom and neglect, and seduction.

CONCLUSION

Discussions of therapists' emotional responses to their clients during a session are as old as the profession of psychotherapy. These discussions, however, have the potential to contribute to today's research on therapist effects, as well as to help the continued effort to improve the effectiveness of all therapists. For the most part, the discussions about negative reactions have led some to advocate for their suppression as sources of interference, and others to advocate for their use as sources of information that can facilitate treatment. This review of the empirical and clinical literature supports both views. One of the conclusions that we have derived is that the expression of anger and frustration toward a client compromises the therapeutic relationship and the implementation of specific techniques. This could in part explain a disconcerting aspect of therapist effects: Some therapists are harmful to some of their clients. In addition, therapists are likely to become more effective by adopting a posture of participant–observers to their clients, themselves, and the psychotherapy relationship, monitoring and managing their internal process and their interactions.

Therapists' experience of their own feelings during a psychotherapy session is part of a complex of therapist factors that include presence and immediacy. Every professional faces challenges in working with difficult clients, but when the focus of the interaction is helping individuals manage their own affective lives, how we as psychotherapists understand and manage our own affective lives makes our field unique among professions. Making therapists more effective means using our experience of negative emotions in more meaningful and less shameful ways and constructively using this experience in the service of the treatment.

The challenges of effective psychotherapy are summarized in the oft-cited question posed 50 years ago by Gordon Paul (1967): "What treatment, by whom, is most effective for this individual with that specific problem, and under which set of circumstances?" "By whom" refers to the importance of the person of the therapist. We believe that one of the main qualities of therapists is their ability to be aware of themselves as a people. Therapists' awareness and emotional experiences are, of course, complex phenomena. If there is a topic on which practicing therapists and researchers can and should learn from each other, it is how to better understand and deal with frequently intense and confusing reactions to clients.

REFERENCES

Binder, J. L., & Strupp, H. H. (1997). "Negative process": A recurrently discovered and underestimated facet of therapeutic process and outcome in the individual psychotherapy of adults. *Clinical Psychology: Science and Practice, 4*, 121–139. http://dx.doi.org/10.1111/j.1468-2850.1997.tb00105.x

Brody, E. M., & Farber, B. A. (1996). The effects of therapist experience and patient diagnosis on countertransference. *Psychotherapy: Theory, Research, Practice, Training, 33*, 372–380.

Castonguay, L. G., Boswell, J. F., Constantino, M. J., Goldfried, M. R., & Hill, C. E. (2010). Training implications of harmful effects of psychological treatments. *American Psychologist, 65*, 34–49. http://dx.doi.org/10.1037/a0017330

Castonguay, L. G., Goldfried, M. R., Wiser, S., Raue, P. J., & Hayes, A. M. (1996). Predicting the effect of cognitive therapy for depression: A study of unique and common factors. *Journal of Consulting and Clinical Psychology, 64*, 497–504. http://dx.doi.org/10.1037/0022-006X.64.3.497

Crits-Christoph, P., & Gibbons, M. B. (2002). Relational interpretations. In J. C. Norcross (Ed.), *Psychotherapy relationships that work: Therapist contributions and responsiveness to patients* (pp. 285–300). New York, NY: Oxford University Press.

Dalenberg, C. J. (2004). Maintaining the safe and effective therapeutic relationship in the context of distrust and anger. *Psychotherapy: Theory, Research, Practice, Training, 41*, 438–447. http://dx.doi.org/10.1037/0033-3204.41.4.438

Freud, S. (1933). Dora: Fragment of an analysis of a case of hysteria. In J. Strachey (Ed. & Trans.), *The standard edition of the complete psychological works of Sigmund Freud* (Vol. 7, pp. 15–122). London, England: Hogarth Press. (Original work published 1905)

Gelso, C. J., & Hayes, J. A. (2007). *Countertransference and the therapist's inner experience: Perils and possibilities.* Mahwah, NJ: Erlbaum.

Guy, J. D., Poelstra, P. L., & Stark, M. J. (1989). Personal distress and therapeutic effectiveness: National survey of psychologists practicing psychology. *Professional Psychology: Research and Practice, 20*, 48–50.

Hayes, J. A., Gelso, C. J., & Hummel, A. M. (2011). Managing countertransference. In J. C. Norcross (Ed.), *Psychotherapy relationships that work: Evidence-based responsiveness* (2nd ed., pp. 239–258). New York, NY: Oxford University Press. http://dx.doi.org/10.1093/acprof:oso/9780199737208.003.0012

Henry, W. P., Schacht, T. E., & Strupp, H. H. (1990). Patient and therapist introject, interpersonal process, and differential psychotherapy outcome. *Journal of Consulting and Clinical Psychology, 58*, 768–774. http://dx.doi.org/10.1037/0022-006X.58.6.768

Henry, W. P., Schacht, T. E., Strupp, H. H., Butler, S. F., & Binder, J. L. (1993). Effects of training in time-limited dynamic psychotherapy: Mediators of therapists' responses to training. *Journal of Consulting and Clinical Psychology, 61*, 441–447. http://dx.doi.org/10.1037/0022-006X.61.3.441

Kelm, Z., Womer, J., Walter, J. K., & Feudtner, C. (2014). Interventions to cultivate physician empathy: A systematic review. *BMC Medical Education, 14*, 219. http://dx.doi.org/10.1186/1472-6920-14-219

Kiesler, D. J. (1996). *Contemporary interpersonal theory and research: Personality, psychopathology, and psychotherapy.* New York, NY: Wiley.

Kohlenberg, R. J., & Tsai, M. (1991). *Functional analytic psychotherapy: Creating intense and curative therapeutic relationships.* New York, NY: Plenum Press. http://dx.doi.org/10.1007/978-0-387-70855-3

McCullough, J. P. (2006). *Treating chronic depression with disciplined personal involvement.* New York, NY: Springer Science + Business Media.

Muran, J. C., Safran, J. D., & Eubanks-Carter, C. (2010). Developing therapist abilities to negotiate alliance ruptures. In J. C. Muran & J. P. Barber (Eds.), *The therapeutic alliance: An evidence-based guide to practice* (pp. 320–340). New York, NY: Guilford Press.

Muran, J. C., Safran, J. D., Eubanks, C., & Winston, A. (2014, June). *Exploring changes in interpersonal process, intermediate & ultimate outcome in a within-subject experimental study of an alliance-focused training.* Paper presented at the annual meeting of the Society for Psychotherapy Research, Copenhagen, Denmark.

Najavits, L. M. (2000). Researching therapist emotions and countertransference. *Cognitive and Behavioral Practice, 7*, 322–328.

Najavits, L. M., & Strupp, H. H. (1994). Differences in the effectiveness of psychodynamic therapists. *Psychotherapy: Theory, Research, Practice, Training, 31*, 114–123. http://dx.doi.org/10.1037/0033-3204.31.1.114

Paul, G. L. (1967). Strategy of outcome research in psychotherapy. *Journal of Consulting Psychology, 31*, 109–118. http://dx.doi.org/10.1037/h0024436

Piper, W. E., McCallum, M., Joyce, A. S., Azim, H. F., & Ogrodniczuk, J. S. (1999). Follow-up findings for interpretive and supportive forms of psychotherapy and patient personality variables. *Journal of Consulting and Clinical Psychology, 67*, 267–273. http://dx.doi.org/10.1037/0022-006X.67.2.267

Pope, K. S., & Tabachnick, B. G. (1993). Therapists' anger, hate, fear, and sexual feelings: National survey of therapist responses, client characteristics, critical events, formal complaints, and training. *Professional Psychology: Research and Practice, 24*, 142–152. http://dx.doi.org/10.1037/0735-7028.24.2.142

Pope, K. S., Tabachnick, B. G., & Keith-Spiegel, P. (1987). Ethics of practice: The beliefs and behaviors of psychologists as therapists. *American Psychologist, 42*, 993–1006. http://dx.doi.org/10.1037/0003-066X.42.11.993

Safran, J. D., & Muran, J. C. (2000). *Negotiating the therapeutic alliance.* New York, NY: Guilford Press.

Safran, J. D., Muran, J. C., & Eubanks-Carter, C. (2011). Repairing alliance ruptures. In J. C. Norcross (Ed.), *Psychotherapy relationships that work: Evidence-based responsiveness* (2nd ed., pp. 224–238). New York, NY: Oxford University Press. http://dx.doi.org/10.1093/acprof:oso/9780199737208.003.0011

Schut, A. J., Castonguay, L. G., Flanagan, K. M., Yamasaki, A. S., Barber, J. P., Bedics, J. D., & Smith, T. L. (2005). Therapist interpretation, patient–therapist interpersonal process, and outcome in psychodynamic psychotherapy for avoidant personality disorder. *Psychotherapy: Theory, Research, Practice, Training, 42*, 494–511. http://dx.doi.org/10.1037/0033-3204.42.4.494

Stern, D. B. (2010). *Partners in thought: Working with unformulated experience, dissociation, and enactment.* New York, NY: Routledge.

Stolorow, R. D., Brandchaft, B., & Atwood, G. (1987). *Psychoanalytic treatment: An Intersubjective approach.* Hillsdale, NJ: Analytic Press.

Strupp, H. H. (1980). Success and failure in time-limited psychotherapy. Further evidence (Comparison 4). *Archives of General Psychiatry, 37*, 947–954. http://dx.doi.org/10.1001/archpsyc.1980.01780210105011

Strupp, H. H. (1989). Psychotherapy. Can the practitioner learn from the researcher? *American Psychologist, 44*, 717–724. http://dx.doi.org/10.1037/0003-066X.44.4.717

Tasca, G. A., & McMullen, L. M. (1992). Interpersonal complementarity and antithesis within a stage model of psychotherapy. *Psychotherapy: Theory, Research, Practice, Training, 29*, 515–523. http://dx.doi.org/10.1037/0033-3204.29.4.515

Vivino, B. L., Thompson, B. J., Hill, C. E., & Ladany, N. (2009). Compassion in psychotherapy: The perspective of therapists nominated as compassionate. *Psychotherapy Research, 19*, 157–171. http://dx.doi.org/10.1080/10503300802430681

Weiner, B. (1986). *An attributional theory of motivation and emotion.* New York, NY: Springer-Verlag.

Westra, H. A., Aviram, A., Connors, L., Kertes, A., & Ahmed, M. (2012). Therapist emotional reactions and client resistance in cognitive behavioral therapy. *Psychotherapy, 49*, 163–172. http://dx.doi.org/10.1037/a0023200

Williams, E. N., & Fauth, J. (2005). A psychotherapy process study of therapist in session self-awareness. *Psychotherapy Research, 15*, 374–381. http://dx.doi.org/10.1080/10503300500091355

Williams, E. N., Judge, A. B., Hill, C. E., & Hoffman, M. A. (1997). Experiences of novice therapists in prepracticum: Trainees', clients', and supervisors' perceptions of therapists' personal reactions and management strategies. *Journal of Counseling Psychology, 44,* 390–399. http://dx.doi.org/10.1037/0022-0167.44.4.390

Williams, E. N., Polster, D., Grizzard, M. B., Rockenbaugh, J., & Judge, A. B. (2003). What happens when therapists feel bored or anxious? A qualitative study of distracting self-awareness and therapists' management strategies. *Journal of Contemporary Psychotherapy, 33,* 5–18. http://dx.doi.org/10.1023/A:1021499526052

Wolf, A. W., Goldfried, M. R., & Muran, J. C. (2013). *Transforming negative reactions to clients: From frustration to compassion.* Washington, DC: American Psychological Association.

11

PROFESSIONAL EXPERTISE IN PSYCHOTHERAPY

FRANZ CASPAR

Therapist effects refer to the ways in which therapist attributes covary with patient outcome. That therapist effects exist indicates that practitioners are not all equally effective, which in turn suggests at least two important issues for the field to address: (a) We need to understand what makes some therapists better or worse than others, and (b) we should devote efforts to improve therapists' effectiveness (see Chapters 1 and 2, this volume). Typically, therapist and outcome variables are measured over the whole range of variation to find average effects across therapists. Similarly, as far as improvement is concerned, general strategies are the focus of our attention (i.e., we search for strategies aimed at improving therapists as a whole group, as opposed to individual practitioners).

In contrast, this chapter deals with expertise. What concepts of expert performance have been developed, and what has research shown for expertise in general and for fields close to psychotherapy? The lack of systematic research on top performance in psychotherapy suggests the need to learn from findings in other domains, which is in line with a general stance that concepts should not be developed separately for small domains (such as psychotherapy) but rather for larger domains (such as professional performance in general) while paying attention to the specificities of particular professions and activities.

Experts like top athletes, chess masters, or musicians can perform at the Olympic Games, chess championships, or top concerts. In the context of psychotherapy, an interest in top performance may appear elitist and of questionable use, considering the fact that it is impossible for all of the patients in need of psychotherapy to be served by a small group of top performers. Fortunately, research suggests that for most patients, working with outlier therapists, in terms of effectiveness, is not necessary for achieving good outcome (see Chapter 1). One could argue that for the well-being of the majority of patients, what is primarily needed is "highly effective psychotherapists" (Chow et al., 2015) or even "just good enough" therapists. Analysis of the conditions for top performance is, however, also related to the goal of providing insights into how to foster good and very good performance. Just like in sports or music, individuals who will never be top ranked can still learn from top performers. While discussing expertise in this chapter, I will therefore keep in mind that this is not only relevant for a small elite group of therapists. I will discuss how expertise can be defined, how top performers differ from the average therapist, in what phases (before, in, and after formal training) differences develop, and how findings related to top performance can contribute, in the absence of more comprehensive, empirically based models, to training and learning from practice.

WHAT IS EXPERTISE IN PSYCHOTHERAPY?

First, experience is required to acquire expertise, but experience does not equal expertise, nor does it by itself lead to expertise. This is in line with findings in general expertise research (Feltovich, Prietula, & Ericsson, 2006), and we may all know experienced colleagues who seem to develop rather than lose bad habits as they keep working.

Several criteria have been formulated and used in the past to operationalize expertise in psychotherapy. The most important are

- peer nomination as experts or "master therapists" (e.g., Jennings & Skovholt, 1999);
- assessment of adherence and competence, usually by raters;
- performance as measured, for example, by effect sizes of patient change (e.g., Miller, Duncan, & Hubble, 2007);

- quality or special contributions as teachers (Eells, Lombart, Kendjelic, Turner, & Lucas, 2005; Eells et al., 2011; Sperry & Carlson, 2014); and
- ability to deal with particularly difficult patients—to engage them and keep them long enough in psychotherapy (this criterion has never been formally used in research, but is important for the reputation of a therapist among colleagues).

Each of these criteria has advantages and disadvantages. Peer nomination may be affected by impression management vis-à-vis colleagues. Adherence and competence are usually found to be unrelated to outcome (Webb, DeRubeis, & Barber, 2010). Effect sizes may be influenced by the difficulty of patients: The best therapists may get stuck with an overload of difficult patients and/or therapists with the best effect sizes may mainly be good in avoiding difficult-to-treat patients. Assessing therapists' quality as teachers is a complex process, and reaching consensus about what is a good teacher is known to be difficult. Finally, therapists good in dealing with difficult patients may not produce better than average effect sizes with less difficult patients.

The limitations of each criterion relative to the respective research question need to be considered. While striving for the best possible definition and operationalization, it must be accepted that no definition is entirely complete and that combined criteria must be found. Ultimately, it is not the ability to establish a good relationship that matters; nor the ability to develop impressive case formulations; nor the ability to impress patients, colleagues, or raters, but rather the ability to facilitate patient improvement. Everything else may be important, but only so far as it is instrumental to this end goal.

WHAT LEADS TO SUPERIOR PERFORMANCE AND EXPERTISE?

The mere notion that there are differences is of limited relevance. What is relevant are the factors behind these differences and what causes them.

The Importance of Information Processing

The assumption that superior observable skills in conducting psychotherapy play an important role has some plausibility. Yet, Hill and Knox (2013) asserted that although the extent to which skills are mastered may explain differences between bad and good therapists, they do not account for excellence. Even at the graduate level, there already may be ceiling effects for basic skills (Hill & Knox, 2013). Sperry and Carlson (2014) mentioned exceptional skills as a characteristic of master therapists. Although there may be ceiling effects for basic skills, for skills requiring more complexity, such ceiling effects do not seem to exist.

In this respect, psychotherapy could resemble other fields studied in expertise research. Ericsson (2006) posited that it is not talent or mastery of simple, observable skills that differentiates between good and expert performers in sports, music, medicine, and other domains. Expert performers primarily excel in their superior thinking and cognitive representations. This may be particularly surprising for sport performance, but even there, the primary individual differences among soccer players and tennis players concern their ability to react appropriately in complex situations, which allow them to better anticipate rather than relying on faster immediate reactions. Ericsson furthermore argued that the difference between good and top performance reflects skills acquired over extended periods of practice and training rather than innate superior abilities providing superior sight, touch, or hearing. Information processing has more to do with the development of expertise than does basic skill-building.

Several psychotherapy orientations deal with some aspects of therapist information processing (e.g., psychoanalysis with the distortions in information processing because of countertransference, client-centered psychotherapy with more or less favorable conditions for information processing on which empathy is based), but no approach has so far dealt with expert information processing in any comprehensive way. Similarly, many contributions to the issue of therapist effects address therapist information processing (e.g., Tracey, Wampold, Lichtenberg, & Goodyear, 2014), but yet, with their heavy focus on adopting a disconfirmatory approach, they are very selective in what aspects of information processing they emphasize.

Although conceptually, it makes sense that information processing is an important aspect of therapist expertise, progress in investigating and understanding therapists' information processing is impeded by a fundamental problem: It is exceedingly difficult to do research on processes that are hidden in the mind of the therapist and are not directly observable. An initial attempt was made with "clinical judgment" research beginning in the 1950s. However, these experiments typically lacked the external validity needed to study expert performance (Caspar, 1997). Thinking aloud protocols, which are a good solution for some domains, are unfeasible in real psychotherapy sessions. One potentially viable method was put forth by Caspar (1997), who introduced an approach with retrospective reports and stimulated recall, which has similarities to interpersonal process recall (Elliott & Shapiro, 1988). In spite of the obstacles inherent to research, there are concepts and findings of relevance that are reported throughout this chapter.

Skills and information processing are not as separable as it may first seem. In fact, they are interconnected in many ways. The two most important links are that superior mental representations are also based on acquired skills (in a broader sense), such as observation, pattern recognition, hypothesis generation and testing, monitoring, and more. The second is that more sophisticated mental processing, on which top performance seems to depend, requires mental representations and information processing resources, which are simply not available as long as therapists struggle with the acquisition and mastery of basic skills such as filtering and basic organizing of the information coming from the patient or formulating their next statement. In a naturalistic study, Caspar (1995) found that in a group of very inexperienced behavior therapists, not one of them paid conscious attention to nonverbal patient behavior, although they had learned in their training how important such behavior cues are. All their thinking was focused on tasks such as formulating their next verbal response to the patient, with nothing left for attending to the nonverbal behavior. Although these findings are not based on data from experts, they illustrate with beginners—the opposite of experts—a precondition for superior performance (i.e., that information processing is freed from dealing with basics in favor of more advanced and subtle information processing). In the same study, it was also found that experienced therapists (of whom many can be considered experts on the basis of their recognition as outstanding therapists among colleagues) were more likely to consciously refer to concrete theoretical concepts of relevance in the situation while working with their patients. It seems as though the novice therapists used their information processing resources for basic skills, whereas the experienced therapists had mastered these more basic skills and could allocate their information processing resources to more nuanced and complex aspects of working with their patients.

In another naturalistic investigation, Kern and McColgan (2015) found that inexperienced therapists lacked information processing capacity for monitoring the psychotherapy process (observing and reflecting what happens in the moment, how this can be related to their view of patients, and whether their work is on track) as compared to more experienced therapists. Additionally, experienced therapists also reported a greater ability to withdraw attention from less important aspects, a precondition for greater flexibility in allocating attention. Popp-Liesum (2005) also found that experienced cognitive–behavioral therapists are able to better recognize patterns and to solve problems faster, and this was also related to a higher degree of automatization. Novice therapists describe problems in a less systematic way; they have a limited readiness to revise hypotheses and they do less planning ahead (Popp-Liesum, 2005).

Although none of the previously mentioned studies collected independent outcome data, they suggest, as a whole, that experts differ from novices and that the mastery of skills frees resources needed for expert information processing. These two empirically derived conclusions, in turn, raise the possibility that identified differences are related to differences in patient outcome.

As a further hint for the importance of information processing, Hill and Knox (2013) argued "that every client is different, and thus, that therapists must respond to each client's needs" (p. 779). Therefore, the ability to develop good case formulations requires particular attention. Expert therapists (defined by Eells et al., 2011, as therapists who are particularly engaged with case formulation) develop richer hypotheses while grounding them in descriptive information, monitor their own information processing, and are aware of information they would need to develop an even better view of patients (Eells et al., 2011). Caspar (1997) found similar effects for a convenience sample of experienced therapists, including a large proportion of experts.

A General Model for the Development of Experts' Ability to Consider Specific Details

A general model of expertise dealing with the increasing ability to consider patients' details and concrete circumstances was presented by Dreyfus and Dreyfus (1986). This model, developed outside the clinical domain, covers the development of expertise from novice to expert (see Figure 11.1).

Several aspects of this model are important:

- Expertise is developed in several steps, a process that can be made more efficient but not abbreviated.

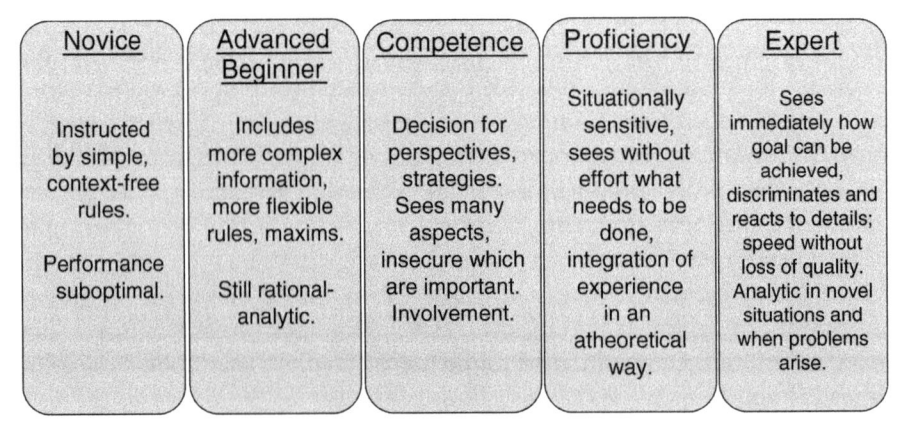

Novice	Advanced Beginner	Competence	Proficiency	Expert
Instructed by simple, context-free rules. Performance suboptimal.	Includes more complex information, more flexible rules, maxims. Still rational-analytic.	Decision for perspectives, strategies. Sees many aspects, insecure which are important. Involvement.	Situationally sensitive, sees without effort what needs to be done, integration of experience in an atheoretical way.	Sees immediately how goal can be achieved, discriminates and reacts to details; speed without loss of quality. Analytic in novel situations and when problems arise.

Figure 11.1. Development of expertise. Data from Dreyfus and Dreyfus (1986) and Dreyfus (2004). A similar phase model for psychotherapists has been presented by Rønnestad and Skovholt (2003).

- Novices have to simplify reality to some extent, which does not imply that more experienced therapists have to pretend that patients and their problems, as well as therapist tasks and psychotherapeutic procedures, are simple in reality.
- Novices simplify reality by applying unconditional, overgeneralized rules (as in some manuals), as opposed to considering specificities of patients, problems, and situations.
- When a novice realizes that his or her responsibility is not only to apply simple rules correctly but also to understand specificities and to decide on the right model and a differentiated procedure, he or she is commonly unsettled. Although most therapists-in-training expect a linear increase of subjective security with training/experience, Dreyfus and Dreyfus (1986) cited evidence from nursing that admitting such insecurity is positively correlated with further development of expertise.
- Experts process information more intuitively, as a prerequisite for fast, holistic processing. Such expert intuition is different from novice intuition, although both are subjectively experienced as intuition. It builds on processing developed through countless instances of deliberate, stepwise, conscious processing. Dreyfus and Dreyfus (1986) were concerned that in a professional world in which justifications are always required (e.g., evidence-based medicine), the development of professional intuition might be suppressed.

The Dreyfus and Dreyfus (1986) model has a number of implications. First, if it is the amount of overall complexity (and avoidance of overload) that determines the extent to which therapists can consider specificity, the bearable amount of specificity depends on their ability to reduce complexity by organizing details in smart case formulations. Therefore, the case formulation is an essential skill to develop in training. Second, temporarily increasing insecurity is a well-known phenomenon in psychotherapy. Therapists-in-training should be prepared to tolerate such insecurity and understand that acknowledging it is an important step in the process of developing expertise. Third, models should be taught for using intuition along with rational analytic thinking.

Intuition

As intuitive processing appears typical for experts (Dreyfus & Dreyfus, 1986; Glaser & Chi, 1988), it is discussed here in more detail. Therapists typically cannot imagine surviving a day without clinical intuition, whereas for science, especially cognitive psychology, intuition has been considered a nonissue, or at best, a type of processing defined negatively by the absence of rational-analytic thinking. To acknowledge that expert performance is partly based on intuition is difficult, as long as intuitive processing is seen as an opposite to rational thinking. Luckily, the rigid academic rejection of intuitive processing has weakened (Eells et al., 2011; Gigerenzer, 2009; Kahneman, 2003), in part because of the availability of psychological models, such as connectionist or neural network models (parallel distributed processing), that provide a more accurate understanding of processes underlying intuition than provided by traditional models (Caspar, Rothenfluh, & Segal, 1992).

It is important to see that deliberate/conscious and intuitive processing do not work against each other. Cognitive scientist Juan Pascual-Leone (1990) has (with reference to the clinical domain) emphasized that neither rational-analytic nor intuitive information processing is superior, but that best performance is related to combining the advantages of each type of information processing, as well as to compensating for the disadvantages of each by using the respective other type. Best performance is reached when a person is flexible in switching between these two modes of information processing.

I have found evidence that such combining is actually possible and happens in psychotherapy (Caspar, 1997; Itten, 1994). In a naturalistic study of psychotherapy intake interviews, reconstructions of therapists' inner processes were rated for indicators of rational-analytic and intuitive thinking, and the ratings were factor analyzed. The first factor includes Application of Rules, Conscious Processing, Reflecting Reasons for Procedure, and Meta-analytic Information Processing. This factor has been labeled Conscious-Analytic processing. The second factor includes Holistic Processing, the Global Intuition rating, Search for Alternatives, and Therapist Emotional Arousal. This factor has been labeled Positive, Holistic Intuition. The third and final factor includes only Automatization (processing information routinely, without special mental efforts in the particular situation) and has been labeled accordingly.

These factors were found to be in an orthogonal structure. What does this orthogonality mean? The time units on which the ratings were based are important: A unit was a turn (a patient and the subsequent therapist utterance). Within such a unit, there is space for some rational-analytic and some intuitive information processing. The empirical question is whether such "coexistence" actually occurs with some frequency, with the alternative of an information processing system being either in one or the other mode for a longer time. The latter would lead to a bipolar factor with intuition on one end and rational-analytic thinking on the other. This would correspond to widespread views of intuitive and rational thinking. In contrast, the orthogonality indicates an independent variation within our units. This means that therapists can process either in a conscious-rational or intuitive manner, or a combination of both, or neither one nor the other clearly. The relevance of such a finding is high: Therapists seem to combine intuitive and rational-analytic processing, and if it is believed, as Pascual-Leone (1990) proposes, that such a combination is advantageous for expert performance, therapists can be instructed and trained to deliberately switch between the two modes within short segments of time. In line with Dreyfus and Dreyfus (1986), it is not plausible that the development of professional intuition can be sped up substantially by mere instruction, but rather it is possible that the *deliberate use* of professional intuition a therapist has developed to this point can be trained. Although it has not been tested whether this leads to better performance, it has been shown that training in switching between intuitive and rational-analytic processing results in more frequent switching between the two modes (Alder, 1999).

As mentioned previously, Automatization, a concept that has been related to intuition in the cognitive literature, has landed on a third independent factor. In our interpretation, this does not contradict the notion that some automatization is needed for expert intuition. But information processing capacity saved by automatization can be used for intuitive as well as for rational-conscious processing, which would account for the statistical independence. For rational-conscious processing, which is slow and resource-consuming, the freeing of resources by automatization can also be crucial.

The relative independence of the factors is in line with impressions from clinical practice: Reluctance of using of rational-analytic thinking (e.g., arguing that it gets in the way of spontaneous empathy) in no way guarantees good clinical intuition. It is also in line with the impression that brilliant therapists often proceed in a way that is very rational, analytic, and conscious, and yet also intuitive. As far as differences between the groups of experienced versus inexperienced therapists in our study are concerned, experienced therapists processed information more intuitively, but their intuition was characterized by Automatization (Factor 3) rather than by an absence of Conscious-Analytic Processing (Factor 1; Caspar, 1997). For example, pattern recognition is known as a largely intuitive ability, which is normally not based on deliberate search; it just pops up and is in this sense automatized. Within the time unit used in our study (i.e., one turn), a flexible therapist can easily switch from intuitive pattern recognition to rational-analytic processing of the recognized patterns, which would contribute to statistical independence. This is in line with findings in research on expertise, which show that experts think rather intuitively, but not at the expense of rational thinking. Ericsson (2015) emphasized that expert performance goes along with deautomatization in some tasks, but this is compatible with automatization in others.

Although the advantages of intuitive thinking have so far not been demonstrated convincingly for psychotherapeutic information processing, general research on expertise shows advantages in terms of speed and economic use of information processing resources, dealing with soft information, uncertainty, multiple constraint satisfaction, pattern recognition, and checking for inconsistencies. All of these are skills of obvious relevance for psychotherapy (e.g., Nakash & Alegría, 2013). It is plausible that these abilities also enable experts to deal with unfamiliar conditions and probabilities as opposed to yes/no facts.

SOURCES OF EXPERT PERFORMANCE

We discuss three sources of expert performance: what characteristics future therapists have already and bring into training, how therapists are trained, and whether and how therapists are able to learn from practice after the termination of formal training.

What Pretraining Characteristics Are Favorable?

Ericsson, Krampe, and Tesch-Römer (1993) posited that it typically takes many years and/or thousands of hours of practice to develop the highest levels of performance in most domains of expertise, whereas the importance of talent is, according to them, generally overrated. Some future therapists do develop some relevant skills and abilities in their private life before entering psychotherapy training. For example, a future therapist growing up in a family with psychological problems may develop a superior ability in observing and interpreting nonverbal signals. Sperry and Carlson (2014) reported that master therapists have often experienced a challenging, yet not overwhelming, youth.

Similarly, Hill and Knox (2013) theorized that certain abilities are prerequisites for beginner therapists. They mentioned cognitive complexity, emotional intelligence, receptivity to feedback, flexibility, and the ability to engage in introspection. Social skills have also been emphasized (Anderson, Ogles, Patterson, Lambert, & Vermeersch, 2009). On the basis of diverse pertinent literature, I would also include in this list additional characteristics and attributes, such as personal security/low level of interpersonal anxiety, readiness to expose oneself to criticism, ability to tolerate tensions, generalized self-efficacy expectation, adaptive attributional style, and independence from unsatisfied (i.e., narcissistic) needs to be satisfied by patients.

Our confidence in the ability of these characteristics to predict top performance is impaired by the lack of prospective studies. Therapists who are considered master therapists today have not undergone systematic assessment at the beginning of their career, and trainees who have been systematically assessed in empirical investigations have not been tested later on to see if they developed into master therapists. Still, some studies have assessed the role of characteristics before training in the development of therapists. Eversmann (2008) studied the correlation between psychotherapy-relevant interpersonal behavior and training effects after 5 years through rating videotaped group interactions in structured and semistructured situations. She found that the ability to communicate in an unambiguous and clear way, empathy, respectful warm contact, the ability to deal with criticism, the ability to cooperate, and above all, interpersonal competence were correlated with fewer dropouts and better outcomes for patients.

A study of correlations of pretraining variables with training success is currently underway in our research group. Interpersonal functioning, social intelligence, life goal attainment, tolerance of ambiguity, and cognitive complexity are being assessed. A video recording of a role-play with a patient (played by a research assistant) will also be rated for several variables. Currently, the study is waiting for these trainees to terminate training: The inherent requirement of time for such studies is a reason for why they are rare.

Some of the characteristics mentioned in this section can be described as skills, whereas others are states or attitudes. Although this has not yet been demonstrated empirically, it is conceivable that several of these properties and abilities could play an amplifying role in the development of expertise, as they can serve as the basis for intense learning, before, in, and after training. Overall, however, it is plausible that not all abilities required to be a master, or even a successful, therapist have to be developed in training—some may never be acquired and/or developed unless they are present before training begins. Which of the abilities/attitudes/states are needed to profit from training, and which are needed directly to be a good therapist is still unknown.

What Training Leads to Expertise?

It is, by and large, unknown what kind of training leads to expert performance in psychotherapy, which underlines the need to learn from professional training in other fields. Few empirical findings exist relative to training elements in psychotherapy. There is, for example, a substantial amount of research on training of helping skills (Hill & Knox, 2013). Although past and current studies have shed light on the development of basic counseling skills in beginning therapists, a considerable number of questions have yet to be answered, even those related to such a relatively straightforward part of training (for details, see Hill & Knox, 2013).

If we draw on findings from general research on the development of expertise, the most effective avenue to expertise appears to be deliberate practice (Ericsson, 2009). Deliberate practice was first identified in students at a music academy who were meeting regularly with their master teacher for assessment and identification of goals and tasks for improving certain aspects of their performance. A recent review of the development of expert performance in medicine provides examples of deliberate practice in medicine and other professional domains (Ericsson, 2015). Important elements of deliberate practice include the following:

- Learners are motivated to deal with the task and to develop efforts to improve their performance.
- The learning goal is clearly defined, and a correct understanding of goal and task after brief instruction is possible.
- The design of the task considers the existing knowledge of the learner.
- Immediate, informative feedback is provided.
- The same or similar tasks can be repeated and errors can be corrected.

Figure 11.2 illustrates a systematic, deliberate practice-oriented procedure over time. Once a learning goal is reached, the next goal and task are defined and learned, in a process of ever-improving performance, although later goals are achieved with decreasing speed.

If these conditions are applied to regular, existing psychotherapy training, findings show that they are not frequently met. The mechanisms of change in psychotherapy are far from being understood so clearly and comprehensively that a training program could be designed with built-in deliberate practice. It is evident, however, that the provision of feedback, especially related to more complex tasks, is a critical point. It should be recognized that it is difficult to provide relevant feedback in psychotherapy, as intrinsic feedback (feedback information accessible without additional assessment or other action; not to be confused with intrinsic motivation) is rare. In many other professional domains, intrinsic feedback is available (e.g., a surgeon immediately sees whether a cut was right, whether a flow of blood has been stopped successfully). In psychotherapy, when expert performance is largely based on the adaptation of therapeutic action to very specific requirements of a case and/or a situation, it would be ideal to have a master therapist watch a trainee's performance and give feedback for much of the training. Many trainees do have supervisors who provide such feedback, but usually it is only partially

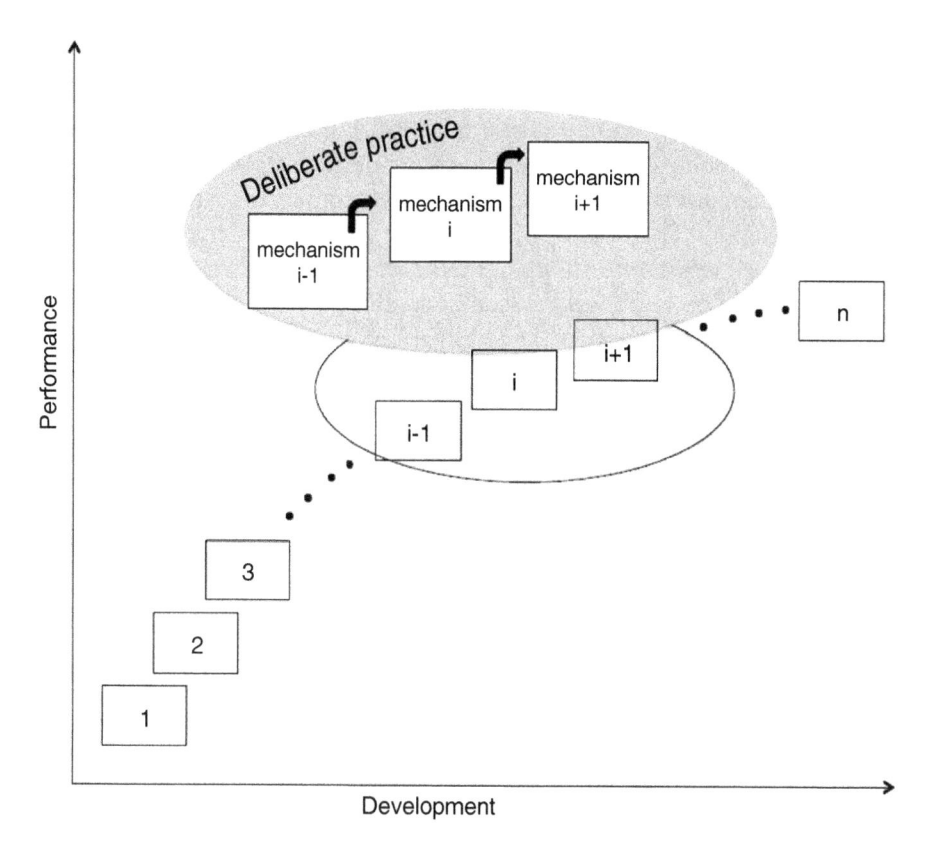

Figure 11.2. Learning the use of different mechanisms over time. Mechanisms are components of a professional activity; they can be defined and learned (or improved) one by one. Once one mechanism is mastered, the next can be dealt with. Mechanisms must be clearly defined, then trained with fast, explicit feedback. From *Expert Performance in Sports: Advances in Research on Sport Expertise* (p. 70), by J. L. Starkes and K. A. Ericsson (Eds.), 2003, Champaign, IL: Human Kinetics. Copyright 2003 by Human Kinetics. Reprinted with permission.

based on direct observation, it is most often not related to previously defined clear learning goals, it is time delayed, and it is not possible to act immediately again in a version improved on the basis of feedback, and get new feedback again. To some extent, live supervision, especially with a bug in the ear or in the eye (by written feedback on a monitor during the session) is an exception, but it is seldom used (Weck et al., 2016).

One method to allow for deliberate practice would be to split up complex performance into modules to make it easier to assess goals and mastery of skills and provide feedback. Computer support can help to make this possible, while sparing the time of master teachers. As an illustration, Caspar, Berger, and Hautle (2004) developed and evaluated a training module that draws heavily on cognitive science and is a straightforward realization of deliberate practice. The goal of the module is to improve therapists' ability to come up with simple case formulations of intake interviews by observing a video recording and comparing their case formulation with those of experts.

The therapist types a report, which the computer compares with themes from expert texts. There are typically about 15 case specific themes identified (e.g., patient's relation to his or her mother, the therapeutic relationship). The therapist gets graphical feedback regarding the extent to which he or she has addressed these topics. The feedback might indicate that only 30% of issues identified by experts have been covered on the topic of the therapeutic relationship, for example. From this feedback, the therapist amends his or her conceptualization, which then becomes the target of another wave of computer feedback. Within this context, an increase of covered percentage represents an immediate reinforcement. Once the therapist thinks that his or her possibilities of completing the formulation are exhausted, the computer gives access to the expert texts. Empirically, it has been found that the use of this program leads to a greater breadth and completeness in the therapist's clinical views of video recorded cases (Caspar et al., 2004).

Despite efforts toward developing deliberate practice, the lack of prescriptive models for much of what makes up expert performance in psychotherapy remains a major problem. For instance, although superior ability to establish and maintain a good therapeutic relationship is a pivotal part of expertise (Sperry & Carlson, 2014), a good relationship is a marker of improvement—confounding training elements and (intermediate) outcome. Therefore, as a basis for training, the ingredients of a good relationship need to be clear: What do therapists need to provide to patients? When it comes to the bond, for example, therapists need a good understanding of patients' interpersonal needs and limitations (which is part of a good case formulation), they need good heuristics for deriving strategies from this understanding, and they need certain abilities (such as always considering relational aspects in every intervention while communicating with a convincing non- and paraverbal behavior; Caspar, 2007). Some therapists may be able to perform well on an intuitive base, but others need explicit, teachable concepts. Unfortunately, there are only a few prescriptive models covering at least part of the relevant ingredients. Two models with experimental evidence exist: alliance ruptures (Safran, Muran, & Eubanks-Carter, 2011) and the motive-oriented therapeutic relationship (Caspar, 2008; Kramer et al., 2014). More such models are needed before a comprehensive conceptual basis of deliberate practice can be created.

A last topic to be covered in this section is the individualization of training. Chow et al. (2015) suspected that a reason for the limited evidence for training effects might be that training has not been sufficiently adapted to individual therapists. Therapists-in-training particularly appreciate when trainers address their individual needs (Nerdrum & Rønnestad, 2002). The issue is not only what they like: Therapists-in-training are able to distinguish between what satisfies them the most in psychotherapy (self-experience) and what contributes the most to competence (individual supervision; Belz, Bayer, & Bengel, 2010). Both are the most individualized part of training. Why does it matter whether they like it? Learning in general, and even more so its special form of deliberate practice, requires motivated learners. That they are most motivated for the most individualized parts is an additional argument in favor of individualizing.

How Can Therapists Learn From Practice After Training?

General research on expertise suggests that excellence cannot be reached at the end of a few years of formal training (Ericsson, 2009). The issue of how to learn from subsequent practice is therefore highly relevant. On this issue, Tracey et al. (2014) argued that

> there is no demonstration of accuracy and skill that is associated with experience as a therapist [and that] over the course of one's professional practice as a psychotherapist, there is little development of expertise. We posit that this lack of expertise development (i.e., greater skill with greater experience) is attributable to the lack of information available to individual therapists regarding the outcomes of their interventions, the lack of adequate models about how psychotherapy produces benefits, and the difficulty of using the information that does exist to improve one's performance over time. (pp. 1–2)

Tracey and colleagues' (2014) assertion is in line with what is known about requirements for deliberate practice: The lack of appropriate models of how psychotherapy works, a possible lack of motivation, and the lack of useful feedback are the main reasons for the difficulty of learning from practice. A requirement for feedback to be useful is that it provides information regarding whether a current intervention actually contributes to some successful outcome, however small it may be. As stated earlier, this is more complicated in psychotherapy than in other fields. A therapist may notice a deep breath or a happy or tense facial expression, but it is not always clear if the intervention to which the patient is reacting will contribute to positive outcome. Findings suggest that excellent therapists are good at reading and evaluating/interpreting subtle signs, but it needs to be acknowledged that this is more demanding compared with professions with more explicit intrinsic feedback. Experts in many domains are better in self-monitoring (Glaser & Chi, 1988), and self-monitoring skills appear to be both a precondition for, and a consequence of, learning from experience. The question, however, is whether psychotherapy practice provides sufficient opportunities to develop such abilities.

Therapists depend more than other professionals on extrinsic (artificially created) feedback, such as patient questionnaires. Extrinsic feedback is usually delayed in time and hard to relate to what the therapist has done. It is revealing to look at which kind of physicians improve with experience: Although performance deteriorates in many medical disciplines with distance from medical school, surgeons' performance improves (Ericsson, 2004). As previously mentioned, the most obvious explanation is the availability of immediate feedback, possibly in combination with a chance of corrected action and immediate new feedback.

Some therapists (good ones, arguably) may seek out feedback from their clients, either directly, by asking them about their reactions to treatment, or indirectly, by assessing nonverbals or reading between the lines of what the client says. Although this sort of feedback may certainly be useful, it is also subjective, and its usefulness may depend on how honest the client chooses to be. Hill, Thompson, Cogar, and Denman (1993) found that in single sessions of psychotherapy, over half of the clients withheld reactions from their therapists, and less than one third of therapists could identify that their client was withholding something. Therefore, this form of feedback may not provide dependable data about the effectiveness of psychotherapy or of specific interventions.

There is a line of research emphasizing feedback on the basis of patient questionnaires (see Chapter 16, this volume; Lutz, De Jong, & Rubel, 2015). Although such assessment and feedback are seen as important, particularly when giving warning signs in the case of a problematic psychotherapy, it cannot be expected to provide sufficient feedback for deliberate practice. Effects captured by the Outcome Questionnaire-45, for example, are only loosely related to therapist action; they can alert therapists and point out what kind of change is missing, but they cannot inform their information processing and acting at a level corresponding to feedback needed for deliberate practice. This may also be responsible for the fact that, although there is good evidence for the use of routine outcome monitoring, there are also contradictory findings (Strauss et al., 2015).

Even if therapists were to have extensive follow-up data available, deliberative practice would still require them to rely on comprehensive and highly detailed models of therapeutic change. Such models, however, as emphasized already, are at best partially available. What the literature on expertise suggests is that the best chance of optimally learning from experience exists when therapists have clear, explicit, theoretically driven, individual case conceptualizations serving as a basis for interpreting information emerging in the course of psychotherapy. Master therapists have indeed a deeper understanding of their cases (Sperry & Carlson, 2014), as they are observing and comparing new information constantly with what they already know

(Miller et al., 2007), and experts in general have been found to invest more than novices into developing a deep, qualitative understanding of problems (Glaser & Chi, 1988).

Formulation, it is claimed, enhances psychotherapy effectiveness because symptoms and problems are understood and organized by a coherent theoretical structure (Benjamin, 2002; Bieling & Kuyken, 2003; Eells et al., 2011), which may then inform treatment planning. Proficiency in case formulation is not only viewed as an ingredient to success in ongoing therapies (for which additional evidence is needed), but it may also be a prerequisite for optimal learning in favor of future cases, as well as for becoming an expert. Eells et al. (2005) found that experts (defined as therapists developing or intensely teaching case formulation concepts) develop superior abilities, whereas nonexpert therapists may lose abilities or develop maladaptive idiosyncrasies with increased experience and distance from training.

In addition to useful feedback and helpful models, expertise requires an ongoing effort to increase and maintain excellence (Ericsson, 2009). Master therapists are "voracious learners" (Sperry & Carlson, 2014). With the suboptimal learning conditions of psychotherapy practice in mind, one could say that they are obviously able and highly motivated to make the best of a difficult situation. Therapists intrinsically dedicated to deliver good psychotherapy may not be necessarily motivated or able to invest much into additional training. There are all kinds of honorable motives (e.g., family) competing for therapists' time, and the job situation may force them to struggle for survival rather than invite them to care about excellence. In addition, the overconfidence of a majority of therapists reported by Tracey et al. (2014) is not an ideal precondition for extra investment of unpaid time. In terms of extrinsic motivation, additional training is not likely to lead to better payment, and the enhanced status that such training could potentially provide is only remotely related to independently assessed success. The situation of psychotherapists is fundamentally different from that of musicians and athletes in this respect (Ericsson, 2006).

Despite less than optimal conditions for seeking additional and/or formal training, some therapists do invest into learning from experience: Najavits and Strupp (1994) reported a study on psychodynamically oriented therapists that showed the more effective therapists made significantly more self-critical comments concerning their performance. In a study by Chow et al. (2015), the top 25% (e.g., most effective therapists) spent, on average, 2.8 times more hours per week engaged in deliberate practice activities (e.g., reviewing difficult/challenging cases alone, attending training workshops for specific models of psychotherapy, mentally running through and reflecting on the past sessions in their mind, mentally planning for future sessions) aimed at improving effectiveness than the other 75% of therapists. Although the data are self-reported and retrospective, they are in line with findings in other domains. Ericsson (2006) reported that, for example, master chess players deteriorate if they "only" play against excellent players. They need very specific (self-) training to further improve.

CLOSING COMMENTS

Although research has yet to provide clear answers to the questions of how to identify expert therapists and how expertise develops in psychotherapists, the broader literature on expertise offers some promising clues to understanding these specific aspects of therapist effects. Although not all therapists may achieve expert status, understanding how expert performance develops may also inform us how to support the development of all good therapists.

There are indicators that individualized treatments for patients have better outcome. There is also good reason to assume that our therapist training needs individualization, for which Caspar (1997) described a utopia of individualized, concept-informed, and empirically based training. This can only be realized, if at all, once more empirical knowledge is gathered and more comprehensive models are developed for how expertise develops in psychotherapy. I contend, however, that even now the situation can be improved by following more of the principles of deliberate practice—in training (formulating more precise, individualized learning steps and providing feedback) and in psychotherapy practice (creating extrinsic feedback and by teaching how to better use the scarce intrinsic feedback that is available)—as master therapists seem to do.

REFERENCES

Alder, J. (1999). *Der Einfluss eines Trainings zur intuitiven und rational-analytischen Informationsverarbeitung auf das Denken und Erleben von Psychotherapeuten und Psychotherapeutinnen* [The impact of a training for intuitive and traditional-analytic information-processing on thinking and experiencing of psychotherapists]. Unpublished doctoral dissertation, University of Bern, Bern, Switzerland.

Anderson, T., Ogles, B. M., Patterson, C. L., Lambert, M. J., & Vermeersch, D. A. (2009). Therapist effects: Facilitative interpersonal skills as a predictor of therapist success. *Journal of Clinical Psychology, 65,* 755–768. http://dx.doi.org/10.1002/jclp.20583

Belz, M., Bayer, J., & Bengel, J. (2010, June). *Which parts of psychotherapy training contribute most to the development of psychotherapeutic expertise?* Paper presented at the meeting of the Society for Psychotherapy Research, Pacific Grove, CA.

Benjamin, L. S. (2002). Structural analysis of social behavior (SASB). In M. Hersen & W. Sledge (Eds.), *Encyclopedia of psychotherapy* (Vol. 2, pp. 707–713). San Diego, CA: Academic Press.

Bieling, P. J., & Kuyken, W. (2003). Is cognitive case formulation science or science fiction? *Clinical Psychology: Science and Practice, 10,* 52–69.

Caspar, F. (1995). Hypothesis-generation in intake interviews. In B. Boothe, R. Hirsig, A. Helminger, B. Meier, & R. Volkart (Eds.), *Perception—evaluation—interpretation* (pp. 3–11). Ashland, OH: Hogrefe & Huber.

Caspar, F. (1997). What goes on in a psychotherapist's mind? *Psychotherapy Research, 7,* 105–125. http://dx.doi.org/10.1080/10503309712331331913

Caspar, F. (2007). Plan Analysis. In T. Eells (Ed.), *Handbook of psychotherapeutic case formulations* (2nd ed., pp. 251–289). New York, NY: Guilford Press.

Caspar, F. (2008). Motivorientierte Beziehungsgestaltung [Motive oriented therapeutic relationship]. In M. Hermer & B. Röhrle (Eds.), *Handbuch der therapeutischen Beziehung* [Handbook of therapeutic relationship] (pp. 527–558). Tübingen, Germany: DGVT-Verlag.

Caspar, F., Berger, T., & Hautle, I. (2004). The right view of your patient: A computer-assisted, individualized module for psychotherapy training. *Psychotherapy: Theory, Research, Practice, Training, 41,* 125–135. http://dx.doi.org/10.1037/0033-3204.41.2.125

Caspar, F., Rothenfluh, T., & Segal, Z. V. (1992). The appeal of connectionism for clinical psychology. *Clinical Psychology Review, 12,* 719–762. http://dx.doi.org/10.1016/0272-7358(92)90022-Z

Chow, D. L., Miller, S. D., Seidel, J. A., Kane, R. T., Thornton, J. A., & Andrews, W. P. (2015). The role of deliberate practice in the development of highly effective psychotherapists. *Psychotherapy, 52,* 337–345. http://dx.doi.org/10.1037/pst0000015

Dreyfus, H., & Dreyfus, S. (1986). *Mind over machine: The power of human intuition and expertise in the era of the computer.* New York, NY: Blackwell.

Dreyfus, S. E. (2004). The five-stage model of adult skill acquisition. *Bulletin of Science, Technology & Society, 24,* 177–181. http://dx.doi.org/10.1177/0270467604264992

Eells, T. D., Lombart, K. G., Kendjelic, E. M., Turner, L. C., & Lucas, C. P. (2005). The quality of psychotherapy case formulations: A comparison of expert, experienced, and novice cognitive-behavioral and psychodynamic therapists. *Journal of Consulting and Clinical Psychology, 73,* 579–589. http://dx.doi.org/10.1037/0022-006X.73.4.579

Eells, T. D., Lombart, K. G., Salsman, N., Kendjelic, E. M., Schneiderman, C. T., & Lucas, C. P. (2011). Expert reasoning in psychotherapy case formulation. *Psychotherapy Research, 21,* 385–399. http://dx.doi.org/10.1080/10503307.2010.539284

Elliott, R., & Shapiro, D. A. (1988). Brief structured recall: A more efficient method for studying significant therapy events. *The British Journal of Medical Psychology, 61,* 141–153. http://dx.doi.org/10.1111/j.2044-8341.1988.tb02773.x

Ericsson, K. A. (2003). The development of elite performance and deliberate practice: An update from the perspective of the expert-performance approach. In J. L. Starkes & K. A. Ericsson (Eds.), *Expert performance in sport: Recent advances in research on sport expertise* (pp. 49–81). Champaign, IL: Human Kinetics.

Ericsson, K. A. (2004). Deliberate practice and the acquisition and maintenance of expert performance in medicine and related domains. *Academic Medicine, 79*(10, Suppl.), S70–S81. http://dx.doi.org/10.1097/00001888-200410001-00022

Ericsson, K. A. (2006). The influence of experience and deliberate practice on the development of superior expert performance. In K. A. Ericsson, N. Charness, R. R. Hoffman, & P. J. Feltovich (Eds.), *The Cambridge handbook of expertise and expert performance* (pp. 683–703). New York, NY: Cambridge University Press. http://dx.doi.org/10.1017/CBO9780511816796.038

Ericsson, K. A. (2009). Enhancing the development of professional performance: Implications from the study of deliberate practice. In K. A. Ericsson (Ed.), *Development of professional expertise: Toward measurement of expert performance and design of optimal learning environments* (pp. 405–431). Cambridge, England: Cambridge University Press.

Ericsson, K. A. (2015). Acquisition and maintenance of medical expertise: A perspective from the expert-performance approach with deliberate practice. *Academic Medicine, 90,* 1471–1486. http://dx.doi.org/10.1097/ACM.0000000000000939

Ericsson, K. A., Krampe, R. T., & Tesch-Römer, C. (1993). The role of deliberate practice in the acquisition of expert performance. *Psychological Review, 100,* 363–406. http://dx.doi.org/10.1037/0033-295X.100.3.363

Eversmann, J. (2008). *Psychometrische Überprüfung eines Auswahlverfahrens psychotherapeutischer Ausbildungsteilnehmer* [Psychometric evaluation of a selection procedure for participants in psychotherapy training]. Unpublished doctoral dissertation, University of Osnabrück, Osnabrück, Germany.

Feltovich, P. J., Prietula, M. J., & Ericsson, K. A. (2006). Studies of expertise from psychological perspectives. In K. A. Ericsson, N. Charness, R. R. Hoffman, & P. J. Feltovich (Eds.), *The Cambridge handbook of expertise and expert performance* (pp. 41–68). New York, NY: Cambridge University Press. http://dx.doi.org/10.1017/CBO9780511816796.004

Gigerenzer, G. (2009). Bounded rationality. In D. Sander & K. R. Scherer (Eds.), *The Oxford companion to emotion and the affective sciences* (pp. 79–80). New York, NY: Oxford University Press.

Glaser, R., & Chi, M. T. H. (1988). Overview. In M. T. H. Chi, R. Glaser, & M. J. Farr (Eds.), *The nature of expertise* (pp. xv–xxviii). Hillsdale, NJ: Erlbaum.

Hill, C. E., & Knox, S. (2013). Training and supervision in psychotherapy. In M. J. Lambert (Ed.), *Bergin and Garfield's handbook of psychotherapy and behavior change* (6th ed., pp. 775–811). Hoboken, NJ: Wiley.

Hill, C. E., Thompson, B. J., Cogar, M. C., & Denman, D. W. (1993). Beneath the surface of long-term therapy: Therapist and client report of their own and each other's covert processes. *Journal of Counseling Psychology, 40*, 278–287. http://dx.doi.org/10.1037/0022-0167.40.3.278

Itten, S. (1994). *Intuitives Informationsverarbeiten in klinischen Erstgesprächen* [Intuitive information processing in intake interviews]. Unpublished master's thesis, University of Bern, Bern, Switzerland.

Jennings, L., & Skovholt, T. M. (1999). The cognitive, emotional, and relational characteristics of master therapists. *Journal of Counseling Psychology, 46*(1), 3–11. http://dx.doi.org/10.1037/0022-0167.46.1.3

Kahneman, D. (2003). A perspective on judgment and choice: Mapping bounded rationality. *American Psychologist, 58*, 697–720. http://dx.doi.org/10.1037/0003-066X.58.9.697

Kern, A., & McColgan, D. (2015). *Monitoring in der Psychotherapie: Untersuchung einer metakognitiven Fähigkeit des Therapeuten* [Monitoring in psychotherapy: Study on a metacognitive ability of psychotherapists]. Unpublished master's thesis, University of Bern, Bern, Switzerland.

Kramer, U., Kolly, S., Berthoud, L., Keller, S., Preisig, M., Caspar, F., . . . Despland, J.-N. (2014). Effects of motive-oriented therapeutic relationship in a ten session general psychiatric treatment of borderline personality disorder: a randomized controlled trial. *Psychotherapy and Psychosomatics, 83*, 176–186.

Lutz, W., De Jong, K., & Rubel, J. (2015). Patient-focused and feedback research in psychotherapy: Where are we and where do we want to go? *Psychotherapy Research, 25*, 625–632. http://dx.doi.org/10.1080/10503307.2015.1079661

Miller, S. D., Duncan, B., & Hubble, M. (2007, November/December). Supershrinks: What is the secret of their success? *Psychotherapy Networker*, 27–56.

Najavits, L. M., & Strupp, H. H. (1994). Differences in the effectiveness of psychodynamic therapists: A process-outcome study. *Psychotherapy: Theory, Research, Practice, Training, 31*, 114–123. http://dx.doi.org/10.1037/0033-3204.31.1.114

Nakash, O., & Alegría, M. (2013). Examination of the role of implicit clinical judgments during the mental health intake. *Qualitative Health Research, 23*, 645–654. http://dx.doi.org/10.1177/1049732312471732

Nerdrum, P. & Rønnestad, M. H. (2002). The trainee's perspective: A qualitative study of learning empathic communication in Norway. *The Counseling Psychologist, 30*, 609–629.

Pascual-Leone, J. (1990). An essay on wisdom: Toward organismic processes that make it possible. In R. Sternberg (Ed.), *Wisdom: Its nature, origins, and development* (pp. 244–278). Cambridge, MA: Harvard University Press. http://dx.doi.org/10.1017/CBO9781139173704.013

Popp-Liesum, M. (2005). *Aufmerksamkeitssteuerungsprozesse von erfahrenen und unerfahrenen Psychotherapeuten* [Control of attention with experienced and inexperienced psychotherapists]. Uelvesbüll, Germany: Der Andere Verlag.

Rønnestad, M. H., & Skovholt, T. M. (2003). The journey of the counselor and therapist: Research findings and perspectives on professional development. *Journal of Career Development, 30*, 5–44.

Safran, J. D., Muran, J. C., & Eubanks-Carter, C. (2011). Repairing alliance ruptures. *Psychotherapy, 48*, 80–87. http://dx.doi.org/10.1037/a0022140

Sperry, L., & Carlson, J. (2014). *How master therapists work*. New York, NY: Routledge.

Strauss, B. M., Lutz, W., Steffanowski, A., Wittmann, W. W., Boehnke, J. R., Rubel, J., . . . Kirchmann, H. (2015). Benefits and challenges in practice-oriented psychotherapy research in Germany: The TK and the QS-PSY-BAY projects of quality assurance in outpatient psychotherapy. *Psychotherapy Research, 25*, 32–51. http://dx.doi.org/10.1080/10503307.2013.856046

Tracey, T. J., Wampold, B. E., Lichtenberg, J. W., & Goodyear, R. K. (2014). Expertise in psychotherapy: An elusive goal? *American Psychologist, 69*(3), 218–229. http://dx.doi.org/10.1037/a0035099

Webb, C. A., DeRubeis, R. J., & Barber, J. P. (2010). Therapist adherence/competence and treatment outcome: A meta-analytic review. *Journal of Consulting and Clinical Psychology, 78*(2), 200–211. http://dx.doi.org/10.1037/a0018912

Weck, F., Jakob, M., Neng, J. M. B., Höfling, V., Grikscheit, F., & Bohus, M. (2016). The effects of bug-in-the-eye-supervision on therapeutic alliance and therapist competence in cognitive-behavioral therapy: A randomized controlled trial. *Clinical Psychology & Psychotherapy, 23*, 386–396. http://dx.doi.org/10.1002/cpp.1968

12

GAINING THERAPEUTIC WISDOM AND SKILLS FROM CREATIVE OTHERS (WRITERS, ACTORS, MUSICIANS, AND DANCERS)

BARRY A. FARBER

"Every specialist, owing to a well-known professional bias, believes that he understands the entire human being, while in reality he only grasps a tiny part of him" (Carrel, 1935, p. 43). And so, despite their extensive education, caring attitude, genuine curiosity, and wish to help, therapists very likely understand less than they believe they do about their clients. The question, then, is what kinds of therapists do understand a bit more about human behavior and are able to help somewhat more than others?

There are myriad reasons why some therapists are more effective than others. As the chapters in this book note, some therapists are more present, focused, self-aware, interpersonally skilled, responsive, attuned, persistent, optimistic, and/or more open to feedback than others, allowing them to more effectively intervene and facilitate change in their clients' lives.

The hypothesis posed in this chapter is that, in general, more effective therapists are those who are most flexible and/or creative—not in the

http://dx.doi.org/10.1037/0000034-013
How and Why Are Some Therapists Better Than Others? Understanding Therapist Effects, L. G. Castonguay and C. E. Hill (Eds.)
Copyright © 2017 by the American Psychological Association. All rights reserved.

sense necessarily of a great degree of theoretical eclecticism, of combining the best ideas from multiple clinical sources, as useful as that strategy might be (e.g., Castonguay et al., 2010)—to the extent that they are able to adopt strategies and perspectives of creative, wise individuals in diverse fields of knowledge, especially in the arts. I argue for privileging wise therapists over smart therapists. Although therapists in both these categories are admirably knowledgeable and worthy of respect, I draw a distinction between those who are open to multiple and varied perspectives on change and those who are highly knowledgeable about the use of a single paradigm (and perhaps some variants) to understand and intervene across a range of problems and disorders. That said, it should be clear that this distinction is best seen as existing on a continuum—most therapists fall somewhere in the middle ground of clinical flexibility and creativity—and that wisdom can be found in many places. It should also be clear, then, that I am concerned in this chapter with the question of effective therapists rather than the more research-focused question of therapist effects.

This chapter is somewhat influenced by the research and reflections of those who have written about the need for creativity in the field, but it is primarily based on interviews that my graduate students and I conducted. Some of those whom we interviewed are artists and creative types outside the field of psychology who have been therapy clients, and some are therapists with a background in the arts. To be sure, the same or similar arguments about enhancing clinical skills could be made on behalf of the proposition that clinical advantages accrue among those therapists with backgrounds in any number of extra-clinical experiences other than the arts, including those that are academically related (e.g., the study of philosophy or anthropology), spiritually related (e.g., work in a religious or spiritual setting), or community related (e.g., volunteer work as a community organizer or with a humanitarian agency). Nevertheless, for purposes of this chapter, the specific emphasis will be on how clinical effectiveness may be abetted by an understanding of the perspectives offered by two general types of creative individuals: those with a background in writing and dramatic performance and those with a background in music and dance.

I rarely come across therapists who are not well intentioned and genuinely interested in helping others, nor ones who are not convinced that their method for treating clients was not the best available. The problem here is reflected in Maslow's (1966) oft-cited quote: "If the only tool you have is a hammer, you tend to see everything as if it were a nail" (p. 1). Therapists may well get stuck, at least at times, by their insistence on sticking with what is familiar and comfortable. Extending this notion, a recent meta-analysis of psychotherapist effects concluded that "effective therapists seem to transcend the ideological mantra that is typically perpetuated by focusing on treatments"

(Owen, Drinane, Idigo, & Valentine, 2015, p. 327). The mounting interest in eclectic forms of psychotherapy over the past few decades suggests that therapists are aware of the problems and limitations of ideological inflexibility; many have seemingly moved from an entrenched rigidity in their thinking to a greater fluidity of intellectual and emotional thinking as they become older.

Although therapists have traditionally sought new knowledge about how best to work with their clients (even when not explicitly required to do so in the service of a required course or for licensure renewal), for the most part, this admirable quest has been narrowly defined. Therapists tend to learn from those in their own profession, and even more so from those sharing their own theoretical vision, via journals and books, professional conferences, graduate and postgraduate courses, personal therapy, and supervision. There are significant advantages to this approach, including those related to professional socialization and those associated with learning a common language and common paradigms, excellent bases from which to further one's already-established understanding and skills. However, there are also significant disadvantages to this strategy, including the adoption of a narrow epistemological base and the exclusion of acquired wisdom about human nature and change from multiple other, potentially rich sources.

In part, I came to this understanding after a particularly wise teacher asked us to read Stanislavsky's (1936) *An Actor Prepares* for a graduate class I attended in clinical psychology as a means for extending our awareness of the ways in which individuals could convey multiple aspects of experience, including genuine emotion and disingenuousness. The book, while describing the experiences of a fictional acting student, is essentially autobiographical, and deals with such issues as motivation, concentration and attention, imagination, unconscious forces, inner monologues, and body language. In fact, this professor frequently had us read books outside the "canon" of established and well-regarded psychology texts, including books that would have been shelved in the history, sociology, education, and fiction sections of a library. Perhaps it was no accident that despite his prodigious reputation in the field he was somewhat of an outcast in the department itself, relegated to an office several blocks away from the rest of the tenured faculty.

I also come to this position—that of extolling the virtues of understanding psychological phenomena through varied means and the study of varied creative enterprises—through the experience of interviewing candidates for our doctoral program in clinical psychology. Many of our candidates, and seemingly most of our favored candidates, have not only studied psychology but have backgrounds in the arts, including theater, music, writing, and dance. That they did so well in our program (and after) seems attributable not just to their beginning their doctoral studies as somewhat older, more mature students, but to a general flexibility of thinking, and a willingness and ability to understand and help individuals through multiple channels, most of which have never shown up in a course curriculum. These burgeoning therapists seem particularly apt at recognizing their own and others' false notes, disjointed presentations, halting narratives, and emotional missteps. They seem to have a talent to be usefully self-critical and to adjust their efforts accordingly.

This is not to say that a background in the arts is either necessary or sufficient to becoming an effective therapist—my own therapy hero, Carl Rogers, was not especially inclined in this way—but rather that the creativity nourished by the arts or otherwise extra-psychological discipline may provide the extra boost that differentiates the good-enough therapist from the especially effective practitioner, perhaps especially in complex cases where traditional patterns of thinking have often failed in the past. It is also important to note that there can be too much of a good thing—therapists, regardless of their experience level, can rely too much on their creativity and artistic inspiration to the detriment of structure and consistent clinical focus.

"PSYCHOTHERAPY IS AN ART BASED ON A SCIENCE THAT DOESN'T EXIST"

This often heard (and unattributed) comment made by therapy critics is hyperbole, of course—among other scientific principles used by psychotherapists are those based on learning theory (e.g., operant conditioning, extinction). Although there may be a small kernel of truth in this assertion—there are surprisingly few well-established principles and mechanisms of change—a more widely accepted proposition is that psychotherapy can be seen as containing elements of science and art, structure and flexibility, classical composition and "all that jazz." All who understand well, or have even mastered, the therapeutic principles they have been taught, do not perform clinical work equally well. Most therapists would agree that there is something beyond technical skills necessary to perform therapeutic work in an expert manner; some have written about this quite passionately (e.g., McWilliams, 2005; Norcross, 2011). McWilliams (2005), for example, while touting the importance of learning the basic principles of clinical work, contended that the "practice of psychotherapy is an art, and as such can be compared more aptly to disciplines of musical expression than to medical treatments" (p. 25).

Although recent empirical work has indicated that adherence to a treatment manual is unrelated to outcome (e.g., Webb, DeRubeis, & Barber, 2010), others, including Wampold (2001) in his influential book, *The Great Psychotherapy Debate*, have argued that such adherence stifles therapists' artistry. Perhaps the resolution to these contrasting perspectives lies in Goldfried, Raue, and Castonguay's (1998) research indicating that expert therapists use manuals differently than others; similarly, it may be the case that adherence to manuals stifles creativity (and perhaps effectiveness) with some therapists working with some specific (i.e., particularly challenging) clients.

As a famous pianist, Artur Schnabel, is reputed to have said, "The notes I handle no better than many pianists. But the pauses between the notes—ah, that is where the art resides." Those pauses, whether in music or psychotherapy, may take more than technical skill to finesse. Therapy manuals drive up the mean effectiveness score of a random sample of therapists, but at the expense of constricting the effectiveness of those who would have performed higher than the mean had they not adhered to the manual. Great interpersonal competence is likely one significant discriminant between average therapists and excellent ones, but the ability to listen and respond to more than the manifest content of the words—to listen for narrative shifts, pauses, tonal variations, emotional coloring, plot lines, minor characters, and false notes, and to intervene flexibly with knowledge of such shifts and the nonlinearity of change (all things that artists and other creative individuals do so well)—is arguably another variable that separates the good from the great therapist. And although these characteristics are neither sufficient nor necessary in regard to therapeutic expertise—there are clinicians with artistic talents that are mediocre in their work, and there are multiple pathways to such therapeutic virtues as empathy, sensitivity, and clinical flexibility—there are distinctive advantages to being able to draw on an artistic sensibility in at least certain cases at certain times.

There are, of course, those who practice forms of psychotherapy that are explicitly associated with and mediated by the expressive arts, including dance, music, and art therapists. And there are those, most notably the late Natalie Rogers (daughter of Carl Rogers), who practice what they call *expressive arts therapy* (e.g., Rogers, 1993), a blend of humanistic therapy and various expressive arts modalities (e.g., music, art, movement, guided imagery, drama). But what of more "mainstream" therapists—those who are not affiliated with the expressive or creative arts but have rather been trained in more traditional psychodynamic, cognitive–behavioral therapy (CBT), or humanistic modalities—what might they learn from artists and creative others that might contribute to their clinical effectiveness?

BEING A MORE EFFECTIVE THERAPIST: LEARNING FROM WRITERS AND ACTORS

> I remember two summers when I went through all the Russians . . . feeling a sense of connection with Dostoevsky, Tolstoy, Checkhov, and Turgenev. Love and death. My early answers to the question, "What is healing?" came from these stories. (Shem, 2002, p. 934)

As a group, writers have long had a conflicted relationship with the practice of psychotherapy. Although many have embraced its virtues and been ardent advocates, at least some have been vitriolic in their criticism. Those in the latter group, most notably D. H. Lawrence (1921/1960), have contended that understanding one's inner life neutralizes the demonic forces that give rise to artistry. Still, for the most part, writers have suggested that their own psychotherapy has enhanced their creativity and generated new and innovative ways of expressing human nature (e.g., Farber & Green, 1993).

But what of the converse? What are the ways in which an understanding of writing and/or literature might increase the effectiveness of a therapist? Jacqueline Sheehan, a novelist and therapist, was one of several people interviewed for an article in the American Psychological Association's *Monitor on Psychology* on psychologist–novelists (Winerman, 2014). She noted that her early reading of Edgar Allan Poe and his great awareness of the emotion of grief had "an early imprint on me, that writing and literature can help you process emotions and feelings" (Winerman, 2014, p. 69). Noted psychoanalyst Thomas Ogden "looks as much to poetry as to psychoanalytic literature when he wants to deepen his understanding of human predicaments" (McWilliams, 2005, p. 69).

In fact, multiple possibilities present themselves in terms of how reading or writing can contribute to therapists' skills: a profound appreciation of the great themes in life, virtually all of which will be observed clinically (e.g., identity, intimacy, meaning, family and community, responsibility and agency, freedom, birth and death); an understanding of the competing states of consciousness and multiple self-states; an awareness of primitive feelings and their press for expression; an awareness of repetitive patterns of behavior and respect for the difficulty of enduring change; an appreciation of the dialectic between public and private selves, and that between the anticipation of shame and the need for self-expression; and a belief in the need for and power of narrative, including the possibility of reshaping one's story.

These foci of awareness can be present in those without considerable literary knowledge or ability, especially in those who tend to be psychologically minded for whatever the reason (Farber & Golden, 1997). Still, it seems plausible, and even likely, that a lifelong passion for reading or writing would not only propel some to the study and practice of mental health—"being a writer and a psychologist comes from the same place" (Winerman, 2014, p. 70)—but that once in the field, such individuals would benefit from their knowledge and awareness of human nature, as well as their ability to extract, summarize, and integrate information. One of my doctoral students admitted "that the way I ask questions is totally shaped by my past as a newspaper writer. In both professions . . . questions are about providing a prompt for the client (or source) to speak more, provide more details, open up, help us both understand what happened." A former writer noted, "There are books and literature and poems that let you see into the soul of the writer, and so sometimes, you see patterns . . . later, you're able to see patterns in therapy sessions and see patterns in the lives of your clients."

The recent psychotherapeutic focus on narrative (e.g., Angus & McLeod, 2003)—on understanding and expanding or otherwise collaboratively altering clients' stories in more realistic and adaptive directions—is particularly consonant with a literary perspective. A narrative approach to therapy assumes that our identities and behavior are shaped by the stories we tell ourselves and others and narrative therapists act as investigative reporters, helping clients examine and reshape their relationship to a problematic aspect of their lives. As the novelist David Lodge (2001) noted, "Of course one can argue that there's a basic need for narrative: it's one of our fundamental tools for making sense of experience—has been back as far as you can go in history" (p. 83). Therapists of diverse theoretical orientations often attempt to change clients' narratives, especially those that are limiting and/or self-deprecating (e.g., with clients with an abuse history); an appreciation for the power, as well as the mutability of literary narratives, may well increase the ease and effectiveness of these approaches.

I interviewed a TV writer, someone with a good deal of success in a highly competitive line of work, and asked him what his writing emphasizes more than his therapy emphasizes. His answer was

> people's fundamental destiny or story . . . their spiritual meanings and beliefs, though not necessarily God. . . . I'm surprised that I've never been asked by a therapist about my belief system or existential questions . . . what am I here for? What is my legacy in life? How does my life have value or meaning?

I followed up by asking what else his own therapy does not sufficiently emphasize. His answered: "How an individual's journey is mediated through community. We live together, even if we die alone."

A colleague of mine, whose previous life was as a writer, suggested that reading good books "forced" him to revise his "too-optimistic" stance on people and that he was now better able to acknowledge the "dark side" of humanity. "I think people are selfish by nature and that avoiding this part of life is understandable but far too easy . . . I think reading, especially the Russian novelists, and writing have deepened my work." Rogers was, in fact, often confronted with the charge that he couldn't accept or deal with humanity's "heart of darkness," a charge he essentially acknowledged late in his career (Zeig, 1987). A student therapist who had been a novelist earlier in life offered that this pretherapy career furthered her appreciation for the power of imagination and fantasy. "I'm intrigued by people's fantasies and hopes for their lives and often ask questions about that. Although most of the time people don't end up doing what they imagine they'd like to do with their lives, they appreciate these kinds of discussion, and it does seem to open new possibilities for them." She added another perspective as well: "As a former struggling novelist, I understand fear and failure quite well, I think. I'm not afraid of going there with my clients and I can easily empathize with the failures and dashed hopes in their lives."

In a similar vein, several former actors (some colleagues, some students in clinical psychology programs) suggested that their acting experience greatly enhanced their ability to empathize with an endless diversity of experiences and feelings. Typically, these individuals had learned to display a wide range of emotions and had portrayed characters with many different emotional and behavioral features, some of which reflected notable pathologies found in the *Diagnostic and Statistical Manual of Mental Disorders*. One former actor went so far as to proclaim that "actors thrive on misery. They need it for their work . . . [it] makes it easier for me to understand others' misery." Another actor I interviewed suggested that actors themselves tended to be temperamental and difficult, providing a "training ground for subsequent clinical work with clients with fragile egos." Furthermore, the actors she knew and worked with often felt "unreal" and confused about their identity, value, and role and purpose in life—issues that often came up in clinical work with people who "felt lost and confused."

Another former actor added that learning improvisational skills helped her cope with difficult moments during therapy: "If a client throws something at you that you have never heard before, I'm reasonably able to think on my feet." This same actor also noted that there was something about learning pacing as part of playing a character (i.e., character development) that has helped her to stay patient when a client has struggled to open up to her: "I don't force the issue. I know there's likely to be an Act II and an Act III." Another former actor felt that she was more comfortable with humor in sessions that many of her contemporaries, suggesting that it was easier for her to view the use of client humor in therapy as something other than a defense: "Humor has the ability to coddle the ego, yet also tell you the truth . . . I think I'm reasonably good at teasing out the truth beneath the surface" (see also Chapter 15, this volume, for a discussion of therapist-initiated humor). Many of the putative advantages that accrue to psychotherapists as a result of immersion in the theater arts were summarized beautifully by an early career therapist who studied classical theater before entering a doctoral program in clinical psychology:

> We learned something called "repetition," sitting across from someone else, noticing things about their physicality, their tone of voice, their emotional tenor . . . monitoring their changing emotional verbal and

nonverbal landscape, as well as our own. It probably remains the most helpful training I've had in how to sit with another human as they have a real emotional experience. We also learned in-depth script and character analysis (What in this character's past brought him to this moment? How do these two characters interact and how do each of their unique pasts contribute to their interaction?). I learned to ask the questions I am still learning to ask. . . . I am also more attuned to the performative aspects of therapy, to the nuances of nonverbal expression, and am better able to contain and monitor my own emotional experience while simultaneously engaging with someone else's. . . . [As] an example, S is a woman in her early 40s with whom I have been working for over 2 years in psychodynamic psychotherapy. [She] displays a wide and extreme range of emotions in session, . . . [and] I am able to sit with her while remaining present and reflect to her moments where I find her display genuine or disconnected. We can then reflect together about why that might be.

Writing and acting plumb the depths of the human spirit; good writing and good acting are particularly effective means for understanding and accepting the complexities and uncertainties of most people's lives. Hollywood endings notwithstanding (e.g., *Good Will Hunting*), enduring change is neither linear nor the result of an insight-driven epiphany, and the awareness of the difficulties of people's lives, the tangled nature of interpersonal relationships, and the difficulty of change can certainly be heightened by immersion in art forms that emphasize these dynamics.

LEARNING FROM PERFORMANCE ARTISTS: MUSICIANS, SINGERS, AND DANCERS

Of all the themes that our interviewees expressed about the ways in which their background in music or dance has influenced their clinical work, the focus on awareness of physicality in the therapeutic setting was, by far, cited the most often. Here's one excellent example:

The experiences I had during my 11-year career as a professional dancer have greatly informed my work as a therapist. My lifelong training in dance has provided me with an intimate understanding of the mind–body connection and the ways in which movement and physicality affect mental states and, similarly, how mental states may impact physiological processes. I try to bring this awareness into the therapy room, where I find so many [clients] lack attunement to their bodies and physical sensations. I believe that the body is a rich resource for clinical data and, for many [clients], a powerful vehicle for accessing latent thoughts and experiences.

A variation on the theme of being attuned to nonverbal aspects of clients' experiences was provided by another therapist who had been a professional dancer. Here she emphasizes movement and other artistic expression not as a diagnostic tool but rather as a means to healing:

> I do know what it feels like to connect with my body, not through words, but through dance, and the rawness and rooted-ness that movement can provide. It cuts through thought, through stress, [and] through anxiety, and allows for a purer form of expression that creates simplicity and calm. In my clinical work, I think my experiences allow me to pick up on, highlight, and encourage whatever form of artistic expression a client may cherish or express interest in, and respect this interest as a piece of an identity and a tool for healing.

A former musician, now a therapist, offered a somewhat different perspective on how a background in the arts could provide an additional clinical edge. Therapists with musical backgrounds, she contended, may be particularly attuned to clients whose narrative is not linear or detail-oriented but rather ambiguous in tone or diffuse in content. As she explained,

> Many of the clients I see at our community-based clinic have been struggling artists—a freelance fashion designer, a filmmaker, a former actor, and an opera singer—and others have been artistic "souls," regardless of their profession, who feel deeply and often express themselves impressionistically, even poetically.

For those many therapists who tend to be more left-brained than otherwise (i.e., more attuned to and comfortable with listening in a detail-oriented manner), the ability to listen effectively and helpfully with clients with quite different verbal styles is a great advantage. In some ways, this is akin to being multilingual, a skill that is of particular value in community clinics serving a great diversity of clients.

A doctoral student of mine, a professional cellist before entering grad school, felt strongly and wrote compellingly about the positive effects his musical training had on his ability to listen clinically in open ways:

> When I think about how being a musician has informed my clinical work, I associate to Bion's advice to enter each therapeutic hour "without memory or desire." For me, that means something akin to "don't force it—let it come to you"—loosen your internal boundaries just enough to allow yourself to be open to discovering the unfamiliar in the familiar.

He also wrote about the ways in which musical performance open one up to new possibilities in familiar material:

> In music, there are endless possibilities to discover newness and aliveness in the routine. The notes never change. We practice them over and over and over again. It is up to the musician to discover something new—be it in him or in concert with his chamber group or orchestra—that permits

the emergence of a different outcome. For me, this is one of the biggest change mechanisms/goals of therapy. How to replay the past in the present and in the future with a different outcome.

Yet another theme, proposed by another dancer, was that of expanding one's own creativity and perspectives through exposure to other creative individuals:

> My years as a professional dancer . . . brought me into contact with a great range of creative individuals, including choreographers, musicians, photographers, costume designers, filmmakers, sculptors, and curators. . . . I connected with individuals whose backgrounds, cultures, values, and ideologies differed significantly from mine. As a result, I became aware of the commonalities in human experience, as well as the idiosyncrasies that make each individual unique. I feel that this exposure has benefitted my work as a therapist, because it taught me to reach beyond conventional, mainstream ideologies to search for meaning and purpose. In my work with my [clients], I try to bring the openness, curiosity, and creativity that I observed and appreciated in so many of the artists with whom I collaborated.

A student in the program in which I teach wrote so eloquently about the ways in which listening, especially the mutuality of attuned and responsive listening, is a shared feature of playing music and doing therapy. His words make ever more poignant my own regret at not learning how to play a musical instrument—a regret that now extends from my previous sense of what I was missing esthetically (as I am a music lover) to the new awareness of how this skill, this experience, especially in the context of playing with others, might have further extended my clinical range.

> Music is an intimate thing. As a musician, although I achieved my own entrance to a rarefied music school for the study of jazz violin performance, I didn't thrive in the sometimes competitive atmosphere of music school. Part of this was where I was personally at the time, but the deeper rejection of this model of musical achievement came from what I loved most about music—the listening. Rather than the practice room for 8 hours, I preferred the actual musical encounter of a group of musicians playing a familiar tune, improvising, listening, calling, and responding. In this way, music is very much like therapy.
>
> Music is like therapy in other important ways. There is a canon, and there are tomes worth of thematic variations upon that canon. There is the postmodern anti-canonical music, and the droll, insipid elevator music, but ultimately at its core, music is a conversation—two people riffing on each other's contributions. The back and forth of therapy is like jazz musicians trading fours. Sometimes we mirror the first soloist's exact contribution—"did I get that right?" Other times we expand, reimagine,

and reinterpret what the client said. But at its height, therapy, like music, is a merging of two souls. Sometimes the boundary between you and I disappears and we are just listening to each other . . . the caller and the responder lose their concrete meaning and there is just a creative experience and exploration.

CONCLUSIONS AND CLINICAL IMPLICATIONS

The rich material offered by these artist–therapists reflects their passion for their new work as therapists and their great appreciation for the ways in which their artistic past (and present in many cases) has provided them with a profound awareness of the complexities of life, the diversity of ways that people express themselves, the strands of meanings and emotions in virtually every communication, and the possibilities in all of us for playfulness, intimacy, and creative change. More specifically, several themes were emphasized in these therapists' attempts to articulate how their creative sensibilities have made them more effective therapists:

- a greater awareness of existential themes (e.g., identity, intimacy, family, community, agency and responsibility, fear and failure, the complexities and uncertainties of life, the universality of tragedy and grief);
- a greater awareness of one's own and others' motivations;
- a greater awareness of patterns of behavior and the possibility and difficulty of change;
- a greater awareness of multiple self-states and competing needs;
- a greater awareness of the conflict between public and private selves;
- a greater awareness of the power of narrative to shape one's life;
- a greater ability to understand fragmented, nonlinear, or diffuse narratives;
- a greater appreciation of the power of humor, imagination, and fantasy;
- a greater ability to empathize with a variety of perspectives (other than one's own);
- a greater ability to understand and process emotions, including intense, "primitive" feelings;
- a greater ability to remain patient and cope with one's own emotions while doing therapy;
- a greater attentiveness to nonverbal aspects of clients (e.g., body language, tone of voice); and

- a greater ease with encouraging artistic expression in clients and, in general, being more creative clinically.

During the interviews for this chapter, I surely pulled for these positive effects (e.g., by asking, "How has your clinical work has been affected—assumedly enhanced—by your background in the arts?"). In addition, these interviews were not subject to rigorous qualitative analysis (e.g., through consensual qualitative research methodology), a limitation consistent with the maxim that "the plural of anecdote is not data." There was also no control group—no means of determining whether a background in any field, including banking, cooking, teaching, law, or computer programming, wouldn't have yielded similarly glowing testaments to the clinically enhancing abilities of one's former profession. Perhaps maturity or number of years between the completion of one's undergraduate degree and the beginning of a doctoral program is primarily what drives beginning therapists' sense of relative competence. Nevertheless, I come away from reading and rereading these responses with a strong belief that though artistic experience is not the only means to therapeutic expertise, this background and sensibility in otherwise healthy and wise individuals does serve as an enhancement, increasing the probability of therapeutic success.

This belief should, of course, be subject to empirical scrutiny and possible validation. Comparing outcomes of matched cases between those therapists (controlling for experience) with and without artistic or literary backgrounds would provide preliminary (though hardly conclusive) data; somewhat more persuasive data could be obtained by analyzing clinical transcripts to determine whether certain classes of therapist interventions (i.e., those that coders deemed reflective of artistic or literary sensibilities) yield clinically and/or statistically significant differences on a variety of outcome measures.

But if this basic hypothesis is correct—that there are clinical advantages to a creative (artistic/literary) sensibility, what might be the clinical implications? For those with a more psychodynamic bent, a willingness to be open and playful as a therapist, and to encourage the same in clients, seems indicated. Winnicott (1953) wrote about "transitional space," suggesting that creativity and playfulness should be considered integral components of the process and outcome of psychotherapy. He believed that the goal of therapy should be not just the removal of symptoms, but it should promote clients' ability to be creative and playful; only through these means could an individual truly discover the self. "We are poor indeed, if we are only sane" (Winnicott, 1945, p. 139). From this perspective, being a more effective psychotherapist entails great awareness of all the parts of a client—not just his or her symptom picture but an appreciation for and encouragement of artistic and other creative aspects of a person—including the ways these play out in the relational world—that provide joy and meaning in life. Although this could be manifest in specific clinical activities offered by the therapist (e.g., Winnicott's, 1971, use of the Squiggle game with children and adolescents), it is far more about a sensibility, a way of being in the world. Such a sensibility can be fostered by a clinician's willingness to immerse him- or herself in the world of artistic expression—either by direct involvement in a specific art or creative enterprise (e.g., dance, sculpture, writing), through reading about the creation and inspiration underlying the creation and performance of influential pieces of music, ballets, paintings, plays, or movies, or through exposure to artistic works by attending performances, going to museums and exhibits, or participating in a book group.

And for those clinicians who are more CBT oriented, the perspectives of those interviewed for this chapter lead to the following suggestion: to consider not just clients' needs for symptom relief, as important as this might be to many, but also the ways they express themselves and the possible constrictions in their style (e.g., ways of speaking, body language) that might be impeding the realization of their goals. Practice and/or homework assignments might well include an appreciation of the elements of an individual's unique style, including opportunities for creative or artistic ways of completing this work. Doing so just might attenuate a significant problem in CBT, that of noncompliance with regard to homework (e.g., Callan et al., 2012; Engle & Arkowitz, 2006). Notably, too, there are CBT-related techniques that already include some artistic elements: Trauma-focused CBT (Cohen, Mannarino, & Deblinger, 2006) incorporates the use of "artistic narrative" within its protocol, reflecting the fact that art and play can be a part of a CBT approach. Furthermore, dialectical behavior therapy explicitly encourages "irreverence" on the part of the therapist, suggesting that such a stance (including humor, purposeful naivete, and feigned surprise) may be an effective means to force the client to adopt an alternative way of thinking.

Both these sets of suggestions (i.e., those aimed at more psychodynamically oriented therapists as well as more CBT-oriented therapists) bring to mind Messer's (1986; Messer & Winokur, 1980, 1984) articulation of four distinct "visions of life"—romantic, ironic, tragic, and comic—that underlie distinct theoretical orientations and guide therapists' interventions. According to this perspective, psychodynamically oriented therapists are far more influenced by a tragic vision of life—one that emphasizes human complexities and the near-impossibility of successful resolution of problems—than are behavioral and CBT therapists, who are more likely to hold to a "comic vision" of life that allows for the possibility of successful resolution of difficulties. In this regard, therapists might well find artistic experiences that would foster their creativity along the lines of their "preferred vision" (e.g., psychodynamically oriented therapists reading the works of Eugene O'Neill);

in addition, though, they might well develop their awareness and sensitivity about dimensions of human functioning reflected in art that emphasizes other visions (e.g., CBT therapists studying the work of Jackson Pollock or the movies of Ingmar Bergman; psychodynamic therapists exploring the power of spiritual quests embodied in the works of Paulo Coelho).

The comments of a former student, a fine musician, synthesize many of the points made in this chapter:

> I think the essence of art (including music, painting, theater, or literature) is about the appearance of truth. . . . In this regard, the right "setting" to allow for the emergence of truth is one of openness, flexibility, and creativity. Therapists with a background in the arts are arguably more able to capture truth in its infinite modes of appearance (insights, contradictions, jokes, feelings, mistakes, slips, impasses, etc.). A background in the arts, I think, deploys the idea that truth is multifaceted, emergent, contradictory, confusing, and surprising.

Although those with backgrounds in the arts arguably have an advantage in performing psychotherapeutic work, others can certainly adopt practices that reflect these skills. Both components of psychotherapeutic practice—art and science—can be improved through attention to issues relate to narrative, pace, tone, physicality, and the overall complexity of individuals' presentation of self to another. "Isn't it possible," asked Lewis Aron (2015), a noted contemporary psychoanalyst and amateur rock guitarist, "that rich immersion in literature or poetry or the arts is actually a better preparation for clinical psychoanalytic practice than studying abstract theory and philosophy?" (p. 153). He may well be right, though the assumption he makes is likely to hold true for therapists of all persuasions.

REFERENCES

Angus, L. E., & McLeod, J. (2003). *The handbook of narrative and psychotherapy: Practice, theory, and research.* Thousand Oaks, CA: Sage.

Aron, L. (2015). Race, roots, and rhythm: Riffing on rock 'n' roll: An introduction. *Psychoanalytic Dialogues, 25,* 153–162. http://dx.doi.org/10.1080/10481885.2015.1013827

Callan, J. A., Dunbar-Jacob, J., Sereika, S. M., Stone, C., Fasiczka, A., Jarrett, R. B., & Thase, M. E. (2012). Barriers to cognitive behavioral therapy homework completion scale—Depression version: Development and psychometric evaluation. *International Journal of Cognitive Therapy, 5,* 219–235. http://dx.doi.org/10.1521/ijct.2012.5.2.219

Carrel, A. (1935). *L'homme, cet inconnu* [Man, the unknown]. New York, NY: Harper.

Castonguay, L. G., Boswell, J. F., Zack, S. E., Baker, S., Boutselis, M. A., Chiswick, N. R., . . . Holtforth, M. G. (2010). Helpful and hindering events in psychotherapy: A practice research network study. *Psychotherapy: Theory, Research, Practice, Training, 47*, 327–344. http://dx.doi.org/10.1037/a0021164

Cohen, J. A., Mannarino, A. P., & Deblinger, E. (2006). *Treating trauma and traumatic grief in children and adolescents.* New York, NY: Guilford Press.

Engle, D., & Arkowitz, H. (2006). *Ambivalence in psychotherapy: Facilitating readiness to change.* New York, NY: Guilford Press.

Farber, B. A., & Golden, V. (1997). Psychological mindedness in psychotherapists. In M. McCallum & W. E. Piper (Eds.), *Psychological mindedness: A contemporary understanding* (pp. 211–235). Hillsdale, NJ: Erlbaum.

Farber, S., & Green, M. (1993). *Hollywood on the couch: A candid look at the overheated love affair between psychiatrists and moviemakers.* New York, NY: William Morrow.

Goldfried, M. R., Raue, P. J., & Castonguay, L. G. (1998). The therapeutic focus in significant sessions of master therapists: A comparison of cognitive-behavioral and psychodynamic-interpersonal interventions. *Journal of Consulting and Clinical Psychology, 66*, 803–810. http://dx.doi.org/10.1037/0022-006X.66.5.803

Lawrence, D. H. (1960). *Psychoanalysis and the unconscious, and fantasia of the unconscious.* New York, NY: Viking. (Original work published 1921)

Lodge, D. (2001). *Thinks.* New York, NY: Viking.

Maslow, A. H. (1966). *The psychology of science: A reconnaissance.* New York, NY: Harper.

Messer, S. B. (1986). Behavioral and psychoanalytic perspectives at therapeutic choice points. *American Psychologist, 41*, 1261–1272. http://dx.doi.org/10.1037/0003-066X.41.11.1261

Messer, S. B., & Winokur, M. (1980). Some limits to the integration of psychoanalytic and behavior therapy. *American Psychologist, 35*, 818–827. http://dx.doi.org/10.1037/0003-066X.35.9.818

Messer, S. B., & Winokur, M. (1984). Ways of knowing and visions of reality in psychoanalytic therapy and behavior therapy. In S. B. Messer & H. Arkowitz (Eds.), *Psychoanalytic therapy and behavior therapy: Is integration possible?* (pp. 63–100). New York, NY: Plenum. http://dx.doi.org/10.1007/978-1-4613-2733-2_5

McWilliams, N. (2005). Preserving our humanity as therapists. *Psychotherapy: Theory, Research, Practice, Training, 42*, 139–151. http://dx.doi.org/10.1037/0033-3204.42.2.139

Norcross, J. (2011). *Psychotherapy relationships that work* (2nd ed.). New York, NY: Oxford University Press. http://dx.doi.org/10.1093/acprof:oso/9780199737208.001.0001

Owen, J., Drinane, J. M., Idigo, K. C., & Valentine, J. D. (2015). Psychotherapist effects in meta-analyses: How accurate are treatment effects? *Psychotherapy, 52*, 321–328.

Rogers, N. (1993). *The creative connection: Expressive arts as healing.* Palo Alto, CA: Science and Behavior Books.

Shem, S. (2002). Fiction as resistance. *Annals of Internal Medicine, 137*, 934–937. http://dx.doi.org/10.7326/0003-4819-137-11-200212030-00022

Stanislavsky, K. (1936). *An actor prepares.* New York, NY: Theater Arts.

Wampold, B. E. (2001). *The great psychotherapy debate: Models, methods, and findings.* Mahwah, NJ: Erlbaum.

Webb, C. A., DeRubeis, R. J., & Barber, J. P. (2010). Therapist adherence/competence and treatment outcome: A meta-analytic review. *Journal of Consulting and Clinical Psychology, 78*, 200–211. http://dx.doi.org/10.1037/a0018912

Winerman, L. (2014). Fascinated by people, on and off the page: Understanding human motivation drives these psychologist-novelists. *Monitor on Psychology, 45*, 69–71.

Winnicott, D. W. (1945). Primitive emotional development. *The International Journal of Psychoanalysis, 26*, 137–143.

Winnicott, D. W. (1953). Transitional objects and transitional phenomena: A study of the first not-me possession. *The International Journal of Psychoanalysis, 34*, 89–97.

Winnicott, D. W. (1971). *Therapeutic consultations in child psychiatry.* London, England: Hogarth Press.

Zeig, J. K. (1987). *The evolution of psychotherapy.* New York, NY: Brunner/Mazel.

III
EMPIRICAL CONTRIBUTIONS

13

EFFECTIVE THERAPISTS IN PSYCHODYNAMIC THERAPY FOR DEPRESSION: WHAT INTERVENTIONS ARE USED AND HOW?

NADIA KUPRIAN, HAROLD CHUI, AND JACQUES P. BARBER

It is not uncommon in the field of psychotherapy to hear comments such as "She is a very good clinician" or "He is an excellent therapist." It is often assumed that a therapist receives this praise from colleagues on the basis of the outcome of patients under his or her care. But how could anyone really know another colleague's work given that the work of psychotherapy is protected by confidentiality agreements and we rarely have access to the outcome of a specific therapist's patients? Positive remarks about a colleague's work may be related to the therapist's years of experience, credentials, or reputation in the field, or how much one likes this therapist personally. However, what does a good therapist actually do in the therapy room that differentiates him or her from other therapists? This is not only an important and practical question but also a research topic that has yet to yield clear answers.

http://dx.doi.org/10.1037/0000034-014
How and Why Are Some Therapists Better Than Others? Understanding Therapist Effects, L. G. Castonguay and C. E. Hill (Eds.)
Copyright © 2017 by the American Psychological Association. All rights reserved.

In the literature, therapist effects have been discussed as characteristics of a therapist, as well as particular interventions that a therapist practices in his or her sessions (Baldwin & Imel, 2013; Lutz, Leon, Martinovich, Lyons, & Stiles, 2007; Saxon & Barkham, 2012). There also may be qualitative differences and nuances in how different therapists could apply the same techniques. These nuances and inclinations can be broadly defined as the therapist's "style"—something about the therapist that makes psychotherapy work, patients engage, and the therapeutic process flourish. It could also be that different therapists are better at handling different kinds of patients (Barber, 2009). In this chapter, we try to uncover the use of specific techniques and identify what makes one therapist better than another, using the data from a randomized clinical trial (RCT) for depression conducted at the University of Pennsylvania (Treatments for Depression [TDS]; Barber, Barrett, Gallop, Rynn, & Rickels, 2012). In this RCT, patients were assigned randomly to receive an active medication, a placebo pill, or supportive–expressive therapy (SET).

We focus on patients in the SET condition, a form of psychodynamic psychotherapy that attends to patients' unconscious motivations, intra- and interpersonal conflicts, and experiences with others that underlie maladaptive patterns of behaviors (Luborsky et al., 1995). All therapists were experienced clinicians and adhered to the SET treatment manual (Luborsky, 1984; Luborsky et al., 1995). Although the manual prescribed which techniques to use, participating therapists still had the freedom to choose which ones to use at a certain moment, how frequently and how intensively to use them; and they could bring in their own knowledge, expertise, and clinical intuition, and apply the interventions that they felt were pertinent for each particular case or phase of treatment. Given that we know which of the therapists in this study were more or less successful in terms of the final outcomes of their patients, we can identify through statistical analysis the interventions that contributed to the "magic ingredients" of their work.

We hypothesize that successful therapists focused their interventions more on their patients' relationships and interpersonal functioning. This hypothesis stems from our understanding of psychopathology as largely an interpersonal phenomenon, the approach that has been gaining much attention since mid-20th century (Greenberg & Mitchell, 1983; Horowitz, 2004; Sullivan, 1953; Weissman, Markowitz, & Klerman, 2008). From this perspective, it is possible but not necessary to assume that interpersonal problems of depressed patients beget interpersonally oriented interventions to address their core problems. The validity of this point is explored further in this chapter.

THE INTERPERSONAL THEORY OF PSYCHOPATHOLOGY AND THE VICIOUS CYCLE OF DEPRESSION

According to Harry Stack Sullivan (1953), psychopathology arises from life experiences that involve relationships with other people and other interpersonal events throughout the lifespan. This means that even the most avoidant, schizoid, or antisocial person has to deal with other people on a daily basis. Today, we understand humans as fundamentally social beings from birth (Beebe & Lachmann, 1998; Bowlby, 1969/1982; Fiske, 2009; Sullivan, 1953). Attempting to understand "the human condition" as it relates to depression without acknowledging the core, universal need to belong would be a serious omission. Therefore, we chose to look at depression it its interpersonal context.

Interpersonal difficulties are discussed in clinical and research literature as a precipitant and as a consequence of depression (Joiner & Timmons, 2002). There is no consensus on whether it is the deficits in interpersonal functioning that lead to depression or that depression makes people feel isolated and misunderstood (Hames, Hagan, & Joiner, 2013). Perhaps the most comprehensive and viable theory is that depression creates a negative feedback loop. People with depression influence their environment, and the environment in turn makes them more depressed (Blatt & Zuroff, 1992; Hames et al., 2013). Specifically, depressed individuals tend to be much more negative in their topics of conversation and tend to self-disclose negative feelings or excessively seek reassurance, which puts them at risk of social rejection and loneliness (Segrin, 2000; Segrin & Rynes, 2009). Furthermore, as in insecure attachment, people with depression want constant feedback and reassurance of closeness and intimacy, yet are never satisfied by what they get, and push others away with their clingy behaviors (Mikulincer & Shaver, 2007). According to the cognitive–affective cross-fire model (Joiner, Alfano, & Metalsky, 1993), people with depression with negative self-views excessively seek reassurance to improve their affect, and as they receive it, it comes in conflict with their cognitions (i.e., self-perception), and they then seek negative feedback to validate their self-perception. Once they receive negative feedback, they become more depressed and more self-critical, their mood deteriorates, and once again they seek reassurance to cope with it. Such behaviors eventually aggravate people around them, and leave them feeling rejected and isolated, leading to greater depression. Additionally, people with depression were found to be either excessively submissive or excessively hostile/dominant, which contributes to their interpersonal difficulties (Constantino et al., 2008). There are reasons to hypothesize that to be successful, therapists may tap into those vicious cycles of depression and maladaptive interpersonal styles, increasing patients' insight and promoting change.

INTERPERSONALLY ORIENTED INTERVENTIONS IN CLINICAL PRACTICE

SET used in the TDS study focuses on exploration and interpretation of patients' interpersonal difficulties. The SET therapist helps patients become aware of these repetitive patterns and arrive at an understanding of their possible origins. The increase in self-understanding is assumed to help patients make more adaptive choices and achieve better psychological functioning. This approach is based on the interpersonal theory of psychopathology and of change, and the SET therapist attends to patients' past relationships (mainly with caregivers) and current relationships with others, including the therapist. The therapist tries to identify common themes across multiple relationships that are associated with psychological symptoms. However, our examination of relationship-oriented interventions goes beyond adherence to the SET manual; we hypothesize that identifying recurrent relationship themes as prescribed by the SET treatment manual may not cover the full spectrum of interpersonally oriented techniques used in practice. For example, there may be more directive or action-oriented techniques that are not typical of psychodynamic psychotherapy, yet address patients' interpersonal functioning.

When mentioning interpersonal functioning in psychotherapy, the reader may automatically think of evidenced-based interpersonal psychotherapy (IPT), which focuses on solving current interpersonal problems associated with patients' life events which are a precursor of depression (Gotlib & Hammen, 2008; Weissman et al., 2008). IPT emphasizes life events such as grief (i.e., complicated bereavement), role disputes (i.e., relationship conflicts), role transitions (i.e., meaningful changes in life), and interpersonal deficits (i.e., social impoverishment, inadequate or sustaining personal relationships). However, the IPT therapist does not necessarily explore the root causes of patients' social problems outside of their current social structure, does not take into account past relationships unless it is absolutely necessary (if patients are isolated and do not have sustainable current relationships to explore), nor does the therapist focus on transference interpretations. Therefore, the IPT therapist looks at depression more from the outside-in rather than inside-out, which makes this approach rather sociological in nature, when external circumstances and social structures are assumed to affect people's lives more than their own maladaptive relational patterns, or what they themselves bring to their conflicts. Additionally, the focus of IPT interventions is different from what we know from research on interpersonal aspects of depression (e.g., negative feedback seeking, social inhibition, avoidance, excessive hostility or submissiveness, excessive reassurance seeking; Gotlib & Hammen, 2008).

Because SET and IPT may not fully capture all the interpersonally oriented interventions used in practice (and that the therapists in the TDS study might have applied), we therefore took a broader, cross-theoretical approach to assessing relationship-oriented techniques and their contribution to differences in therapist performance. With the expert input of experienced therapists and psychotherapy researchers, we created a Relationship-Oriented Subscale (ROS) within a well-validated psychotherapy research measure of therapeutic interventions from eight theoretical orientations, which will be described in the Method section. This newly created subscale was used for coding therapeutic interventions in this study, with the goal of relating the techniques to the outcome and perhaps differentiating between a more and less successful therapist. Specifically, we formulated three hypotheses for this study:

- *Hypothesis 1*: A therapists with good patient outcomes would differ from a therapist with poor patient outcomes in his or her use of relationship-oriented interventions (i.e., a therapist with better outcomes would use ROS more frequently and more intensively).
- *Hypothesis 2*: There will be a direct relation between the use of relationship-oriented interventions and symptom change, with higher ROS predicting lower depression symptoms at a later time.
- *Hypothesis 3*: The use of relationship-oriented interventions would be related to greater decrease in interpersonal distress.

Clinical examples from the transcripts of the TDS study are provided to gain a deeper understanding of how interpersonal and other techniques were used by successful versus less successful therapists.

METHODS

Participants

Therapists

Four doctoral-level clinical psychologists (three women and one man, all Caucasian) served as therapists in the TDS study. These therapists had at least 15 years of experience providing psychodynamic psychotherapy and at least 10 years of experience providing SET. One therapist was excluded because the therapist treated only two cases, both of whom dropped out before the end of active treatment. The remaining three therapists had 20, 12, and 12 cases.

Patients

Fifty-one patients were randomly assigned to receive SET (Barber et al., 2012). Five patients did not show after randomization, and 13 patients dropped out before the end of 16 weeks of active treatment (nine left before Week 8 and four left between Weeks 8 and 16). Of the 33 treatment completers, seven patients could not be included because there were no usable video recordings of the sessions, and four patients could not be included because they did not have a score from the Hamilton Rating Scale for Depression (HRSD) at Week 32, which was used to define treatment outcome. This resulted in a total sample of 22 patients. Compared with dropouts, treatment completers had lower baseline depression severity as measured on the HRSD (completers: $M = 18.97$, $SD = 3.63$; dropouts: $M = 21.39$, $SD = 4.01$; $t(49) = -2.19$, $p = .03$, $d = 0.63$) but similar levels of interpersonal distress (completers: $M = 1.69$, $SD = 0.51$; dropouts: $M = 1.67$, $SD = 0.65$; $t(47) = 0.15$, $p = .88$). Among all treatment completers (patients included in the final sample total and patients who were excluded), there was no difference in baseline depression severity (patients included: $M = 18.50$, $SD = 3.97$; patients excluded: $M = 19.91$, $SD = 2.77$; $t(31) = -1.05$, $p = .30$) or levels of interpersonal distress (patients included: $M = 1.69$, $SD = 0.55$; patients excluded: $M = 1.71$, $SD = 0.47$; $t(31) = -0.10$, $p = .92$). Among the 22 patients included in this study, 11 were Caucasian, eight were African American, two were Asian, and one was Latino. No significant differences were found in the demographic and psychiatric severity makeup across the three groups of patients (i.e., therapist caseloads).

Treatment

Treatment included 16 weeks of time-limited SET (Luborsky, 1984; Luborsky et al., 1995), with a focus on core conflictual relationship themes. Each session was 45 to 50 minutes in length, which occurred twice a week in the first 4 weeks, and then once a week in the remaining 12 weeks. After Week 16 (i.e., the end of the active treatment phase), up to four booster sessions were provided between Weeks 16 and 32, as needed.

Measures

Multitheoretical List of Therapeutic Interventions

The Multitheoretical List of Therapeutic Interventions (MULTI; McCarthy & Barber, 2009) is a 60-item observer-rated measure of therapist interventions. The 60 items include therapist interventions from a broad range of theoretical perspectives (behavioral, common factors, cognitive, dialectical–behavioral, interpersonal, person centered, psychodynamic, and process-experiential). Each item is rated by at least two observers on a 5-point Likert scale (1 = *not at all typical of the session* to 5 = *very typical of the session*). For this sample, the mean intraclass correlation coefficient (ICC; Shrout & Fleiss, 1979) between raters on the total scale was .86 (range: .69–.94), evidencing good to excellent interrater reliability.

Development of the Relationship-Oriented Subscale

For this study, the ROS was created from the MULTI to assess the use of therapeutic interventions that pertain to patients' interpersonal functioning. Eleven psychotherapy researchers/clinicians were asked to review the 60 MULTI items and select items that "tap into patients' interpersonal functioning inside and outside of therapy regardless of theoretical orientations." Nine items had over 70% agreement (i.e., at least eight out of the 11 clinicians thought that an item described an intervention that addressed the interpersonal domain) and were included in the new ROS. Of these nine items, five came from the interpersonal subscale, three from the psychodynamic subscale, and one came from the dialectical–behavioral subscale, suggesting the ROS consists of items that span different theoretical orientations. Cronbach's alpha for the ROS ranged between .82 and .86 for each of the four observed time points ($M = .85$, $SD = .02$), evidencing good internal consistency for the new subscale.

Specifically, the following items were included in the ROS:

- The therapist pointed out recurring themes or problems in patients' relationships.
- The therapist made connections between the way patients act or feel toward the therapist and the way that patients act or feel in their other relationships.
- The therapist tried to help patients better understand how they relate to others, how this style of relating developed, and how it causes patients' problems.
- The therapist focused on a specific concern in patients' relationships, like disagreements or conflicts, major changes, loss of a loved one, or loneliness.
- The therapist encouraged patients to explore ways in which patients could make changes in their relationships, like ways to resolve a conflict in a relationship, fulfill a need, establish new relationships or contact old friends, or avoid problems experienced in previous relationships.
- The therapist encouraged patients to examine their relationships with others, like positive and negative aspects of their

relationships, what patients want from others and what others want from them, and the way patients act in relationships.
- The therapist encouraged patients to think about ways in which they might prepare for major changes in their relationships, like learning new skills or finding new friends.
- The therapist encouraged patients to identify situations in which patients' feelings were invalidated, like times when a significant other told the patient his or her feelings were incorrect or when patients had strong feelings that seemed inappropriate.
- The therapist tried to help patients better understand how their problems were due to difficulties in their social relationships.

Hamilton Rating Scale of Depression

The 17 item-HRSD (Hamilton, 1967), an observer-rated measure of depression severity, was used as the primary outcome measure in the TDS study and was administered at intake and throughout the course of therapy (Weeks 2, 4, 6, 8, 12, 15, and 16, and at booster sessions). The raters were six experienced master's or doctoral level diagnosticians. Interrater reliability as calculated using the intraclass correlation was .92 for the full sample in the trial.

Response to treatment was defined as HRSD score ≤ 9, or as a 50% reduction of HRSD score from intake and HRSD score ≤ 12 at the same time point. Remission was defined as the absence of a diagnosis for major depressive disorder according to the Structured Clinical Interview for the *Diagnostic and Statistical Manual of Mental Disorders, Fourth Edition* (DSM–IV; First, Spitzer, Gibbon, & Williams, 1995) and HRSD < 8 at the end of active treatment (Barber et al., 2012).

Patients were considered to have good treatment outcome if they achieved a strict criteria (i.e., remission—they achieved response as well) at the end of active treatment, and sustained it at Week 32.

Inventory of Interpersonal Problems–64

The Inventory of Interpersonal Problems–64 (IIP-64; Alden, Wiggins, & Pincus, 1990; Horowitz, Alden, Wiggins, & Pincus, 2000) is a 64-item self-report questionnaire measuring interpersonal difficulties and sources of distress. There are two types of items: interpersonal behaviors that are "hard for you to do" (e.g., "It's hard for me to be self-confident when I am with other people") and interpersonal behaviors that "you do too much" (e.g., "I open up to people too much"). Participants are asked to rate how distressing these problems are for them on a 5-point scale ranging from 0 = *not at all* to 4 = *extremely*. The IIP-64 was administered at intake and at Weeks 8, 16, and 32. Psychometric properties of the IIP-64 are well documented (Alden et al., 1990; Horowitz et al., 2000). For the current sample, Cronbach's alpha for the IIP-64 at intake was .93, suggesting excellent internal consistency.

Procedure: Coding of Therapist Interventions

For each of the 22 patients who completed the treatment, we rated four sessions: the second, fourth, eighth, and the second-to-last session or the next closest session when unavailable. Because we were interested in the interventions used in ongoing therapy, we excluded the first and last treatment sessions from coding because these sessions are typically different (e.g., discussion of treatment frame at the beginning and termination issues at the end). Each session was rated independently by at least two reliably trained judges, with the exception of a foreign-speaking patient who was rated by one judge. The raters were clinical psychology doctoral students with more than 200 hours of training on the MULTI. Ratings for each subscale of the MULTI, for each session, were averaged for further analyses.

RESULTS

Patient Outcome and Therapist Success

Across the three therapists, patients had comparable mean levels of depression at baseline (Therapist A: $M = 17.44$, $SD = 2.01$; Therapist B: $M = 20.86$, $SD = 5.21$; Therapist C: $M = 17.33$, $SD = 3.98$, $F(2, 19) = 1.98$, $p = .17$). Ten patients (six from Therapist A, three from Therapist B, and one from Therapist C; 45.5% overall) were responders, and seven patients (five from Therapist A, two from Therapist B, and none from Therapist C; 31.8% overall) remitted by Week 16. At Week 32, 12 patients (six from Therapist A, two from Therapist B, and four from Therapist C; 54.5% overall) were responders, and 10 patients (six from Therapist A, two from Therapist B, and two from Therapist C; 45.4% overall) were remitters. On the basis of stringent criteria of requiring remission at Week 16 and at Week 32, six out of the 22 patients were considered to have achieved good treatment outcome. Of these good outcome cases, five came from Therapist A (55.6% of caseload), one came from Therapist B (14.3% of caseload), and none came from Therapist C (0% of caseload). Rates of good treatment outcome were significantly different among therapists ($\chi 2(2) = 6.48$, $p = .04$). Because of the small sample, we also conducted bootstrapping (1,000 samples) to obtain more accurate estimates. We found a moderate to large effect (Cramer's $V = .54$, 95% CI: [.27, .89]) of therapist on patient outcome. Nevertheless, given the similar rates of remission for Therapists B and C, we considered Therapist A to be more successful and Therapists B and C to be less successful.

It should be noted that patients of Therapist A did not differ significantly from patients of Therapists B and C in terms of change in HRSD scores adjusted for baseline severity (i.e., measured by the standardized residuals obtained by regressing HRSD at Week 32 on HRSD at baseline; Therapist A: $M = -0.13$, $SD = 1.26$; Therapists B and C: $M = -0.01$, $SD = 0.74$, $t(20) = 0.26$, $p = .80$, $d = 0.11$). The lack of difference is also illustrated by the low therapist-level variability in HRSD (ICC = .02) obtained using multilevel modeling (controlling for baseline HRSD). Given that the stringent criterion of sustained remission at two time points (Weeks 16 and 32) was determined a priori and required the absence of a DSM–IV diagnosis of major depression, which may not be reflected in HRSD scores, this categorical difference will be used as an indicator of outcome.

It should also be noted that, within Therapist A, patients with good treatment outcome did not differ from those with poor treatment outcome in terms of age, sex, race, marital status, baseline depression severity, or the presence of a personality disorder (all $p > .28$). These patient characteristics did not seem to distinguish good versus poor treatment outcome for Therapist A.

Relationship-Oriented Intervention by Therapist and Time

Factorial repeated measures analysis of variance showed that more and less successful therapists differed significantly in their use of relationship-oriented interventions as measured using the ROS (Therapist A: $M = 2.78$, $SD = 0.20$; Therapists B and C: $M = 2.46$, $SD = 0.39$; $F(1, 21) = 5.29$, $p = .03$, $\eta_p^2 = 0.21$, large effect), and that the effect of time was significant (Time 1: $M = 2.85$, $SD = 0.63$; Time 2: $M = 2.71$, $SD = 0.71$; Time 3: $M = 2.55$, $SD = 0.59$; Time 4: $M = 2.27$, $SD = 0.56$, $F(3, 63) = 3.84$, $p = .01$, $\eta_p^2 = 0.16$, large effect; see also Figure 13.1). However, there was no significant interaction between time and therapist ($F(3, 63) = 1.18$, $p = .33$). These results suggest that the more successful therapist used more relationship-oriented interventions and that all therapists used fewer relationship-oriented interventions over time.

Post Hoc Analyses

Additional post hoc analyses were conducted at the item level to examine specific interventions within the ROS that might be driving the observed results. Therapist A scored significantly higher than Therapists B and C on only one of the nine ROS items: Item 60: *The therapist tried to help patients better understand how patients' problems were due to difficulties in their social*

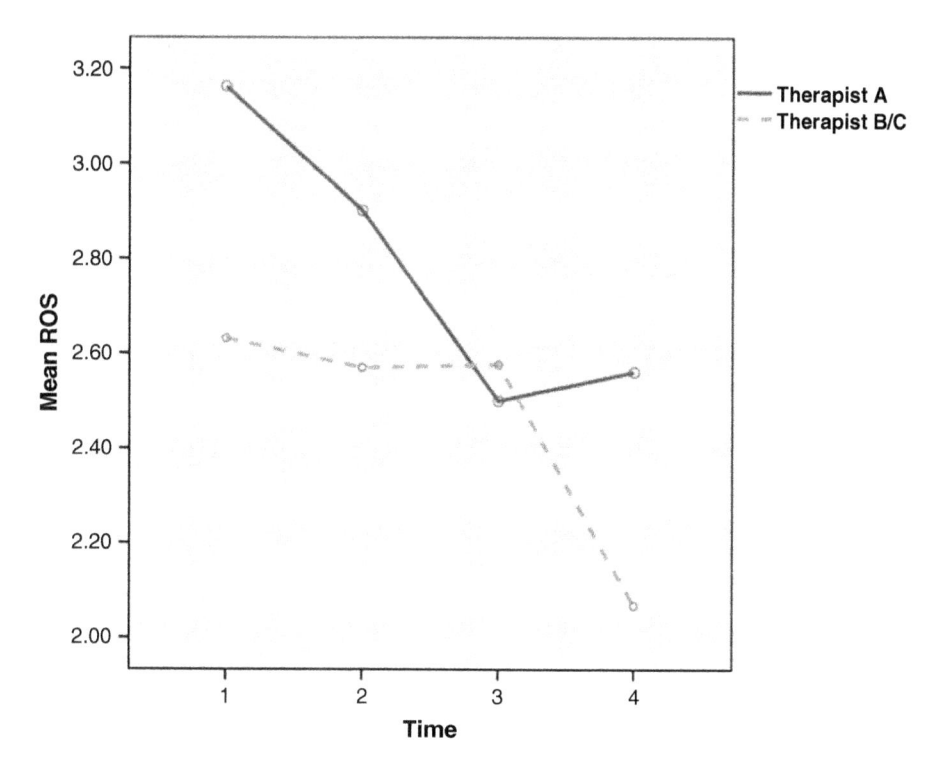

Figure 13.1. Relationship-Oriented Subscale (ROS) scores over time for more successful (A) versus less successful (B and C) therapists.

relationships (Therapist A: $M = 3.53$, $SD = 0.46$; Therapists B and C: $M = 2.92$, $SD = 0.60$, $t(20) = 2.56$, $p = .02$, $d = 1.14$).

Relationship-Oriented Interventions and Change in Depression

Whereas in the previous section we addressed whether mean levels of used relationship-oriented intervention differed between more and less successful therapists, here we looked at the relation between ROS use and the change in depressive symptoms. Using multilevel modeling, mean ROS score (average for each client across four time points) did not predict level of HRSD ($\gamma = -0.73$, $p = .81$) but marginally predicted the slope of HRSD over time ($\gamma = -3.52$, $p = .05$), while controlling for baseline HRSD. This suggests that higher ROS predicted a greater reduction in depressive symptoms over the course of therapy. However, the effect size was small: ROS only accounted for 1.6% of the variance in HRSD when added to the model.

Next, we examined the temporal relation to see if the use of relationship-oriented interventions (on the basis of ROS scores) can predict reduction in subsequent levels of depression (on the basis of HRSD scores). To set up this analysis, we matched each of the four ROS scores with an HRSD score that was obtained closest in time when the ROS was coded. One patient had a missing HRSD score at Time 2, but this patient's HRSD scores at Time 1 and Time 3 were the same. As such, we used those scores to fill in the missing Time 2 score.

Cross-Lagged Analysis

We conducted a cross-lagged panel analysis using structural equation modeling to take into account the temporal relation between variables. Specifically, we predicted HRSD score at time T from ROS score at T-1, while controlling for HRSD score at time T-1. We also predicted ROS score at time T from HRSD score at T-1, while controlling for ROS score at time T-1. In addition, the model took into account correlations between HRSD and ROS at the four time points. This model was performed using the *lavaan* package (Rosseel, 2012) of the statistical software environment R (http://cran.r-project.org/). We used this model to test our hypothesis that more intensive interventions at one time point would predict lower depression symptoms at a subsequent time point, while controlling for symptoms at the prior time point and for reverse causation (i.e., symptom predict subsequent intervention). This model is similar to the model in Zilcha-Mano, Dinger, McCarthy, and Barber (2014) that examined the temporal relation between working alliance and depression symptoms.

We did not find support for our hypothesis. Specifically, ROS at Time 1 did not predict HRSD at Time 2 ($\beta = 0.18$, $p = .37$) while controlling for HRSD at Time 1; ROS at Time 2 did not predict HRSD at Time 3 ($\beta = -0.31$, $p = .10$) while controlling for HRSD at Time 2; and ROS at Time 3 did not predict HRSD at Time 4 ($\beta = 0.06$, $p = .76$) while controlling for HRSD at Time 3. The lack of findings did not generally seem to be related to the possibility of reverse causation: HRSD at Time 1 did not predict ROS at Time 2 ($\beta = -0.13$, $p = .52$) while controlling for ROS at Time 1; HRSD at Time 2 did not predict ROS at Time 3 ($\beta = 0.00$, $p = 1.00$) while controlling for ROS at Time 2. Interestingly, HRSD at Time 3 predicted ROS at Time 4 ($\beta = -0.52$, $p = .01$) while controlling for ROS at Time 3, with higher depression symptoms at midtreatment predicting lower use of relationship-oriented interventions at follow-up.

Relationship-Oriented Intervention and Change in Interpersonal Distress

Using multilevel modeling, mean ROS score (average for each client across four time points) did not predict level of IIP ($\gamma = 0.01$, $p = .98$) or slope of IIP over time ($\gamma = -0.07$, $p = .46$) while controlling for baseline IIP. Hence, therapist use of relationship-oriented interventions did not seem to be related to patient changes in levels of interpersonal distress.

Clinical Examples

To bring therapists' style and interventions to life, we selected two patients per therapist who had a complete set of transcripts (four sessions per patient, 24 transcripts in total), focusing on good outcome patients from Therapist A and poor outcome patients from Therapists B and C. Special attention was paid to interpersonally oriented interventions with the goal of identifying clinical nuances of how these interventions were used and how this differentiated the more successful therapist from the less successful ones.

From the quantitative analysis, we know that the more successful therapist (Therapist A) scored significantly higher than Therapists B and C on the ROS item: *The therapist tried to help patients better understand how their problems were due to difficulties in their social relationships*. Therapist A's tendency to steer the conversation in the interpersonal domain was also notable in the transcripts. Therapist A proactively identified patients' recurrent relationship themes, such as not standing up for themselves, bottling up their feelings and then exploding, expecting only negative feedback (and believing positive feedback to be dishonest), and feeling abandoned and let down. Therapist A often ended these summaries of relationship themes with a statement that connected patients' interpersonal problem and being depressed, as can be seen in the following examples from the transcripts: "I think there is a connection between your loss and you feeling very, very sad. This loss brought up a lot of feelings in you, and you are feeling overwhelmed" and "When you are surrounded by people and there is a lot going on, that gives you a high. And then, when it's gone, you kind of sink."

The explicit connection between interpersonal problems and symptoms illustrates that Therapist A not only followed the prescribed techniques of SET (Luborsky, 1984) but also was more proactive than other therapists in tapping into the elements of the vicious cycle of depression, such as lack of assertiveness, negative feedback seeking, and isolation. Going back to the interpersonal models of depression discussed in the beginning of this chapter, Therapist A seemed to pay more attention to how patients were responsible for a negative feedback loop (Joiner et al., 1993) that aggravated their depressive symptoms. Although no significant difference was found in the use of transference interpretation by the three therapists, it was noteworthy how Therapist A brought the aforementioned relationship themes into the in-session relationship, asking if patients felt the same way toward the therapist.

Consider the following example from the transcript of one of Therapist A's sessions with a patient:

> *Patient:* I don't know very much what it's about, like it's about not trusting other people, it's like about . . . about what everybody thinks badly about you.
>
> *Therapist A:* But, you don't know that. You assume we do, you assume that if I don't share that with you, I simply am holding that back from you, but I must be thinking something negative.
>
> *Patient:* That, that's why it's like very important to give, give knowledge. That's when I need feedback.
>
> *Therapist A:* Well, you don't accept feedback if it's not critical because that's all you can really trust.
>
> *Patient:* Yeah, I guess for some reason . . .
>
> *Therapist A:* I think that has a lot to do with your depression and anxiety.

What was also interesting and perhaps not fully captured by the quantitative coding, was that many of the interventions that were not explicitly interpersonal and were not rated as such by our experts when developing the ROS (and therefore were not included in the ROS of the MULTI), were used by Therapist A with an interpersonal focus—Therapist A made them interpersonal.

Paraphrasing

When choosing to paraphrase, Therapist A seemed to be more selective as to which aspects of patients' narratives and affective experiences to summarize, choosing to focus on relationship themes more than other material brought by patients. In contrast, the other two therapists showed less inclination to connect those affective experiences with interpersonal situations and relationship issues. They empathically repeated what the patient said without a specific thematic focus. In the following dialogue, Therapist A redirects the focus to the patient's relationships.

> *Patient:* Sometimes I feel like something bad is going to happen if I tell something and then I would, like, stop feeling. Whenever I was invested in an emotion, whenever I was doubting something, in the middle it was just, like, cut off. So, I would just like . . . like there is no room for feeling anymore.
>
> *Therapist A:* And that's how you usually feel when you go out and talk to people, is this what you are saying? When you interact

with people or tell them a story, at some point you feel disconnected from your feelings?

Moment-to-Moment or Here-and-Now Interventions

These interventions tended to focus on the patient–therapist relationship, a recent interaction between the two, or patients' in-the-moment feelings about a past relationship. Consider the following examples Therapist A used in session: "How do you feel right now? Are you feeling detached? Do you feel connected to any of what you're describing?" "How are you feeling now as you are thinking about her?"

Cognitive Interventions

These interventions entailed challenging the patients' beliefs or discovering flaws in the patients' reasoning, and discussing consequences of irrational beliefs. In all these cases, the beliefs emphasized by the therapist were interpersonal in nature and involved patients' relationships. In the following example, Therapist A challenges a patient's view about criticism from others.

Therapist A: I think that what you're saying is, that I, with me, maybe in those situations, you do assume that there is some criticism, some feeling that's not so positive. If you don't hear about it, it's just being withheld from you and it's very hard to trust that if it's not there, you're really not getting the whole picture, you're really not getting the whole truth.

Patient: Yeah, yeah.

Therapist A: It really puts you in a position to, to always question the way you can trust what you're hearing.

In another example, Therapist A helps a patient reconsider how to honor past memories.

Therapist A: You're not hurting the other memory, while creating the new memory and engaging in new relationships. And I think you're not believing that, you may be at a, you know, at a rational level, but not with your heart, you don't believe you can have it. You don't accept it, you think engaging in new relationships would mean betraying the memories of your grandfather. That it takes something from it by competing with it, and I think that rationally you know this isn't true because it is there and nobody can touch it, yet emotionally, you feel that these memories need you.

Therapist's Self-Disclosure

Therapist A often disclosed personal feelings during the interaction with patients, which showed that Therapist A's style tended to be more relational rather than classically psychodynamic. In the transcripts, it became clear that Therapist A was creating space for honest, yet often uncomfortable, conversations about the patient–therapist relationship, which ultimately deepened the alliance.

Therapist A: I'll share with you what my reaction was. It was more that when you say to me things sound illogical, it sounds to me like, again you go with your thinking rather than with your feeling and there is a "but" there. You know, it's like, "yes I can see where you're coming from, but, I'm not really there." And that may be very valid, I mean it tore me off, but it also may be that there is a part of you that does not want me to know it.

Exploring Past or Childhood Experiences

Therapist A tended to relate patients' history with their present problems in a manner that also tended to have an interpersonal focus. Consider the following example from one of Therapist A's sessions:

Therapist A: If you are aware that a lot of what happened—things that you bring with you into relationships with men—that makes you extremely sensitive to how they treat you, especially with regard to how much respect you're really getting in that, and that's a lot to walk with in the new relationship. Right?

Patient: Right.

Therapist A: And if you have difficulties trusting because of your relationship with your father, you can be very aware of it in your new relationship, without necessarily changing your relationship with your father. I mean it may change too, but just knowing what was so damaging, that's what you're bringing to the new relationship, this will be extremely helpful.

Giving Advice and Practical Solutions

Even though it is not common practice for psychodynamic therapists, all three therapists at some point shared their opinion about what they thought would be best for patients. However, when Therapist A gave advice, it once again tended to focus on patients' relationships. Especially toward the end of the treatment, in the context of approaching termination, Therapist A often engaged in something similar to interpersonal coaching (i.e., teaching the patients to deal with their relationship issues and recurrent patterns on their own). In other words, Therapist A was "launching" the patients into the world, so that they would not be dependent on their therapist going forward. As observed in the transcripts, the two other therapists' advice usually concerned patients' daily living (e.g., which jobs to apply for, what items to pack while moving, how to start a business). Our hypothesis is that this kind of handholding can foster patient dependency and submissiveness, which was identified as a common interpersonal problem in depression earlier in this chapter. However, Therapist A prepared patients to deal with future challenges, especially in the interpersonal context and after the termination of therapy. Several examples of Therapist A's advice are as follows:

Therapist A: That's right, this is how you feel, there's no wrong or right, it's valid. The question is what do you do with it?

Patient: Yeah . . . I don't know what I'm gonna do with it I guess, put it back where it was. Just throw it back on a shelf and [laughs] just go on the same way [laughs] which probably isn't good.

Therapist A: Well, it depends.

Patient: I don't, I mean that, I can't, I don't see anything else to do.

Therapist A: Unless, you do. [You can] continue what you started in other relationships and that is, express how you feel

***

Therapist A: So how are you going to handle it? How are you going to manage that closeness?

***

Therapist A: You can always choose not to argue, but on the other hand, there are certain things that you don't want to have with her. How can you protect yourself? Because to keep it all in and then explode, or feel resentful, is it going to feel good?

***

Therapist A: You're on your own, making your decisions. So yes, you can, but it's almost like you need the permission in a way.

Patient: [Permission] to be, to be strong

> *Therapist A:* To, to set your limits, to speak up. To, to be, to standing up for yours, to stand up for yourself.
>
> ***
>
> *Therapist A:* And I think that waiting until you feel calmer, it's a wonderful thing to be able to do. The problem with many people is that they can't and they're getting [in] violent arguments, verbally or nonverbally. They get out of control.
>
> ***
>
> *Therapist A:* And so it's important that you will allow yourself to talk with her openly, but I think that if sometimes you get too upset, too emotional, it's good to wait for a while before you say it. But if you keep it all bottled in because you are too concerned about hurting her, or . . . you're not going to do any good for yourself.

The two less successful therapists in this study (Therapists B and C) applied many similar techniques as Therapist A, but there were some nuances about their chosen interventions and communication style that could perhaps be problematic, and could, hypothetically, explain the worse outcomes of their patients. These include the following:

- Not meeting patients where they were. A telling clinical example of such behavior was when a patient was opening up after the initial resistance, Therapist C became very excitable and interrupted the patient, finishing her sentences and thoughts. If the patient began to hesitate slightly or even take the time to think about an answer or try to look inward to find an answer, the therapist immediately jumped in and either asked another question or tried to insert the therapist's opinion. Rather than listening and letting the patient arrived at her own conclusions, possible conclusions were mapped out for her and then the therapist asked, "do you agree?" or "right?"
- Discussing other people's relationships (in great detail) that were not relevant to the suffering or interpersonal problems of the patient. Therapist B on these occasions often engaged into a question-and-answer mode about different people in the patient's story, and expressed curiosity that seemed merely conversational (i.e., chatty) rather than exploratory or therapeutic.
- Pushing a traumatized patient to talk about the trauma too early in the treatment. We believe that a certain level of trust needs to be developed before exploring the traumatic experience.
- Using obscure analogies and making assumptions that can get quite lost on patients and derail patients' flow of thoughts and feelings.

SUMMARY AND DISCUSSION

The goal of this study was to test whether greater use of relationship- and interpersonally-oriented techniques by therapists was related to better psychotherapy outcome and could be an underlying reason for the presence of therapist effects. Our first hypothesis, that a more successful therapist used relationship-oriented interventions more frequently and more intensively, was confirmed. The therapist with a significantly better caseload outcome used significantly more relationship-oriented interventions. Although this finding does not imply a causal relation between interventions and outcome, it indicates an association between the interpersonally oriented style of the more effective therapist and good performance.

It was somewhat surprising that for all three therapists the use of relationship-oriented interventions decreased over time. One would imagine that therapists and patients more often discuss relationships later rather than earlier in the course of therapy as they become more familiar with each other. Our interpretation, derived from a cursory reading of the transcripts, is that patients learned to bring up and explore their relationship themes and patterns in the later stages of therapy. If this is correct, those self-generated discussions were not considered therapist interventions because therapists were not the ones who initiated them, even if they engaged in them.

Our findings addressing the second hypothesis about the causal relation between the use of ROS and reduction in depression scores were inconclusive. The therapist's use of relationship-oriented interventions at one time point did not predict lower depression symptoms at a subsequent time point. However, higher ROS marginally predicted a greater reduction in depressive symptoms over the course of therapy, with a very small effect size (1.6% of the variance in HRSD was account by ROS). Possible explanations for those findings include that our hypothesis was incorrect and interpersonal interventions were not related to a better outcome. Given the small sample and the large number of variables, the study was underpowered for the cross-lagged panel analysis. However, because we have established that the more successful therapist used relationship-oriented interventions more frequently and more intensively, there may be alternative explanations. One possibility is patient variables (e.g., comorbid personality disorders) that were not accounted for in this study. Another possibility could be qualitative differences in the use of seemingly similar relationship-oriented interventions (i.e., how exactly they were used and what exactly was said) that could not be captured by the quantitative analysis. For example, Crits-Christoph (1998) showed that accurate interpersonal interpretations are related to better outcome. This means that although the therapists could have used similar relationship-oriented interventions, some of them may not have been accurate, may not have had the same therapeutic value, or may even have negatively impacted the treatment. In this study, we did not determine the accuracy of interpretations. However, we did observe in the transcripts that one of the less successful therapists often formulated interpretations in a "multiple choice" form, not giving the patient enough space for introspection or even a thoughtful response to these "interpretation options." It might be possible that more compliant patients agreed with the therapist's interpretations even when they did not ring true.

Interestingly, higher depression symptoms at midtreatment (Time 3) predicted lower use of relationship-oriented interventions at follow-up (Time 4). It is possible that therapists focused less on relationships when they saw their patients struggling with more severe depression symptoms, and instead chose to help them manage and reduce the symptoms. Additional analysis of behavioral and symptom-oriented techniques used at these time points would be needed to test this hypothesis.

Our third hypothesis was to see if the use of ROS was related to decrease in interpersonal problems of the patients. This hypothesis was not confirmed. Even though most of the patients who improved on their depression scores also demonstrated a reduced level of interpersonal distress, there was no significant correlation between the ROS and those interpersonal changes as measured by the IIP (Horowitz et al., 2000). One of the possible explanations could lie in the stable nature of interpersonal problems or at least of the measurement of those problems. According to the authors of the interpersonal circumplex (Horowitz, 2004), they represent stable interpersonal patterns (i.e., traits) that do not change quickly over time. Slower interpersonal gains have been observed in other studies (Barkham, Rees, Stiles, Hardy, & Shapiro, 2002; Vromans & Schweitzer, 2011), suggesting that perhaps changes in interpersonal problems depend on the dosage of treatment, and short-term therapies might not be sufficient to result in significant reduction in interpersonal distress. The restricted range of change might have limited our ability to detect correlation between interventions and change in IIP. Nonetheless, this finding is puzzling given that the IIP has been widely used as an outcome measure (Lambert, Horowitz, & Strupp, 1997), and has been shown to have good sensitivity to change (Huber, Henrich, & Klug, 2007).

Additionally, our exploratory quantitative analysis revealed that the most successful therapist differed from the less successful ones on the use of a specific relationship-oriented technique: Therapist A scored significantly higher than the other two therapists on the item connecting problematic social relationships to patients' depressive symptoms. This intervention, although created within IPT, is consistent with SET and is also relevant to the interpersonal theory of psychopathology at large. Because it was used significantly more often and more intensively by the more successful therapist, it is possible to conclude that this therapist's partiality toward the interpersonal theory could help understand this therapist effect.

Some observations were made from the selected transcripts. Therapist A tended to add an interpersonal focus to the interventions that were not considered interpersonal per se; Therapist A targeted more actively the interpersonal vicious cycle of depression described in the beginning of this chapter (i.e., negative feedback seeing, submissiveness, and self-isolation), and overall had a more relational style than the other two therapists, actively encouraging patients to speak up about their feelings about the therapist and therapy, and sharing Therapist A's own feelings in response.

This study had some methodological limitations. First of all, small sample size and only three therapists limit our ability to generalize. Second, only one modality of psychotherapy was used—SET with psychodynamically oriented therapists. Even though a multitheoretical measure was used to code the sessions, the psychodynamic focus of this treatment might have prevented us from seeing the full spectrum of interpersonally oriented work that therapists from other theoretical orientations do. Finally, the clinical materials used to highlight some of our quantitative findings might contain authors' bias. More rigorous coding and qualitative analysis of transcripts from a different team of researchers unaware of the quantitative results might offer more impartial conclusions.

CONCLUSION

The findings of this study suggest that psychodynamic therapists who focus on their patients' interpersonal functioning may be more effective in treating depression, at least in a controlled setting. However, we did not find conclusive evidence that the use of interpersonally oriented interventions is directly related to improvements in depressive symptoms and interpersonal functioning. This finding suggests that therapists who use more interpersonal interventions may have characteristics not yet examined in this study (e.g., therapist personality, communication style) that bring about patient change. A direction for future research could be a theory-building case study (Fishman, 2009; McLeod, 2010; Stiles, 2007) aimed at developing clinical implications for untangling the vicious cycle of depression in therapy with depressed patients. This could help to further develop aspects of the theory and practice of SET for depression and better connect what we know from research on the vicious cycle of depression to what is clinically prescribed by the SET.

REFERENCES

Alden, L. E., Wiggins, J. S., & Pincus, A. L. (1990). Construction of circumplex scales for the Inventory of Interpersonal Problems. *Journal of Personality Assessment, 55,* 521–536. http://dx.doi.org/10.1207/s15327752jpa5503&4_10

Baldwin, S., & Imel, Z. E. (2013). Therapist effects: Findings and methods. In M. J. Lambert (Ed.), *Bergin and Garfield's handbook of psychotherapy and behavior change* (6th ed., pp. 258–297). New York, NY: Wiley.

Barber, J. P. (2009). Toward a working through of some core conflicts in psychotherapy research. *Psychotherapy Research, 19*(1), 1–12. http://dx.doi.org/10.1080/10503300802609680

Barber, J. P., Barrett, M. S., Gallop, R., Rynn, M., & Rickels, K. (2012). Short-term dynamic psychotherapy versus pharmacotherapy for major depressive disorder: A randomized placebo-controlled trial. *The Journal of Clinical Psychiatry, 73,* 66–73. http://dx.doi.org/10.4088/JCP.11m06831

Barkham, M., Rees, A., Stiles, W. B., Hardy, G. E., & Shapiro, D. A. (2002). Dose effect relations for psychotherapy of mild depression: A quasi-experimental comparison of effects of 2, 8, and 16 sessions. *Psychotherapy Research, 12,* 463–474. http://dx.doi.org/10.1093/ptr/12.4.463

Beebe, B., & Lachmann, F. M. (1998). Co-constructing inner and relational processes: Self-and mutual regulation in infant research and adult treatment. *Psychoanalytic Psychology, 15,* 480–516. http://dx.doi.org/10.1037/0736-9735.15.4.480

Blatt, S. J., & Zuroff, D. C. (1992). Interpersonal relatedness and self-definition: Two prototypes for depression. *Clinical Psychology Review, 12,* 527–562. http://dx.doi.org/10.1016/0272-7358(92)90070-O

Bowlby, J. (1982). *Attachment and loss: Vol. 1. Attachment.* New York, NY: Basic Books. (Original work published 1969)

Constantino, M. J., Manber, R., Degeorge, J., McBride, C., Ravitz, P., Zuroff, D. C., . . . Arnow, B. A. (2008). Interpersonal styles of chronically depressed outpatients: Profiles and therapeutic change. *Psychotherapy: Theory, Research, Practice, Training, 45,* 491–506. http://dx.doi.org/10.1037/a0014335

Crits-Christoph, P. (1998). The interpersonal interior of psychotherapy. *Psychotherapy Research, 8*(1), 1–16. http://dx.doi.org/10.1080/10503309812331332157

First, M. B., Spitzer, R. L., Gibbon, M., & Williams, J. B. (1995). *Structured clinical interview for DSM–IV axis I disorders.* New York, NY: New York State Psychiatric Institute.

Fishman, D. B. (2009). Using case studies to develop theory: Roadmap to a dialogue. *Pragmatic Case Studies in Psychotherapy, 5*(3), 1–8. http://dx.doi.org/10.14713/pcsp.v5i3.972

Fiske, S. T. (2009). *Social beings: Core motives in social psychology.* Danvers, MA: John Wiley & Sons.

Gotlib, I. H., & Hammen, C. L. (Eds.). (2008). *Handbook of depression.* New York, NY: Guilford Press.

Greenberg, J. R., & Mitchell, S. A. (1983). *Object relations in psychoanalytic theory: Interpersonal psychoanalysis* (pp. 79–115). Cambridge, MA: Harvard University Press.

Hames, J. L., Hagan, C. R., & Joiner, T. E. (2013). Interpersonal processes in depression. *Annual Review of Clinical Psychology, 9*, 355–377. http://dx.doi.org/10.1146/annurev-clinpsy-050212-185553

Hamilton, M. A. X. (1967). Development of a rating scale for primary depressive illness. *British Journal of Social and Clinical Psychology, 6*, 278–296. http://dx.doi.org/10.1111/j.2044-8260.1967.tb00530.x

Horowitz, L. M. (2004). *Interpersonal foundations of psychopathology*. Washington, DC: American Psychological Association. http://dx.doi.org/10.1037/10727-000

Horowitz, L. M., Alden, L. E., Wiggins, J. S., & Pincus, A. L. (2000). *Inventory of interpersonal problems*. Odessa, FL: The Psychological Corporation.

Huber, D., Henrich, G., & Klug, G. (2007). The Inventory of Interpersonal Problems (IIP): Sensitivity to change. *Psychotherapy Research, 17*, 474–48.

Joiner, T. E., Jr., Alfano, M. S., & Metalsky, G. I. (1993). Caught in the crossfire: Depression, self-consistency, self-enhancement, and the response of others. *Journal of Social and Clinical Psychology, 12*, 113–134. http://dx.doi.org/10.1521/jscp.1993.12.2.113

Joiner, T. E., Jr., & Timmons, K. A. (2002). Depression in its interpersonal context. In I. H. Gotlib & C. L. Hammen (Eds.), *Handbook of depression* (pp. 322–339). New York, NY: Guilford Press.

Lambert, M. J., Horowitz, L. M., & Strupp, H. H. (1997). Conclusions and recommendations. In H. H. Strupp, L. M. Horowitz, & M. J. Lambert (Eds.), *Measuring patient changes in mood, anxiety, and personality disorders: Toward a core battery* (pp. 491–502). Washington, DC: American Psychological Association. http://dx.doi.org/10.1037/10232-019

Luborsky, L. (1984). *Principles of psychoanalytic psychotherapy: A manual for supportive-expressive treatment*. New York, NY: Basic Books.

Luborsky, L., Mark, D., Hole, A. V., Popp, C., Goldsmith, B., & Cacciola, J. (1995). Supportive-expressive dynamic psychotherapy of depression: A time-limited version. In J. P. Barber & P. Crits-Christoph (Eds.), *Dynamic therapies for psychiatric disorders (Axis I)* (pp. 13–42). New York, NY: Basic Books.

Lutz, W., Leon, S. C., Martinovich, Z., Lyons, J. S., & Stiles, W. B. (2007). Therapist effects in outpatient psychotherapy: A three-level growth curve approach. *Journal of Counseling Psychology, 54*, 32–39. http://dx.doi.org/10.1037/0022-0167.54.1.32

McCarthy, K. S., & Barber, J. P. (2009). The multitheoretical list of therapeutic interventions (MULTI): Initial report. *Psychotherapy Research, 19*, 96–113. http://dx.doi.org/10.1080/10503300802524343

McLeod, J. (2010). *Case study research in counselling and psychotherapy*. London, England: Sage. http://dx.doi.org/10.4135/9781446287897

Mikulincer, M., & Shaver, P. R. (2007). *Attachment in adulthood: Structure, dynamics, and change*. New York, NY: Guilford Press.

Rosseel, Y. (2012). *Lavaan: An R package for structural equation modeling and more. Version 0.5–12 (BETA)*. Ghent, Belgium: Ghent University.

Saxon, D., & Barkham, M. (2012). Patterns of therapist variability: Therapist effects and the contribution of patient severity and risk. *Journal of Consulting and Clinical Psychology, 80*, 535–546. http://dx.doi.org/10.1037/a0028898

Segrin, C. (2000). Social skills deficits associated with depression. *Clinical Psychology Review, 20*, 379–403. http://dx.doi.org/10.1016/S0272-7358(98)00104-4

Segrin, C., & Rynes, K. N. (2009). The mediating role of positive relations with others in associations between depressive symptoms, social skills, and perceived stress. *Journal of Research in Personality, 43*, 962–971. http://dx.doi.org/10.1016/j.jrp.2009.05.012

Shrout, P. E., & Fleiss, J. L. (1979). Intraclass correlations: Uses in assessing rater reliability. *Psychological Bulletin, 86*, 420–428. http://dx.doi.org/10.1037/0033-2909.86.2.420

Stiles, W. B. (2007). Theory-building case studies of counselling and psychotherapy. *Counselling & Psychotherapy Research, 7*, 122–127. http://dx.doi.org/10.1080/14733140701356742

Sullivan, H. S. (1953). *The interpersonal theory of psychiatry*. New York, NY: Norton.

Vromans, L. P., & Schweitzer, R. D. (2011). Narrative therapy for adults with major depressive disorder: Improved symptom and interpersonal outcomes. *Psychotherapy Research, 21*, 4–15. http://dx.doi.org/10.1080/10503301003591792

Weissman, M. M., Markowitz, J. C., & Klerman, G. (2008). *Comprehensive guide to interpersonal psychotherapy*. New York, NY: Basic Books.

Zilcha-Mano, S., Dinger, U., McCarthy, K. S., & Barber, J. P. (2014). Does alliance predict symptoms throughout treatment, or is it the other way around? *Journal of Consulting and Clinical Psychology, 82*, 931–935. http://dx.doi.org/10.1037/a0035141

14

EFFECTIVE AND LESS EFFECTIVE THERAPISTS FOR GENERALIZED ANXIETY DISORDER: ARE THEY CONDUCTING THERAPY THE SAME WAY?

SOO JEONG YOUN, HENRY XIAO, HANJOO KIM,
LOUIS G. CASTONGUAY, ANDREW A. McALEAVEY,
MICHELLE G. NEWMAN, AND JEREMY D. SAFRAN

At its core, this book is guided by simple but disarming questions: What are therapist effects? What might they look like? Previous studies exploring similar questions have highlighted the importance of attending to the interaction between therapist and client, and the impact that interventions have on eliciting change in the client's cognitions, emotions, behaviors, and self-perceptions (Strupp, 1980a, 1980b, 1980c, 1980d). In this chapter, we examine client–therapist interactions to investigate the processes that might differentiate therapists in the effective implementation and enhancement of empirically supported treatments.

The current study uses data from a randomized controlled trial (RCT) aimed at determining whether cognitive–behavioral therapy (CBT) for generalized anxiety disorder (GAD) could be improved by the addition of techniques targeting GAD difficulties not systematically addressed in traditional CBT. Briefly, research suggests that individuals with GAD worry, in part, to avoid emotional processing (Borkovec, Alcaine, & Behar, 2004; Newman & Llera, 2011). Interestingly, research and conceptual critiques of CBT (e.g., Mahoney, 1980; Wiser & Goldfried, 1993) point out that interventions in this approach are used to control or reduce affect, thereby reinforcing the maladaptive function of worry—the primary symptom of GAD. In addition, research has demonstrated that GAD is associated with a wide range of past and current interpersonal problems, and that a high level of interpersonal difficulties post CBT-treatment is linked with higher relapse (Newman, Castonguay, Borkovec, & Molnar, 2004). Process research shows that CBT tends to focus more on intrapersonal (e.g., thoughts) than on interpersonal issues (e.g., Castonguay, Hayes, Goldfried, & DeRubeis, 1995), thereby reducing its ability to address variables involved in the etiology or maintenance of GAD. Aggregating these psychopathology and psychotherapy factors together, one way to improve the efficacy of CBT for GAD would be to add humanistic, psychodynamic, and interpersonal interventions to its protocols, developed to foster the deepening of emotions and to facilitate the fulfillment of interpersonal needs. On the basis of this reasoning, a theoretically driven combination of CBT and non-CBT interventions was built in an integrative therapy manual (which is described in the Method section of this chapter and more fully in Newman et al., 2004).

Despite the promising results of a preliminary open trial of the integrative therapy (Newman, Castonguay, Borkovec, Fisher, & Nordberg, 2008), a subsequent RCT (from which this study is based) failed to find significant differences between the integrative treatment and the control condition (Newman et al., 2011). However, recent analyses suggest that the predicted superiority of the integrative treatment was obfuscated by differences in therapists. Although all three therapists were adherent to the integrative and control conditions, the clients of one of the three therapists in the study had significantly inferior outcomes compared with the clients of the other two. Furthermore, when this less effective therapist was removed from the analyses, the integrative therapy was significantly better than the control condition at posttreatment and 6-month follow-up.

These results obviously raise the question of what the less effective therapist might have done differently from the other two. Sessions of three client–therapist dyads were assessed via a combination of quantitative and qualitative methods to understand what the effective therapists might have done, or avoided doing, to foster positive outcome in their clients, as well as explore how the less effective therapist may have inhibited or interfered with optimal therapeutic change.

METHOD

Data Set

Data for this study were derived from the treatment condition of an RCT for GAD that explored the efficacy of augmenting CBT treatment with interpersonal and emotional processing (I/EP) interventions. Using an additive design, individuals with GAD received 2-hour sessions of integrative therapy for 14 weeks. The first 50-minute segment focused on CBT techniques, whereas the second segment involved the use of I/EP techniques. Each 50-minute segment was followed by a period of 10 minutes to complete process measures.

Participants

Three clients were selected, one seen by each of the therapists involved in the RCT. The three protocol therapists, all with doctoral degrees in clinical psychology, had extensive postdoctorate clinical experience. Prior to the RCT, they had received intensive training in and had conducted all components of the additive design delivered in the preliminary open trial mentioned previously (Newman et al., 2008). During the RCT, the three therapists met an a priori set of criteria for adherence and competence of the CBT and I/EP components of the integrative therapy (Newman et al., 2011).

Research Team

Coders

The first three authors of this chapter were the coders for this study—one female and two male doctoral students, all of them Asian American. The female coder had 3.5 years of clinical experience, and the two male coders had 1.5 years of clinical experience at the start of the study. In terms of theoretical orientation, the female coder described herself as integrative, whereas the male coders identified as psychodynamic and cognitive–behavioral. Following Hill's (2012) recommendation, the coders discussed their overall biases and experiences that could have influenced their assessments prior to commencing the coding process, including biases regarding the effectiveness of the treatments, differences in clinical experience within the coding team that may affect the discussion process, and potential cultural biases because of the ethnic background of the coders.

The coders were aware of the overall treatment effectiveness results of the RCT, namely, that there were no significant outcome differences between the integrative (CBT+I/EP) and control conditions. However, to decrease biases in the coding, they did not know the differences among the three therapists in the RCT, and were not aware of the individual results of the clients selected for this study. In other words, the coders did not know which of the therapists achieved better or worse outcomes, the reason why the three clients had been selected, or the outcome for any of the three clients. The results were revealed to the coders once all of the coding had been completed.

Auditors

The auditors for this study, the fourth and fifth authors of this chapter, included a professor who was one of the investigators on the trial from which the dyads were selected. It also should be noted that this auditor was one of the supervisors with whom the study therapists met weekly to discuss treatment adherence and competence, as well as client progress. He was aware of the outcome differences among the three therapists, as well as the general outcome of each of the three selected clients. The other auditor was a doctoral student with 5.5 years of clinical experience at the start of this study, and he was also aware of the differences between the therapists and clients. Before starting the project, the auditors discussed their overall biases, including how their knowledge of the dyads may influence the auditing process, and these biases were shared with the coders once the coding was completed.

Measures

A number of outcome measures were used at different phases of the RCT (pretreatment; posttreatment; 6-, 12-, and 24-month follow-ups; see Newman et al., 2011, for a detailed description). Two instruments assessing anxiety symptoms were therapist administered and rated: The Hamilton Anxiety Rating Scale (Hamilton, 1959) and the Clinician Severity Rating for GAD from the Anxiety Disorders Interview Schedule for the *Diagnostic and Statistical Manual of Mental Disorders, Fourth Edition* (Brown, Di Nardo, & Barlow, 1994). Two self-report measures of anxiety were completed by the clients: the Penn State Worry Questionnaire (Meyer, Miller, Metzger, & Borkovec, 1990), and the State-Trait Anxiety Inventory–Trait Version (Spielberger, Gorsuch, Lushene, Vagg, & Jacobs, 1983). The clients also completed a measure assessing relaxation-induced anxiety (The Reactions to Relaxation and Arousal Questionnaire; Heide & Borkovec, 1983). At the end of each session's therapy components (CBT, I/EP), the client and the therapist also completed modules of the Therapy Session Report (TSR; Orlinsky & Howard, 1966), a self-report instrument measuring diverse aspects of the therapy.

Treatment

CBT

The techniques used in the CBT segment included self-monitoring of anxiety cues, relaxation methods, self-controlled desensitization, and cognitive restructuring. During CBT, therapists were allowed to address only the learning and application of these methods as they related to intrapersonal anxious experiences, such as the challenge of irrational thoughts or the reduction of anxiety symptoms.

I/EP

To address interpersonal problems and facilitate emotional processing, the techniques in the I/EP segment included the therapists' use of their own emotional experience to identify interpersonal markers, the use of the therapeutic relationship to explore affective processes and interpersonal patterns, the provision of emotional corrective experiences via the repair of alliance ruptures, the processing of clients' affective experiencing in relation to past and current interpersonal relationships, and the use of skill training methods to provide more effective behaviors to satisfy identified interpersonal needs.

Procedure

Dyad and Session Selection From Archival Data

After consultation with an expert (Clara Hill) in qualitative research methodology, the auditors selected one session from each of the three dyads for intensive case study analyses. The three clients were chosen on the basis of stringent criteria of treatment response called *end-state functioning*, which was used for each of the five outcome measures described previously. For four of these outcome measures, high end-state functioning was defined as a score in the nonclinical range. For the fifth measure, the clinician severity rating, end-state functioning was defined as a score exceeding a face valid level of meaningful change, as normative data are not available (see Newman et al., 2011, for more details). Specifically, for the two most effective therapists (Therapists A and B), the clients chosen met criteria for high end-state functioning in four of the five outcome measures, at posttreatment, as well as at 6-, 12-, and 24-month follow-ups. For the less effective therapist (Therapist C), the client chosen failed to meet criteria for high end-state functioning on all but one outcome measure at a 6-month follow-up (see Table 14.1). In sum, the clients selected for the two effective therapists were treatment responders, whereas the client chosen for the less effective therapist was a non–treatment responder.

TABLE 14.1
Therapy Session Report (TSR) Ratings for the Selected Session,
and Level of Functioning at Posttreatment and Follow-Up

Client/ therapist	TSR for selected session		End-state			
	Client-rated	Therapist-rated	Posttreatment	6-month follow-up	12-month follow-up	24-month follow-up
Sharon/ Therapist A	1.5	4	5	5	4	5
Kate/ Therapist B	2	3	5	5	5	5
Ana/ Therapist C	2.5	4.5	0	1	0	0

Note. The ratings are the average for the CBT and I/EP segments, ranging from 1 (*perfect*) to 7 (*very poor*). The end-state data are the number (out of five) of measures on which clients met high level of functioning at each respective assessment point.

To provide a fair comparison of the therapeutic processes of the two responsive clients and the nonresponsive client, the session analyzed for each client was chosen because it had the highest combined helpfulness score across the two segments (CBT and I/EP), as rated by the client and the therapist on the following item of the TSR: "How do you feel about the session which you have just completed?" (ranged from 1 [*perfect*] to 7 [*very poor*]). All the sessions chosen were also within the middle phase of therapy (between Sessions 7 and 9). TSR ratings for the selected sessions are shown in Table 14.1. Coders were unaware of the reason for choosing the sessions.

Combined Methods Analysis: Quantitative and Qualitative

The three videotaped sessions selected by the auditors were transcribed verbatim, had identifying information removed, and were analyzed using a combined quantitative and qualitative methods approach. The qualitative portion was guided by consensual qualitative research–case study (CQR-C), which specifically applies to case analyses (Jackson, Chui, & Hill, 2012). Starting with one randomly selected dyad, the three coders independently watched the first session of therapy, the session prior to the selected session, and the selected session itself. They wrote down their initial impressions of the dyad, with special attention to the therapists and their use of interventions and interactions with their clients. The coders then met and discussed initial impressions and potential biases that may have impacted their assessments. The selected session was then independently watched again and coded following guidelines of CQR-C, and the coders discussed the results of their coding until a consensus was achieved and sent to the auditors for further review. Consistent with CQR-C, the team of coders engaged in open discussion and interpretation to arrive at a consensus for each of the analytic steps:

1. Domain coding involved organizing the data into meaningful, unique, and discrete topic areas. When coding for the domains, coders were guided by the Coding System of Therapist Focus (Goldfried, Newman, & Hayes, 1989), as well as the general ways by which the therapists interacted with their clients. This process resulted in eight domains of therapist–client interaction.
2. The data within each domain were summarized to capture their essence, including the context and content of what the client and the therapist discussed.
3. The summarized data were cross-analyzed to develop and understand the interventions used across the three cases during each of the CBT and I/EP portions of treatment. The interventions were used to highlight similar and different techniques used by the therapists across their clients.
4. To differentiate the effectiveness of the interventions (and the therapists), the research team categorized the interventions into three codes based on their impact on the client (Strupp, 1980a, 1980b, 1980c, 1980d):
   - *Positive*—Interventions that were deemed highly impactful and were followed by noticeably positive or active responses from the client, such as corrective experiences, increased insight, behavioral changes, or skill acquisition.
   - *Neutral*—Interventions that had an average level of impact. These interventions did not lead to negative outcome, but on their own did not lead to the type of significant changes that followed the interventions with positive impact.
   - *Negative*—Interventions that had an absence of an impact or seemed to lead to a mismatch between therapist and client in terms of their experience of the intervention.

The auditors provided feedback after each of the steps, which was then further discussed by the coders and auditors until a consensus was achieved before moving to the next step. This process was repeated for all three dyads.

RESULTS

Findings are divided into two sections. First, the within-dyad results are presented to understand each therapist's style and focus of intervention. Within this section, a broad description of the therapist's relational style is provided, followed by the most frequently used interventions for the top three domain areas for each dyad (see Table 14.2 for the number and percentage of interventions per domain by each of the therapists).

Second, between-therapists comparisons are drawn for each domain and during each treatment segment (CBT and I/EP), to highlight similarities between the two successful cases, and differentiate these from the unsuccessful case to address the goal of this chapter: What are some of the ways that therapists intervene and interact with clients that might explain, at least in part, therapist effects.

Within-Dyad Results: Qualitative Description and Quantitative Results

Dyad 1: Sharon and Therapist A

"Sharon" is a White, heterosexual, married woman in her early 40s living with her husband and child. Therapist A is a White, male therapist in his early 40s. He identifies primarily as a CBT therapist but has expressed strong interest in learning and augmenting his treatment with exploratory interventions.

Qualitative Description. Overall, Therapist A was judged as reinforcing and validating, especially with regard to the changes that Sharon accomplished. He continually facilitated Sharon's progress by supportively challenging her to entertain alternative views to distressing thoughts and interpretations, as well as by attempting to open new directions for exploration. Although the therapist was adherent to the treatment protocol (in terms of the focus of the content and techniques prescribed), the judges viewed him as generally nondirective and instead, mainly as using explorations of new client experiences in a curious and nonskeptical way. Therapist A did not talk over Sharon, and although his interventions were not always synchronized with Sharon's affective state in session, there were also no overt alliance ruptures. Therapist A did, however, use lengthy interventions at times with little active client interaction. Sharon appeared comfortable in the room. For example, during the second half of the session, she found it difficult to control her laughter, and Therapist A's repeated attempts to explore the affect in the room did not have the desired effect of productively using this positive emotion to facilitate increased understanding of self or insight. Nevertheless, Sharon was in high spirits during the session, and Therapist A's attunement to this positive emotion seemed aligned with her experience, as also assessed by Sharon's TSR session rating of *excellent* to *perfect*.

Quantitative Results. Overall, Therapist A spoke nearly 50% more than Sharon in terms of number of words in the selected session. Almost half of all the interventions focused on Sharon's emotional processes. Over half of the interventions in this domain consisted of reflections that were judged

TABLE 14.2
Number (and Percentage) of Interventions per Domain of Functioning for Each of the Three Dyads

Therapist	Domains of functioning n (%)							Total
	A	C	E	I	P	SL	TP	TPP	
A	1 (0.39)	47 (18.29)	118 (45.91)	16 (6.23)	8 (3.11)	36 (14.01)	21 (8.17)	10 (3.89)	257
B	7 (2.39)	118 (40.27)	57 (19.45)	14 (4.78)	43 (14.68)	20 (6.83)	11 (3.75)	23 (7.85)	293
C	12 (4.55)	149 (56.44)	55 (20.83)	27 (10.23)	5 (1.89)	12 (4.55)	0 (0.00)	4 (1.52)	264
Total	20 (2.46)	314 (38.57)	230 (28.26)	57 (7.00)	56 (6.88)	68 (8.35)	32 (3.93)	37 (4.55)	814

Note. Domains: A = action, C = cognitive processes, E = emotional processes, I = intentions/needs, P = psychophysiological processes, SL = supportive listening, TP = therapist presence, TPP = therapy protocol procedures. Total refers to the total number of interventions used by each therapist or per domain.

to match Sharon's affect, as she discussed her developing awareness of her emotions. Therapist A also seemed to use clarifications to increase his and Sharon's understandings of these emotions, and validations to further support Sharon's new understandings. Although these interventions were deemed to more likely promote Sharon's interactivity in the session, they also were at times mismatched with Sharon's experience, particularly during the second half of the session (the I/EP segment), during which Sharon found it difficult to control her laughter. During this part of the session, Therapist A's reflections, validations, and clarifications, which were judged as helpful earlier on, were instead coded as highlighting a discrepancy in Therapist A's interventions and Sharon's response in the room. Overall, although these mismatches did occur, Therapist A's emotionally based interventions were largely judged as helpful, and he encouraged Sharon to talk about her emotional experiences in a supportive manner.

One third of all interventions addressed Sharon's cognitive processes. Therapist A adopted a more exploratory style, and primarily used clarifications and reflections within this domain to better understand Sharon's difficulties. These interventions were also judged to be more likely to help Sharon gain new insight and understanding of her difficulties. Within this domain, Therapist A used different interventions frequently and therefore was viewed as being varied and flexible in his technique use.

Finally, Therapist A also used his own experience of the therapy process as interventions and provided Sharon with feedback. He would refer to his own thoughts when he described the present-moment impact of Sharon's responses, although this was deemed as not fostering emotional growth or interactive discussion. Specifically, these interventions seemed to occur when he tried to refocus the session. Therapist A also frequently used supportive listening as a way to provide supportive statements and gather information in a nonspecific manner.

Dyad 2: Kate and Therapist B

"Kate" is a White, heterosexual, single woman in her early 30s. Therapist B is a White, female therapist in her late 30s. She describes herself primarily as psychodynamic, but she has extensive CBT training and served as a protocol therapist in a CBT trial for panic disorder.

Qualitative Description. Overall, Therapist B was judged as very active, focused, and adherent to the protocol in her treatment delivery, but also flexible and attuned to Kate's concerns and markers prescribed by the protocol within the session. Therapist B was directive, especially during the first half of the session (CBT), but in a collaborative and attentive manner, rather than being domineering or overpowering Kate and session content. She was deemed as reinforcing and validating of Kate's changes, but she also continuously challenged the client using interventions that were consistent with mechanisms of change underlying both treatments. These interventions were viewed as encouraging Kate to continue with her process of change in an empathic and affirming manner. The coders and auditors judged all aspects of the working relationship in the dyad, bond, tasks, and goals as strong, with no alliance ruptures, and Kate and Therapist B appeared to work collaboratively on the same issues in a consistent manner. This positive overall judgment was further corroborated by Kate's TSR rating of the session as *excellent*.

Quantitative Results. Overall, Therapist B spoke almost 40% more than Kate in terms of total number of words in the selected session. Almost half of the interventions were targeting Kate's cognitive processes. Therapist B actively used Socratic questioning to challenge and clarify Kate's thoughts in the session, and these interventions were judged to be facilitative of positive changes, including new understandings of the self and behavioral changes. Therapist B seemed to increase Kate's ability to effectively use anxiety coping skills through flexible use of various interventions, including validations, reflections, and instructions on how and when to apply these skills.

Therapist B also used session time to address Kate's emotional processes. One of Kate's difficulties in this area was her inability to stay with her emotions. She appeared to have a tendency to cognitively analyze her emotions and remove herself from the experiential level. Therapist B directed Kate's attention to this tendency in an emphatic manner through a variety of interventions, such as clarifications of her emotions, metacommunication, and gently, yet firmly, pointing out Kate's avoidant tendencies when she shifted her focus away from her affect to her cognition and worries. Also, Therapist B facilitated Kate's experiential processes by providing her with feedback of the impact that this tendency had on others, including Therapist B and their relationship. For example, Therapist B encouraged Kate to be spontaneous in the session, sharing that she felt more connected with Kate. The dyad successfully used this intervention to foster changes in the interpersonal patterns in Kate's relationships with Therapist B, as well as with others outside of the session.

Therapist B's interventions also frequently focused on Kate's psychophysiological processes. She included relaxation training in the session, as well as outside of session, and seemed to work collaboratively with Kate to identify when and how to apply the various anxiety coping skills tailored to Kate's unique psychophysiological experiences so as to effectively manage her anxiety symptoms. For instance, Therapist B helped Kate identify that the most common psychophysiological presentation of her anxiety was through stomach discomfort, and she instructed the client to apply the relaxation skills learned in treatment to diverse situations in which she noticed these symptoms, such as at work or in interpersonal situations.

Dyad 3: Ana and Therapist C

"Ana" is a White, heterosexual, single woman in her mid-30s who was pursuing a doctoral degree at the time of the RCT trial. Therapist C is a White, male therapist in his mid-40s. His theoretical orientation is primarily psychodynamic, but he also has experience with CBT.

Qualitative Description. Overall, Therapist C was judged as highly directive and adherent to the protocol, and he was viewed as less collaborative and more leading and controlling than the other two therapists. Therapist C identified and noted areas of distress for Ana, but, with the exception of segments during the latter part of the CBT hour, the coders and auditors agreed that he was not able to engage Ana in initiating and fostering active work on her side. Instead, Ana seemed to passively follow Therapist C's lead and failed to bring about change for herself in these areas of difficulty. Therapist C repeatedly reminded Ana to apply her new skills, but he did not follow by describing how to use these interventions effectively in her life or what obstacles have made it difficult for her to readily use these skills outside of session. Despite his apparent domineering and frequently interruptive presence in the session, Therapist C was reflecting, validating, and normalizing of Ana's experience, especially surrounding an interpersonal fear, as she described feeling understood by the therapist (which may help in understanding Ana's TSR rating of the session as *very good* to *excellent*). However, Therapist C was judged as not fostering specific change, emotionally or behaviorally, but rather remaining focused on global issues in Ana's life (e.g., her sense of loneliness), which inadvertently seemed to support Ana's lack of agentic initiative for change. Notably, Therapist C focused substantially on the cognitive aspect of Ana's experience during the I/EP section, providing new intellectual rationale or insight rather than fostering emotional deepening.

Quantitative Results. Overall, Therapist C spoke 10% less than Ana in terms of number of words in the selected session. More than half of the interventions were targeting Ana's cognitive processes. Therapist C actively used Socratic questioning to challenge and clarify Ana's thoughts in the session, but these interventions were judged to more likely have a neutral level of impact in Ana and not necessarily facilitate or encourage new change processes. Ana seemed attuned to what Therapist C was saying, but the coders and auditors did not view the interventions as fostering active meaningful changes in Ana at the emotional, cognitive, or behavioral level. There were a few instances in which Therapist C's cognitive restructuring was deemed to increase self-awareness in Ana, but Therapist C seemed to have difficulty continuing any behavioral or emotional changes in relation to this new self-understanding. In addition, Therapist C provided a lot of psychoeducation of anxiety coping skills, and instructed Ana to apply these in her life outside of session, but he did not work with her to determine when or how to use these skills, nor did he discuss and remediate possible obstacles that limited their use in Ana's life.

Therapist C also actively addressed Ana's emotional processes during the session, mainly through clarifications and reflections of her emotions. These interventions seemed to allow Ana to express her feelings, including frustrations and fears in the context of romantic relationships, and Ana seemed relieved at being able to share these emotions with Therapist C without reservation or judgment. However, overall, the coders and auditors did not view the interventions as fostering additional processes of change, such as deepening her emotional experience or exploring unfulfilled needs in Ana's relationships, that would have allowed Ana to further use this experience. Therefore, Therapist C and Ana were viewed as stuck in a cycle in which Ana talked about her feelings but failed to fully experience these and use them to bring about changes in session or address her distress in the relationships outside of session. Ana even asked Therapist C for specific skills to increase her chances of successful interactions with potential partners, but he was not able to link these to her understanding of her anxiety symptoms or to ways to bring about changes for herself.

Therapist C's interventions also frequently explored Ana's intentions and needs through clarifications, reflections, and validations. However, as noted previously, he was not able to work with Ana to enhance her understanding of her unmet needs or develop new ways to have these met in a fulfilling manner. The inquiries in this area seemed metacognitive, with limited affect involvement on Ana's part, and therefore appeared to increase the client's self-understanding but with no significant changes occurring in conjunction or resulting from this knowledge.

Between-Dyads Results: Domain-Specific Comparisons

In this section, a brief description of each domain is presented, followed by a comparison of intervention use and their impact on the client by each of the therapists during the CBT and I/EP treatment segments. The domains are listed in order of most number of interventions used across therapists. See Table 14.2 for the number and percentage of interventions per domain for the three dyads, and Table 14.3 for the number and percentage of positive, neutral, and negative interventions per domain for the three dyads.

Cognitive Processes

This domain included interventions that addressed client thoughts and cognitive processes. As expected, the majority of the cognitive processes interventions occurred during the CBT segment of treatment for all three

TABLE 14.3
Number of Positive, Neutral, and Negative Interventions per Domain
of Functioning for Each of the Three Dyads

Domain of functioning	Codes	Therapists n (%)			Total (%)
		A	B	C	
C	Positive	8 (17.0)	25 (21.2)	13 (8.7)	46 (14.67)
	Negative	2 (4.3)	0 (0)	0 (0.0)	2 (0.6)
	Neutral	37 (78.7)	93 (78.8)	136 (91.3)	266 (84.7)
E	Positive	19 (16.1)	11 (19.3)	5 (9.1)	35 (15.2)
	Negative	9 (7.6)	0 (0)	0 (0.0)	9 (3.9)
	Neutral	90 (76.3)	46 (80.7)	50 (90.9)	186 (80.9)
SL	Positive	2 (5.6)	1 (5.0)	0 (0.0)	3 (4.4)
	Negative	0 (0.0)	0 (0.0)	1 (8.3)	1 (1.5)
	Neutral	34 (94.4)	19 (95.0)	11 (91.7)	64 (94.1)
I	Positive	6 (37.5)	7 (50)	0 (0.0)	13 (22.8)
	Negative	0 (0.0)	0 (0)	0 (0.0)	0 (0.0)
	Neutral	10 (62.5)	7 (50)	27 (100)	44 (77.2)
P	Positive	0 (0.0)	1 (2.3)	1 (20.0)	2 (3.6)
	Negative	0 (0.0)	0 (0)	0 (0.0)	0 (0.0)
	Neutral	8 (100)	42 (97.7)	4 (80.0)	54 (96.4)
TPP	Positive	0 (0.0)	3 (13.0)	0 (0.0)	3 (8.1)
	Negative	0 (0.0)	0 (0)	0 (0.0)	0 (0.0)
	Neutral	10 (100)	20 (87.0)	4 (100)	34 (91.9)
TP	Positive	0 (0.0)	1 (9.1)	0 (0.0)	1 (3.1)
	Negative	6 (28.6)	0 (0)	0 (0.0)	6 (18.78)
	Neutral	15 (71.4)	10 (90.9)	0 (0.0)	25 (78.1)
A	Positive	0 (0.0)	2 (28.6)	1 (8.3)	3 (15.0)
	Negative	0 (0.0)	0 (0.0)	0 (0)	0 (0.0)
	Neutral	1 (100)	5 (71.4)	11 (91.7)	17 (85.0)

Note. Domains: A = action, C = cognitive processes, E = emotional processes, I = intentions/needs, P = psychophysiological processes, SL = supportive listening, TP = therapist presence, TPP = therapy protocol procedures. Total refers to the total number of interventions per code per domain, and the corresponding percentage out of the total number of interventions per domain.

therapists. Therapist C was coded to have the most interventions in this domain. However, Therapist B had the most positive interventions in this domain, with 21% of her interventions judged to facilitate positive changes in Kate. Therapist A was also judged to have no negative interventions in this domain. Despite the low overall number of interventions, Therapist A was also deemed to use the most diverse types of interventions, rarely using the same type twice. Therapists B and C on the other hand, were similar in their flexibility of cognitive interventions used.

Clarifications related to the clients' cognitive processes, such as (a) increasing the clients' awareness of their thought processes in general, as well as the ways in which their distressing thought patterns changed, and (b) facilitating an understanding of the clients' use of anxiety coping skills, including cognitive restructuring, were judged to yield the most positive results across all therapists. It also appeared that the therapist's actively challenging the client's thoughts in session facilitated positive change in the latter.

Emotional Processes

This domain included interventions targeting emotions and emotional processing. As would be expected, most of the interventions in this domain occurred during the I/EP segment of treatment for all three therapists. Therapist A was judged to have more than double the number of interventions in this domain compared with the other two therapists. However, Therapist B had the highest percentage of interventions coded as positive, with almost 20% of her interventions facilitating a significant change in Kate. Interestingly, however, Therapist A was the only one with interventions coded as negative, and these comprised about 8% of his interactions with Sharon in this domain. This may have been due to the fact that, as mentioned previously, Sharon spent a big portion of the session laughing, and Therapist A attempted to redirect her multiple times without success. Therefore, the impact of these types of interventions was coded as "negative" because there was no change in the client at all. The three therapists were comparable in the variety of interventions used.

The therapists' clarifications and reflections of their clients' emotions seemed to facilitate the most significant positive change. These interventions were judged as not only aiding clients to become aware of their emotional processes but also fostering a newer self-understanding. Interestingly, this domain, especially when focused on by these specific interventions, had the highest consensus in terms of facilitating positive client change across the three therapists, with emotion clarifications coded as the most positive for Therapists B and C, and one of the highest for Therapist A. Therapist A used significantly more reflections when processing Sharon's feelings compared with other interventions within the dyad, and also when compared with the other two therapists. These interventions were deemed to facilitate the most positive change with Sharon but were also coded as the most frequently used negative intervention.

Supportive Listening

These were both general and supportive interventions. Therapists used interventions in this domain regardless of segment of treatment: Therapist A was coded to use them most in the CBT segment, Therapist C used them most in the I/EP segments, and Therapist B used them evenly across the two treatments. Therapist A had almost one and a half times more interventions than Therapist B, and almost two and a half times more than Therapist C. However, Therapists A and B were judged to have comparable numbers of positive interventions, whereas Therapist C had none, and was coded to have delivered the only negative intervention in this domain. In other words, this type of intervention was deemed to yield different reactions by dyad.

Most of the interventions in this domain involved the therapists' gathering factual information from their clients and providing supportive statements. This domain was mutually exclusive from others and was purposefully designed to include only a limited number of specific types of interventions, explaining the lack of diversity among therapists.

Intentions/Needs

This domain included interventions that focused on clients' needs, wants, and intentions. Therapist A was coded to use more interventions in this domain during the CBT segment, whereas Therapists B and C used more interventions during the I/EP segment. Therapist C had almost double the amount of interventions in this domain than the other two therapists. However, none of Therapist C's interactions with Ana in this domain were coded as positive, and instead, were all rated as neutral. In other words, Therapist C was successful at capturing Ana's intentions and needs but was not viewed as being able to use this awareness to foster significant changes. In contrast, 50% of Therapist B's and 38% of Therapist A's interventions were coded as positive for their clients in this area of functioning. It is notable that no interventions were coded as negative in this domain across all three therapists. Furthermore, Therapists A and B were coded to have used a diversity of types of interventions, rarely using the same more than twice, whereas Therapist C used a limited repertoire of interventions in this domain.

Similar to the emotional processes domains, the therapists' clarifications and reflections of the clients' intentions were judged to yield the most positive results across Therapists A and B. These therapists seemed to increase their clients' awareness of intentions in interpersonal relationships, as well as changes in intentions associated with previously distressing areas.

Psychophysiological Processes

These interventions focused on the psychophysiological reactions of the clients. As expected given the therapists' high adherence to the protocol, 98% of interventions in this domain occurred during the CBT segment, with only one intervention during the I/EP segment by Therapist B. A significant difference in intervention use was apparent in this domain, with Therapist B using 5 times more interventions than Therapist A and almost 9 times more than Therapist C. Most notably, the majority of Therapist B's interventions in this domain involved providing her client psychoeducation regarding the anxiety coping skills targeting Kate's physiological symptoms, such as progressive muscle relaxation, and working with Kate to consistently apply these skills in session, as well as outside of it. Therapists B and C were deemed to have one intervention rated as positive, which was instructing their clients to apply the anxiety coping skills learned. Therapist B used more than double the types of interventions as Therapist A, and almost 4 times as many types compared with Therapist C.

It should be noted, however, that the limited number of positive changes linked to this intervention during session may have been due, at least for Therapist B, to the fact that these skills had already made an impact on Kate's functioning in prior sessions. When instructed to apply these skills outside of session in a variety of situations by Therapist B, Kate said that she was consistently practicing and using the relaxation skills already, to which she attributed her decreased anxiety symptoms. This suggests that helping clients apply the learned skills in various situations in and outside of session can lead to change as clients become more agentic in their ability to manage their own anxiety symptoms through increased awareness and successful application of these skills.

Therapy Protocol Procedures

This domain addressed homework and other such assignments. Overall, most of the interventions in this domain were coded during the CBT segment of treatment. Therapist B seemed to apply the most interventions within this domain, more than double Therapist A and more than 5 times compared with Therapist C. Notably, Therapist B was deemed to also use these interventions to have a positive impact on Kate, facilitating significant change. For example, through the assignment of homework, Therapist B's interactions with Kate facilitated positive changes on three occasions, especially in terms of increasing the client's awareness of the change within herself in her ability to successfully monitor her anxiety symptoms and apply the skills learned in session to applicable situations. Interestingly, Therapists A and B were judged to use a comparable number of types of different interventions within this domain.

Therapist Presence

These interventions included utterances that revealed therapists' experience of clients. Consistent with treatment protocol, most of the interventions in this domain were during the I/EP segment. Only Therapists A and B were coded to use interventions targeting this domain, and the former had double the number of interventions. However, despite the majority, Therapist A did not have any interventions coded as positive, and in fact, almost a third of the interventions were coded as negative. All of the negative interventions resulted from Therapist A's sharing his experience of the therapy process with Sharon, such as expressing his confusion about whether to let Sharon continue to laugh or redirect treatment to explore potential areas of difficulties. Therapist B, on the other hand, was coded to have one intervention rated as positive, which involved her checking in with Kate about her reaction to the therapist's intervention.

Interestingly, this domain had the lowest diversity in terms of types of interventions, with only four. Of these, the two therapists' sharing their own experiences of the therapy processes were used the most frequently. Most of the interventions were targeted at increasing clients' awareness of their impact on the other person, in this case on the therapists.

Action

This domain included interventions focused on actual physical actions taken by the client. As revealed by the coding, Therapist A's only intervention in this domain occurred during the CBT segment, whereas Therapists B's and C's interventions were during the I/EP portion of treatment. Therapist C had the most interventions addressing this area. Therapists B and C had a comparable overall number and number of different types of interventions coded as positive.

The interventions most widely used within this domain included clarifications of clients' behaviors, reflections, and validations related to these actions and changed behaviors. Compared with the other areas of functioning, the therapists appeared to address this domain the least, with the fewest overall number of interventions targeting it. From these, the interventions coded as positive were clarifications surrounding clients' actions and changed actions, and validation of these changes.

Comparisons Across Domains

All three therapists used a similar number of interventions during the allotted session time, ranging between 257 (Therapist A) and 293 (Therapist B). The interventions coded most frequently across the three therapists targeted clients' cognitive processes (Therapists B and C) and emotional processes (Therapist A). Except for these, the three therapists appeared to be differentially attuned to their client's areas of functioning, with Therapists A and B significantly addressing all areas and Therapist C more selective in his interventions. Table 14.2 shows the total interventions per therapist for each domain, as well as the percentage of the total number of interventions per domain.

All three therapists were judged to use interventions that were highly impactful; about 13% of all interventions across all three therapists facilitated noticeably positive changes in the clients. However, there were also differences between the three therapists in this area. Therapist B seemed to have the most of these types of interventions, with almost 18% having a positive effect on Kate, followed by Therapists A and C. Notably, Therapist B had no interventions that were rated as negative. Interestingly, Therapist A, deemed to have the second-highest percentage of positive interventions across all domains of functioning, also had a substantial number of interventions that were rated as negative in terms of client response—in fact, this therapist accounted for 95% of these types of interventions. The three therapists were evenly distributed in terms of interventions that were rated as neutral, and these accounted for about 85% of all interventions across all areas of functioning. As expected, the vast majority of interventions were neither positive nor negative. But it is important to note that each of these therapists did indeed make impactful interventions. What seemed to differentiate Therapists A and B as more effective than Therapist C was their use of these impactful interventions to elicit clients' engagement in the treatment's prescribed mechanisms of change.

DISCUSSION

The goal of this chapter was to shed light on therapist effects by investigating interventions and therapist–client interactions that took place in an RCT in which there were noticeable outcome differences among the therapists. These differential outcomes were observed despite the fact that treatment was closely monitored for adherence to the study protocol, and the fact that all therapists received the same training, as well as same type and level of supervision during the study. Therapist differences are not only important for research purposes but also have significant conceptual consequences. Although ignoring therapist effects typically leads to overestimation of the magnitude of treatment effects (Baldwin & Imel, 2013), the therapist effects reported here seem to hide predicted treatment differences: The primary outcome paper of the RCT did not take into account therapist effects, which appears to have led to the inaccurate conclusion that the CBT+I/EP integrative treatment was not superior to CBT alone (Newman et al., 2011). On the basis of analyses conducted on therapist outcomes, a more accurate conclusion might have been that CBT for GAD can be improved by the assimilation of humanistic, psychodynamic, and interpersonal techniques—at least when the integration of these different interventions is practiced by some therapists. In our attempt to assess what therapist effects look like, at least within the context of a particular treatment for a specific disorder, we conducted intense analyses of the best sessions from two treatment responders (each seen by one of the two more effective therapists) and one nonresponding client (treated by the less effective therapist).

First, it is important to note common themes that emerged from our analyses of the three dyads, as these highlight possible heuristics for the process of change in general. Not surprisingly, most therapist interventions were judged as neutral. This should be expected, as it would be unrealistic to anticipate that most interventions of a therapist would be characterized as a "lightbulb" moment, nor should we assume sessions would be filled with non sequiturs and incoherent, hostile, or otherwise negative statements. However, there were differences in the frequency of positive and negative types of interventions.

A second theme that cuts across the cases involves the techniques used and their relationship with the domains and impact of interventions. The results show that the therapists used different types of interventions when they focused on each of the domains that were coded in this study. This is consistent with Goldfried et al.'s (1989) assumption that a diversity of interventions (within and across different approaches) can be used to serve the same function or to target the same aspect of functioning (e.g., emotion, thought, action). However, our findings also suggest that, in particular contexts, some interventions may be better than others. Specifically, the kinds of interventions that were deemed positive seem to correlate with the treatment modality. For example, the most impactful interventions in the CBT portion of treatment focused on clarifications and challenges of thoughts, and the interventions in the I/EP portion focused on clarifications and reflections of emotions were particularly impactful. It would seem that a wide range of techniques can be used when working with one client, but that these techniques may be especially helpful when they are consistent with the conceptual framework that has been established with the client. Put in terms of a general, yet tentative guideline: Many interventions are available to therapists, but they should aim to use what is best to activate the mechanism of change that they are supposed to foster. Finally, and again not surprisingly, the relationship matters. In all cases, and in both therapy segments, we observed therapists being respectful and attentive, as well as frequently offering supportive and validating statements. As for the interventions used and their impact, however, differences in the way the therapists interacted with their clients were observed.

How did the dyads differ? There was certainly variation in terms of focus on domains. Therapist C directed more attention to cognitions, whereas Therapist A focused more on emotions. But these differences, taken alone, are not necessarily meaningful. In fact, Therapist C was coded to have the lowest percentage of positive interventions in the cognitive domain, and

Therapist A had the highest percentage of negative interventions in the emotion domain. Consistent with previous findings, the frequency of certain interventions appeared to have been less important than whether or not the interventions worked (Strupp, 1980a). The therapist effects observed in the study were not due to a mysterious, unknown factor, but instead were best explained as the summation of many individual interventions, some of which were helpful and others of which were not. This suggests that training therapists in specific skills and techniques can potentially lead to improvements.

On the basis of all the information (quantitative and qualitative) gathered, the most meaningful difference between the dyads observed can be summarized as follows: Compared with the two treatment responders, Ana, the nonresponsive client, did not show as frequent or as deep engagement in the mechanisms of change targeted during each treatment segment of the integrative therapy. Even though the least effective therapist, Therapist C, used interventions that were permitted by the treatment protocol, these interventions, and the way they were used, did not appear to lead to the therapeutic effect at which they were aimed—whether cognitive, emotional, and/or behavioral change. The lack of intended impact is evidenced by the fact that Therapist C showed a distinct lack of positive interventions compared with the other therapists across all domains.

Bringing our quantitative and qualitative findings together, we argue that this lack of impact resulted from two broad types of therapeutic mistakes: errors of commission and omission. One commission error repeatedly observed relates to the use of technical interventions. Specifically, during the I/EP segment, Therapist C seemed to focus on what Ana worried about, as he was supposed to do, but rather than exploring the emotions underlying Ana's concerns, he most frequently provided interpretations. In doing so, Therapist C replaced the worry, a cognitive process, with another cognition. This is not only inconsistent with, but opposite to, the process or mechanism of change that I/EP interventions are aimed at activating. As noted in the introduction of this chapter, I/EP has been built on research findings that worry is used by individuals with GAD to avoid emotions. By providing interpretations, Therapist C essentially reinforced Ana's cognitive avoidance of her emotional experience. Ana had some insights and felt understood, which likely explains the high helpfulness score she gave for the session, but she remained in "her head" rather than fully experiencing the painful affect triggering her worries.

Another type of commission error relates to the way the therapists used the techniques prescribed by the protocols. In what could be viewed as a breach of alliance, Therapist C repeatedly interrupted Ana. Although providing useful psychoeducation, clarifications, and reflections, his delivery of interventions often superseded Ana's attempts to react and respond. And although Ana frequently agreed with Therapist C, what was perceived as a jarring and controlling manner of intervening may have been counterproductive and, as such, could in part explain the lack of impactful interventions observed and coded.

With regard to errors of omission in the therapeutic interaction, a number of content markers that the therapist did not respond to with interventions prescribed by the treatment were observed. For example, Ana frequently referred to her anxiety and sadness about being single. Rather than inquiring about her interpersonal needs and exploring ways to fulfill them, Therapist C simply reflected what she already knew—that she was sad. At other times Ana brought up specific relational situations, which Therapist C could and should have used as markers for social skills training. Again, however, he reformulated Ana's situation without providing ways to change it. Although the errors of commission appeared to have interfered with the process of change, these errors of omission reflected missed opportunities for change. In both cases, the interventions did not have the most desirable impact.

Interestingly, negative interventions can and do occur, but they may not necessarily represent irreversible failures. Therapist A was found to perform over 90% of the mismatched interventions observed during the coded sessions, yet he also achieved a favorable outcome. In contrast, Therapist C was coded to have only one negative intervention. The difference appears to be that Sharon and Therapist A were fully engaged in the therapeutic processes that were meant to be activated. The mismatched interventions represented moments of lack of synchronicity that importantly, did not derail the therapeutic impact of therapy. One lesson that could be derived from this is that a faux pas or lack of perfect attunement does not necessarily represent a therapeutic mistake. Not everything in the treatment has to flow smoothly, especially if the relationship is solid and if healthy processes of change (e.g., experiencing positive emotions related to more adaptive and fulfilling interpersonal relationships) have been facilitated by the therapy.

LIMITATIONS

The sample size of this study was small, and only included three therapists that were providing treatment to clients that met criteria for GAD within the context of an RCT. Therefore, the findings of this study were limited in their generalizability. Additionally, only one session midtreatment was selected for coding for each dyad. Even though the coders were not aware of the reason for selection, the content discussed during these sessions may have impacted the results observed. Furthermore, future studies should look at additional clients interacting with these therapists to investigate the presence, or lack of mechanisms of change identified in this chapter, not only to assess the reliability of our findings but also to assess the variance accounted for by the therapists and the clients in outcome.

CONCLUSIONS

Approaching our findings from a global perspective, our analyses suggest two general conclusions. First, therapist effects may well be nested within a client–therapist dyad. Just looking at what the therapists do or fail to do may not be enough to explain outcome differences. Crucial to our understanding was the impact that the therapist had on a client—whether the therapist allowed, fostered, or interfered with activation of the process or mechanism of change targeted by therapy. Second, the most effective therapists, or each therapist at his or her best, are not likely to be defined by the use of specific sets of interventions. Rather, some of the qualities of the most skillful therapists, or when a therapist is particularly effective, entail (a) knowing when to use particular interventions to start and deepen a process of change, (b) knowing how to validate and consolidate changes that have taken place, (c) knowing when not to continue to intervene when the desired changes have been achieved (i.e., when health has replaced pathology in the session), (d) knowing what mechanisms of change should be activated to facilitate change, (e) knowing when and why the interventions do not have an impact on these mechanisms, and (f) knowing how to repair errors of commission and omission that may have prevented or hindered the process of change. The manner in which these qualities present themselves in a given dyad will vary by client, but the underlying characteristics of what makes a therapist effective seem to transcend the therapy dyad.

REFERENCES

Baldwin, S. A., & Imel, Z. E. (2013). Therapist effects: Findings and methods. In M. J. Lambert (Ed.), *Bergin and Garfield's handbook of psychotherapy and behavior change* (6th ed., pp. 258–297). Hoboken, NJ: Wiley.

Borkovec, T. D., Alcaine, O. M., & Behar, E. (2004). Avoidance theory of worry and generalized anxiety disorder. In R. G. Heimberg, C. L. Turk, & D. S. Mennin (Eds.), *Generalized anxiety disorder: Advances in research and practice* (pp. 77–108). New York, NY: Guilford Press.

Brown, T. A., Di Nardo, P. A., & Barlow, D. H. (1994). *Anxiety disorders interview schedule for DSM–IV*. New York, NY: Oxford University Press.

Castonguay, L. G., Hayes, A. M., Goldfried, M. R., & DeRubeis, R. J. (1995). The focus of therapist's intervention in cognitive therapy for depression. *Cognitive Therapy and Research, 19*, 485–503. http://dx.doi.org/10.1007/BF02230510

Goldfried, M. R., Newman, C. E., & Hayes, A. M. (1989). *The coding system of therapeutic focus.* Unpublished manuscript, University of Stony Brook, Stony Brook, NY.

Hamilton, M. (1959). The assessment of anxiety states by rating. *The British Journal of Medical Psychology, 32,* 50–55. http://dx.doi.org/10.1111/j.2044-8341.1959.tb00467.x

Heide, F. J., & Borkovec, T. D. (1983). Relaxation-induced anxiety: Paradoxical anxiety enhancement due to relaxation training. *Journal of Consulting and Clinical Psychology, 51,* 171–182. http://dx.doi.org/10.1037/0022-006X.51.2.171

Hill, C. E. (Ed.). (2012). *Consensual qualitative research: A practical resource for investigating social science phenomena.* Washington, DC: American Psychological Association.

Jackson, J., Chui, H., & Hill, C. E. (2012). The modification of CQR for case study research: An introduction to CQR-C. In C. E. Hill (Ed.), *Consensual qualitative research: A practical resource for investigating social science phenomena* (pp. 285–303). Washington, DC: American Psychological Association.

Mahoney, M. J. (1980). Psychotherapy and the structure of personal revolutions. In M. J. Mahoney (Ed.), *Psychotherapy process: Current issues and future directions* (pp. 157–180). New York, NY: Plenum Press. http://dx.doi.org/10.1007/978-1-4615-9125-2_11

Meyer, T. J., Miller, M. L., Metzger, R. L., & Borkovec, T. D. (1990). Development and validation of the Penn State Worry Questionnaire. *Behaviour Research and Therapy, 28,* 487–495. http://dx.doi.org/10.1016/0005-7967(90)90135-6

Newman, M. G., Castonguay, L. G., Borkovec, T. D., Fisher, A. J., Boswell, J. F., Szkodny, L. E., & Nordberg, S. S. (2011). A randomized controlled trial of cognitive-behavioral therapy for generalized anxiety disorder with integrated techniques from emotion-focused and interpersonal therapies. *Journal of Consulting and Clinical Psychology, 79,* 171–181. http://dx.doi.org/10.1037/a0022489

Newman, M. G., Castonguay, L. G., Borkovec, T. D., Fisher, A. J., & Nordberg, S. S. (2008). An open trial of integrative therapy for generalized anxiety disorder. *Psychotherapy: Theory, Research, Practice, Training, 45,* 135–147. http://dx.doi.org/10.1037/0033-3204.45.2.135

Newman, M. G., Castonguay, L. G., Borkovec, T. D., & Molnar, C. (2004). Integrative therapy for generalized anxiety disorder. In R. G. Heimberg, C. L. Turk, & D. S. Mennin (Eds.), *Generalized anxiety disorder: Advances in research and practice* (pp. 320–350). New York, NY: Guilford Press.

Newman, M. G., & Llera, S. J. (2011). A novel theory of experiential avoidance in generalized anxiety disorder: A review and synthesis of research supporting a contrast avoidance model of worry. *Clinical Psychology Review, 31,* 371–382. http://dx.doi.org/10.1016/j.cpr.2011.01.008

Orlinsky, D. E., & Howard, K. I. (1966). *Therapy session report, forms P and T.* Chicago, IL: Institute of Juvenile Research.

Spielberger, C. D., Gorsuch, R. L., Lushene, R., Vagg, P. R., & Jacobs, G. A. (1983). *Manual for the state-trait anxiety inventory STAI (form Y)*. Palo Alto, CA: Mind Garden.

Strupp, H. H. (1980a). Success and failure in time-limited psychotherapy. A systematic comparison of two cases: Comparison 1. *Archives of General Psychiatry, 37*, 595–603. http://dx.doi.org/10.1001/archpsyc.1980.01780180109014

Strupp, H. H. (1980b). Success and failure in time-limited psychotherapy. A systematic comparison of two cases: Comparison 2. *Archives of General Psychiatry, 37*, 708–716. http://dx.doi.org/10.1001/archpsyc.1980.01780190106013

Strupp, H. H. (1980c). Success and failure in time-limited psychotherapy. With special reference to the performance of a lay counselor. *Archives of General Psychiatry, 37*, 831–841. http://dx.doi.org/10.1001/archpsyc.1980.01780200109014

Strupp, H. H. (1980d). Success and failure in time-limited psychotherapy. Further evidence (Comparison 4). *Archives of General Psychiatry, 37*, 947–954. http://dx.doi.org/10.1001/archpsyc.1980.01780210105011

Wiser, S., & Goldfried, M. R. (1993). Comparative study of emotional experiencing in psychodynamic-interpersonal and cognitive-behavioral therapies. *Journal of Consulting and Clinical Psychology, 61*, 892–895. http://dx.doi.org/10.1037/0022-006X.61.5.892

15

SOMETHING TO LAUGH ABOUT: HUMOR AS A CHARACTERISTIC OF EFFECTIVE THERAPISTS

SARAH KNOX, MEGHAN C. BUTLER, DAKOTA J. KAISER, GRAHAM KNOWLTON, AND CLARA E. HILL

We know that therapist effects exist (e.g., Crits-Christoph & Mintz, 1991), such that not all therapists act the same in therapy nor elicit the same outcomes. We know much less, however, about what contributes to therapist effects. Given that most of what has been studied about therapist effects examines trait factors (e.g., demographics, training, personality styles; Baldwin & Imel, 2013), more research is needed regarding what therapists do in psychotherapy that is perceived as effective, as well as what they do that is perceived as ineffective or unhelpful. Many therapists, for instance, talk about using themselves as "the tool" of effective interventions (Yalom, 1980). In so doing, therapists use their humanness to form relationships with clients. We suggest that one potentially effective element of this personhood involves therapists' use of humor.

The final draft of this chapter was updated and approved by the study participants, especially regarding whether their confidentiality had been adequately protected.

http://dx.doi.org/10.1037/0000034-016
How and Why Are Some Therapists Better Than Others? Understanding Therapist Effects, L. G. Castonguay and C. E. Hill (Eds.)
Copyright © 2017 by the American Psychological Association. All rights reserved.

DEFINING HUMOR

Defining *humor* is surprisingly difficult. Indeed, "hardly a word in the language ... would be harder to define with scientific precision than [humor]" (Sully, 1902 as cited in Kuhlman, 1984). Merriam-Webster's dictionary defines humor as "a funny or amusing quality," and "the mental faculty of discovering, expressing, or appreciating the ludicrous or absurdly incongruous" ("Humor," n.d.). The Association for Applied and Therapeutic Humor (n.d.) defines therapeutic humor as follows:

> Any intervention that promotes health and wellness by stimulating a playful discovery, expression or appreciation of the absurdity or incongruity of life's situations. This intervention may enhance health or be used as a complementary treatment of illness to facilitate healing or coping, whether physical, emotional, cognitive, social or spiritual. (para. 2)

Therefore, humor consists of an internal recognition of the incongruities of life, as well as an ability to look on these incongruities with an attitude of appreciation, amusement, or play. In addition, humor varies across cultures and between individuals (Bell, 2007; Martin & Sullivan, 2013) and is socially constructed (Bell, 2007).

HUMOR IN THERAPY

Therapists' use of humor in therapy is controversial (Shaughnessy & Wadsworth, 1992). Whereas psychoanalytically oriented theorists have historically, though not universally (Blevins, 2010; Killinger, 1987), frowned on using humor in therapy (Kubie, 1970; Pritzker, 1999), other theoretical orientations such as Gestalt, behavior, and Adlerian therapy, use elements of humor in their interventions (Corey, 2005; Fry & Salameh, 1987; Gelkopf & Kreitler, 1996). Haig (1986), for instance, acknowledged that humor may possess constructive and destructive aspects. According to Haig, humor may strengthen the therapeutic alliance, break through resistance, reduce anxiety, release affect, assist in diagnosis, and assist therapists in dealing with painful situations or frustrating clients. On the other hand, humor may have destructive aspects as well, including denial, repression, serving as a "cover" for hostility, and undermining the seriousness of the therapeutic endeavor. Humor's varied potential impacts, then, may well help explain the controversy that surrounds its use in therapy, and may also be related to its being socially constructed (Bell, 2007).

In the only quantitative study we found examining therapists' interventions preceding clients' laughter, Falk and Hill (1992) reported that therapists' humor rarely led to clients' laughter. Rather, clients' laughter was associated with therapists' interventions designed to release tension.

In one qualitative study, Bennett (1996) found that clients reported that humor helped them change their behavior in positive ways, improved the therapeutic relationship, helped them continue therapy, reduced tension or stress, changed their perceptions, reduced their use of defense mechanisms, or opened them to new ideas. In addition, humor was sometimes evaluated positively and sometimes evaluated negatively, and was sometimes not experienced in therapy. Clients who had worked with multiple therapists also reported that they left therapists who did not engage in humor during therapy. In addition, Bennett collected short surveys from therapists (eight identified as behavioral, cognitive, or cognitive–behavioral; three as eclectic; two as psychodynamic; and four as various other orientations), and found that they had used humorous interventions in spontaneous and planned fashions, and that their clients appreciated both kinds of humor.

Given the paucity of empirical data regarding humor, and the lack of focus on therapists' perspectives, our goal in the present study was to focus on therapists' perceptions of the use and impact of humor in therapy. We used consensual qualitative research (CQR; Hill, 2012) to gather rich data about the therapists' experience of using humor in therapy.

METHOD

Participants

Therapists

Eleven therapists (six men, five women; all Caucasian) from across the United States participated in this study, ranging in age from 31 to 65 years ($M = 53.8$, $SD = 11$). Seven were licensed psychologists, two were licensed professional counselors or licensed mental health counselors, and two were licensed clinical social workers. For theoretical orientation (nonmutually exclusive), six identified as psychoanalytic/psychodynamic, six as cognitive–behavioral, four as integrative/eclectic, three as person-centered, two as spiritual, one as existential, one as family systems, one as relational, one as solution-focused, and one as supportive. They had been seeing clients for between three and 38 years ($M = 23.7$, $SD = 12.1$). A 12th therapist was dropped from the analysis because no specific examples of using humor in therapy were offered.

Clients

According to therapists' descriptions of the 11 clients who had positive experiences with humor, six were women and five were men, they ranged in age from 18 to mid-60s, the length of therapy ranged from 12 weeks to 3 years, and most were seen on a weekly basis. The clients' presenting problems included adjustment disorder, Axis II disorders, bipolar disorder, dysthymia/depression, obsessive–compulsive disorder, and problems with relationships, substance abuse, and trauma/abuse. The five clients who had negative experiences with humor were all women, they ranged in age from early 30s to early 60s, length of therapy ranged from 6 months to a few years, and some were seen weekly and some biweekly. The clients' presenting problems included adjustment disorder, Asperger's, depression, paranoia, and problems with relationships and substance abuse.

Interviewers and Judges

Four researchers (a 52-year-old Caucasian, female professor of counseling psychology, a 26-year-old Caucasian, female doctoral student of counseling psychology, a 25-year-old Caucasian, male master's student of mental health counseling, and a 28-year-old Caucasian, male master's student of mental health counseling) interviewed therapists and served as judges on the primary team. A 65-year-old Caucasian, female professor of counseling psychology served as the auditor. All are authors of this chapter. All but two of the graduate students had prior experience with CQR. The team had good professional relationships with each other.

Measures

Demographic Form

This form asked for age, sex, race/ethnicity, highest academic degree, credential/license, practice experience, and theoretical orientation.

Interview Protocol

All researchers collaborated in developing the preliminary protocol, which was piloted on three nonparticipant volunteers who met the participation criteria, and altered on the basis of their feedback. The resulting semistructured protocol (i.e., each participant was asked a standard set of questions, and researchers pursued additional topics on the basis of participant answers) began with opening questions about participants' overall use of humor (e.g., how they tend to use humor with clients, how they define "use of humor," to what extent they adjust their use of humor with different clients, how important they consider the use of humor in therapy, what they had learned in their training about using humor in therapy). Therapists were then asked to discuss one specific instance in which they used humor and it had positive/helpful effects. They were asked to describe the relationship with the client, what they said or did that was humorous, what was going on in the therapy just prior to the humor event, what their intentions were for using humor, whether this was the first time they had used humor with this client, how the client responded to the humor, what they perceived to be the effect of the humor on the client, what they would have done differently, and how the event influenced their later use of humor with this or other clients. They were then asked the same questions about a different humor event that had negative/harmful effects, along with descriptions of attempts to recover from the negative event. The final questions asked generally about the use of humor in therapy, what type of training they thought would be helpful regarding use of humor in therapy, and why they chose to participate in the study.

Procedures

We recruited therapists via relevant email lists, electronic bulletin boards, and professional organizations; we also used snowball techniques in which we asked therapists if they knew of others who might be interested in and eligible to participate in the study. In each such communication, we provided information about the study and participation criteria (i.e., participants must be credentialed psychotherapists [e.g., licensed psychologists, counselors, social workers]; they must have been devoting at least 25% of their professional time to psychotherapy practice). Those interested in participating were directed to contact the primary investigator, who then emailed them a letter fully describing the study, the demographic and consent forms, and the interview protocol. When the completed demographic and consent forms were received, a primary team member contacted the therapist and scheduled the interview.

Each member of the primary team conducted a 50-min audiotaped phone interview with two to four therapists. All interviews were transcribed verbatim (other than minimal encouragers, silences, or stutters). Any identifying information was deleted, and each therapist was given a code number to protect confidentiality.

Data were analyzed using CQR (Hill, 2012; Hill et al., 2005; Hill, Thompson, & Williams, 1997), in which research team members reach consensus through discussion of data classification and interpretation as they complete the three steps of analysis (domain coding, through which data are organized into topic areas; core ideas, through which data in each domain for each participant are abstracted to capture their essence; and cross-analysis, through which core ideas within each domain, but across cases, are compared to reveal common themes); the auditor reviewed each step of the data analysis process.

RESULTS

We followed CQR guidelines in labeling category frequencies (Hill, 2012). Findings that emerged in all or all but one case were labeled *general*, those that emerged in more than half and up to all but two cases were labeled *typical*, and those that emerged in a least two and up to half the cases were labeled *variant*. Findings that emerged in only a single case were not included. We report only general and typical findings in this section (unless a domain yielded only variant findings), although all findings are reported in this chapter's tables.

Contextual Findings

Table 15.1 shows the findings that emerged when therapists discussed their overall experience of using humor in therapy.

Why Therapists Use Humor in Therapy

Therapists generally used humor to ease clients' tension or anxiety, or to lighten the mood. For example, one therapist noted that humor "de-escalates the situation and eases tension," and another stated that humor enables clients "to look more lightly on [their] own and other people's foibles."

In addition, participants generally asserted that they used humor to strengthen the therapy relationship and humanize themselves as therapists. One therapist commented on using humor to show that she was "more than one dimension . . . and a real person," and another asserted that "humor is bonding if two people find something funny together."

Participants typically also used humor to provide a new perspective or insight. One therapist remarked that he used humor to reframe and shift the context so that clients obtain a new perspective on what they are doing; another noted that she used humor "to provide insight or to complement serious insight . . . to provide clients with new ways of understanding."

Types of Humor Used

Typically, participants used sarcasm, irony, or dry humor. One therapist noted that she used "cynical, sarcastic, or dry wit," and another reported using "irony and snide remarks."

Modifying Humor for Different Clients

Generally, participants modified their use of humor to be responsive to clients' openness to humor. One therapist noted that if her clients have a sense of humor, she "goes for it." Another therapist stated that he "follows

TABLE 15.1
Therapists' Overall Use of Humor in Therapy: Contextual Findings

Domain	Category	Frequency
Why T uses humor in PT (purpose, function, intention)	Ease C tension/anxiety; lighten mood	General
	Strengthen relationship/humanize T	General
	Provide new perspective/insight	Typical
	Humor is healing	Variant
	Keep T engaged in PT	Variant
	Soften the blow of difficult material	Variant
	Exaggerate absurdity to C	Variant
	Not always intentional	Variant
Types of humor used	Sarcastic/ironic/dry humor	Typical
	Tease C	Variant
	Self-effacing remarks	Variant
	Use of media/other materials	Variant
	Stories/anecdotes	Variant
	Humorous use of language	Variant
	Does not use jokes	Variant
	Not to denigrate others	Variant
Modifying humor for different Cs	Accommodates to C's use of or openness to humor	General
	Depends on relationship with C	Typical
	Depends on type and severity of presenting issue	Typical
	Adjusts based on other C variables	Typical
T personal factors that influence use of humor in PT	Part of T personality	Typical
	Family/culture	Typical
	Theoretical orientation	Variant
Thoughts about use of humor in PT	Humor important in PT	General
	Humor should be used with caution	Typical
	Humor should only be used if part of T personality	Typical
	Although important, humor not essential	Variant

Note. General = 10–11 cases; Typical = 6–9 cases; Variant = 2–5 cases; T = Therapist; PT = Psychotherapy; C = Client.

the client's lead and tests the waters with a mild humorous comment" to see how the client responds.

Typically, therapists also adapted their use of humor on the basis of their relationship with the client. One therapist asserted that he and his client "must have a good bond" for him to use humor, and another stated that she uses teasing humor with clients whom she has been seeing for a long time and with whom she has a "firm therapeutic alliance."

In addition, therapists typically adjusted their humor on the basis of the type and severity of clients' presenting issues. One therapist did not use humor with clients experiencing major depression, PTSD, or acute grief because she did not want to make light of their symptoms. Similarly, another therapist noted that "the more serious the disturbance," the less likely he is to use humor.

Other client variables also influenced the type of humor. One therapist altered her humor on the basis of clients' cognitive functioning, another on clients' "worldview," and another did not use humor with clients who are not "emotionally regulated."

Therapist Personal Factors That Influence Use of Humor in Therapy

Typically, therapists noted that humor had to be a part of the therapist's personality. One therapist saw herself as someone who has a sense of humor in many settings and liked to give herself permission to be occasionally silly. Another remarked that because humor is "part of how I function as a human being," not using humor would be incongruent with his personal style.

Family or culture also typically influenced therapists' use of humor. One therapist described herself as coming from a Jewish background in which "ironic Jewish black humor" was not unusual. Another therapist noted that he learned humor from growing up with a teasing father and brothers.

Thoughts About Use of Humor in Psychotherapy

Generally, participants felt that humor was important in therapy, with one asserting that she "knew from the day that [she] became a therapist that humor was going to be an extremely important part of [her] therapy." Another commented that "we all will need healing at some point, and humor is a big part of that," and a third referred to humor as "life-saving at times" when it prevents clients from exacerbating their concerns.

Therapists also, however, typically asserted that humor should be used with caution. One participant emphasized that humor should be used "only with clients whom the therapist feels would welcome and feel comfortable with humor." Likewise, another stated that he wanted to remain "judicious about the use of intentional humor and remember that it is not always appropriate." Typically, as well, participants stated that humor should only be used if it was part of the therapist's personality, as evidenced by the therapist who remarked that if someone does not have a good sense of humor and tries to force it in therapy, "it can be a disaster." Instead, humor must be "part of the therapist's style."

Positive/Helpful Humor Event

Relationship Between Therapists and Clients

Generally, therapists described good relationships with the clients for whom humor was a positive or helpful event (see Table 15.2). One therapist

TABLE 15.2
Therapists' Use of Humor With Particular Therapy Clients: Specific Event Findings

Domain	Category	Positive/Helpful Event Frequency	Negative/Harmful Event Frequency
Relationship between T and C	Good	General	—
	Guarded; tenuous	Variant	—
	Formal; weak	—	Typical
	C had hard time "socializing to PT"	—	Typical
Precipitant/stimulus for using humor	C discussing/demonstrating symptoms/problems	General	Typical
	T noticed C nonverbals	Variant	—
What T said/did	Shared media (cartoon/story) that paralleled C situation	Variant	—
	Made bold/direct statement; used catchy language	Variant	—
	Commented on/responded to C nonverbal	Variant	—
	Made light of a difficult situation	—	Typical
T intent	Stimulate insight/growth	Typical	—
	Build relationship; support C	Variant	Typical
	Normalize/reduce C anxiety; lighten mood	Variant	Variant
	Catharsis	Variant	—
C observed/immediate response	Laughed; appreciated humor	Typical	—
	Negative reaction	—	Variant
Impact			
Perceived impact on C	Opened up C/PT	Typical	—
	Provided insight/perspective	Variant	—
	Felt misunderstood/confused	—	Typical
	Terminated PT	—	Variant
Impact on T	Reinforced/affirmed appropriate use of humor	Typical	—
	No impact	Variant	—
	More aware of/cautious about use of humor	—	General

(continues)

TABLE 15.2
Therapists' Use of Humor With Particular Therapy Clients: Specific Event Findings *(Continued)*

Domain	Category	Positive/Helpful Event Frequency	Negative/Harmful Event Frequency
What Ts would do differently	Nothing	Typical	—
	Explore event more with C	Variant	—
	Would use different intervention	—	Typical
	Take more serious/careful stance	—	Typical
	T misunderstood C/Cs presenting problem	—	Typical
Reason event was negative or harmful/what went wrong (negative/harmful events only)			
Attempts to recover (negative/harmful events only)	P directly discussed rupture with C		Typical
	T sought more understanding of C perspective		Variant
What T learned from event (negative/harmful events only)	Important to be careful in use of humor		Typical

Note. Positive/helpful events: General = 10–11 cases; Typical = 6–9 cases; Variant = 2–5 cases. Negative/harmful events: General = 5 cases; Typical = 3–4 cases; Variant = 2 cases. T = Therapist; PT = Psychotherapy; C = Client.

reported that she and her client enjoyed mutual respect for and trust in each other, that the client "worked her tail off," and that the relationship was "productive." Another therapist similarly noted that he and his client sometimes "bantered" and had a good working alliance.

Precipitant/Stimulus for Using Humor

The general precipitant for the humor was clients discussing or demonstrating symptoms or problems. In one case, the client described a "long laundry list of symptomology." Another client told his therapist "what a loser [the client] was, how he never made it in the corporate world, never made enough money, never married."

What Therapists Said/Did

Three variant categories emerged here. First, therapists shared something from the media that paralleled the clients' situation. One therapist, for example, asked his client with which character in *Seinfeld* the client most identified. When the client responded with "George," the therapist said, "Well, I suggest you switch to Kramer," because George, according to the therapist, was always complaining and thought that all that he did was wrong, whereas Kramer felt no need to be successful and did not care about the opinions of others. A second participant shared an adult-oriented cartoon from Matt Groening's (2004) book *School Is Hell* with a client struggling in graduate school.

Therapists also delivered bold and direct statements or used catchy language. As an illustration, one therapist stated to his client, "It sucks to be you." Another said to her client, using language from *Star Trek*, "It sounds like you're deciding to become humanoid."

In the final variant category, therapists commented on or responded to their clients' nonverbal behaviors. Here, for instance, one therapist mirrored her client's crossed arms, stuck-out tongue, and pouting expression and said, "This is what you look like."

Therapists' Intent

Participants typically used humor to stimulate insight or client growth. For instance, one therapist sought to help her client realize that she looked foolish and could change her behavior; another hoped to illuminate the client's distortions and challenge the client's thinking patterns.

Clients' Observed/Immediate Response

Typically, therapists reported that clients' immediate response to the humor was laughter or appreciation. In one case, therapist and client looked at each other and "could not stop laughing"; in another case, therapist and client laughed and smiled, which the therapist interpreted as a signal that "they were okay."

Impact of Event

We also asked about the longer term impact of the humor event. Specifically, we focused on the impact on clients and therapists, as well as on what, if anything, the therapists might have done differently with regard to this humor event.

Perceived Impact on Clients. Participants typically perceived that the humor event opened up the client or the therapy. One therapist, for instance, noted that after the event, his client was more willing to discuss the theme identified in the humor event; another reported that the event "became a venue" for getting the work done.

Impact on Therapists. Typically, these positive events reinforced or affirmed participants' appropriate use of humor. One therapist said the event "gave the green light that humor would be an okay intervention to use with this client." Similarly, another noted that the event helped her understand that, "this [was] good," and could work with other clients as well.

What Therapists Would Do Differently. Typically, therapists asserted that they would do nothing differently with regard to this event, because it "worked" and "was effective."

Positive/Helpful Example

To illustrate the results and protect anonymity, we created a composite example from several cases, focusing primarily on general and typical findings.

Dr. "X" described his relationship with his client, "Pam," as quite strong. They had reached "a comfortable point" in their work so that they could laugh together, and their rapport was such that Dr. X felt safe using humor with Pam. They "had a humorous attitude" with each other from early in their work together. Prior to this specific instance of humor, Dr. X noticed that Pam was deeply mired in her symptoms and was presenting a lengthy list of ongoing concerns, leading her to feeling overwhelmed and discouraged as she battled "the dragons." Hearing Pam's distress, Dr. X said to her, "You sound very wobbly today, like a chair that somebody has cut off one of the legs," hoping to provide support for Pam and also to lighten the mood of the session. In addition, he sought to use a "fun" word (i.e., "wobbly") to re-label Pam's distress and "make a sea of problems become one." Pam responded immediately with laughter and a smile, and seemed to "brighten up" a bit. Over the long term, this use of humor helped Pam calm down and talk more openly and deeply about the concerns that brought her to therapy. In addition, Dr. X and Pam began to use a "wobble index" in their work together, and it became "part of our own secret language." For Dr. X, the event provided "positive reinforcement" about the effectiveness of appropriate humor as a possible tool in therapy. Dr. X remarked that he did not consider other interventions at the time of the event nor would he want to change any part of the event.

Negative/Harmful Humor Event

Because only five therapists reported negative/harmful specific event findings, general categories required data from all cases, typical categories required three to four cases, and variant categories required two cases.

Relationship Between Therapists and Clients

Participants typically described a formal or weak relationship with clients who experienced a negative humor event. One therapist, for instance, stated that she and her client had a "stilted" relationship and a "weak connection from the start." Another therapist noted that he and his client had a "strictly professional" relationship in which the client "saw [the therapist] as a psychologist as opposed to another human on the planet." Therapists also typically reported that these clients had difficulties "socializing to therapy," as evidenced by the therapist who found her client "hard to reach . . . because he was not psychologically minded," and by another therapist whose client was "very concrete."

Precipitant/Stimulus for Using Humor

The typical precipitant for using humor was the client discussing or demonstrating symptoms or problems, as was the case with the positive humor events. One therapist commented that her client was discussing struggles with alcohol and drug dependence, as well as dysfunctional family relationships; another was presenting with symptoms of depression and was experiencing "horrible" and distressing thoughts.

What Therapists Said/Did

Participants' humor intervention typically made light of clients' difficult situations. For instance, one therapist remarked that his client's complicated family "would make alcohol look good to just about anyone." Another therapist, in trying to discern whether the client ever had enjoyable thoughts, asked the client if she ever felt like a particular character from a famous musical, and then sang a song from that musical.

Therapists' Intent

Typically, participants' intention was to build the relationship and support clients. One therapist sought to "meet the client where she was and go with that, go with the grain instead of against the grain," and to be supportive of the client and use humor "to build rapport." Another therapist indicated that he used humor "to build the relationship and let the client know that the therapist liked the client."

Clients' Observed/Immediate Response

The immediate variant response to the humor was negative. One therapist, for instance, noted that his client "did not smile," and another client evinced a "crinkled face" of confusion.

Impact of Event

Typically, therapists perceived that the use of humor led clients to feel misunderstood or confused. In one case, the client said she felt that the therapist "did not take her seriously and [she] felt totally misunderstood, insulted, and belittled." In another case, the client was confused by the therapist's remark, and then began to educate the therapist about the causes of alcoholism.

After these negative events, participants generally became more aware of and cautious about the use of humor in therapy. One therapist commented that the event "jump started" her awareness, and she became "more sensitive to remembering to make sure that clients can tolerate humor." Another therapist stated that he became "more wary" of using humor with clients.

What Therapists Would Do Differently

Therapists typically wished they had used a different intervention. One therapist wished she had used a different technique to express empathy, and another noted that he would have "commanded the client to go deeper instead of using humor." Therapists also typically wished they had taken a more serious and careful stance. One therapist wondered if "being more professional would have been better" with the client, and another suggested that he should have been more careful.

Reason Event Was Negative or Harmful/What Went Wrong

Typically, participants asserted that the event was negative/harmful because they misunderstood clients and their presenting problems. In one case, the therapist "completely misread the client's facial expression," interpreting the expression as evincing humor when, in fact, it was not. Another therapist acknowledged that he did not understand 12-step programs (in which the client was highly involved), and admitted that "there are too many therapists who are familiar with [such programs] for it to be worth the client's time to teach [me] about [them]." Furthermore, the therapist did not realize that his comment regarding alcohol looking good to anyone, given the client's family dynamics, "was like suggesting abortion."

Attempts to Recover

Therapists typically tried to discuss the rupture created by the humor event. For instance, one therapist apologized when the client brought up the event later, acknowledged that he made a "therapeutic flaw," and invited the client to talk about how the event made the client feel. In another case, the therapist admitted to the client that she should not have made light of what the client was discussing with the therapist.

What Therapists Learned From the Event

Typically, participants reported that they learned the importance of being careful when using humor in therapy. One therapist commented that humor "is not always perceived as lightheartedness," and she must first assess the client's "capacity to smile" and to receive the humor as it was intended. Another therapist realized that he was "too light and too permissive" in the event and got "sucked into the client's coping strategy."

Negative/Harmful Example

Dr. "L" described her relationship with her client, "Alex," as weak and difficult. They had a tenuous connection, perhaps because of "personality disorder characteristics," and Dr. L found Alex "hard to reach." Prior to the humor event, Alex was discussing persistent symptoms of depression and anxiety that were affecting Alex's ability to function and throwing Alex "off balance." Alex commented, as one possible means of managing these difficulties, of "wishing I was God, without all the responsibilities." In responding to Alex's distress, and in seeking to strengthen their rapport and lighten the mood, Dr. L giggled while stating, "Well, that could be pretty scary." Alex responded with confusion, and at the end of the session asked Dr. L what she meant by "scary." Alex said s/he had been thinking about what Dr. L said and thought that Dr. L wanted Alex to see God as scary, which Alex did not consider funny "in the least bit."

The event helped Dr. L understand that she "has to be more aware of what each client needs." She also realized that "she wasn't serious enough at that point" and needed to "put the brakes on [her]self." Were Dr. L to alter the event, she would have been more careful and chosen a different intervention to encourage Alex to explore more deeply. The event was the first, and only, time Dr. L used humor with Alex. Dr. L believed that the event was negative/harmful because she misread Alex's facial expression and did not realize how "brittle" Alex was. Dr. L did discuss the event with Alex, clarifying her intent in what she said and apologizing for her therapeutic error.

Influence of Gender and Theoretical Orientation

Although our sample was small, we noted some intriguing findings related to client gender and therapist theoretical orientation.

Of the positive/helpful events, six involved female and five involved male clients, six dyads were same gender and five dyads were mixed gender. Hence, gender effects did not seem to be prominent in the positive events. Of the negative/harmful events, however, all five clients were women, three of whom saw female therapists and two of whom saw male therapists. We cannot draw definite conclusions from such preliminary findings, but wonder whether female clients might be more sensitive to misunderstandings related to humor.

Regarding theoretical orientation, only three participants identified a single theoretical approach as their orientation, whereas other therapists integrated more than one orientation. In their descriptions of humor, theoretical orientation did not emerge as a salient factor. Although therapists who espouse "purist" forms of psychoanalytic/psychodynamic and cognitive–behavioral approaches may reflect different thoughts about therapist use of humor in therapy, these therapists' actual practice did not evince a conscious effort to use humor in a way that would be consonant with their stated theoretical orientation.

DISCUSSION

The therapists described humor as a potentially useful intervention. Although they asserted that humor should be used carefully, they suggested that it can ease client anxiety, lighten the mood, enhance the therapy relationship, and render the therapist more human, findings consistent with existing theory (Bader, 1994; Gelkopf & Kreitler, 1996; Godfrey, 2004; Haig, 1986) and research (Bennett, 1996; Falk & Hill, 1992; Golan, Rosenheim, & Jaffe, 1988; Megdell, 1984; Rosenheim & Golan, 1986; Rosenheim, Tecucianu, & Dimitrovsky, 1989). They also occasionally used humor to nurture insight or a new perspective, again consistent with existing literature (Bennett, 1996; Gelkopf & Kreitler, 1996). Their actual humor interventions were sarcastic, ironic, or dry, which we cannot compare to previous literature because no other researchers have empirically examined types of therapist humor.

Therapists wisely adjusted their humor to be responsive to their clients, and in doing so sought to facilitate more constructive effects of humor (Haig, 1986). In addition, therapist personality, family, and culture influenced use of humor. By allowing their "humanness" to emerge (Bader, 1994, p. 25), therapists seemed to model humor for clients, in the hope that clients' fostered use of humor might coincide with a return to health (Dziegielewski, Jacinto, Laudadio, & Legg-Rodriguez, 2003; Goldin & Bordan, 1999).

In looking at the results from the specific humor events, the therapy relationship emerged as key in how clients experienced therapist humor. Strong relationships provided fertile soil for such interventions, soil that may be even further enriched when therapists allow their own humanity to emerge through humor (Bennett, 1996; Gelkopf & Kreitler, 1996; Godfrey, 2004; Goldin & Bordan, 1999; Haig, 1986; Sala, Krupat, & Roter, 2002). Weaker relationships, on the other hand, may not be able to tolerate such divergence from "orthodox" therapeutic interventions (Franzini, 2001; Goldin & Bordan, 1999; Goldin et al., 2006; Haig, 1986; Kubie, 1970), especially if clients perceive the humor as making light of their concerns, and then feel confused and misunderstood. In such instances, therapists misread their clients, and in their attempt to introduce some levity, actually exacerbated clients' distress.

Adjustments to clients' receptiveness to humor are therefore essential (Bell, 2007; Lynch, 2010; Martin & Sullivan, 2013). Therapists indeed must be responsive to whether clients appreciate and value humor in the therapy setting, and in so doing, aspire to uphold the general principles articulated in the *Ethical Principles of Psychologists and Code of Conduct* (American Psychological Association, 2010).

Finally, humor must fit with therapists' personality. With those for whom humor arises as a natural part of their personality, appropriate use of humor may well yield positive effects in therapy; with those to whom such humor does not come naturally, not engaging in humor may be the better course.

Limitations

Our sample was balanced with respect to gender, but it consisted primarily of Caucasian therapists, and we do not know the extent to which the findings might apply to a more culturally diverse sample. We also have only therapists' perspectives here, and relied on their ability to recall and describe their use of humor with clients. Therapists received the protocol prior to the interview so that they could reflect on their experiences; those who received the protocol but chose not to take part in the study may have had different experiences. Because we used neither process nor outcome measures, conclusions regarding the effects of humor, whether positive or negative, must be tentative.

Implications

With regard to guidelines for how therapists might most effectively use humor to foster client change, our findings indicated that in the context of good therapy relationships and with therapists for whom humor fits their personality, judicious use of humor intended to reduce clients' anxiety, lighten clients' mood, nurture clients' insight/provide a new perspective, or make therapists seem more human, may be effective. When the therapy relationship is weak, however, even benignly intended humor may yield damaging effects, and must be used with extreme caution. Furthermore, and as is true for other interventions (e.g., therapist self-disclosure; Hill & Knox, 2002), humor's impact may well depend on its infrequent use, and therapists should be careful not to overuse humor in therapy.

In terms of future research, it would be interesting to observe and examine the actual use of humor in ongoing therapy. In this study, we asked therapists about their memories of using humor; it would be equally interesting to interview therapists and clients after sessions in which humor actually occurred. Likewise, as a complement to our focus on therapist-initiated humor, we wonder about the process and effects of client-initiated humor.

In addition, given that therapists indicated that they and their clients had to be amenable to humor, it would be intriguing to determine whether we can identify the "humor" personality, in therapists and clients. And when therapists' use of humor, despite their benevolent intentions, does not elicit the anticipated response in clients, how do clients experience this intervention, and how does it affect the therapy? Furthermore, to what extent is humor actually intentional in therapy, and to what extent is it more an intervention of "spontaneous combustion" (L. Angus, personal communication, April 4, 2014)? For instance, do therapists consciously and at least somewhat planfully use their clinical judgment to weigh whether to use humor versus a different clinical skill before deciding to deliver a humor intervention, or do humor interventions arise as more in-the-moment responses that may not be as deliberately considered? Falk and Hill (1992) found, for example, that client laughter was rarely preceded by therapist use of humor interventions, and instead seemed to have a more spontaneous flavor. What, then, might be the link, if any, between therapist humor and client laughter, and how might a deeper understanding of such a potential link inform therapy? Moreover, to what extent might therapist use of humor arise from difficulty tolerating some affect or theme present in the room? Might such discomfort elicit "nervous" humor?

Finally, it would be interesting to examine the possible role of gender, culture, and theoretical orientation in the delivery and experience of humor. Female and male therapists from different cultures may well use different types of humor, and female and male clients from different cultures may well respond differently to different types of humor. Similarly, adhering to the values of a particular theoretical orientation may influence therapists' enactment of their natural tendencies, although this influence may evolve over the course of therapists' careers.

REFERENCES

American Psychological Association. (2010). *Ethical principles of psychologists and code of conduct (2002, Amended June 1, 2010)*. Retrieved from http://www.apa.org/ethics/code/index.aspx

Association for Applied and Therapeutic Humor (AATH). (n.d.). *General information*. Retrieved from http://www.aath.org/general-information

Bader, M. (1994). The analyst's use of humor. In H. Strean (Ed.), *The use of humor in psychotherapy* (pp. 25–44). Scranton, PA: Haddon Craftsmen.

Baldwin, S. A., & Imel, Z. E. (2013). Therapist effects: Findings and methods. In M. J. Lambert (Ed.), *Bergin and Garfield's handbook of psychotherapy and behavior change* (6th ed., pp. 258–297). Hoboken, NJ: Wiley.

Bell, N. (2007). Humor comprehension: Lessons learned from cross-cultural communication. *Humor: International Journal of Humor Research, 20*, 367–387. http://dx.doi.org/10.1515/HUMOR.2007.018

Bennett, C. E. (1996). *An investigation of clients' perception of humor and its use in therapy* (Doctoral dissertation). Retrieved from ProQuest Dissertations and Theses. (304345043).

Blevins, T. L. (2010). *Humor in therapy: Expectations, sense of humor, and perceived effectiveness* (Doctoral dissertation). ProQuest Dissertations and Theses. (768030904).

Corey, G. (2005). Gestalt Theory. In L. Gebo & S. Gesicki (Eds.), *Theory and practice of counseling and psychotherapy* (7th ed., pp. 192–223). Belmont, CA: Brooks/Cole.

Crits-Christoph, P., & Mintz, J. (1991). Implications of therapist effects for the design and analysis of comparative studies of psychotherapies. *Journal of Consulting and Clinical Psychology, 59*, 20–26. http://dx.doi.org/10.1037/0022-006X.59.1.20

Dziegielewski, S. F., Jacinto, G. A., Laudadio, A., & Legg-Rodriguez, L. (2003). Humor: An essential communication tool in therapy. *International Journal of Mental Health, 32*, 74–90. http://dx.doi.org/10.1080/00207411.2003.11449592

Falk, D. R., & Hill, C. E. (1992). Counselor interventions preceding client laughter in brief therapy. *Journal of Counseling Psychology, 39*, 39–45. http://dx.doi.org/10.1037/0022-0167.39.1.39

Franzini, L. R. (2001). Humor in therapy: The case for training therapists in its uses and risks. *Journal of General Psychology, 128*, 170–193. http://dx.doi.org/10.1080/00221300109598906

Fry, W. F., & Salameh, W. A. (1987). *Handbook of humor and psychotherapy: Advances in the clinical use of humor*. Sarasota, FL: Professional Resource Exchange.

Gelkopf, M., & Kreitler, S. (1996). Is humor only fun, an alternative cure or magic? The cognitive therapeutic potential of humor. *Journal of Cognitive Psychotherapy, 10*, 235–254.

Godfrey, J. R. (2004). Toward optimal health: The experts discuss therapeutic humor. *Journal of Women's Health, 13*, 474–479. http://dx.doi.org/10.1089/1540999041280972

Golan, G., Rosenheim, E., & Jaffe, Y. (1988). Humour in psychotherapy. *British Journal of Psychotherapy, 4*, 393–400. http://dx.doi.org/10.1111/j.1752-0118.1988.tb01041.x

Goldin, E., & Bordan, T. (1999). The use of humor in counseling: The laughing cure. *Journal of Counseling & Development, 77*, 405–410. http://dx.doi.org/10.1002/j.1556-6676.1999.tb02466.x

Goldin, E., Bordan, T., Araoz, D. L., Gladding, S., Kaplan, D., Krumboltz, J., & Lazarus, A. (2006). Humor in counseling: Leader perspectives. *Journal of Counseling & Development, 84*, 397–404. http://dx.doi.org/10.1002/j.1556-6678.2006.tb00422.x

Groening, M. (2004). *School is hell: A cartoon book*. New York, NY: Harper Collins.

Haig, R. A. (1986). Therapeutic uses of humor. *American Journal of Psychotherapy, 40*, 543–553.

Hill, C. E. (Ed.). (2012). *Consensual qualitative research: A practical resource for investigating social science phenomena*. Washington, DC: American Psychological Association.

Hill, C. E., & Knox, S. (2002). Self-disclosure. In J. C. Norcross (Ed.), *Psychotherapy relationships that work: Therapist contributions and responsiveness to patients* (pp. 255–265). Oxford, England: Oxford University Press.

Hill, C. E., Knox, S., Thompson, B. J., Williams, E. N., Hess, S. A., & Ladany, N. (2005). Consensual qualitative research: An update. *Journal of Counseling Psychology, 52*, 196–205. http://dx.doi.org/10.1037/0022-0167.52.2.196

Hill, C. E., Thompson, B. J., & Williams, B. N. (1997). A guide to conducting consensual qualitative research. *The Counseling Psychologist, 25*, 517–572. http://dx.doi.org/10.1177/0011000097254001

Humor. (n.d.). In *Merriam-Webster's online dictionary* (11th ed.). Retrieved from http://www.merriam-webster.com/dictionary/humor

Killinger, B. (1987). Humor in psychotherapy: A shift to a new perspective. In W. F. Fry & M. A. Salameh (Eds.), *Handbook of humor and psychotherapy* (pp. 21–41). Sarasota, FL: Professional Resource Exchange.

Kubie, L. S. (1970). The destructive potential of humor in psychotherapy. *The American Journal of Psychiatry, 127*, 861–866. http://dx.doi.org/10.1176/ajp.127.7.861

Kuhlman, T. L. (1984). *Humor and psychotherapy*. Homewood, IL: Dow Jones-Irwin.

Lynch, O. (2010). Cooking with humor: In-group humor as social organization. *Humor: International Journal of Humor Research, 23,* 127–159. http://dx.doi.org/10.1515/humr.2010.007

Martin, G. N., & Sullivan, E. (2013). Sense of humor across cultures: A comparison of British, Australian and American respondents. *North American Journal of Psychology, 15,* 375–384.

Megdell, J. (1984). Relationship between counselor-initiated humor and client's self-perceived attraction in the counseling interview. *Psychotherapy: Theory, Research, Practice, Training, 21,* 517–523. http://dx.doi.org/10.1037/h0085997

Pritzker, S. R. (1999). The effect of Groucho Marx glasses on depression. *Psychology Today, 32,* 88.

Rosenheim, E., & Golan, G. (1986). Patients' reactions to humorous interventions in psychotherapy. *American Journal of Psychotherapy, 40,* 110–124.

Rosenheim, E., Tecucianu, F., & Dimitrovsky, L. (1989). Schizophrenics' appreciation of humorous therapeutic interventions. *Humor: International Journal of Humor Research, 2,* 141–152. http://dx.doi.org/10.1515/humr.1989.2.2.141

Sala, F., Krupat, E., & Roter, D. (2002). Satisfaction and the use of humor by physicians and patients. *Psychology & Health, 17,* 269–280. http://dx.doi.org/10.1080/08870440290029520

Shaughnessy, M. F., & Wadsworth, T. M. (1992). Humor in counseling and psychotherapy: A 20-year retrospective. *Psychological Reports, 70,* 755–762. http://dx.doi.org/10.2466/pr0.1992.70.3.755

Yalom, I. (1980). *Existential psychotherapy.* New York, NY: Basic Books.

IV
IMPLICATIONS AND CONCLUSIONS

16

THE IMPLICATIONS OF THERAPIST EFFECTS FOR ROUTINE PRACTICE, POLICY, AND TRAINING

JAMES F. BOSWELL, DAVID R. KRAUS, MICHAEL J. CONSTANTINO, MATTEO BUGATTI, AND LOUIS G. CASTONGUAY

Despite considerable research demonstrating the significance of the individual psychotherapist for mental health treatment outcomes (Baldwin & Imel, 2013), we have witnessed some researchers reacting to the findings on therapist effects with mild amusement, taking the position that these findings are interesting only insofar as they exemplify what can be done statistically with a large enough sample. Others have stated that the fact that there are differences between therapists is plainly obvious and not particularly interesting. Although admittedly anecdotal, the common thread between these viewpoints appears to be: "So what? I don't see how this is clinically useful."

We believe that efforts to address the implications of therapist effects are long overdue. In this chapter, we attempt to address the "so what?" question of therapist effects by discussing (a) what can and should (or should not) be done with process and outcome information collected in routine clinical practice, and (b) the challenges and potential solutions in conducting

http://dx.doi.org/10.1037/0000034-017
How and Why Are Some Therapists Better Than Others? Understanding Therapist Effects, L. G. Castonguay and C. E. Hill (Eds.)
Copyright © 2017 by the American Psychological Association. All rights reserved.

relevant assessments and in using the resulting information. We hasten to say, however, that when addressing these issues, at least as many questions will be raised as tentative answers offered. Furthermore, we appreciate that the solutions offered should be considered tentative until stronger empirical evidence supports them.

WHAT CAN AND SHOULD BE DONE

The ultimate goal of psychotherapy researchers and practitioners should be to foster treatment success and avoid harm (Castonguay, Boswell, Constantino, Goldfried, & Hill, 2010). Within that context, once it is clear which treatment variables explain between-therapist effects (see Chapters 2 and 3, this volume, for a discussion of candidate variables for explaining therapist differences), the field should move toward integrating these variables within different facets of mental health care. This could involve adapting training programs, supervision routines, and standard referral practices to maximize therapist effectiveness and minimize client deterioration. This is especially true for those outcome variables for which therapists makes a clear and consistent contribution.

With the proper measurement and estimation of therapist contributions to treatment outcomes, provider effectiveness data have the potential to improve the quality of care. Multiple studies involving large samples have demonstrated that individual therapist effectiveness is relatively stable across time and clients (e.g., Kraus et al., 2016; Wampold & Brown, 2005; see also Chapter 2, this volume). Therapist effects, therefore, appear to be predictable. On the basis of real-world data, simulations suggest that treatment effect sizes would increase significantly by matching or referring clients to the most effective therapists. For example, Imel, Sheng, Baldwin, and Atkins (2015) conducted a Monte Carlo simulation to examine the impact of removing therapists with the worst outcomes, defined as performing in the bottom 5% of the sample. Extrapolating over 10 years, they found significantly higher response rates when the lowest performing therapists were removed and replaced with a random sample of therapists from the better performing population, translating into thousands of additional treatment responders over time. Although the data on effective therapists have so far been based almost exclusively on symptom measures (as opposed to other aspects of functioning, such as personality reorganization, that many insight-oriented clinicians perceive as an important focus of change), we view these empirical results as highly meaningful clinically, and as one very compelling answer to the "so what?" question. We also believe that this and other findings about therapist effects (see Chapters 1, 2, and 3) provide an empirical basis to our own question: What can be done with data gathered through routine outcome monitoring? In our view, one way that such an assessment can (and should) be used is to help identify the therapists to whom we most want to refer clients (not to dictate, but to provide relevant information). Such an assessment can also identify the therapists likely to be more effective with particular clients and the therapists who are unlikely to best serve particular clients (at least in the current phase of their career and/or without additional training and supervision).

The identification of stable outcome differences among providers and services is already being harnessed in other areas of health care. In medicine, treatment providers and hospital systems are often ranked on the basis of established criteria (http://www.leapfroggroup.org/), and this information is disseminated in various ways to stakeholders and decision makers (Scanlon, Lindrooth, & Christianson, 2008). Behavioral health care, however, has received virtually no attention in this area. It seems important to consider the feasibility and merit of using similar methods, as the predominant existing methods of referring clients to therapists are based on questionable assumptions, to say the least (e.g., the therapist's availability, reputation, or connection with a referring provider).

It should be recognized that strategies for making effectiveness data available for health care decisions are complex, with many options, but few good ones, at least partially because of the diversity of stakeholders (e.g., clients, therapists, hospitals, payers, trainers, state licensing boards). For example, although online provider ratings have become more common, they are typically based on self-selecting clients' general impressions that generate a certain number of endorsed "gold stars" with highly questionable validity (Boswell, Constantino, Kraus, Bugatti, & Oswald, 2016).

Each stakeholder group has its own unique needs and interests in the use of therapist effectiveness data, and these needs and concerns may not always align. Moreover, each stakeholder is confronted with several unresolved issues regarding use of such data. Although the discussion is far from exhaustive, we explore some of the needs of and problems faced by four critical stakeholder perspectives: payers (e.g., insurance companies), clients, therapists, and trainers. A consideration of these distinct needs and problems will help clarify not only what can (and should) be done with data monitoring but also what should not be done.

Payers

Payers are motivated to improve the efficiency and effectiveness of treatment. In the rapidly changing health care landscape, payers have been under increasing pressure from self-insured employers to tier their networks (Scanlon et al., 2008) and to display outcome "report cards" (Chernew, Gowrisankaran, & Scanlon, 2008). In a *tiered network*, health insurance plan providers or hospitals are separated into different levels on the basis of established cost and quality metrics. In such a system, individuals can choose to seek services from a lower tier provider or hospital, but they will be responsible for a higher copayment relative to seeking services from a Tier 1 provider or hospital. As alluded to previously, quality data from hospital systems are already being used to inform health care decision making at the client, employer, and insurance levels. One could argue that therapist effectiveness data could be similarly useful and valuable. To be of optimal value from the payer perspective, however, collection and access to these data would need to influence payment and payment models. A major movement is to pay out more to the providers who demonstrate consistently positive outcomes (Greene & Nash, 2008). Different labels are used for this approach, including pay-for-performance and performance-based incentives (Bremer, Scholle, Keyser, Knox Houtsinger, & Pincus, 2008).

This approach, as we discuss next, raises serious fears for providers. From a public health perspective, one could argue that a pay-for-performance approach on the basis of demonstrated change could disincentivize therapists from seeing more difficult clients. Clinical experience and research reveal subgroups of clients who demonstrate relatively flat change trajectories even after a significant dose of treatment. It may be the case that therapy offers a stabilizing function that reduces the risk of inpatient hospitalization or self-harming behaviors, rather than demonstrable improvements in symptoms and functioning on the basis of standard measurement tools. This raises an understandable concern regarding performance-based payment models. However, models could be constructed that adjust for client characteristics that are associated with attenuated response. In these models, the trajectory of clients with poorer prognosis would not be compared with the expected trajectory of motivated and less impaired clients, because these would not represent a relevant benchmark. Decreased frequency or absence of inpatient hospitalization could also function as a key performance indicator.

Nevertheless, a number of critical issues need to be addressed before performance-based payment models and incentives could be safely and fairly implemented in mental health practice, including the reliability and validity of outcomes measurement, and the selection of outcomes that are of greatest value. For example, should payers reimburse therapists for providing an established, evidence-based treatment with a high level of fidelity and/or for demonstrating significant functional improvements in individual clients on the basis of standardized self-report measures? There are no doubt inherent limitations to relying solely on self-report measures. To muddy the waters further, the results from Kraus, Castonguay, Boswell, Nordberg, and Hayes (2011; see also Kraus et al., 2016) indicate that a "better therapist" is relative to the client problems one is treating and an individual therapist should be considered *better matched* rather than generally "better" in an absolute sense. In addition, if a good therapist match exists, the referral system within the payer network would need access to the outcome data within whatever referral procedures the payer has in place (e.g., an online referral database with distance to travel and other selection criteria).

Finally, with regard to payers, one might wonder about the significance of an effect that appears to explain between 5% and 8% of the variance in client outcomes. The results of Imel et al. (2015) demonstrate that removing underperforming therapists translates into thousands of additional treatment responders, which would significantly improve public health. Other research (e.g., Kraus et al., 2016) demonstrates larger outcome effect sizes for therapists who are labeled *above average* on the basis of their performance track records. It is certainly the case that the importance of therapist differences should be weighed in the context of what we know about other treatment factors, such as client characteristics and interventions effects. In this respect, the size of the therapist effect is notable and should not be discounted. Furthermore, if a payer is in the hypothetical position of choosing between paying attention to therapist differences or mandating the use of empirically supported treatments (ESTs), it is considerably more cost-effective and logistically feasible to identify effective therapists on the basis of their observed performance on standardized measures than it would be to confirm the presence or absence of therapist EST certification and assess intervention-specific adherence and competence on an ongoing basis.

Clients

We have collected survey data demonstrating that clients struggle to find good-fitting therapists and highly value the idea of using therapist performance information when selecting therapists (Boswell et al., 2016). However, clients are more ambivalent about needing or wanting direct access to therapist effectiveness information. Although speculative, this may be because clients are less confident in their own ability to interpret or make use of therapist performance information. However, what is clear from the survey data is that an overwhelming majority of clients want assurances that those helping them find the right therapist are using such data, if the data are available.

If we can identify therapist effects in specific outcome domains, research highlights the outcome implications of steering clients to more effective therapists (e.g., Imel et al., 2015), and the preliminary evidence cited previously indicates that clients favor using such information. From the perspective of client treatment benefit and choice, we can and should use therapist effectiveness data to inform mental health care decisions. However, other research findings underscore the importance of client preferences and the relative values clients place on different treatment characteristics. For example, Swift and Callahan (2010) found that clients were willing to discount a significant percentage of benchmarked intervention empirical support for assurances that they could develop a positive therapeutic relationship with therapists. Although this study focused on attitudes toward ESTs, the implications logically extend to "empirically supported providers." The point here is that outcome data should not be viewed as the sole basis for referral or matching. Rather, the data should be viewed as one source of information to support these crucial decisions (as well as other important decisions that must be made once treatment has begun; see Castonguay, Barkham, Lutz, & McAleavey, 2013).

In addition, it is unclear which dissemination and implementation methods for provider effectiveness information are optimal. For example, just as there are multiple EST lists available in the literature, multiple versions of report cards could be established by a health plan, hospital system, or trade association (e.g., American Psychological Association). Furthermore, if there are relative effectiveness ratings by problem category (e.g., mood vs. substance use) or another domain classification system, how does a client know which one to prioritize, particularly when problem comorbidity is the rule?

Therapists

The term *accountability* has been used extensively in discussions about routine outcome monitoring (ROM) and therapist effectiveness, yet calls for increased accountability rarely originate from the therapist perspective. They are more likely to come from policy experts, payers, and clients. Understandably, therapists have concerns regarding outcome data, performance measurement, and report cards. Interestingly, in the same survey previously referenced (Boswell et al., 2016), therapists reported generally positive attitudes toward ROM. In fact, most therapists welcomed the idea of having a system that could help them "find" clients with whom they have a high likelihood of success. Relatedly, most therapists endorsed the belief that they are more or less effective with different types of clients.

Supporting the need for a system to assist therapists in identifying well-matched clients, research has shown that therapists tend to overestimate their own general effectiveness with clients, as well as their effectiveness relative to that of other therapists (e.g., Walfish, McAlister, O'Donnell, & Lambert, 2012). Traditional alternatives to ROM-based therapist effectiveness information include peer identification (or self-identification) as an *expert*, *master*, or a *specialist* in a particular area. It is not uncommon for such labels to be conferred on treatment developers. Even when a particular treatment has demonstrated efficacy in controlled research, it is taken for granted that the treatment developer, in particular, is an effective therapist. In the absence of systematically tracking the outcomes of this therapist's clients, this assertion is highly speculative. For example, it is unlikely that all of the inventors of surgical devices are outstanding surgeons, although it is most likely that they are surgeons.

In short, it has historically been common practice to make anecdotal claims about one's own or another therapist's effectiveness. This implies that therapist effectiveness information is valued at some level. It seems reasonable to expect that such assertions are based on the best available empirical evidence. The availability of such evidence is itself a critical issue. Depending on the clinical contexts that lead certain therapists to use routine outcome assessment, outcome databases may include a selective sample of providers and clients. For example, more seasoned therapists who see primarily self-paying clients may be less likely to routinely monitor their clients' progress and would not be represented in data repositories.

Regardless of one's professional stage or typical payment practices, we believe that therapists should be aware of their own relative areas of strength and weakness; however, if individual therapist effectiveness data are used in a way that is clearly detrimental to therapists' livelihoods, there will be no motivation for therapists to cooperate. For example, therapist effectiveness information could be published for the general public's consumption, mirroring one approach already being implemented in medicine (Henderson & Henderson, 2010). However, we caution against publishing individual therapist effectiveness data. Rather than focus on therapists' strengths, we believe this would lead to a greater focus on therapists' weaknesses. Although therapist effectiveness, as typically measured, is relatively stable across time, there is emerging research implying that therapists can achieve better outcomes when they engage in more deliberative practice activities. A highly innovative study by Chow et al. (2015) found that therapists' reported time spent engaging in deliberative practice related to their work with clients was significantly associated with their clients' outcomes. Interestingly, no significant associations were observed between specific activities (e.g., attending a training workshop) and outcome. However, the amount of reported cognitive effort exerted while reviewing therapist recordings, for example, was significantly correlated with outcome.

In another example, benchmarked outcome reports, which provide information regarding outcomes from a provider or setting relative to an existing standard or similar outcomes from a provider or setting, demonstrated that an adolescent inpatient substance abuse treatment facility was achieving suboptimal outcomes in the area of violence and anger (Adelman, McGee, Power, & Hanson, 2005). Consequently, the program sought additional training for addressing anger. When the targeted training was provided to program therapists, violence outcomes improved.

These findings highlight the importance of exercising caution when responding to observed differential effectiveness among therapists. If therapists can improve their outcomes in a particular domain through additional training and deliberative practice, then at least some who initially demonstrate relative ineffectiveness can become effective therapists. This is one of the reasons why the warning signals from data monitoring may be relevant for some therapists in the current phase of their career (in general or with regard to specific types of clinical problems). Arguably, ongoing postlicense training and supervision is typically unsystematic and underemphasized in the United States. Steering clients to better-matched therapists who have demonstrated effectiveness is only one side of the coin. Therapists who appear to struggle will require additional training and supervision resources.

We think publishing point-in-time therapist effectiveness data would ultimately deter therapist buy-in. Furthermore, we strongly hold that there should be equal public policy emphasis on helping low-performing therapists improve their skills.

Trainers

The studies by Chow et al. (2015) and Adelman et al. (2005) highlight the training implications of "harnessing" therapist effects and identifying effective therapists. In considering the training implications of therapist effects, we once again raise the question of "therapists are effective under what conditions?" For example, it may be the case that effective therapists possess a certain degree of basic interpersonal skills, such as empathic attunement. However, if therapists with very high empathic attunement do not have optimal skills to help clients control impulsive and dangerous behaviors (toward themselves and/or others), therapists may have poorer outcomes with certain types of clients (e.g., clients with problems with substance abuse or violence). We expect that among the population of all therapists, each individual may possess differential patterns of strengths and weaknesses across outcome domains (or clusters of domains) and across the various skills and attributes that are associated with good outcomes.

When coupled with accumulating research findings supporting the importance of deliberative practice and structured supervision for client outcomes, as well as changes in therapist behavior (e.g., Chow et al., 2015; Hill et al., 2015), we believe the utility of routinely evaluating client outcomes and treatment process to support professional development is no longer a matter of debate. Benchmarked outcome information can direct therapists, regardless of career stage, to engage in deliberative practice or seek additional consultation and training in targeted areas of relative ineffectiveness (Castonguay et al., 2010). For example, therapists who are relatively ineffective at improving sleep outcomes can be provided with specific training in evidence-based sleep interventions through training programs or when a workshop is offered at a professional conference.

The tracking of therapist outcomes has additional developmental implications. For example, after a short time in graduate training, therapists-in-training may have concrete data indicating that, compared with other therapists-in-training who treat similar clients, they are less effective with clients presenting with substance abuse issues. This information could motivate particular therapists-in-training to seek additional supervised training experiences with clients experiencing substance abuse and identify substance abuse treatment as an area in need of additional training in predoctoral internship applications. Without improvement, these therapists-in-training might steer away from treating clients with substance abuse altogether.

MAKING USE OF WHAT WE KNOW AND CAN ASSESS: CHALLENGES AND SOLUTIONS

We have focused on the challenges in identifying effective therapists and making use of therapist effectiveness information. In this section, we refocus on some of the big challenges to integrating attention to therapist effects in routine practice, training, and policy, as well as offer potential solutions on the basis of existing research, trends in the field, and our own experience.

Engaging Therapists

Therapists are skeptical of how these data might be used, and they will have little incentive to engage in routine outcome or process assessment if the potential (real and perceived) costs are too high. From a Skinnerian perspective, should highly effective therapists be rewarded (e.g., with increased reimbursement or an enhanced referral stream), or should ineffective therapists (e.g., the 4% with no effective outcome domain in Kraus et al., 2011) be punished (e.g., removed from a network's preferred provider list until they document improvement)? Consistent with Skinner's view on the differential impact of various kinds of contingencies, we believe that a focus on positive reinforcement (see Gates et al., 2005) and therapists' relative strengths will yield greater engagement. Even if therapists are temporarily restricted from treating clients with a certain type of problem (e.g., depression), they could still treat other types of problems (e.g., anxiety) while working on increasing their competency in treating depression. This underscores that therapists are not globally effective or ineffective but are effective or ineffective under certain conditions. This allows positive reinforcement of effective domains and provides markers for additional training in other domains (a frame that we would hope would foster therapist engagement in outcome monitoring and use). However, it will take time and a critical mass of "corrective experiences" related to positive impacts on therapists' practice and clients' outcomes before the collection and use of effectiveness data becomes standard practice.

Socialization in Training

When asked about the factors that shape their professional identity and approach to psychotherapy, therapists often identify experiences during graduate training (e.g., supervision; Goldfried, 2001). Therapy practice and supervision during training creates a schema for conducting therapy, including thinking about client problems, how clients change, and the roles of therapist and client. Simply put, if therapists-in-training are not exposed to integrating routine assessment and data collection in their work with clients or their own development, they will be less likely to integrate routine assessment and data collection as professionals or to be receptive to actuarial feedback. Although we are speculating here, therapists without such exposure may ultimately harbor negative or suspicious views toward such practices.

The earlier that therapist-level effectiveness data and feedback (outcome and process) are introduced in therapists' training, the more likely it is that such assessment will become a part of therapists' routine clinical practice. In line with the recommendations of Barkham, Lutz, Lambert, and Saxon (Chapter 1, this volume), a potential solution is the early introduction of data-driven self-reflection and supervision in graduate training, which is transtheoretical and transdiagnostic (Constantino, Boswell, Bernecker, & Castonguay, 2013). Early socialization to this level of feedback may not only enhance the impact of training but also foster positive attitudes toward measurement-based care. Training directors and supervisors are likely to see benefit in making such routine assessment a standard part of the training curriculum. At the very least, it provides an opportunity for ongoing program evaluation. This would include making review of information from routine monitoring (process and/or outcome) an explicit part of supervision. A supervisor's valuing of such information and feedback might serve as a model for enhancing treatment responsiveness through discussions of what to do, and what not to do, in response to the obtained feedback.

That said, the use of relative effectiveness information to direct deliberative practice experiences is not limited to therapists' graduate training.

Rather, we envision this information being directly linked to continuing education experiences as a professional. In fact, reflective practice/self-assessment is a competency benchmark according to the American Psychological Association (Kaslow et al., 2009). The validity of this approach for training and professional development is dependent on the use of performance benchmarks that control for client characteristics that are systematically related to outcome yet are not in therapists' control (i.e., risk-adjustment, baseline severity).

System and Stakeholder Integration

It is a complex task to weigh all of the potential provider selection options, which include such things as the supply of local therapists; the relative skills, strengths, and weaknesses of therapists; the unique needs and problems of each client; and the current capacity of each therapist (e.g., waiting lists), among other factors. Effective communication is vital, and ultimately, information must make its way to the relevant decision makers. We do not see how direct-to-consumer or even direct referral source access to raw therapist effectiveness data will be the most efficient way to improve population outcomes. Therefore, a solution will require some type of "expert system," either the use of a computerized expert system and/or a health care expert (e.g., a primary care physician) that could help clients interpret the data.

We envision the following use of therapist effectiveness data that meet the various anticipated needs of key stakeholders. Clients desiring a scientifically based referral to a well-matched therapist would take their first multidimensional outcome assessment, not just before the start of treatment but also before a referral is made. For a system-wide application across an entire health plan using the same outcome system, this could work on the payer's website where the payer lists and helps clients find specialists, where the system is connected to a primary care physician's office, and where the client–therapist match could be completed online before the client's visit to the physician's office. For more localized applications, the system could sit within a group practice, community mental health system, or hospital-based practice where clients are to be matched to therapists within the localized practice setting.

Results of this assessment would be scored by a central processing system and be augmented with a list of well-matched therapists. This list could be geographically boundless (in the case of telemedicine) or as restricted as the client requires (e.g., within a few blocks of a public transportation stop). It would also include all of the typical filters for things such as type of insurance accepted, age of the therapist, and therapist degree/orientation. The feedback could encourage the user to relax their criteria so that at least three options are delivered, allowing for choice. Payers could receive a signal that a therapist (or a short list of therapists) was "well matched," triggering a higher rate of reimbursement suggested for top-tier network providers. Therapists would be incentivized to participate because their strengths would be rewarded with higher pay and they would automatically receive referrals that are in their "wheelhouse." With funding from the Patient-Centered Outcomes Research Institute, we are conducting a mixed-method study, including a randomized controlled trial, to examine the feasibility and impact of this approach. To our knowledge, this will be the first randomized controlled trial for a referral process in any field of medicine and may shed light on how health care can be improved by creating real-world applications of therapist effect data. This study will be based in the largest primary care outpatient practice in New England, but the same methodology should be applicable to all of the settings described previously.

Policymakers

Finally, keeping decision makers informed so that enacted policies are empirically based and result in sufficient benefit to relevant stakeholders represents a core challenge. For example, if clients do not value therapist performance information or problem-domain–based matching, then they will not be motivated to access an "expert system." We simply do not know if relative to other therapist characteristics (e.g., experience), clients would prefer to be assigned or referred to therapists on the basis of therapist effectiveness. This should be investigated, as should the possibility that the quality of the therapeutic relationship might overcome initial apprehensions that clients may have about the way they were referred to therapists.

Another key example comes from the adherence–competence literature. A high level of adherence and competence in applying an evidence-based treatment does not guarantee a better client outcome (Webb, DeRubeis, & Barber, 2010), yet state licensing boards appear to be more focused on therapist fidelity than therapist effectiveness. These are far from mutually exclusive and may often be positively correlated; however, policymakers must be educated on the complexities of behavioral health treatment outcomes. This will require input from not only researchers but also therapists and clients. Consequently, one solution is to support the active participation of diverse stakeholders in this ongoing discussion. In addition, implementation interventions and policy initiatives can themselves be a focus of research (Boswell, Kraus, Miller, & Lambert, 2015).

CONCLUSION

In answer to the "so what?" question posed throughout this chapter, we believe that therapist effect data may have an important place in transforming and improving the health care system. We believe that the positive implications of therapist effects for routine practice, training, and policy will be maximized by taking a multidimensional and pantheoretical approach to measurement that involves diverse outcome and process domains. For example, future work should prioritize the identification and measurement of processes and outcomes that are more directly linked with psychodynamic and humanistic therapies, such as enhanced reflective functioning and self-actualization. Although data monitoring should never by viewed as the only basis for mental health care decisions, we believe it can provide information to improve referral practice, training programs, and supervision routines, as well as to maximize and enhance therapist effectiveness. Furthermore, we believe that decision making and policy initiatives that are informed by observed therapist effects should focus on therapists' relative strengths and disseminating easily interpretable information to relevant stakeholder(s). Conversely, observed relative ineffectiveness should trigger targeted training and consultation resources to providers and care systems.

Of course, all of this is easier said than done. We end this chapter after having raised more questions than answers. Considerable work will be required to realize the potential implications of therapist effects. For example, stakeholders must carefully examine the relative value of different outcome and process domains where the identification of therapist differences are most meaningful. Symptom-based outcomes may be more relevant in certain contexts or psychotherapy approaches, whereas other psychological constructs (e.g., self-actualization) may be more important in others. In addition, research is sorely needed on the client-level outcomes of performance-based incentives for therapists, or, conversely, the use of penalties for therapists for lack of demonstrated effectiveness. In our view, the best way to face these challenges and find actionable and retainable solutions that may improve health care is to pursue them through active partnerships between researchers, therapists, clients, and policymakers.

REFERENCES

Adelman, R., McGee, P., Power, R., & Hanson, C. (2005). Reducing adolescent clients' anger in a residential substance abuse treatment facility. *Joint Commission Journal on Quality and Patient Safety, 31,* 325–327.

Baldwin, S. A., & Imel, Z. E. (2013). Therapist effects: Findings and methods. In M. J. Lambert (Ed.), *Bergin and Garfield's handbook of psychotherapy and behavior change* (6th ed., pp. 258–297). Hoboken, NJ: John Wiley & Sons.

Boswell, J. F., Constantino, M. J., Kraus, D. R., Bugatti, M., & Oswald, J. (2016). The expanding relevance of routinely collected outcome data for mental health care decision making. *Administration and Policy in Mental Health, 43,* 482–491.

Boswell, J. F., Kraus, D. R., Miller, S. D., & Lambert, M. J. (2015). Implementing routine outcome monitoring in clinical practice: Benefits, challenges, and solutions. *Psychotherapy Research, 25,* 6–19. http://dx.doi.org/10.1080/10503307.2013.817696

Bremer, R. W., Scholle, S. H., Keyser, D., Knox Houtsinger, J. V., & Pincus, H. A. (2008). Pay for performance in behavioral health. *Psychiatric Services, 59,* 1419–1429. http://dx.doi.org/10.1176/ps.2008.59.12.1419

Castonguay, L. G., Barkham, M., Lutz, W., & McAleavey, A. (2013). Practice-oriented research. In M. J. Lambert (Ed.), *Bergin and Garfield's handbook of psychotherapy and behavior change* (6th ed., pp. 85–133). Hoboken, NJ: John Wiley & Sons.

Castonguay, L. G., Boswell, J. F., Constantino, M. J., Goldfried, M. R., & Hill, C. E. (2010). Training implications of harmful effects of psychological treatments. *American Psychologist, 65,* 34–49. http://dx.doi.org/10.1037/a0017330

Chernew, M., Gowrisankaran, G., & Scanlon, D. P. (2008). Learning and the value of information: Evidence from health plan report cards. *Journal of Econometrics, 144,* 156–174. http://dx.doi.org/10.1016/j.jeconom.2008.01.001

Chow, D. L., Miller, S. D., Seidel, J. A., Kane, R. T., Thornton, J. A., & Andrews, W. P. (2015). The role of deliberate practice in the development of highly effective psychotherapists. *Psychotherapy, 52,* 337–345. http://dx.doi.org/10.1037/pst0000015

Constantino, M. J., Boswell, J. F., Bernecker, S. L., & Castonguay, L. G. (2013). Context-responsive integration as a framework for unified psychotherapy and clinical science: Conceptual and empirical considerations. *Journal of Unified Psychotherapy and Clinical Science, 2,* 1–20.

Gates, L. B., Klein, S. W., Akabas, S. H., Myers, R., Schawager, M., & Kaelin-Kee, J. (2005). Outcomes-based funding for vocational services and employment of people with mental health conditions. *Psychiatric Services, 56,* 1429–1435. http://dx.doi.org/10.1176/appi.ps.56.11.1429

Goldfried, M. R. (Ed.). (2001). *How therapists change: Personal and professional reflections.* Washington, DC: American Psychological Association. http://dx.doi.org/10.1037/10392-000

Greene, S. E., & Nash, D. B. (2008). Pay for performance: An overview of the literature. *American Journal of Medical Quality, 24,* 140–163. http://dx.doi.org/10.1177/1062860608326517

Henderson, A., & Henderson, S. (2010). Provision of a surgeon's performance data for people considering elective surgery. *Cochrane Database of Systematic Reviews, 11,* CD006327. Advance online publication.

Hill, C. E., Baumann, E., Shafran, N., Gupta, S., Morrison, A., Rojas, A. E., . . . Gelso, C. J. (2015). Is training effective? A study of counseling psychology doctoral trainees in a psychodynamic/interpersonal training clinic. *Journal of Counseling Psychology, 62,* 184–201. http://dx.doi.org/10.1037/cou0000053

Imel, Z. E., Sheng, E., Baldwin, S. A., & Atkins, D. C. (2015). Removing very low-performing therapists: A simulation of performance-based retention in psychotherapy. *Psychotherapy, 52,* 329–336. http://dx.doi.org/10.1037/pst0000023

Kaslow, N. J., Grus, C. L., Campbell, L. F., Fouad, N. A., Hatcher, R. L., & Rodolfa, E. R. (2009). Competency assessment toolkit for professional psychology. *Training and Education in Professional Psychology, 3,* S27–S45. http://dx.doi.org/10.1037/a0015833

Kraus, D. R., Bentley, J. H., Alexander, P. C., Boswell, J. F., Constantino, M. J., Baxter, E. E., & Castonguay, L. G. (2016). Predicting therapist effectiveness from their own practice-based evidence. *Journal of Consulting and Clinical Psychology, 84,* 473–483. http://dx.doi.org/10.1037/ccp0000083

Kraus, D. R., Castonguay, L., Boswell, J. F., Nordberg, S. S., & Hayes, J. A. (2011). Therapist effectiveness: Implications for accountability and patient care. *Psychotherapy Research, 21,* 267–276. http://dx.doi.org/10.1080/10503307.2011.563249

Scanlon, D. P., Lindrooth, R. C., & Christianson, J. B. (2008). Steering patients to safer hospitals? The effect of a tiered hospital network on hospital admissions. *Health Services Research, 43,* 1849–1868. http://dx.doi.org/10.1111/j.1475-6773.2008.00889.x

Swift, J. K., & Callahan, J. L. (2010). A comparison of client preferences for intervention empirical support versus common therapy variables. *Journal of Clinical Psychology, 66,* 1217–1231. http://dx.doi.org/10.1002/jclp.20720

Walfish, S., McAlister, B., O'Donnell, P., & Lambert, M. J. (2012). An investigation of self-assessment bias in mental health providers. *Psychological Reports, 110,* 639–644. http://dx.doi.org/10.2466/02.07.17.PR0.110.2.639-644

Wampold, B. E., & Brown, G. S. (2005). Estimating variability in outcomes attributable to therapists: A naturalistic study of outcomes in managed care. *Journal of Consulting and Clinical Psychology, 73,* 914–923. http://dx.doi.org/10.1037/0022-006X.73.5.914

Webb, C. A., DeRubeis, R. J., & Barber, J. P. (2010). Therapist adherence/competence and treatment outcome: A meta-analytic review. *Journal of Consulting and Clinical Psychology, 78,* 200–211. http://dx.doi.org/10.1037/a0018912

17

THERAPIST EFFECTS: INTEGRATION AND CONCLUSIONS

CLARA E. HILL AND LOUIS G. CASTONGUAY

After the previous chapters of this book were written, we held a meeting with a large number of the authors who contributed to them to determine what we know about therapist effects and what could be done to improve our understanding about them. Discussion was lively, given that the researchers involved varied in theoretical orientation, engagement in clinical practice, and preferred research methods (e.g., qualitative, quantitative). There were essentially two camps: those who believed that a phenomenon of therapist effects had been detected and established via sophisticated statistical methods, and those who were more cautious and skeptical about the state of our knowledge given the many methodological and clinical problems with the research to date.

We would like to acknowledge the people who attended the session where we arrived at the conclusions presented in this chapter. They reviewed this chapter and provided suggestions to ensure that all perspectives were included. In alphabetical order, they are Timothy Anderson, Jacques P. Barber, James F. Boswell, Franz Caspar, Michael J. Constantino, Barry A. Farber, Charles J. Gelso, Marvin R. Goldfried, Jeffrey A. Hayes, Martin grosse Holtforth, Sarah Knox, David R. Kraus, Michael J. Lambert, Wolfgang Lutz, J. Christopher Muran, Michelle G. Newman, Jeremy D. Safran, William B. Stiles, Bruce E. Wampold, and Abraham W. Wolf.

http://dx.doi.org/10.1037/0000034-018
How and Why Are Some Therapists Better Than Others? Understanding Therapist Effects, L. G. Castonguay and C. E. Hill (Eds.)
Copyright © 2017 by the American Psychological Association. All rights reserved.

Bruce Wampold, one of the participants, noted that the discussion about therapist effects was heated because the topic is highly personal. Given that all present had spent many years in training to become therapists, most currently were therapists, and most also currently supervised therapists-in-training, it was challenging to grapple with the findings related to therapist effects. Despite the professional, if not existential, weight carried by these issues, all viewpoints were respectfully heard and valued.

In the final chapter of this volume, we integrate the perspectives aired during our meeting. Three questions were considered: How are therapist effects defined, and what is the evidence for therapist effects? What therapist variables might account for therapist effects? And what are the next steps in the research on therapist effects? Although we did not discuss them at our meeting, there are also clear implications for the research on therapist effects, which we address in this chapter as well.

THERAPIST EFFECTS

By definition, *therapist effects* are present when some therapists consistently achieve superior performance and others consistently achieve poorer performance than other therapists. Although therapist effects could emerge for many variables, we are most interested in therapist effects as reflected in changes in client mental health (e.g., symptom relief, interpersonal functioning, social role performance, well-being, quality of life), such that some therapists have better client outcomes (in terms of psychological improvement) than do others. Moreover, as Constantino, Boswell, Coyne, Kraus, and Castonguay (Chapter 3) summarized, therapists can have relative strengths and weaknesses in treating different types of mental health problems within their own caseloads.

Differences between therapists have been observed since the beginning of the field of psychotherapy. There has also been considerable research on therapist variables (see the review in Beutler et al., 2004). Yet, the recent surge of interest in this phenomenon is due to findings from sophisticated statistical analyses (e.g., hierarchical linear modeling [HLM]) involving large numbers of therapists and clients. HLM is particularly appropriate for psychotherapy research because it models how clients are nested within therapists. Nesting is especially important for understanding variables such as the alliance and outcome, as clients and therapists contribute to the effects. HLM allows for statistically disentangling clients' and therapists' contributions to the alliance, which then allows determination of how these two sources predict outcome.

As Barkham, Lutz, Lambert, and Saxon (Chapter 1) noted, a substantial body of research using HLM analyses has established that about 5% to

8% of the variability in client outcome is attributable to therapists. Although smaller than the proportion of variability attributable to clients, Barkham et al. suggested that this proportion is important statistically and clinically, indicating that some therapists are consistently better and some are consistently worse than others. These therapist effects appear to be most pronounced with clients who are more challenging and distressed relative to other more highly functioning clients.

Major caveats to these findings about therapist effects, however, are that our current knowledge about therapist effects is mainly based on specific populations, treatment approaches, measures, and methods. In other words, most of this research has been conducted in very large databases that typically involve either university counseling centers or managed care clients. Therefore, data may not be representative of clients seen in long-term psychotherapy. Relatedly, more data are available for short-term, manualized, and cognitive–behavioral treatments than for longer term insight-oriented treatments. In addition, most measures used to assess outcome involve client self-report of symptomatology, social role performance, and interpersonal functioning, whereas measures associated with depth psychology (e.g., defenses, character structure, meaning in life) have rarely been assessed (though, if these constructs can be reliably assessed, they can be examined for therapist effects). Finally, much of this research has not considered the complexity of the change process, such as the intertwining of therapist and client variables and the many moderators and mediators of change. We would note that this lack of inclusion of specific populations, treatment approaches, measures, and methods is not a fault of the statistical methods, which are indeed value neutral, but arise more because many of the complexities of the therapy situation have not been validly measured and included in analyses.

An additional caveat is that HLM-demonstrated therapist effects may reflect differences in therapists' ability or tendency to responsively "do the right thing at the right time," where the right thing varies with shifting client requirements, therapeutic approach, and other circumstances. In that case, variables that simply describe therapist characteristics and behaviors would not be expected to be predictive of outcomes. Variables that evaluate the therapists or the process (i.e., considering whether the actions and timing were appropriate) tend to be more successful in predicting outcome.

Hence, current results of therapist effects must be interpreted with caution given these caveats. With these caveats in mind, however, we can assert that we have considerable evidence about the role that therapists play in client improvement. Table 17.1 summarizes the findings about the outcome variance explained by therapist effects, as well as some of the clinical implications that have been derived from these results.

TABLE 17.1
Summary of Chapters in This Volume Describing the Current State of Empirical Literature on Therapist Effects in Terms of Quantitative Findings and Methods

Chapter	Findings and methods	Clinical implications
1	Therapist effects explain between approximately 5% and 8% of client outcome variance; with higher effect sizes found in naturalistic studies than in randomized clinical trials. In general, most therapists seem to be equivalent in terms of therapeutic benefits experienced by their clients. However, 15% to 20% appear to be consistently and distinctively more effective, whereas 15% to 20% appear to be consistently and distinctively less effective than other therapists. Therapist effects also appear to be stronger with highly distressed or impaired clients.	Implications of these results include the need to focus on therapist effects early in treatment (to predict dropout and quick therapeutic change), to provide outcome monitoring and feedback during training (to foster therapeutic improvement and decrease deterioration), and to examine the work of exceptional therapists (to better predict and explain therapist effects).
2	Four variables have received empirical support in explaining why some therapists are better than others. First, strong evidence has been found for therapists' ability to establish a positive therapeutic alliance. More limited evidence exists for the other three variables: therapists' facilitative interpersonal skills, self-doubt, and engagement in deliberative practice. It is also important to note that several variables have not been found to be responsible for therapist effects: demographics (e.g., age, gender), self-reported interpersonal skills, theoretical orientation, experience, adherence to a treatment protocol, and rated competence performing a particular treatment.	As ways to increase their effectiveness, therapists should strive to become better at developing, maintaining, and repairing the alliance with clients. They should also make use of and enhance their verbal and emotional expressiveness, motivational skills (persuasiveness and hopefulness), warmth and empathic attitude, and problem focus. Moreover, they should adopt and/or maintain a sense of humility toward their ability to help their clients. When not working with clients, therapists should also repeatedly and consistently devote time to improve their work, such as thinking about difficult cases, preparing and reflecting on sessions, and attending training workshops.

| 3 | Despite the existence of therapist effects, little is known about why some therapists are more effective than others, or why some therapists are good at treating some clients but not others within their caseloads. It important to uncover such determinants empirically within diverse outcome domains (e.g., depression, substance abuse). Two promising categories of such determinants that have received the most empirical support to date are (a) individual characteristics of the therapist (e.g., amount of deliberate practice) and (b) characteristics manifested in therapy sessions (e.g., alliance). Multilevel statistical modeling is the most appropriate method for disentangling between-therapists and within-therapist variability in psychotherapy processes and outcomes to isolate, predict (including in interaction with possible moderator variables), and explain (through the use of therapist-level mediational models) between-therapists effects on client outcomes. | The selection and training of therapists is crucial. Therapists should engage in deliberate practice and foster the alliance to enhance their clinical services. |

THERAPIST VARIABLES THAT MIGHT ACCOUNT FOR THERAPIST EFFECTS

We have three sets of findings to consider here. The first set involves data about therapist variables collected prior to the development of HLM analyses, typically using simple correlational analyses and not considering that clients are nested within therapists. The second set includes data about therapist variables associated with therapist effects, in which clients' and therapists' contributions to outcomes are disentangled using HLM. The third set involves many potential candidates for therapist variables that have not yet been adequately tested as determinants of between-therapists effects with HLM analyses.

Data on Therapist Variables Prior to Hierarchical Linear Modeling Analyses

On the basis of decades of research on therapist variables, Norcross (2002, 2011) compiled considerable evidence about relationship (process) variables that have been linked to client outcomes. These results tend to be based on total correlational analyses of relationship variables in relation to client outcomes. As noted previously, these correlational analyses fail to disentangle within-therapist (between-clients) variability, between-therapists variability, or the interaction between within-therapist and between-therapists variability in the correlations between relationship variables and outcomes. In these reviews, Norcross demonstrated that there is evidence that the following therapist-related variables are related to positive outcomes: alliance, cohesion, empathy, goal consensus and collaboration, positive regard and affirmation, congruence/genuineness, collecting client feedback, repairing alliance ruptures, managing countertransference, self-disclosure, and relational interpretations.

Although no doubt was expressed at the meeting about the relationship between process variables (e.g., therapist empathy) and client outcome, some participants noted that research conducted on most of them thus far has not shown, statistically, that they are responsible for why some therapists are better than others (see Chapter 3). It should be noted, furthermore, that some therapist variables are difficult to include in HLM analyses because it is not frequency of the variable as much as timing and quality that matters, and these contextual considerations are much harder to measure and include in statistical analyses. A good example is therapist self-disclosure, as it is not frequency of self-disclosure that matters in terms of effectiveness as much as it is type, timing, quality, and context (see Pinto-Coelho, Hill, & Kivlighan, 2016, for an example of a mixed-methods study of self-disclosure).

Data About Therapist Variables From Multilevel Statistical Analyses

Wampold, Baldwin, Holtforth, and Imel (Chapter 2) and Constantino, Boswell, Coyne, Kraus, and Castonguay (Chapter 3) indicated that there is good evidence from several HLM analyses that therapist ability to establish a therapeutic alliance and demonstrate facilitative interpersonal skills accounts for differential therapist effectiveness. In addition, Wampold et al. cited more limited evidence (i.e., not yet enough studies from different research teams) for therapist self-doubt and engaging in deliberate practice. These findings reflect the current status of what we know, quantitatively, about what explains therapist effects—what accounts for the fact that some therapists are better and some are worse than others (these findings and some of their clinical implications are presented in Table 17.1). Importantly, though, work on therapist-level predictors of systematic differences in therapists' outcomes is just beginning. Not only do more variables need to be examined, but existing findings need to be replicated. Underscoring the need for replication, Constantino et al. pointed out that the therapist's contribution to alliance quality is variable across studies, meaning that alliance may not be a consistently good indicator of how more versus less effective therapists attain their personal effectiveness status.

In addition, several therapist variables—age, gender, race/ethnicity, theoretical orientation, experience, or professional degree—were noted by Wampold et al. (Chapter 2) as not predicting therapist effects in the HLM analyses, as similar to findings in non-HLM research (see Beutler et al., 2004). We hasten to say, however, that there is considerable controversy about the evidence related to some of these variables, particularly experience, given that cross-sectional studies and an intensive longitudinal study (Goldberg et al., 2016) found no effects of experience, and yet others (Hill, Spiegel, Hoffman, Kivlighan, & Gelso, in press) have noted major problems with the definition and measurement of experience.

Potential Therapist Variables That May Be Related to Therapist Effectiveness

Many additional therapist-level variables that are potential candidates for determining therapist effects are presented in chapters of this book. Evidence for these variables comes primarily from clinical practice and therapist training, as well as from research-based evidence not restricted to the paradigm of using client outcomes as the sole dependent variable or on the basis of analyses that isolate therapists' contribution, as is done with HLM. Table 17.2 shows a summary description for each chapter of how these respective therapist variables might be linked to therapist effects on adaptive

TABLE 17.2
Summary of Chapters in This Volume Presenting Factors Potentially Explaining Therapist Effects

Chapter	Therapist variables potentially associated with therapist effects	Implications for therapists
4	Therapist effects are due, in part, to therapists' ability to be appropriately responsive to clients' needs.	Within the framework of their theoretical orientation, personality, and skills, as well as in consideration of a wide range of contextual variables (e.g., client diagnostic, values, therapeutic progress, preceding events, history of the therapeutic relationship), effective therapists flexibly attune the choice, dose, manner of implementation, and timing of their interventions to fit clients' moment-to-moment needs. By optimizing their responsiveness, effective therapists foster good therapeutic process, which leads to positive outcome.
5	More effective therapists reach, maintain, and appropriately convey higher levels of presence (awareness of, openness to, and centered on their experience and the experience of their client) during therapy, allowing them to be more empathic than less effective therapists.	To improve their effectiveness, therapists should identify, before and during therapy sessions, factors that can signal and/or increase their difficulty to be fully present (e.g., distraction, preoccupation, intellectualization, anxiety). Considering a number of possible strategies (e.g., self-observation, self-trust, intentionality and mindfulness, meditation, management of anxiety and countertransference, improving one's own mental health), therapists should focus and sustain their attention to internal and interpersonal experiences taking place in the here and now of therapy.
6	Therapist effects can be explained, in part, by clinicians' ability to be aware of, regulate, and use their inner experience (e.g., affect, cognition) during therapy to help foster clients' change.	Therapists are likely to be more effective when they successfully communicate empathy, prizing, and genuineness to their clients. Therapist effectiveness may also be improved by a recognition, acceptance, regulation, tolerance (not acting out), and use of negative and positive reactions (e.g., hate and love) to better understand their clients and their relationships with others. Furthermore, therapists are likely to increase their effectiveness when they can manage their countertransference.

7. Therapist attachment characteristics contribute to therapist effects. Whereas therapist secure attachment has been linked with positive alliance, therapist insecure attachment has been associated with negative therapeutic process. Therapist secure attachment has also been related to positive outcome with highly distressed and impaired clients. Complementarity between client and therapist attachment styles may also explain differences in client outcomes.

As a way to improve their effectiveness, therapists might raise awareness of their own attachment patterns and that of their clients. They can use this awareness to avoid engaging in negative processes, as well as to help clients modify maladaptive ways of regulating emotions and relating to others.

8. The fact that some therapists are more (or less) effective than others may be in part due to the competent delivery of technical, relational, conceptual, and cultural skills. In particular, helping and facilitative interpersonal skills (e.g., empathy; alliance related skills; interventions aimed at increasing hope, expectation, insight, behavioral changes) are likely to account for some of the outcome variance observed between therapists. Rather than a single skill (or a whole set of them), however, the integration of skills and other variables may provide a better explanation of therapist effects. For example, adherence to techniques prescribed by treatment and the use of helping skills may have an indirect impact on outcome, given that their effect could be moderated or mediated by relationship variables (e.g., quality of alliance), therapist characteristics (e.g., allegiance, internalized hostility), and client variables (e.g., involvement in the treatment process).

To improve their effectiveness, therapists should strive to responsively and appropriately use technical, relational, conceptual, and cultural skills that they learn and deliberately practice. The competent delivery of technical and relational skills is likely to be enhanced if based on a comprehensive case formulation, used in response to immediate markers for interventions, and implemented with therapists' awareness of their own internal experience and cultural awareness. In addition to implementing these skills in an interpersonal facilitative way and culturally sensitive manner, therapists are likely to improve client outcomes by paying attention to the client response as a way to decide to pursue, modify, or refrain from continuing to use specific skills.

9. Some therapists are better than others, in part because of their ability to work with clients from a wide range of cultures and their ability to address cultural issues in therapy.

When working with clients (irrespective of ethnicity, race, religion, gender, sexual orientation, age, or disability status), therapists may improve their effectiveness by integrating in their practice an attitude of humility and openness toward cultural issues (acknowledging and tolerating lack of specific knowledge), by creating or making use of opportunities to address cultural issues, by addressing these issues as comfortably as possible (as by avoiding or repairing cultural microaggressions).

(continues)

TABLE 17.2
Summary of Chapters in This Volume Presenting Factors Potentially Explaining Therapist Effects *(Continued)*

Chapter	Therapist variables potentially associated with therapist effects	Implications for therapists
10	The experience of negative emotional reactions on the part of therapists (e.g., frustration, anger) toward clients, and the ways such reactions are dealt with during sessions, could account for a portion of the observed therapist effects. By potentially impeding the therapeutic process, negative reactions might be particularly relevant in explaining why some therapists have worse outcomes than others.	To improve their effectiveness, therapists need to engage in a participant–observer stance during therapy (which includes self-awareness), control the expression of negative reactions they have toward clients (regulate and contain), and use helpful strategies to work with these internal and relational experiences. These strategies include a reattribution of the meaning of clients' behavior that may have triggered the negative reaction, as well as techniques to temper these reactions and to repair resulting alliance ruptures. When implemented successfully, these strategies may not only lead to a reduction of toxic interactions but may also provide the opportunity to correct client maladaptive interpersonal patterns that might, in part, be triggering such negative reactions.
11	The outcome of better therapists may be explained, in part, by what has been observed in experts, or top performers, in different domains such as sports, music, and chess. These observations include (a) automatization of basic skills, (b) superior abilities in complex skills such as information processing (intuitive and rational-analytic mode of thinking) and appropriate reactions to complex situations, (c) repeated and deliberate practice of these complex skills over a long period of time, and (d) use of feedback to acquire and improve these complex skills.	Therapists might improve their effectiveness by following guidelines for expertise and deliberate practice. During training, these include the definition of learning steps and provision of feedback. Over years of practice, these guidelines include the development of abilities to process clinical information (e.g., sharpening case formulation skills, using their intuitive and analytic modes of thinking), and the use of feedback obtained after sessions and observed during sessions.

12	Some therapists are more effective than others in part because they adopt, in their practice, creative and flexible ways of thinking and being that are akin to perspective and strategies of artists. Therapists are likely to increase their effectiveness, at least for some clients, if they develop a creative (artistic/literary) sensibility that allows them to be aware, open to, and work with different aspects of the clients' life (e.g., existential issues, meanings, emotions, multiple sides and states of self, humor, imagination, fantasies), needs (e.g., playfulness, intimacy, creative change), and ways of communicating and expressing themselves (e.g., narratives, body language, tone of voice). They can foster this creative sensibility by engaging in artistic activities or by being exposed to artistic work.
13	Therapist outcome differences in psychodynamic therapy for depression could partially be explained by the use of relationship-oriented interventions. As a way to improve their effectiveness when working with depressed clients, psychodynamic therapists should focus on client interpersonal functioning inside and outside therapy, such as helping clients to better understand how their difficulties in social relationships may contribute to their problems.
14	What, in part, may explain therapist effects in the treatment of generalized anxiety disorder is the extent to which therapists facilitate client activation of the mechanisms of change in the theoretical approach being implemented (at least in cognitive–behavioral and interpersonal/emotion-focused therapies). In particular, less effective therapists may miss opportunities to foster client engagement in targeted mechanisms, may interfere with such engagement, and/or may intervene in ways that are contrary with the mechanism of change targeted by the treatment. Ways by which therapists may improve their effectiveness include being cognizant and aware of mechanisms of change driving the successful implementation of the treatment used; responding with appropriate techniques to markers of interventions that are consistent with targeted mechanism of change; and using techniques in affiliative, noncontrolling, and responsive manners (including knowing when to stop using some techniques). Moreover, therapists should ensure that these interventions are activating the targeted mechanisms (e.g., emotional deepening) and not fostering processes that are in opposition to these mechanisms (e.g., using interpretation in ways that reinforce cognitive avoidance of emotions). In addition, therapists should correct technical and/or relational mistakes that may interfere with positive therapeutic process.

(*continues*)

TABLE 17.2
Summary of Chapters in This Volume Presenting Factors Potentially Explaining Therapist Effects *(Continued)*

Chapter	Therapist variables potentially associated with therapist effects	Implications for therapists
15	Part of the therapist effects may be due to the use of humor in a manner that is responsive to the client's needs and view of humor, as well as consistent with the therapist's personality.	If it fits who they are, if the therapeutic relationship is strong, and if the client values humor, therapists may improve their effectiveness by using humor (often ironic or dry humor) in response to clients' discussing or demonstrating symptoms or problems. Used in a careful and responsive way, humor could reduce clients' anxiety, enhance the therapeutic climate and bond, and foster clients' acquisition of new perspectives. Humor can lead to increased distress if used when the relationship is weak, and/or in ways that make client feel uncared for, misunderstood, or confused.

treatment processes and outcomes, as well as implications for how therapists can improve their own effectiveness.

Some of these variables are traits or stable personality characteristics, such as therapist attachment style (Chapter 7); or creativity, openness, and flexibility (Chapter 12). The rest are situational variables that vary according to context, such as

- technical skills (Chapters 8 and 13);
- relational skills (Chapters 6 and 8);
- conceptual skills (Chapter 8);
- cultural awareness (Chapters 8 and 9);
- responsiveness to client needs (Chapter 4);
- attentiveness to inner experiences/emotional reactions (Chapters 6 and 10);
- presence (Chapter 5);
- automatization of basic skills, superior abilities in complex skills such as information processing and appropriate reactions to complex situations, deliberate practice of skills, use of feedback (Chapter 11);
- humor if used in a genuine manner and fits therapist's personality (Chapter 15); and
- fostering client engagement in treatment-related activities (Chapter 14).

Of course, there are many more potentially relevant therapist variables that were not addressed in the chapters in this book (e.g., use of immediacy, compassion, burnout, humility, curiosity, persuasiveness/confidence).

IMPLICATIONS OF THERAPIST EFFECTS

As mentioned previously, a number of clinical implications have been derived from the current research on therapist effects (see Table 17.1). Boswell, Kraus, Constantino, Bugatti, and Castonguay (Chapter 16) identified additional implications related to different facets of mental health practice; these implications and some of the challenges involved in implementing them are summarized in Table 17.3. For example, given that variability in therapist effectiveness on client outcomes (in relation to other therapists in general, and with regard to different types of outcomes in one's own caseload) can be detected with routine outcomes monitoring data, we can use such data to inform the referral of clients to the therapist who is most likely to be successful. Such evidence-informed matching might be especially important for low-functioning clients, or for specific types of outcomes, where the person of the

TABLE 17.3
Summary of Chapter in This Volume Describing Implications of Therapist Effects on Different Facets of Mental Health Practice

Chapter	Implications for mental health practice
16	On the basis of monitoring of treatment outcomes, research has demonstrated that therapists show relatively stable patterns of effectiveness. Assessing therapist outcomes in routine practice settings can provide helpful information to identify therapist strengths and limitations across numerous clients, guide referral practices and case assignments, as well as to improve supervision and professional development during and after training. However, successful implementation of outcome monitoring requires paying attention to the various needs and concerns of several stakeholders in the mental health field (payers, clients, therapists, and trainers), as well as to several challenges to be expected in day-to-day clinical work (therapist engagement), training (socialization to outcome feedback), organization functioning (management and interpretation of outcome data), and policymaking (informing decision makers about empirical data on therapist effects).

therapist seems to have a more pronounced influence on treatment outcome. How exactly to disseminate information on therapist personal effectiveness, however, remains an open and empirical question.

In addition, if we can identify specific and consistent therapist-level *characteristics* that are responsible for differential between-therapists effectiveness, we could select students for therapist-training programs using those variables as criteria. Similarly, if we can identify specific and consistent therapist-level *behaviors* that are responsible for differential between-therapists effectiveness, we can implement targeted training on these actions for novice and experienced therapists (recalling that experience, as currently measured, does not explain differences in therapist effectiveness; Chapter 2).

Finally, awareness of therapist effects (relative to self and others) can help clinicians manage their own clinical services in a way that counteracts inherent bias and overestimation of general effectiveness. As it is a statistical impossibility that all therapists are above average, tracking and digesting outcome data seems useful. Of course, as Boswell et al. (Chapter 16) noted, many questions remain unanswered with regard to optimizing measurement-informed care.

NEXT STEPS IN RESEARCH ON THERAPIST EFFECTS

In the meeting, there was strong consensus about the next steps for research on therapist effects. In addition to advocating for the field to see therapists as a crucial focus of psychotherapy research (in addition to treatment and client, see Chapter 1), perhaps the strongest sentiment was expressed for encouraging research using many paradigms. At this stage in research, we firmly believe that the use of multiple designs and methods is needed.

Discovery-oriented designs (e.g., consensual qualitative research, correlational process studies) and designs that seek verification (experimental designs) may be mutually beneficial toward advancing our understanding of therapist effects (which may be translated as bottom up and top down, respectively). For example, we could conduct qualitative analyses of clients who have seen many different therapists and ask about variables that they believe caused them to continue with some therapists rather than others. Or we can conduct studies of therapist use of different types of interventions, such as immediacy, in different contexts (e.g., Hill et al., 2014). Furthermore, we are most likely to find meaningful results if findings replicate across different methods.

In the context of experimental research that seeks verification, researchers can use sophisticated statistical designs such as HLM to test those variables that were identified in the context of discovery. Therefore, we strongly encourage researchers to add variables such as therapist humor, presence, and humility in HLM analyses. By including specific therapist variables in datasets with large numbers of therapists, each seeing large numbers of clients, we are most likely to verify the effects of specific variables, especially if we include many of the relevant moderator and mediator variables identified in the qualitative analyses. In other words, these HLM tests are not likely to be simple tests of straightforward or direct variables, but need to include clinical nuances. New designs and statistical methods also need to be developed to further enable researchers to include clinical nuances (e.g., context, timing, quality of interventions) and contextual factors (e.g., setting).

A special word needs to be said about developing and including measures that reflect more in-depth outcomes, such as those that are targeted in exploratory- or insight-oriented therapies (psychodynamic, humanistic) and/or long-term approaches. We do a disservice to the field if the only variables we include in investigations involve measures of symptom relief. Relatedly, we need to include more than just client self-report, given that therapists, external assessors, and significant others have important perspectives about client change (Chapter 10; see also Strupp & Hadley, 1977). We also need to be particularly attentive to negative changes and deterioration effects, given the realization that some therapists are indeed harmful (Castonguay, Boswell, Constantino, Goldfried, & Hill, 2010). Importantly, though, whatever the outcome and whoever the rater, the chapters in this volume remind us of the importance of determining if therapists systematically differ on particular variables (e.g., some therapists may be consistently more likely to foster a reduction in client use of defenses as rated by a therapist or significant others). This outcome would be a therapist effect just the same as self-reported outcomes and would therefore require understanding its determinants.

Furthermore, as Constantino et al. (Chapter 3) discussed, we need to investigate therapist effects on process variables that consistently explain between-therapists differences on outcomes. And these relations may be complex. For example, we need to understand why some therapists foster alliances so competently, whereas others do not. It could be, for example, that therapists who use more immediacy promote better alliance formation, which then promotes better outcomes for those therapists. This would reflect a therapist-level mediational model, which Constantino et al. argued is an important next wave of therapist effects research. Similarly, it would be fruitful to examine therapist differences in responding competently and successfully to markers of change, some markers specific to particular orientations (e.g., Greenberg, 2015) and others common across approaches (e.g., Constantino, Boswell, Bernecker, & Castonguay, 2013; Messer, 1986). Finally, in conducting future research, it is important to remain aware of long-standing myths of uniformity, and search for differential therapist effectiveness within particular contexts (e.g., specific forms of therapy, particular types of clients, specific types of symptoms, dimensions of functioning, clients' concerns). We also need, of course, to be aware of possible myths related to differences (e.g., differences related to therapist theoretical orientation and sex) and change our thinking or design more valid research studies to better understand these variables.

We are excited about the advances in knowledge regarding therapist effects. We hope that continued research using sophisticated statistical analyses and qualitative methods, with attention to the complexities and nuances of the psychotherapy process, will help us understand why some therapists are better than others, which in turn may lead us to improve the effectiveness of psychotherapy.

REFERENCES

Beutler, L. E., Malik, M., Alimohamed, S., Harwood, T. M., Talebi, H., Noble, S., & Wong, E. (2004). Therapist variables. In M. J. Lambert (Ed.), *Bergin and Garfield's handbook of psychotherapy and behavior change* (5th ed., pp. 227–306). New York, NY: Wiley.

Castonguay, L. G., Boswell, J. F., Constantino, M. J., Goldfried, M. R., & Hill, C. E. (2010). Training implications of harmful effects of psychological treatments. *American Psychologist, 65,* 34–49. http://dx.doi.org/10.1037/a0017330

Constantino, M. J., Boswell, J. F., Bernecker, S. L., & Castonguay, L. G. (2013). Context-responsive integration as a framework for unified psychotherapy and clinical science: Conceptual and empirical considerations. *Journal of Unified Psychotherapy and Clinical Science, 2,* 1–20.

Goldberg, S. B., Rousmaniere, T., Miller, S. D., Whipple, J., Nielsen, S. L., Hoyt, W. T., & Wampold, B. E. (2016). Do psychotherapists improve with time and experience? A longitudinal analysis of outcomes in a clinical setting. *Journal of Counseling Psychology, 63*(1), 1–11. http://dx.doi.org/10.1037/cou0000131

Greenberg, L. S. (2015). *Emotion-focused therapy: Coaching clients to work through their feelings* (2nd ed.). Washington, DC: American Psychological Association. http://dx.doi.org/10.1037/14692-000

Hill, C. E., Gelso, C. J., Chui, H., Spangler, P. T., Hummel, A., Huang, T., . . . Miles, J. R. (2014). To be or not to be immediate with clients: The use and perceived effects of immediacy in psychodynamic/interpersonal psychotherapy. *Psychotherapy Research, 24,* 299–315. http://dx.doi.org/10.1080/10503307.2013.812262

Hill, C. E., Spiegel, S. B., Hoffman, M. A., Kivlighan, D. M., Jr., & Gelso, C. J. (in press). Therapist expertise in psychotherapy revisited. *The Counseling Psychologist.*

Messer, S. B. (1986). Behavioral and psychoanalytic perspectives at therapeutic choice points. *American Psychologist, 41,* 1261–1272. http://dx.doi.org/10.1037/0003-066X.41.11.1261

Norcross, J. C. (Ed.). (2002). *Psychotherapy relationships that work: Therapist contributions and responsiveness to patients.* New York, NY: Oxford University Press.

Norcross, J. C. (2011). *Psychotherapy relationships that work: Evidence-based responsiveness.* New York, NY: Oxford University Press. http://dx.doi.org/10.1093/acprof:oso/9780199737208.001.0001

Pinto-Coelho, K., Hill, C. E., & Kivlighan, D., Jr. (2016). Therapist self-disclosures in psychodynamic psychotherapy: A mixed methods investigation. *Counselling Psychology Quarterly, 29,* 29–52. http://dx.doi.org/10.1080/09515070.2015.1072496

Strupp, H. H., & Hadley, S. W. (1977). A tripartite model of mental health and therapeutic outcomes. With special reference to negative effects in psychotherapy. *American Psychologist, 32,* 187–196. http://dx.doi.org/10.1037/0003-066X.32.3.187

INDEX

AAI (Adult Attachment Interview), 123, 124, 126–128
Accountability, 314
Ackerman, S. J., 141
Action (cognitive–behavioral therapy for generalized anxiety disorder), 276
Action skills, 151
An Actor Prepares (K. Stanislavsky), 217
Actors, 219–223
Adelman, R., 316
Adelson, J. L., 20
Adlerian therapy, 286
Adult Attachment Interview (AAI), 123, 124, 126–128
Advice-giving, 250–251
Affect
   and attachment, 117
   regulation of, 184–185
Agape, 109–110
Age, therapist, 38, 47, 48, 331
Agentic self, 119
Agras, W. S., 75
Agriculture, 38
Ahmed, M., 182
Alliance. *See* Therapeutic alliance
Alliance-focused training, 81
Allison, L., 119
American Psychological Association (APA)
   competency benchmarks of, 319
   and conventions on therapist negative reactions, 177
   and data analysis, 38
   and multidimensional outcome assessment, 55
   and therapeutic wisdom from creative others, 220
Anderson, T.
   and assessment of outcome, 59
   and effective therapists, 44, 45, 48
   and therapist skills, 145, 152–153
Anger, 177–178, 187–188
Anxiety
   attachment, 120, 121, 125
   behavioral exposure for, 147, 149–150
   and insecure attachment style, 128–129
   therapist, 91, 112, 184–185
Anxiety Disorders Interview Schedule, 262
APA. *See* American Psychological Association
Appropriate responsiveness, 71–81
   implications of, 80–81
   and process–outcome research, 74–78
   and responsiveness, 71–73
   and therapeutic alliance, 75, 78–79
   tools for measurement of, 73–74
Aron, Lewis, 229
Arredondo, P., 144
Artists, 223–225
Asian cultures, 144
Assessment reports, 143
Association for Applied and Therapeutic Humor, 286
Atkins, D. C., 29, 310
Attachment, 117–132
   and helping alliance, 124–125
   in psychotherapy research, 120–122
   and specific disorders, 128–129
   as theoretical model in psychotherapy, 118–120
   and therapist as attachment figure, 122–123
   and therapist attachment style, 123–128
Attachment anxiety, 120, 121, 125
Attachment match, 128–129
Attachment security, 119
Attitudes, 38
Aviram, A., 77, 182
Avoidant attachment style, 127–128
Azim, H. F., 181–182

Baldwin, S. A.
   and therapeutic alliance, 42, 63, 79
   and therapist effects, 19, 20, 29, 310
Barker, C., 125
Barkham, M., 21
Bates, B., 122
Behavioral exposure, 147, 149–150

Behavioral health care, 311
Behaviorism, 181, 286. *See also*
　　Cognitive–behavioral therapy
Benjamin, L. S., 142
Bennett, C. E., 287
Berger, T., 205–206
Bernecker, S. L., 120
Between-therapist variability
　　in correlational research on therapist variables, 330
　　defined, 39
　　in process and outcome research, 61–64
　　and process variables, 340
　　and treatment variables, 310
Beutler, Larry, 38, 39, 42, 146
Bielefeld Questionnaire of Partner Expectations, 129
Binder, J. L., 178
Bolt, D. M., 19
Borderline personality disorder (BPD), 106–107
Boredom, 86, 183–184
Boswell, J. F., 47, 182, 312
Bowlby, J., 117–118, 122–123, 131–132
BPD (borderline personality disorder), 106–107
Brief Symptom Inventory, 25
Brown, G. S., 18, 47
Buchheim, A., 124
Budge, S. L., 165

Callahan, J. L., 91, 314
Campbell, C., 119
Caritas, 109–110
Carlson, J., 195, 202
Carpenter, J. S. W., 124
Carrel, A., 215
Carter, J. A., 107
Caspar, F., 196–198, 205–206, 210
Castonguay, L. G.
　　and appropriate responsiveness, 75
　　and contextual model, 146
　　and nonuniformity of therapist effects, 47
　　and relativity of "better therapist," 312
　　and therapist negative reactions, 182, 187
　　and wisdom from creative others, 218
Caterpillar plot, 21

CATS. *See* Client Attachment to Therapist Scale
CBT. *See* Cognitive–behavioral therapy
CBT for generalized anxiety disorder.
　　See Cognitive–behavioral therapy for generalized anxiety disorder
Change
　　effect sizes of, 194–195
　　empirically supported principles of, 146
　　negative, 339
Childhood experiences, 250
Chow, D. L.
　　and applying research therapist effects, 315, 316
　　and assessment of outcome, 59
　　and deliberate practice, 46, 209
　　on importance of therapist effects, 65
　　and training, 206
CIs (confidence intervals), 21–23, 26–27
Client Attachment to Therapist Scale (CATS), 120, 121, 125, 126
Clinical Outcomes in Routine Evaluation–Outcome Measure (CORE-OM), 21–22, 25
Clinician Severity Rating for GAD, 262
Cogar, M. C., 208
Cognitive Behavioral Analysis System of Psychotherapy, 180–181
Cognitive–behavioral therapy (CBT)
　　appropriate responsiveness to client resistance in, 77
　　client self-expression in, 228
　　conceptualization skills in, 143
　　for eating disorders, 75
　　homework in, 166
　　psychodynamic approach vs., 76
　　and therapeutic wisdom from creative others, 219
　　therapist inner experience in, 102, 106
　　therapist negative reactions in, 180–181, 187
　　trauma-focused, 228
Cognitive–behavioral therapy for generalized anxiety disorder, 259–281
　　limitations in research on, 280–281
　　method for research on, 261–265

overview of therapist factors in, 277–280
results from research on, 265–277
Cognitive interventions, 249
Cognitive processes (cognitive–behavioral therapy for generalized anxiety disorder), 271–273
Cognitive restructuring, 263
Cohesion, 330
Colosimo, K. A., 86
Common cultural processes, 165–166
Common factors, 143–144
Communication
　cultural influences on, 159
　importance of effective, 319
Compassion, 182–186
Competence, 194–195, 320
Competencies, 165, 319. *See also* Multicultural competencies
Conceptualizing ability, 112
Conceptual skills, 139, 142–143, 145–147, 337
Confidence, therapist, 91
Confidence intervals (CIs), 21–23, 26–27
Confrontational ruptures, 180
Congruence
　and therapeutic presence, 87
　and therapist inner experience, 103–105
Connors, L., 182
Consensual qualitative research–case study (CQR-C), 264–265, 287–290
Constantino, M. J., 182
Contextual model of therapist skills, 143–153
CORE-OM (Clinical Outcomes in Routine Evaluation–Outcome Measure), 21–22, 25
Counselor Comfort Scale, 167
Countertransference. *See also* Inner experience of therapist; Negative reactions of therapist
　and attachment, 121, 127
　defined, 179
　hate in, 106–109
　management of, 105–106, 111–113, 184–185, 330
　and therapeutic presence, 94

Countertransference Factors Inventory, 179
Coyle, 150
Crits-Christoph, P., 18, 79, 181, 253
Crowley, M. J., 152
Cultural background of therapist, 38
Cultural comfort, 167–168
Cultural session markers, 169
Cultural skills, 139, 143–147
Culture of client, 159–172, 337
　clinical practices for working with, 168–172
　and evidence-based psychotherapy, 160–161
　and myths about culturally competent therapist, 162–164
　recent research on therapist effects and, 161–162
　and research support for therapists' multicultural orientation, 167–168
　theoretical implications of research on, 164–167

Dancers, 223–225
D'Andrea, M. 144
Deactivating attachment system, 118–119
Defiance, 75–76
Deliberative practice (DP)
　and client culture, 171
　client outcomes with, 315–316
　defined, 46
　elements of, 59
　and professional expertise, 204–206
　as situational variable, 337
　and therapeutic alliance, 62
Del Re, A. C., 44, 79
Denman, D. W., 208
Depression
　psychodynamic therapy for. *See* Psychodynamic therapy for depression
　therapist effects in reduction of, 56–58
　and therapist hostility, 61–62
　vicious cycle of, 237
Desensitization techniques, 263
Deterioration, treatment, 30, 339
Diagnosis, 47

Diagnostic and Statistical Manual of Mental Disorders (DSM), 222, 242, 262
Diener, M. J., 120
Difficult clients, 183, 185, 195, 312
Dinger, U., 124
Dismissing attachment style, 121, 124, 128
Distress level, 47
Doolin, E. M., 104
Dozier, M., 122, 127
DP. *See* Deliberative practice
Dreyfus, H., 198–199, 201
Dreyfus, S., 198–199, 201
Dropout rates
    and client culture, 167–168
    therapist-focused research on, 30
    variability in, 24
Dry humor, 290, 300
DSM (*Diagnostic and Statistical Manual of Mental Disorders*), 222, 242, 262
Dunn, R., 91

Eating disorders, 75
Eckert, J., 123–124
Education, 38
Eells, T. D., 209
Effective therapists, 37–50. *See also specific headings*
    defined, 13–14
    history of research on, 38–39
    identified characteristics and actions of, 42–46
    methodological issues in research on, 39–42
    overview, 16–17
    techniques of, 75–76
    uniformity of characteristics and actions of, 47–48
    and unrelated outcome variables, 48–49
    and variability, 20–21
Efficacy research, 19
Elkin, I., 18, 77
Ellison, W. D., 120
Emotional expression, 144
Emotional processing, 263, 273
Emotion-focused therapy, 80–81
Emotion regulation, 118

Empathy
    compassion vs., 185–186
    correlation between outcomes and, 330
    in countertransference management, 112
    in evidence-based therapy relationships, 78
    and therapeutic presence, 87–90
    and therapist inner experience, 103–104
    and therapist skills, 142, 147
    in therapy process research, 40
Empirically supported treatments (ESTs), 313–314
Encouraging language, 73
End-state functioning, 263
Engagement, treatment, 30, 337
Ericsson, K. A., 196, 201, 202
Eros, 109–110
ESTs (empirically supported treatments), 313–314
Ethical Principles of Psychologists and Code of Conduct, 301
Ethnicity, of therapist, 38, 331
Eurocentrism, 160–161
Evaluative measures, 74
Eversmann, J., 45, 203
Evidence-based psychotherapy, 160–161
Evidence-based therapy relationships, 77–78
Exceptional therapists, 16–17, 31
Existential themes, 226
Experiential approaches, 180
Experimental design, 38
Expertise. *See* Professional expertise
Exploratory skills, 151
Exploratory therapies, 339
Expressive arts therapy, 219
Extraordinary presence, 95–97
Eye contact, 73

Facilitative interpersonal skills (FIS), 44–45, 59, 62, 152–153
Falconnier, L., 18
Falk, D. R., 286, 302
Fallot, R. D., 127
Family background, 292, 301
Fantasy, 226

Farber, B. A., 104
Fatter, D. M., 96
Fear, 177
Fearon, P., 125
Feedback, 207–208
    client, 330
    and depression, 237
    for finding provider, 319–320
    socialization to, 318
FIS. See Facilitative interpersonal skills
Fisher, Ronald, 38
Five-factor theory, 111–113
Flückiger, C., 44, 45, 79
Fonagy, P., 119, 120, 123
Frank, J. B., 143, 145, 152
Frank, J. D., 143, 145, 152
Freud, Sigmund, 105–106, 175
Frustration, 182–188
Fuller, F., 4
Function-based outcomes, 55

Geller, S. M., 88, 89, 90, 91–93
Gelso, C. J., 110, 179, 183, 187
Gender
    as cultural component, 145
    and humor in therapy, 300
    of therapist, 38, 47, 48, 331
Generalized anxiety disorder. See
        Cognitive–behavioral therapy for
        generalized anxiety disorder
Genuineness, 142, 147
Gestalt therapy, 286
Gibbons, M. B., 181
Global outcome indexes, 59
Goal consensus/collaboration, 40, 78, 330
Goheen, M. D., 75–76
Goldberg, S. B., 45
Goldfried, M. R., 146, 182, 218, 278
Gonçalves, M. M., 80
The Great Psychotherapy Debate
        (B. E. Wampold), 18, 218
Greenberg, L. S., 88, 89, 91–93
Grief, 238
Groening, Matt, 295
Group cohesion, 78
Guy, J. D., 178

Hack-Ritzo, S., 161
Haig, R. A., 286

Hamilton Anxiety Rating Scale, 262
Hamilton Rating Scale of Depression
        (HRSD), 242, 245–246
Hatcher, R. L., 72
Hate, 105–111
Hautle, I., 205–206
Hayes, A. M., 182
Hayes, J. A.
    and countertransference, 179, 183,
        187
    and therapeutic presence, 90, 96
    and therapist match, 312
    and uniformity of therapist effects, 47
Healing, 143–144
Health insurance, 311–313
Helping skills model, 151–152
Helping therapeutic alliance, 124–125
Hentschel, U., 118, 119
Here-and-now interventions, 249
Hierarchical linear modeling (HLM),
        326–327, 330, 331, 339
Hill, C. E.
    and attachment, 126
    and cognitive–behavioral therapy for
        generalized anxiety disorder,
        261
    and empathy vs. compassion, 185
    and helping skills, 151–152
    and humor in therapy, 286, 302
    and information in therapy, 4
    and professional expertise, 195, 198,
        202, 208
    and therapist negative reactions, 182
    and therapist techniques, 141
Hilsenroth, M. J., 75, 141
Himawan, L., 152
Hines, C. E., III, 75
HLM. See Hierarchical linear modeling
Höger, D., 123–124
Holmberg, J., 152
Homework, 73, 166
Horvath, A. O., 44, 75–76, 79, 80
Hostility, 61–62, 142
Howard, K., 118, 145–146
Hox, J. J., 29
HRSD (Hamilton Rating Scale of
        Depression), 242, 245–246
Humanistic approach
    conceptualization skills in, 143
    and expressive arts therapy, 219

Humanistic approach, *continued*
  research measures in, 339
  therapist negative reactions in, 180
Humility, 163, 167–168
Humor in therapy, 285–303
  defined, 286
  effects of, 226, 300–301
  existing research on, 286–287
  future directions for research on, 302–303
  method for research on use and impact of, 287–289
  results of research on, 289–300
  as situational variable, 337
Hyperactivating attachment system, 119

ICC (intraclass correlation), 39
Identity, 159
IIP-64 (Inventory of Interpersonal Problems), 25, 242–243
Imagination, 226
Imel, Z. E.
  and alliance-outcome correlations, 79
  and client culture, 161
  and therapist effects, 19, 20, 29, 63, 310, 313
Immediacy, 176
"Inadmissible" therapist states, 105–111
Information processing, 195–198
Inner experience of therapist, 101–113. *See also* Negative reactions of therapist
  attentiveness to, 337
  defined, 102
  and facilitative conditions, 102–105
  feelings of hate and love as part of, 105–111
  and five-factor theory, 111–113
  management of, 111
  and relational skills, 142
Insecure attachment style
  and anxiety, 128–129
  and therapeutic alliance, 120–121
  of therapists, 123–126
Insight-oriented therapies, 339
Insight skills, 151
Insomnia, 76
Insurance plans, 311–313
Intake interviews, 143, 168–169

Intentions (cognitive–behavioral therapy for generalized anxiety disorder), 274
Interpersonal deficits, 238
Interpersonal interpretations, 253, 330
Interpersonally oriented interventions, 238–239
Interpersonal psychotherapy (IPT), 238–239. *See also* Psychodynamic therapy for depression
Interpretations
  interpersonal, 253, 330
  related to alliance strength, 80
  transference, 181–182
Intimacy, 237
Intraclass correlation (ICC), 39
Intuition, 199–202
Inventory of Interpersonal Problems (IIP-64), 25, 242–243
IPT (interpersonal psychotherapy), 238–239. *See also* Psychodynamic therapy for depression
Irony, 290, 300
Irreverence, 228
Ivanovic, M., 91
Ivey, A. E., 144
Ivey, M. B., 144

Jacobson, N. S., 23
Jeong, J., 121
Jones, E. R., 18
Joyce, A. S., 181–182

Kahneman, D., 150
Keith-Spiegel, P., 178
Kelly, S. M., 151
Kern, A., 197
Kertes, A., 182
Kim, D.-M., 19
Kivlighan, D. M., 126
Knox, S., 151, 195, 198, 202
Kohlenberg, R. J., 181
Kohut, Heinz, 103
Korr, W. S., 161
Krampe, R. T., 202
Kraus, D. R., 47, 56, 312

Ladany, N., 185
Lambert, M. J., 18, 44

Lange, J., 45
Larrison, C. R., 161
Lawrence, D. H., 220
Leach, M. M., 168
Levy, K. N., 120
Liebowitz Social Anxiety Scale, 129
Listening, supportive, 273–274
Lodge, David, 221
Love, 105–111
Lunnen, K. M., 145
Lutz, W., 24
Luyten, P., 119

Maas, C. J. M., 29
Mahoney, C., 18
Mallinckrodt, B., 120, 121
Mania, 56
Manualized treatments, 72
Marked-guided interventions, 80–81
Marmarosh, C. L., 121, 127
Martin, A., 124
Martindale, C., 17–18
Martinovich, Z., 19
Maslow, Abraham, 216
Mastery, 150, 194–196, 314–315. *See also* Professional expertise
May, R., 87, 109–110
McCallum, M., 181–182
McClintock, A. S., 152
McColgan, D., 197
MCCs. *See* Multicultural competencies
McCullough, J. P., 180–181
McDavis, R., 144
MCO. *See* Multicultural orientation
McWilliams, N., 218
Meditation, 96
Mentalization, 119–120
Messer, S. B., 228
Meta-analysis, 37
Metacognitive regulation, 119
MI (motivational interviewing), 77
Microaggressions, 145, 170
Minami, T., 18
Mindfulness, 27, 185
Mirroring, 123
Mollen, D., 151
Moment-to-moment interventions, 249
Monroe, J. M., 120
Monsen, J. T., 46

Motivational interviewing (MI), 77
Motive-oriented therapeutic relationship, 206
MULTI (Multitheoretical List of Therapeutic Interventions), 240–241, 243
Multicultural competencies (MCCs)
  disparities in, 164–165
  multicultural orientation vs., 159
  ratings of, 168
Multiculturalism, 143–145
Multicultural orientation (MCO)
  aims of, 167
  disparities in, 164–165
  multicultural competencies vs., 159
  pillars of, 166
  research support for therapists', 167–168
Multilevel models, 41, 102, 331
Multitheoretical List of Therapeutic Interventions (MULTI), 240–241, 243
Muran, J. C., 180, 187
Musicians, 223–225

Najavits, L. M., 179, 187, 209
Narrative approaches, 221, 226
National Institute for Mental Health (NIMH), 18–19
Needs (cognitive–behavioral therapy for generalized anxiety disorder), 274
Negative reactions of therapist, 175–189. *See also* Countertransference; Inner experience of therapist
  implications of empirical and clinical knowledge on, 186–188
  importance of, 175–176
  research on, 177–182
  transformation of, 182–186
  types of, 177
Nesting, 64
Nielsen, S. L., 18
NIMH (National Institute for Mental Health), 18–19
Nissen-Lie, H. A., 46
Nonverbal behavior, 226
Norcross, J. C., 77, 330
Nord, C., 123–124
Nordberg, S. S., 47, 312

Norms, 159
Nowacki, K., 124

Ogden, Thomas, 220
Oghene, J., 90
Ogles, B. M., 18, 44, 145
Ogrodniczuk, J. S., 181–182
Okiishi, J., 18
Online provider ratings, 311
Openness, 163
OQ-45 (Outcome Questionnaire–45), 88–89, 93, 208
Orlinsky, D. E., 118, 145–146
Osler, William, 15
Outcome Questionnaire–45 (OQ-45), 88–89, 93, 208
Outcome research
 on attachment, 120–122
 on deliberative practice, 315–316
 integration of therapist effects into, 55–66, 326–327
 on mentalization-based treatment of personality disorders, 120
 on psychodynamic therapy for depression. See Psychodynamic therapy for depression
 and therapeutic alliance as predictor, 78–79
 on therapist negative reactions, 178–179
 on treatment adherence, 63, 320
 variables in, 330
Owen, J., 20, 75, 145, 166–168

Panic disorder, 128
Paraphrasing, 248–249
Pascual-Leone, Juan, 200, 201
Past experiences, 250
Patient-Centered Outcomes Research Institute, 320
Patient questionnaires, 208
Patients to therapists (PTR), 44
Patterson, C. L., 44, 152
Paul, Gordon, 188
Payers, 311–314, 320
Pay-for-performance, 312
Peer nomination, 194–195
Penn State Worry Questionnaire, 262
Performance artists, 223–225
Performance-based incentives, 312

Persig, R. M., 74
Personality
 changes in, 57
 and humor in therapy, 301
 and relational skills, 142
 of therapist, 38
 and therapist inner experience, 102–103
Personality disorders, 106–107, 120
Petrowski, K., 124
Philia, 109–110
Pincus, A. L., 75
Piper, W. E., 181–182
Plan analysis, 80
Pluralistic therapy, 80
Poe, Edgar Allen, 220
Poelstra, P. L., 178
Pokorny, D., 124
Policy experts, 314
Policymakers, 320
Pope, K. S., 177, 178
Popp-Liesum, M., 197
Pos, A. E., 86, 90
Positive regard. *See* Unconditional positive regard
Practical solutions, 250–252
Preoccupied attachment style
 of therapists, 124, 126, 127
 treatment outcomes with, 120, 121
Prescription therapy (SP), 76
Private selves, 226
Process–outcome research, 74–78, 330. *See also* Outcome research
Process research
 on attachment, 121–122
 and between-therapists differences on outcomes, 340
 integration of therapist effects into, 55–66
 types of variables in, 40
Professional degree, 48, 331
Professional expertise, 150, 193–210
 in data interpretation, 319
 general model for development of, 198–199
 and information processing, 195–198
 and intuition, 199–202
 overview, 194–195
 peer identification of, 314–315
 sources of, 202–210

Professional self-doubt (PSD), 46
Projective identification, 107
Psychoanalysis
    countertransference in, 106
    and humor in therapy, 286
    projective identification in, 107
    therapist negative reactions in, 180
Psychodynamic approach
    and artistic experiences, 228–229
    changes in personality organization in, 57
    conceptualization skills in, 143
    deviations from adherence to, 75
    professional expertise in, 209
    research measures in, 339
    and therapeutic wisdom from creative others, 219
    therapist negative reactions in, 180, 181
Psychodynamic therapy for depression, 235–255
    and interpersonally oriented interventions, 238–239
    methods for research on, 239–243
    results in research on, 243–252
    theoretical foundations of, 237
Psychophysiological processes, 274–275
Psychosis, 56
Psychotherapy research. *See specific headings*
PTR (patients to therapists), 44
Public selves, 226

Race, of therapist, 38, 331
Raue, P. J., 182, 218
Referral practices, 310
Reflective functioning, 119
Reframing, 185–186
Reinforcement, 317–318
Relational interpretations, 253, 330
Relational skills, 139, 142, 145–147, 337
Relationship-Oriented Subscale (ROS), 239, 241–242, 244–246, 253, 254
Relationship Questionnaire, 124
Relaxation exercises, 73, 263
Religion, 168
Residuals (therapist effects research), 21–23
Resilience, 27
Respect, 147

Responsiveness, 71–73, 337. *See also* Appropriate responsiveness
Ribeiro, A. P., 80
Ribeiro, E., 80
Ricks, Frank D., 16–17, 25
Ridley, C. R., 151
Robinson, N., 126
Rogers, Annie, 110
Rogers, Carl
    on necessary and sufficient conditions in psychotherapy, 102–105, 112
    and organismic valuing process, 74
    and relational skills, 142
    and therapeutic presence, 87, 96
Rogers, Natalie, 219
Role disputes, 238
Role transitions, 238
ROM (routine outcome monitoring), 314
Romano, V., 125
Rønnestad, M. H., 46
ROS. *See* Relationship-Oriented Subscale
Roth, T., 125
Routine outcome monitoring (ROM), 314
Rubino, G., 125

Safran, J. D., 180, 187
Sarcasm, 290, 300
Saxon, D., 21
SC (stimulus control therapy), 76
Schizophrenia, 16
Schlosser, L., 151
Schnabel, Artur, 219
School Is Hell (Matt Groening), 295
Schoppelrey, S. L., 161
Schöttke, H., 45, 48
Secure attachment style
    prevalence of, 120
    and therapeutic alliance, 121
    of therapists, 123–126
    therapy behaviors indicative of, 122
Seinfeld, 295
Self-awareness, 176, 183–184
Self-care, 185
Self-disclosure, 250, 330
Self-insight, 111–112
Self-integration, 112
Self-monitoring, 207, 263

Self-reflection, 179, 318
SET. *See* Supportive–expressive therapy
Severity, clients presenting, 24–26
Sexuality
  in therapeutic relationship, 109–111
  and therapist negative reactions, 177
Shauenburg, H., 124
Sheehan, Jacqueline, 220
Shem, S., 219
Sheng, E., 29, 310
A Shining Affliction (Annie Rogers), 110
Simek-Morgan, L., 144
Skills, therapist. *See* Therapist skills
Sleep onset insomnia, 76
Socialization, 318–319
Social phobia, 128, 129
Society for Psychotherapy Research, 55
Song, X., 152
SOPHO-Net study, 129
SP (prescription therapy), 76
Specialization, 314–315
Specific cultural processes, 165–166
Sperry, L., 195, 202
Spirituality, 168
Stakeholders, 319–320
Stanislavsky, K., 217
Stark, M. J., 178
Star Trek, 295
State-Trait Anxiety Inventory–Trait Version, 262
Statistical disaggregation, 41
Statistical methods, 38
Stiles, W. B., 80, 153
Stimulus control therapy (SC), 76
Strange Situation procedure, 123
Stress, 117
Structural Analysis of Social Behavior, 142
Strupp, H. H., 178, 179, 187, 209
Substance use, 56, 79
Sue, D. W., 144, 145
Sullivan, C., 151
Sullivan, Harry Stack, 237
Supershrinks, 16
Supervision, 310, 316, 318
Supportive–expressive therapy (SET), 236, 238–240, 247, 254–255. *See also* Psychodynamic therapy for depression

Supportive listening, 273–274
Swift, J. K., 91, 314
Symonds, D., 44, 79
Symptom outcomes, 55

Tabachnick, B. G., 177, 178
"Talent hotbeds," 150
Taubner, S., 124
Teague, G. B., 127
Technical skills, 139–142, 145–147, 337
Tesch-Römer, C., 202
Theoretical orientation, 331. *See also specific orientations*
Therapeutic absence, 86. *See also* Therapeutic presence
Therapeutic alliance
  across range of patients, 42–44
  and appropriate responsiveness, 75, 78–79
  and attachment, 118, 120–121, 127, 129
  in cognitive therapy, 182
  correlation between outcomes and, 40, 330
  and microaggressions in therapy, 145
  quality of, 61
  research on ruptures in, 180, 206, 330
  therapist interpretations related to, 80
  and therapist negative reactions, 178
  within-therapist and between-therapist effects with, 62–64
Therapeutic presence, 85–97
  in cognitive–behavioral therapy for generalized anxiety disorder, 275–276
  extraordinary, 95–97
  in-session factors in, 92–95
  presession factors in, 91–92
  research on, 87–90
  as situational variable, 337
  and therapist negative reactions, 176
Therapeutic wisdom from creative others, 215–229
  clinical implications of, 226–229
  and criticisms of therapy, 218–219
  and learning from performance artists, 223–225

and learning from writers and actors, 219–223
overview, 215–218
Therapist effects, 13–31, 309–321, 325–340. *See also specific headings*
   applications of research on, 30–31, 310–317
   brief history of research on, 17–19
   challenges and solutions with research on, 317–320
   and clients presenting severity, 24–26
   definitions of, 14–15, 326
   designing research on, 20–24
   and effective therapists, 16–17, 39–40. *See also* Effective therapists
   empirical understanding of, 3–4
   future directions for research on, 26–29, 338–340
   implications of, 337–338
   limitations of existing research on, 327
   overview, 326–329
   possible variables in, 330–337
   and professional expertise, 193
   researcher skepticism on, 309
   and therapist skills, 151–153
   and variability, 15–16
Therapist effects analysis in outcome and process research, 55–66
   complex considerations with, 64
   and individual characteristics of therapist, 58–60
   overview, 55–58
Therapist-focused research
   defined, 14
   history of, 17–19
Therapist inner experience. *See* Inner experience of therapist
Therapist Presence Inventory (TPI), 88–90
Therapist skills, 139–153. *See also* Professional expertise
   conceptual, 139, 142–143, 145–147, 337
   contextual model for integration of, 143–153
   cultural, 139, 143–147, 337
   relational, 139, 142, 145–147, 337
   technical, 139–142, 145–147, 337
   and therapist effects, 151–153
Therapy-interfering behaviors. *See* Negative reactions of therapist
Therapy outcomes, 3. *See also* Outcome research
Therapy process, 3. *See also* Process research
Therapy Session Report (TSR), 262
Thompson, B. J., 185, 208
Tiered networks, 311–313
Tishby, O., 127
Total correlation, 40
TPI (Therapist Presence Inventory), 88–90
Tracey, T. J., 207, 209
Training
   alliance-focused, 81
   and applying research therapist effects, 310
   applying research therapist effects to, 316–317
   and deliberate practice, 46
   for development of professional expertise, 203–207
   directions for future research on, 30
   emphasis on empathy in, 104
   multicultural, 171–172
   postlicense, 316
   socialization in, 318–319
   and therapist skills, 152
   as variable in psychotherapy outcome research, 38
Transference, 73, 121, 141. *See also* Countertransference
Transference interpretations, 181–182
Transforming Negative Reactions to Clients: From Frustration to Compassion (A. W. Wolf, M. R. Goldfried, & J. C. Muran), 177, 182–186
Transitional spaces, 227–228
Trauma, 128, 252
Trauma-focused cognitive–behavioral therapy, 228
Treatment adherence
   and appropriate responsiveness, 75
   to motivational interviewing approach, 77

Treatment adherence, *continued*
    outcome research on, 63, 320
    and professional expertise, 194–195
    and technical skills, 140–141
Treatment Outcome Package, 56, 59
Truax, P., 23
Trust, 93, 252
Tsai, M., 181
TSR (Therapy Session Report), 262
Two-chair dialogue, 73
Tyrrell, C. L., 127

Uhlin, B., 152
Ulleberg, P., 46
Unconditional positive regard (UPR)
    in evidence-based therapy relationships, 78
    and relational skills, 142
    and therapeutic presence, 87, 88
    and therapist inner experience, 103, 104
Uniformity of therapist effects, 47–48, 340
UPR. *See* Unconditional positive regard

Values, 159
Vanderbilt studies, 178–179, 186–187
Variability
    between-therapist, 39, 61–64, 310, 330, 340
    defined, 14
    and effective therapists, 20–21
    in process and outcome variables, 63–64
    and therapist effects, 15–16, 21–23
Verbal response modes (VRMs), 141
Vermeersch, D. A., 44
Vicarious introspection, 103
Vinca, M. A., 88–90, 92, 93
Vivino, B. L., 185
VRMs (verbal response modes), 141

Wampold, B. E., 18, 19, 44, 47, 79, 218
Warmth, 88, 142
Weiner, B., 185
Westra, H. A., 182, 187
Winnicott, D. W., 106–108, 227
Wiseman, H., 127
Wiser, S., 182
Withdrawal ruptures, 180
Within-therapist effects
    in correlational research on therapist variables, 330
    partitioning of, 61
    and therapeutic alliance, 62, 64
Wolf, A. W., 111
"Wounded therapists," 59–60
Writers, 219–223

Yusof, Y., 124

Zajonc, R. B., 74

ABOUT THE EDITORS

Louis G. Castonguay, PhD, completed his doctorate in clinical psychology at the State University of New York, Stony Brook. He completed a clinical internship at the University of California, Berkeley, and he completed his postdoctorate at Stanford University. He is currently a professor in the Department of Psychology at Penn State University. With more than 180 publications (including eight coedited books), his scholarly work and research has focused on different aspects of the process of change and training, especially within the context of psychotherapy integration of psychotherapy. He is also involved in the investigation of the efficacy of new integrative treatments for generalized anxiety disorder and depression, and the development of Practice Research Networks aimed at facilitating collaboration between clinicians and researchers. Dr. Castonguay has received several awards, including the Early Career Contribution Award from the Society of Psychotherapy Research, and the David Shakow Award from Division 12 (Society of Clinical Psychology) of the American Psychological Association (APA). He has also received four recognitions from Division 29 (Society for the Advancement of Psychotherapy) of the APA: the Jack D. Krasner Memorial Award, Distinguished Contributions to Teaching and Mentoring, the Distinguished Research Publications Award, and the Distinguished Psychologist Award for his lifetime contributions to the field of psychotherapy. He also served as president of the North American Society for Psychotherapy Research, as well as the International Society for Psychotherapy Research.

Clara E. Hill, PhD, completed her doctorate in counseling psychology at Southern Illinois University and a clinical internship at the University of Florida. She is currently a professor in the Department of Psychology at the University of Maryland. With 12 books, 74 book chapters, and 215 journal articles, her scholarly work and research has focused on psychotherapy process, therapist interventions, therapist training, dream work, meaning in life, and qualitative research methods. She has received several awards, including the Leona Tyler Award from APA Division 17 (Society of Counseling Psychology), the Distinguished Psychologist Award from APA Division 29 (Society for the Advancement of Psychotherapy), the Outstanding Lifetime Achievement Award from the Section of Counseling and Psychotherapy Process and Outcome Research of the Society for Counseling Psychology, and the Distinguished Research Career Award from the Society for Psychotherapy Research. She served as the editor of the *Journal of Counseling Psychology* and *Psychotherapy Research*, and she also served as the president of the North American Society for Psychotherapy Research, as well as the International Society for Psychotherapy Research.